BARRON'S

HOW TO PREPARE FOR THE
CALIFORNIA STATE UNIVERSITY WRITING PROFICIENCY EXAMS

(or the GWAR—Graduation Writing Assessment Requirement)

2ND EDITION

Fred Obrecht
Professor of English
Los Angeles Pierce College

Revised by
Boak Ferris
Professor of English
California State University, Long Beach

© Copyright 1998 by Barron's Educational Series, Inc.
Prior edition copyright © 1992.

All rights reserved.
No part of this book may be reproduced in any form, by photostat, microfilm, xerography, or any other means, or incorporated into any information retrieval system, electronic or mechanical, without the written permission of the copyright owner.

All inquiries should be addressed to:
Barron's Educational Series, Inc.
250 Wireless Boulevard
Hauppauge, New York 11788
http://www.barronseduc.com

Library of Congress Catalog Card No. 98-35742

International Standard Book No. 0-7641-0464-0

Library of Congress Cataloging-in-Publication Data
Obrecht, Fred.
    How to prepare for the California State University writing proficiency exams
    (or the GWAR—Graduation Writing Assessment Requirement) / Fred Obrecht;
    revised by Boak Ferris. — 2nd ed.
        p. cm.
    ISBN 0-7641-0464-0
    1. English language—Rhetoric—Examinations—Study guides. 2. English language—
      Rhetoric—Study and teaching—Standards—California. 3. Academic writing—
      Examinations—Study guides. I. Ferris, Boak. II. Title.
PE1411.027 1999
808'.042'076—dc21   98-35742
                                                                                                    CIP

PRINTED IN THE UNITED STATES OF AMERICA

9 8 7 6 5 4 3 2

DEDICATION

To my wife Lydia, who was so patient and supportive during this project.

Acknowledgments

Kym Collins, for her cartoon work.
Louise Barbato, Ph.D., for her ESL chapter.
Gary Larson, for permission to use a "Far Side" cartoon.
Barbara Tuchman for permission to use her essay "Mankind's Better Moments."
The California State University, Long Beach Testing Office and
Writing Proficiency Exam Test Development Committee

CONTENTS

Preface   vii
Introduction   ix
Survey of Current CSU Graduation Writing Assessment Requirements   x
How to Use This Book   xi

1. The Testing Mind-Set   1
    Before Taking the Writing Proficiency Exam   2
    Questions to Ask   2
    Tactics on the Day of the Test   3
    Structured and Unstructured Exam Questions   3
        Structured Questions   3
        Unstructured Questions   4
    Key Words Used in Essay Questions   4
    Prewriting Tactics   5
        Listing   5
        Clustering   6
        Freewriting   6
        Mapping   7
        Exemplification   7

2. Essay Types   8
    A Word About Essay-Test Design   8
    Types of Essays   9
    The Personal-Experience Essay   9
    The Comparison/Contrast Essay   12
    The Explanatory/Analytic Essay   15
    The Argument/Persuasion Essay   18
    Length of Prompt   21

3. How to Write an Impromptu Essay   23
    Where Do I Begin?   23
    The Pregnant Sentence   24

4. How Your Essay Will Be Scored   31
    What You Need to Know About Holistic Scoring   31
    What This All Means to You   32
    Representative Scoring Guide   33
        I. Answer the Question, Fully and Completely   34
        II. Be Organized   34
        III. Use College-Level Language   34
        IV. Avoid Errors in Mechanics, Usage, and Sentence Structure   35
        V. Write Legibly   35
        VI. Plan and Use Your Allotted Time Carefully   35
    Prewriting Considerations   36
    A Final Word About Examples   39
    One Type of Procedure for Ensuring a High Quality Response on a One-Hour GWAR   39

5. Thirteen Mistakes That Fail Tests   40
    More on Holistic Scoring   40
    Weights of Specific Errors According to the Holistic Scoring Process   41
        1. Nothing to Say   43
        2. Almost But Not Quite   43
        3. Without Perceptible Direction or Purpose   44
        4. Major Sentence Errors   45
        5. "Bermuda Triangle" Errors   46
        6. Errors in Predication or Mixed Sentences   46
        7. Subject-Verb Agreement Errors   47
        8. Dangling or Misplaced Modifier   47
        9. Misuse or Overuse of Semicolon   47

      10. Problems with Verb Tense 48
      11. Thoughtless Use of the Passive Voice 49
      12. Ineffective Coordination and Subordination 50
      13. Errors in Parallelism 51
6. Representative Essays 53
   Personal Experience 53
   Comparison/Contrast 57
   Explanatory/Analytic 60
   Argument/Persuasion 63
7. Essay-Writing Practice 67
   Personal-Experience Topics 67
   Comparison/Contrast Topics 68
   Explanatory/Analytic Topics 69
   Argument/Persuasion Topics 71
   Essay Based on Reading 72
8. Special Notes and Tips for ESL Students 78
   Preliminary Advice and Strategies for International and ESL Students 78
   Holistic Scoring and ESL Students 78
   A Quick Overview of Subordination and Coordination 79
   A. Linking Words 79
   B. The Usage of the Article 93
   C. A Quick Review of the Major Verb Tenses 101
   D. Learning to Correct Your Composition by Yourself 107
9. Multiple-Choice Tests 113
   Fresno Model 114
   Test of Standard Written English (TSWE) 119
   CAAP Model 125
   Long Beach Model 138
10. English Review and Practice 145
   Usage/Mechanics 145
      Punctuation 145
      Basic Grammar and Usage 157
   Sentence Structure 170
   Rhetorical Skills 190
      Strategy 190
      Organization 193
      Style 197
      Word Choice 199
   Basic Spelling List 202
   Practice Test 212
      Passage I 212
      Passage II 217
11. Sample Tests 222
   Test A 222
   Test B 233
   Test C 244
   Answer Explanations 255
   Test A 255
   Test B 257
   Test C 259
Index 263

PREFACE

In 1975, in response to state-wide and community concerns, the California State University System Chancellor's Office established a task force to investigate a noticeable decline in the quality of student writing. Subsequently, with concerns confirmed, in 1977, the Chancellor's Office mandated that the 19 California State Universities institute a Graduation Writing Assessment Requirement (GWAR) for all students approaching graduation. Each campus, according to region, community, faculty, and administration, devised its own testing process. As a result, the GWAR now varies from campus to campus, consisting of passing a course at one (or challenging the course by an optional exam), writing two essays at a second, taking a short answer test at a third, or passing both objective and essay portions at a fourth. (At many—if not all—of the campuses, transfer and graduate students who have not passed a GWAR also must take the test in order to continue with their course work.)

Most of these campuses prescribe a mandatory impromptu essay that all students must pass in order to receive their diplomas. Each campus carefully designs these essay exams to reveal how well baccalaureate candidates have internalized the writing and thinking skills they will need to perform and compete in the professional white-collar world. Also, to evaluate these essays, many campuses must apply a grading system known as holistic scoring, which has such a high statistical accuracy that recently many professional firms and businesses (using similar evaluation systems) have instituted impromptu essay-tasks for their job applicants. Professional personnel managers have determined that at least one way exists—beyond the job interview—to find out quickly whether candidates and applicants have developed their analytical, comprehension, logic, and communication skills. A recent statistic from *Forbes Magazine* supports this trend: "The average white-collar worker devotes 25% or more of the work week to writing tasks." For you, therefore, investing time in evolving your writing skills will reward you by advancing you toward both your degree and eventual line of work.

This preparation manual provides comprehensive opportunities to delete your error areas and strengthen your skills. Students can best use this preparation manual in conjunction with the sample tests provided by their home universities. (For more information regarding the availability of sample tests on paper and disk, and on-line materials or websites specific to each university, call your testing office. The table at the beginning of the book lists the testing office numbers current as of January 1998.) Be advised, however, that the sample test materials at each institution seldom substitute for a **full** review of potential problem areas as covered in this manual.

For more than thirty years, Professor Obrecht has been a community college English Instructor helping students prepare for upper-division courses, writing standards, and writing proficiency tests. This book presents sound and tested strategies for preparing for both the writing examinations and the objective tests some universities give in addition to the impromptu essays.

Professor Ferris pretested the first California State University, Long Beach Writing Proficiency Exam in 1977, and continues at that university in all phases of the GWAR process, running student workshops, scoring essays, and participating in GWAR test development. According to CSULB testing office statistics, he has outstanding accuracy in holistic scoring, demonstrating his familiarity with CSU writing standards. He has also taught CSU composition at all levels for both ESL students and native speakers since 1974.

INTRODUCTION

The problem of providing sufficient training for university students in writing derives largely from lack of time and funding. Across the country, university administrators and faculty know that students need at least one full year of writing training at the university level, since as students' knowledge and experience evolve, so do professional expectations of their skill in thinking and providing a coherent, clear record of their thinking. But the pressures for universities of ensuring a minimal amount of time to graduation (supposedly four years), a General Education Course Core Requirement to make students "college educated" in a well-informed and globally connected world, and current major classes combined together preclude much more than a single semester of training in writing. Therefore, universities have developed one, two, or three strategies to address the issue. First, they provide remedial classes for lower-level students. Second, they institute exit writing exams. Or third, they are beginning to require upper-division writing classes, or upper-division courses specifying a writing component, perhaps specific to students' major requirements.

Notably, *excellent* high school writers can pass with 90 percent probability a California State University GWAR. Unfortunately, the grades and assessments such students have received from their high school teachers will not adequately inform these students if their skills are adequate for the university level. Only an experienced university teacher of composition, or a composition program director, can inform such students if their essay skills are sufficient. By contrast, meanwhile, *average* high school writers will find their skills do not equate to university-level writing skills.

For students able to pass a first-year university composition with a C or better, statistics of the GWAR tests indicate a high passing rate in the upper 80th and lower 90th percentiles; even ESL students are passing the tests in higher numbers. It is important that students fresh out of first-year composition attempt the GWAR as soon as possible, while their skills have had recent regular practice. Very few of the California State Universities require writing courses beyond the first year, except as might be found in courses with high writing content.

For you, the point of this discussion aims at insecurities you might feel regarding the level of your skills. You know how much writing training you've had, and by the time you face the GWAR at your institution you should have an idea of gaps in your knowledge.

Still, three facts about the test should increase your levels of comfort and confidence. First, it is not a test you can fail. (We define "failure" here as "no second chance.") The CSU's allow you to take the test until you pass it. As mentioned, the majority of students who attempt the test the first time pass, and the majority of students who do not pass the first time pass the next. Second, the GWAR at most of the universities is not run by their respective English departments. (It is a university writing test, not an English test.) It is designed, constantly updated, revised, and scored by faculty from *all* disciplines. The test represents the standards of the whole university, the CSU system, the professional community, and the Chancellor's Office and Trustees for baccalaureate candidates. Therefore, most universities take a democratic and global approach to the design, implementation, and scoring of the exam by including faculty from every department: Engineering, Psychology, Criminal Justice, History, Political Science, Electronic Arts, English as a Second Language, and so on. You are represented by scorers sympathetic to your interests and background in the design and scoring process. Third, you can ready yourself in specific ways. You can sign up for the exam today, no matter what your grade level, and attempt it, and thus familiarize yourself with it. One of the best ways to prepare is to take the exam—preferably after consulting your local sample tests and this preparation manual. If for some reason you don't pass, or haven't passed, don't be hard on yourself, because you have moved directly toward passing the test on your next attempt.

Whatever your circumstances, this book will serve all students who wish to prepare for their writing proficiency exam in an organized and judicious manner.

x CSU — Writing Proficiency Exam

CALIFORNIA STATE UNIVERSITY SYSTEM
SURVEY OF CURRENT CSU GRADUATION WRITING ASSESSMENT REQUIREMENTS

Campus	Exam Required?	Telephone	Acronym	Kind of Exam	Frequency	Essay Type	Multiple-Choice Type
Bakersfield	Optional	805-664-2011 x3373	UDWCE Upper Division Writing Competency Examination	1 90-minute essay	4 per year	PE or E/A	—
Chico	Required	916-898-6218	WEST Writing Effectiveness Screen Test	1 90-minute essay	2/semester	E/A	—
Dominguez Hills	Optional	310-243-3635	GWE Graduation Writing Examination	1 60-minute essay; double time for ESL	2/semester	PE, C/C, or E/A	—
Fresno	Optional	209-278-2457	UDWE Upper Division Writing Examination	2 45-minute essays; and multiple-choice test	5/year	PE or E/A	See Fresno Model Chapter 9
Fullerton	Required	714-278-3838	EWP Examination in Writing Proficiency	1 90-minute essay; and multiple-choice test	15/year	E/A	Test of Standard Written English
Hayward	Required	510-885-3661	WST Writing Skills Test	1 60-minute essay; and multiple-choice test	4/year	PE, C/C, or E/A	CAAP Writing Skills Test
Humboldt	Required	707-826-3611	GWPE Graduate Writing Proficiency Examination	2 45-minute essays	3/year	PE and E/A	—
Long Beach	Required	562-985-4007	WPE Writing Proficiency Examination	1 60-minute essay; multiple-choice test	5/year	PE or E/A	See Long Beach Model Chapter 9
Los Angeles	Required	213-343-3160	WPE Writing Proficiency Examination	1 90-minute essay	4/year	PE or E/A	—
Northridge	Required	818-677-2369	WPE Writing Proficiency Examination	1 60-minute essay	6/year	PE or E/A	—
Pomona	Required	909-869-7659 x3353	GWT Graduation Writing Test	1 60-minute essay	6/year	PE or E/A	—
Sacramento	Required	916-278-6296	WPE Writing Proficiency Examination	1 150-minute essay; 240 minutes for ESL	6/year	PE	—
San Bernardino	Optional	909-880-5045	WREE Writing Requirement Exemption Examination	1 180-minute essay	4/year	PE or C/C	—
San Diego	Optional	619-594-5216	UDWT Upper Division Writing Test	1 60-minute essay	3/semester	PE, E/A, or C/C	—
San Francisco	Required	415-338-2271	JEPET Junior English Proficiency Essay Test	1 60-minute essay	4/year	E/A	—
San Jose	Required	408-924-5980	WST Writing Skills Test	1 60-minute essay; and multiple-choice test	6/year	PE	CAAP Writing Skills Test
San Luis Obispo	Optional	805-756-2067	WPE Writing Proficiency Examination	1 90-minute essay	3/year	E/A or A/P	—
Sonoma	Required	707-664-2947	WEPT Written English Proficiency Test	1 120-minute essay	15/year	PE or E/A	—
Stanislaus	None (Classes required)	209-667-3157	—	—	—	—	—

Key   PE = Personal experience   C/C = Comparison/Contrast   E/A = Explanatory/Analytic   A/P = Argument/Persuasion

Note: Testing patterns may change at any time.

HOW TO USE THIS BOOK

1. Check the brochures and statements issued by your university testing office. Contact the appropriate number in the table on the previous page. Examine the sample essay assignments in your university's sample test package or registration materials that should be available at your university bookstore or testing office. (They may offer a computer disk with a sample objective test, on-line help or a web-site, or even sample student essays in response to their typical essay prompts.) Determine which of the four essay types (discussed in Chapter 3 in this book) your university administers.
2. Find and read the discussion and analysis of the essay type in Chapter 3. Read the model essays and the comments made about them.
3. Look through the other strategies concerning the writing test in Chapters 1–6 of this manual, focusing on tips and suggestions you find helpful and useful for your situation.
4. Practice writing essays of the appropriate type, selecting topics from Chapter 4. Give yourself the same amount of time you will have on the actual exam. Try to apply the six strategies defined in Chapter 4 *as you write your essay*, a mind-juggling maneuver, but one that will become easier with each essay.
5. Find someone at your university who enjoys providing help to students facing the exam, who can be referred to you by your tutorial lab, your English department, or your testing office. You need feedback on each *practice* essay you write, preferably from faculty who actually score the exam at your institution.
6. If your school gives a multiple choice examination, determine which type or types of questions will be on the test. Carefully review the practice questions of that type in Chapter 7.
7. Review all grammar and usage practice questions in Chapters 9–11, even those framed in a format you will not encounter on your test. Each test gives you important practice in English grammar and usage.
8. Spend whatever time you require to master the basic English skills discussed in Chapter 10. You will need time and a determined plan to cover the points made in that chapter effectively. Plan on a measured amount of study and review each day until you finish the chapter.
9. The review of English provided by this book will help you above and beyond your GWAR for your CSU, well into your professional life.

1 The Testing Mind-Set

It's important to realize that this essay exam is not being given to hinder your progress, but to provide some quality control over the writing skills of each graduating class. Begin your preparation by ignoring distracting feelings of annoyance or intimidation; see the test as business, business that you can take care of objectively and without delay. If you have not experienced significant problems writing before, and have passed previous writing classes with a B or better, there is little reason to believe you should not pass the test, particularly if you look over the material in this book.

If, on the other hand, you have taken this exam and not passed, or know from your performance in past English classes that you do not write well, you have some work to do. Many students who write poorly often give up; they compensate for their weaknesses in writing by doing better work in another area. When they are forced to write, they do everything possible to squeeze out of a direct confrontation with it, in Joseph Conrad's words, "the destructive element." They have their spouses write for them, or they go to a friend's house where some misguided people rewrite their papers for them, or they pay ghost writers to write their final draft. But what do such students do when they must face a strictly verified, timed, spontaneous written test? Well, take heart. There is hope aplenty. First of all, a student who has achieved junior status in a state university obviously has real capabilities. Second, the professors who read these tests want to pass you and do not expect a flawless performance from you. If you are an ESL student, your paper is, in most universities, graded by staff who teach ESL students. Finally, there are ways by which you can learn to avoid making the serious sentence errors or lapses in organization that have given you so much trouble in the past. This book clarifies the kinds of errors you need to avoid and gives some means of avoiding them. Meanwhile, if you have a friend or acquaintance who is a "writing person," a writing tutor, a community college English instructor, your high school English teacher, or anyone with the ability and willingness to go through an essay of yours and tell you where you have a fragment, comma splice, lack of coherence, or any of the other errors that are keeping you from passing this test, seek that person's help.

BEFORE TAKING THE WRITING PROFICIENCY EXAM

Many students delay taking the exam, though it is to their advantage to take it as early as possible—even as early as the summer before their junior year—if their school administers it at that early date. There are several reasons why an early testing date works to the advantage of the student. First, a student is closer in time to the semester in which he or she took the freshman composition course, a period when a student's writing skills are at their peak, according to a well-known study at Dartmouth, a peak from which they steadily decline in subsequent semesters. Second, a student may not be able to take an exam that is administered so infrequently every semester, given the emergencies and other priorities that surface so frequently. Third, if you do not pass the test, you need time for the courses and the intensive preparation you must complete before you take it again; and often, more that one semester is needed.

During the months leading up to the exam, improve your prose "ear" by reading good, informative prose under relaxed conditions, perhaps even on a daily, limited basis. (This advice applies especially to ESL students.)

Discuss the test frankly with your English instructor. Ask about your strengths and weaknesses in the skills to be tested. Does your English teacher see anything in your writing habits or work that suggests problems you may have with the test? If so, how can you deal with those problems?

Search out all avenues of help. Perhaps your English professor or writing lab tutor has practice tests or other materials that are helpful. If there is a composition study group, join it by all means. A group of motivated students writing essays and then evaluating them as a group can work miracles. The additional practice will give you confidence, and you will find that sharing problems with other prospective test-takers is another good way to build confidence.

Talk with your friends and family about the test and any fears you might have. This is no time to bottle up dread or panic. Keep in mind that you are able to repeat the exam if you do not pass; do not magnify its importance to the degree that you cannot prepare or perform effectively.

Anxiety affects your perception and use of language. Before you take the exam, you should come to terms in your own mind that you will do your best and that nobody, including yourself, has a right to ask more of you than that.

QUESTIONS TO ASK

Jot answers to the following questions down in your personal calendar.

- What are the testing dates and when are the deadlines for signing up? How does one register for the exam? What does it cost? (Usually ten to thirty dollars per exam.) Where is the test given? What identification must students bring on the day of the exam? How does a student reschedule if the student can't appear for the registered day and time?
- What is the makeup of the test? If it involves writing, how many essays are required, what is the nature of each one, and what sorts of questions can I expect? How much time am I allowed for each essay? If I make notes or an outline before I write, will they be graded? Will the proctor strictly divide the exam into planning, writing, proofing segments or will I be expected to budget time myself? What should I bring to the exam? Are pens or bluebooks required? Is scratch paper supplied? Am I allowed to bring a dictionary or thesaurus?
- If the test or a portion of the exam is objective, what kinds of questions will be asked? Are there sample past exams I can study?

Always be sure to read your university's *current* brochure or bulletin that describes the test. Every year, some universities change the exam configurations, sometimes dramatically.

TACTICS ON THE DAY OF THE TEST

1. **Concentrate**. On the day of the test, reduce as many of your distractions, obligations, and plans as possible. Have no social events planned—either before or after the test—so that you focus full attention on the job you must do. Leave adequate time to arrive at the test center. It is better to be a little bit early. Have a positive mental attitude.
2. **Pace yourself**. Occasionally, stop to check the time to be sure you are working at a good pace and plan on five or six minutes at the end to proof or review your work.
3. **Work carefully**. Listen carefully to any directions given to you by the test proctor. If you are taking a multiple-choice test also, be sure to put each answer in the right space. If you skip a question, be careful to skip the corresponding space on the answer sheet. Focus only on the test; block out any distractions.
4. **Read the question carefully**. Be absolutely sure that you understand what is required of you. Make a few notes; employ appropriate prewriting techniques like listing, mapping, clustering, outlining.
5. **Work smoothly and efficiently**. Once you know what you're going to say, begin writing with cool effectiveness; don't dawdle. Let your communicative "voice" take over, don't mill and fume over each word; don't doubt yourself as you write. Make a strong, clear, unified statement. Write naturally, as to a friend, but with the slang and clichés removed. Use a number 1 or 2 pencil if permitted for ease of erasing and repairing errors.
6. **Keep introductions succinct**. Once you have expressed the topic sentence, look for a quick close of the introductory paragraph. Most of the content of your paper will be carried in the following paragraphs. Don't wander; begin with your main point and stay with it.
7. **Don't editorialize**. Don't take issue with or complain about the question or the test in the context of your paper.
8. **Use the appropriate person**. Don't hesitate to use the first person (*I*) in personal experience essays.
9. **Remain businesslike**. The writing test determines how you handle logic and information in solving a problem or analyzing an idea. The scorers will be looking for a competent statement that is well organized, well detailed, well supported, and generally well written.
10. **Write about what you know**. If you are not able to apply personal experience, use the experience of a family member or friend. Refer to books, films, or interviews where appropriate. Always employ accurate, credible, and straightforward data.
11. **Don't be caught in the "narrative snare."** Many writers have trouble pulling out of a narrative, especially about themselves. Spend more time on explanation, logic, support, and analysis. Always tie experience and narrative to the overall essay topic by frequent connecting sentences and evaluations.
12. **Don't neglect conclusion, but keep it short**. Don't sum up previous points in the last paragraph of an impromptu essay. Instead, answer the last part of the question, suggest a solution, make an appeal, point to the future, or identify a truth or principle.

STRUCTURED AND UNSTRUCTURED EXAM QUESTIONS

Structured Questions

Most of the essay questions you will deal with are *structured*, that is, equipped with directions (called "prompts") that tell you exactly how to organize your answer to the question. This feature is a two-edged sword. While it does provide you with much of the organization you must have in your essay, it sets forth rigid requirements that you must fulfill. If you miss any of them, you might write an incomplete paper, and not pass for that reason. Always read a structured question several times and study it carefully.

Example of a Structured Question

> We all know at least one person among our acquaintances or family who behaves in an unusual manner, or whose lifestyle does not conform to accepted forms of behavior. Write a well-organized essay in which you do the following:
> —Identify and describe an acquaintance or relative you consider unusual or unconventional.
> —Explain what you believe to be unusual about this person.
> —Explain why you believe this person behaves the way he or she does.
> As you can see, this question is beautifully organized for you. Be sure to answer it just as it is formatted, section by section.

Unstructured Questions

Unstructured questions are rare and do not provide a plan. You need to map out your own organizational scheme for this topic. There is no trick in deciding whether or not a question is prestructured or unstructured; if the organization of your essay does not bounce out at you the way it does in the previous example, if it is not immediately evident to you, you need to formulate your own structure. You can do this very easily by breaking a general, unstructured question down into a series of narrower, more focused questions.

Example of an Unstructured Question

> Compare the possible reasons that motivate prolife and prochoice advocates to argue for their respective beliefs.

This question becomes much clearer and much easier to organize if it is broken down into a series of questions:

- What is the prolife position?
- What is the prochoice position?
- What possible reasons lie behind the beliefs of prolifers?
- What possible reasons lie behind the beliefs of the prochoice advocates?
- What examples can you use to illustrate each?

You can see how easy it is now to deal with the original questions, which seemed a little heavy and vague, and how practical it is now to organize an essay with a strong, controlling sentence and specific supporting paragraphs. Any time you encounter an unstructured question, or, for that matter, any essay question that does not seem to have an organizational plan inherent in its wording, break the question into a series of short, sharply focused questions before you organize the essay. Also, consider examples you will need.

KEY WORDS USED IN ESSAY QUESTIONS

Analyze: Literally "loosen up." Break a single thing or idea into its component parts and then show how those parts are related and essential. Explore connections within subject of essay. Examine cause and effect.

Argue: Seek agreement through an appeal to reason, using logic as opposed to emotion. Structure of a classic argumentative essay:

1. State premise clearly.
2. Give opposition's best argument and then counter it.
3. State premise again firmly.

Compare and contrast: These methods are usually linked, but may be used separately. A careful user of language discriminates between them clearly. To compare is to discuss similarities; to contrast is to discuss differences. Comparison-contrast discussions should be balanced.

Define: To set forth the meaning of a thing, idea, or quality by answering the questions, "What is it? What does it mean?" Begin by putting the word into a general classification (anger is an emotion), and then limit its meaning by using description (*How does it look, sound, smell, feel?*), examples (*What other things are like this?*), comparison/contrast, (*How is it like/unlike related things?*), value (*What is its function? How important is it?*), and process (*How is it made?*). A request for a definition is a request for *your* definition.

Describe: To create a verbal picture of the subject by relying on the senses of sight, sound, touch, taste, smell. A careful selection of details is important to satisfy your readers and accomplish your purpose.

Discuss: To raise some important issues about a topic and treat them fully over several paragraphs.

Evaluate: To determine the merit, value, stature, relevance, or truthfulness of a statement or idea. To evaluate a statement, find the *thesis*, determine what points have been made to support the thesis, and then write a statement declaring whether the points are valid (do they really support the thesis? Are they accurate, current, sound? Are they really relevant to the thesis?).

Explain: To clarify an opinion or idea by laying all its parts out, revealing causes, justifications, relevant points.

Identify: To name clearly, to select from a larger group.

Prove: To determine the truth of an assertion or idea by presenting evidence, logical arguments, or corroborative testimony.

Relate: To show how things are associated with each other by comparing, matching, equating, or pairing them (as in a cause-effect relationship).

State: To present the main point clearly and definitively, without much supporting material.

Summarize: To condense an argument or discussion by highlighting its main points, omitting supporting material like examples, details, or illustrations that comprise the body of an essay.

PREWRITING TACTICS

Once you have read your essay assignment, you will want to decide quickly and efficiently what your approach will be—quickly because you don't have that much time; efficiently because you want to emerge from this ruminating stage with a good, developable topic.

There are several widely used prewriting techniques. As we go over them, remember that you will be using them under intense time pressure, so judge each one with that restriction in mind. You will use only one when the time comes; the nature of the question will govern which one you must choose. The best prewriting tactic will work with the recommended essay procedure outlined at the end of Chapter 4.

Listing

By far the most common prewriting technique, listing is a way for writers to determine if the chosen subject is rich enough to be developed. (The wise writer, of course, chooses a topic that he or she knows something about.) Suppose the essay assignment requires that you explain a process, and you have decided to write about how a student can earn an A in a subject. Here's what your list might look like:

1. Select instructor carefully. (Add an example of Professor X.)
2. Audit class one semester before. (Add an example of a specific class.)
3. Buy books early; preread them. (Add specific examples.)
4. Cut schedule down to give yourself time. (Add an experience or example.)
5. Overlearn everything. (Add a specific example.)
6. Join study groups. (Add examples.)
7. Speak to instructor about any unclear concepts. (Offer an example or experience.)
8. Treat final like a war campaign. (Add an example.)

Don't worry about the order or comprehensiveness of the list. Just give yourself some ideas that will set an essay in motion.

Clustering

With the *clustering* approach (which may be time *in*efficient), you put your topic in the center of a sheet of paper, draw a circle around it, and then add other smaller circles radiating around it that represent derivative or developmental ideas. Some of those smaller circles themselves may have subsets of circles branching from them. Suppose, for example, that you have an assignment like the following:

> All human beings, at one time or another, have a crisis. A crisis is a time when we need to stick out our chin, prepare for the worst, and get going. Identify a crisis or series of crises that you had or someone close to you has experienced. Explain the aftermath of the crisis on you and your family.

You decide that you want to write about predictable crises of a college education. Here is a possible cluster diagram for that topic:

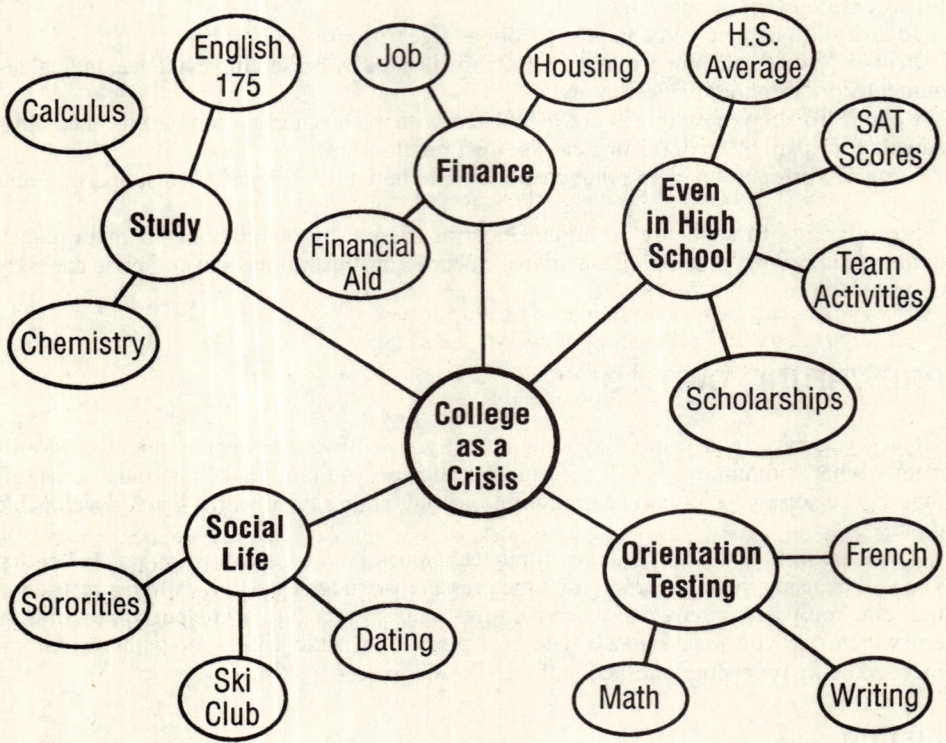

Again, your essay topic will only allow you enough time to develop a specific strand derived from the cluster. You must budget your time and examples accordingly.

Freewriting

Probably better used with much more time, freewriting can allow the writer to evoke creative ideas that lie just below the level of the conscious mind. Allow yourself a short time period (say three minutes). Focus on the question or issue as a beginning point; put your pencil on the paper, write continuously whatever comes into your mind without worrying about punctuation or relevance. The technique is included here, because it can be used as an emergency stopgap if a writer cannot think of a topic at all. Here is an example of how a writer used nonstop writing with the college-as-a-crisis topic:

> In my freshman year, I had imaginary struggles with my professors. My biology professor scared me to death. He always referred to my "beautiful blue eyes" every time he talked about the genetics of rabbits, and then winked at me. My history prof seemed to live in a somnambulant haze and would not even look up from the podium. He would stalk out quickly at the end of every

class. Nobody seemed to know anything about him. He was the "mysterious Dr. B." Then there was Dr. Potts. He assigned us so much work that I was up all night every night that semester. I have never learned so much from anyone, except Dr. P. with whom I fell in love.

Some sort of a topic seems to be developing here. For really desperate cases, it could work. For example, it suggests several possible directions for the essay: "Fear as a motivator in college"; "Imaginary or philosophic alliances with professors as a factor in my success"; "Nonverbal communication by professors"; and others as well.

Mapping

Once writers have an idea for a topic to write on, they need to *map* out or give a rough outline to their ideas and details. Here is a map of the college-as-a-crisis cluster:

Thesis:

Throughout my entire school career, college always took on the proportions of a great crisis.

A. Even in high school, college loomed over me like a threat.
   1. The SAT tests were my first initiation.
   2. College scholarships were a necessity.
   3. Even the applications I filled out were a trial.
B. My social life as a freshman was one predicament after another.
   1. I couldn't make up my mind which sorority to join.
   2. I dated too often and became confused.
   3. I innocently walked into a financial buzz saw when I became treasurer of the ski club.
C. Some courses became a moment of truth for me.
   1. Chemistry 103 robbed me of my self-confidence.
   2. I always thought I could write and read until I hit English 175.
   3. Calculus seemed literally out of this world.

Exemplification

Whichever of these prewriting strategies you find most helpful, they will achieve no effect if unaccompanied by specific examples. So you must incorporate deliberate and conscious exemplification to add the power of illustration to your impromptu writing. Examples expand into sequence and details when developed into paragraphs. And remember, when in doubt about what to write next, include another example relevant to the topic.

2 Essay Types

A WORD ABOUT ESSAY-TEST DESIGN

Test-development committees which oversee the construction of the essay portions of CSU Graduation Writing Assessment Requirements must create essay questions and tasks for students called "prompts." Understanding these committees' concerns will help you anticipate and prepare for the test.

First, the essay test cannot ask an over-specialized question: "Discuss and analyze the architecture of the Intel Pentium II chip." Only computing engineering students would have much chance to talk with authority about such a subject. All essay questions must be accessible to the general body of knowledge available to all university students. However, even in consideration of such generalized knowledge, essay questions still cannot be specialized. For an essay question to provide prompts asking about a recent movie, for example, might serve you well if you go to movies, but penalize another student not interested in films. By contrast, a more global prompt asking about the successes or failures of movies as good art might work, because students could discuss *any* film and generate their own definitions of "good art" to be evaluated in their essay responses.

To put it another way, if a test-development committee wishes to attempt to ask you an essay question regarding specialized information, in philosophical ethics, perhaps, or applications of psychological theory, it must allow you to apply any personally accessible examples in any kind of limited way, as long as you follow the tasks. Therefore, all essay questions on the GWAR must make space for students to refer to personal experience and background, no matter what. Though some students may be unwilling to discuss personal experience, test developers know that the students can refer to others' experience, news items, articles they've read, stories they've heard, and so on.

Second, test developers know that students do not have access to the library or any research for the test. Students bring their skills, their minds, and their memories to the test. These must be sufficient to accomplish the task of passing an impromptu essay. Some tests get around this limitation by first providing a reading the student must evaluate, and then asking an essay question. In those cases, students are expected to refer to the reading along with their own counter examples—as long as they don't copy the language of the reading and use it to substitute for their own writing.

Third, essay questions must be free of bias, including gender bias, racial bias, religious and English as a Second Language bias. For example, the first sentence of the sample essay question from Chapter 1 could have ended with the word "norms": "We all know at least one person among our acquaintances or family who behaves in an unusual manner, or whose lifestyle does not conform to accepted **norms**." But this word *norms* would be quite confusing to international students familiar with statistics, who might interpret the word as "statistical" or mathematical norms, as opposed to "conventional behavior." Test developers are usually sensitive to these issues, and thus must ensure that the question is phrased in the clearest possible language. Essay questions are free to introduce issues of race, gender, and international politics, as long as they do so in a completely unbiased manner, encouraging the student to evaluate one or both sides of an issue.

The upshot of all of the above considerations should be clear. For a test question to successfully assess the range of student writing it must be carefully designed, and it must be pre-tested. It's well known that even test developers overlook exam features they take for granted; to ensure quality control they must pretest the GWAR questions they would like to use on similar bodies of students to uncover any hidden biases. Every question gets pretested, therefore, usually by faculty from sister institutions who—as a courtesy—administer possible tests to their classes as part of their grading criteria. The results are scored, tallied, and assessed, and successful questions go into a pool of thousands of potential essay questions that can be tapped for future GWAR exams.

For you, the above considerations are significant in three ways:

1. Prepare to refer to personal experience, others' experience, and sources you are familiar with to support any claims you make in your essays. Be confident that your realm of experience is acceptable as long as you provide sufficient concrete detail and show the relevance of your experience to both the question and the readers—the scorers in this case.
2. A lot of work has preceded your taking the test to ensure you get fair treatment.
3. If you answer in good faith, your answer will be respected, and with confidentiality.

The Two Hidden Agenda

As a last word about test design, you should know the hidden agenda. Good test questions also teach, and so be prepared for a question that tries to teach you something, or that reveals to you your own wisdom regarding an issue, which your writing skill will unlock and reveal. Also, good questions test the full range of students' abilities, from the most elementary writing skill of introduction (thesis)-examples-recapitulation, to the most complex, insightful analysis. In other words, if you wish to score highly, no matter which of the essay types below that you encounter, think first of examples you can use to support the question, and then try to state how effective those specific examples are and how they are meaningful or applicable to all readers. Be prepared to follow your examples with answers to "Why?" "How did this state result?" "Where to from here?" "What do my examples mean?" "How are my examples significant to larger-scale issues?" Your practice at providing answers to these questions addresses "the implicit analytical task."

In other words, test developers creating essay questions assume a better writer will incorporate an analytical approach, whether or not the question requests it directly.

TYPES OF ESSAYS

1. Personal Experience
2. Comparison/Contrast
3. Explanatory/Analytic
4. Argument/Persuasion

The four essay types listed are the ones most typically found on California State University writing proficiency exams. The time allotted for writing varies from 45 minutes to 3 hours. Any one of the types can be either structured or unstructured, but the majority tend to be structured. You will notice in the following detailed look at each one of these essay types that there is considerable crossover between them.

THE PERSONAL-EXPERIENCE ESSAY

Personal-experience essays are by far the most prevalent, requiring personal narratives and descriptions on the part of the writer. Commonly, the student is asked to draw on his or her personal experiences to write these essays. Topics include reminiscences about people or past events; situations at home, school, or in the community; current events and issues; observations about the media; hobbies; personal successes and accomplishments; changes the writer would like to see made; career choices; and the like. Most of these questions are structured so that the student has no doubt about the task at hand.

Here is an example:

> Identify one person who has had a measurable effect on your life. Describe the person and the effect he or she has generated, the means by which the effect was brought about, and the difference the effect has made in your life.

Sample essay beginning:

There are many people who have had a positive impact on my life, but the one with the most measurable contribution is my high school math teacher, Mr. Newcomb, in whose math classes I spent one semester of my freshman year, and my entire junior and senior years.

(In three developmental sections of the essay, each of which could be written in one or more paragraphs, the writer would then describe Mr. Newcomb and the change he brought about; provide specific and concrete details about the way Mr. Newcomb produced the change, possibly including ways in which he bolstered the self-confidence of the writer, and then detail the difference Mr. Newcomb's contribution has made in the student's life.)

Another example:

There are very few truly solitary individuals today, so insistently are group activities woven into the patterns of American society. Describe some groups you have been part of, explaining which you wish you had never joined and which have had a positive influence on your life. Do not merely list the groups. Be sure to describe them specifically, explaining what you did in each group and why you consider each group a good or bad influence.

Sample essay beginning:

When I was a little girl, my mother eagerly forced me into groups which are to blame for my present feelings of disdain toward softball, gymnastics, karate, and church music. However, I felt I am a stronger, more capable person today because of other groups I was also eagerly forced to join, such as Girl Scouts, 4H, and International Pen Pals.

(In two or three paragraphs for each, the writer can go on to describe the unfavorable groups first, being careful to supply the specific information the question calls for, and then do the same for the beneficial groups, ending the essay with a one- or two-sentence conclusion.)

Here is a full personal-experience question and essay response:

> Describe an incident in which you or someone close to you was "cut" from a team or rejected in some manner from a group or activity. Be sure to explain the logic behind the reasons for the initial rejection, the reasons you feel the refusal was just or unjust, and the long-term effect of the incident upon you and your behavior. (45 minutes)

During my first year in college I was cut from the baseball team. To most people that would be a minor bummer in their lives, but, to me and my family, it was more of a calamity, in fact, more like a death in the family. To explain why, I need to digress here and explain something about my past few years.

All through my life I have played and excelled at ball, from the time I played T-ball at the Sylmar Independent Baseball League to my first year in college. My mother and father were always a part of my experience; in fact, I have *never* played a game without one or the other watching. As long ago as my last year in elementary school I was singled out as a real prospect. Two coaches from different high schools used to keep track of me that year when I was pitching for the Broncos, an independent sports organization in the West

Valley. Curt Daniels, my coach at that time, said that, in his thirty years of coaching, he had never seen a more promising ballplayer. He predicted that I would become a major leaguer before I finished college. In high school, I broke all the redshirt records in my freshman year, and was all-city, all-state, all star, and state champion each of my last three high school years. At Garrison High School in Canoga Park you can still see plaques and cups awarded to me in the trophy room.

During my last season at Garrison High, my coach, Ansel Williams, invited major league scouts to our games. I was offered a job with the Cincinnati and Houston farm systems, but my mother in particular wanted me to go to college. I could have gone practically anywhere, but I settled on USC because of their great baseball tradition.

All this time, I was really playing great. My ERA never dropped below 2.4. The last two seasons of high school ball my elbow had hurt and become swollen after every game, but the pain never kept me from pitching, and the excitement of those years, when I was a hero of the school and even appeared in national sports magazines as a top recruiting prospect, seemed so much more important than a little pain. I never even mentioned the pain to anyone. I just got in the habit of putting ice on my elbow when I got home.

The first practice game I pitched at USC disaster struck. Suddenly my arm hurt so badly that I couldn't even lob the ball. Nothing—rest, massage, heat, ice, nothing—helped. I was sent by the team doctor to an orthopedic surgeon who did a spread of tests and then let me know the bad news. I had literally worn down the cartilage at several key spots in my elbow. There was no quick fix. The elbow could be replaced, but at a cost of two to three hundred-thousand dollars, and, even then, there was no guarantee that I could pitch well. The doc said that I had done all the damage when I was much younger, while the cartilage was being formed on the growing bone. The coach had no option but to cut me from the team. I understood. He had other prospects waiting in line who wanted to play. His job was to put the best team together, not to wipe the noses of those who cannot play.

Meanwhile, I have had a rebirth of sorts. I never had been much of a student, but suddenly I became interested. I learned a lot about anatomy when all those probes and cat scans were made of my elbow. I was fascinated by orthopedic medicine. I determined to become a pre-med major and see what else the world holds for me. So far, it's giving me much more of a kick than baseball.

EVALUATION OF ESSAY

This is a well-organized, well-written, natural-sounding response to the question. The writer spells out the incident straightforwardly and then effectively shifts to the events leading up to the rejection, in the process supplying enough background information to fulfill each of the points requested in the prompt; the reasons for the rejection, the writer's feelings about the equity of the cut, and the long-term effects. Paragraph 1 clearly proclaims the thesis of the entire essay which is unwaveringly addressed in every paragraph.

Faults in the essay are its colloquial style, its use of contractions, for example, and slang terms like *doc* and *bummer*. The final paragraph is so sparse of detail that it seems abrupt.

THE COMPARISON/CONTRAST ESSAY

Though comparison/contrast essays are rare on GWARs, some essay questions focus on how things are alike; in such cases we might choose to develop the entire essay in the comparison pattern. The comparison essay reveals similarities, and the contrast essay shows differences, but the word *comparison* is often used to describe essays that discuss both similarities and differences.

Whenever a writer lines up two things for discussion, he will almost always be comparing and contrasting them. Never forget, however, that for this essay type to be really meaningful, all the subjects must be members of the same group. A writer might profitably compare and contrast a vocational major with an academic major because both are courses of study. Another writer might effectively compare and contrast a vocational course with an industrial training program because both lead to a job. However, it is not likely that any writer could meaningfully compare and contrast an academic major with an industrial training program. When you employ the comparison/contrast mode of writing, be sure the subjects are plainly related.

There are two ways the details in a comparison paragraph may be arranged: the *point-by-point* pattern or the *block* pattern. We will examine the block pattern first because it really is quite simple. To begin, you describe the pertinent points of the first subject; then you describe the pertinent points of the other. You should always try to conclude the essay with a brief statement that brings the two into focus and restates your reason for comparing them. The block pattern is appropriate to use and easy to organize when the subjects are brief and not too complicated. The point-by-point method helps to keep the reader's attention when the material becomes detailed or full of refinements or exceptions.

Please read and give some thought to the following two quotations:
A. "There's one born every minute."—*P. T. Barnum*
B. "You can fool all of the people some of the time, and you can fool some of the people all of the time, but you can't fool all of the people all of the time."
 —*A. Lincoln*

Write an essay on the two statements above in three parts as follows:
1. Compare the statements. Explain what the two statements have in common and how they overlap.
2. Contrast the statements. Explain how the two statements differ.
3. Explain what your position is regarding the two statements by choosing one or describing the favorable and unfavorable aspects of each. Support your view with examples from your personal experience.

Sample essay beginning:

The two quotations above deal with the naiveté and innocence of the public, especially where public pronouncements of famous personalities like politicians and showmen are concerned. However, one quotation differs from the other very clearly because it seems more respectful of the public than the other, and seeks, in fact, to salute it. I believe Lincoln's statement is, upon some analysis, a very astute and credible description of the different stages the public goes through in making political decisions.

(The writer can proceed to develop the three parts called for in the question, a paragraph or two about the similarity of the statements and ways in which they overlap, another paragraph or two about their differences, and finally a section dealing with the relative values of the quotations, supported by specific observations the writer has made about the public and politics.)

Here is an example of another comparison/contrast topic developed into an essay:

"Dreams are but the touchstones of our characters."—*Henry David Thoreau*
(A touchstone is a hard, flintlike stone that for centuries was used to test the authenticity of gold or silver. Now, the word *touchstone* has come to mean any criterion or test used to measure the quality of a thing.)

In a well-structured essay, describe a dream you or someone you know well attempted to fulfill, only to discover that the dream did not match the reality. Compare and contrast the dream with its own fulfillment. Show in what ways your life was changed because of your discovery. (One Hour)

A Partial Dream

Ten years ago, when I finally received permission from the Department of Immigration and Naturalization to move to Los Angeles from my native homeland Seoul, Korea, I thought I was in heaven. Not only was I going to the promised land, America, but I was going to the movie capital of the world, Hollywood. My family and I arrived at Los Angeles International Airport on May 3, 1989, and it was a very few weeks before our lavish dreams were confronted by a very cold reality.

The America I had fabricated in my imagination was the product of American movies, magazines, and advertisements, all a major source of entertainment and information to Koreans. Every day was sunny, and every house was on a beautiful tree-shaded street, each with a large, aquamarine pool in the back yard. The schools (I was a high-school sophomore at the time) were modern facilities with the finest of teachers; standards were high, and the student body was fun-loving, friendly, and eager to learn. How could it be any other way? After all, this was America, the mightiest, the wealthiest, the most scientifically and technologically advanced nation in the history of all mankind. How could such an advanced and learned country possibly maintain itself in such a position of leadership without its young people being students of this quality? In much the same vein, my father, who is a doctor, felt great optimism about the medical system in the United States. As a foreign doctor, even though he had to repeat most of his internship and residency at the USC Medical Center, he felt honored to be given such an opportunity. After all, this was the best health-care system in the world, and the most advanced. This was the world center of medical research, this was the country in which the most doctors per units of population practiced, this was the country where almost ten times per citizen was spent on health care than the amount spend by the Korean government on its own citizens.

Our first shock came when we drove by taxi to our pre-arranged apartment in North Hollywood. The ride itself was not very pretty. Where were the flowers and wide expanses of green grass? Where was the sunshine? The streets leading to our new home were not clean. There was graffiti all over the walls and houses. Young, aimless men stood around doing nothing, some of them drinking from a can or bottle covered by a small paper bag. We were to learn from our new Korean neighbors that the neighborhood was not safe, and that one had to be careful at all times. Yet even this was minor compared to what I discovered about the Los Angeles schools. Unlike the high school in Seoul I had just left, where all students were, to be plain, devoting their entire lives to the business of learning, spending nine-hour days in class six days a week, with virtually no time for play, this school was a place of leisure. Students wandered late into each class, and the instructor often sat in the front of the room doing something at his desk while the students chatted for maybe a third of the period. Once the instruction started, if the teacher began asking questions about the assignment or the topic at hand, almost nobody had done the work. If the teacher called on individual students, one after another would say he had not done the homework. The tests on the subject were so easy that a reasonably smart student who had done most of the very easy homework assigned could earn an "A." Once I began to be familiar with the students in the class, I realized how high the absence rate is, and how tolerated it is by the authorities. Eventually I transferred to a magnet school with honors classes, but, while the situation was better, it was still a school with surprisingly low standards and sadly motivated students compared to the high school I had left back home.

My father also had some shocks in his medical school, especially the state of the emergency room at the USC Medical Center, where seriously ill patients were allowed to sit in the hall for hours until a doctor could get to them, but generally his initiation into American schools was a much better experience than mine.

My general feeling about America is not one of disappointment, as one might expect, but a realization that America needs some help now that maybe I can give. I have chosen education as a career, and I hope that some day I am able to make some changes, even if they are small changes. I hope to be a naturalized citizen soon, and, when I am, I hope to be an active, helpful part of this great nation, and perhaps, just perhaps, move it closer to the ideal I once carried.

EVALUATION OF ESSAY

> The first paragraph introduces the topic by identifying a dream and hinting at the contrasting reality. The thesis is set forth in the sentence "it was a very few weeks before our lavish dreams were confronted by a very cold reality," and it is developed in well-detailed paragraphs. The author employs the block method of writing a comparison/contrast essay, with the second paragraph supplying adequate supporting details about the dream; and the third and fourth dealing with contrasting points about the reality. The last paragraph holds a surprise ending, a positive statement that runs against the negative grain of the essay, yet manages to help unify and finish it. Negative points include the incomplete references to the father's experience and the somewhat disparaging viewpoint.

Here is an example of an essay written in the point-by-point mode. Notice that the details prompted by the topic pretty much require this kind of organization, which allows the author to place the habits and styles of each family, the Gaitanos and the Castillos, side by side.

> Compare one branch of your family with another. Focus on similarities or differences, whichever is greater and more representative of the way things really are. Illuminate your discussion with specific details, anecdotes, or descriptions to support your basic thesis. (One Hour)

Whenever I try to compare my relatives, specifically my mother's family with my father's, I find that similarities are very hard to find. With differences it's another story. The two families are so unlike that it sometimes seems that they belong on different planets. My father's family lives in Venice, and all of its members look to "the old country" as the source of all that is sound and good. My mother's family comes from Mexico, Culiacan, Sinaloa, to be exact, where life is not lavish, but where family is everything. In this essay, I will compare and contrast the habits and preferences of the two groups of relatives, particularly in regard to food and dress.

Before I visit either family, I find it useful to establish a "mind-set" so that I can relax and feel natural. Any celebratory meal partaken with the Gaitanos, my Italian family, is very formal, with the finest of table settings and linens, and the most perfect examples of Italian culinary art. In contrast, any Christmas or Easter meal shared with my Mexican family, the Castillos, is much like a normal evening meal, with very little in the way of special dishes or settings. At the Italian table, silverware is placed just so, and spoons and forks must be used for specific foods like salads, desserts, and meat. At the Castillos', any eating implement is fine; nobody notices or cares. Even plastic utensils sometimes are mixed with metal ones. When one eats dinner at the Gaitanos', one is expected to be formally dressed; at the Castillos', one is merely expected to be wearing something. At the Gaitano table, the meal is always a carefully coordinated assemblage of traditional Italian dishes, with salad, pasta, perhaps a veal roast, ravioli, and then a fine dessert, like pistachio cream cake, all served with a fine table wine. A move to the living room with expresso and liqueur always ends the meal. At the Castillo table, most of the meal is served in bowls or platters on the table at the beginning of the meal, and one helps himself to whatever he feels like eating.

Even though the Gaitano family seems more formal and aristocratic, it is the Castillo family that has the money and education in the family. Yet, when it comes to dress, the Italian contingent of my family pulls all the stops out. When I visit the Gaitanos in Venice, everyone there is dressed as if he or she were royalty. Women routinely wear mink jackets or camel's hair coats. Men routinely wear formal business wear, meticulously tailored for a perfect fit. Everyone who lives in Venice seems to dress to perfection, including the children. In Sinaloa, however, the Castillos are usually in bare feet and loose fitting clothes. In warm weather, which is the rule when I visit, virtually all of the boys and young men do not wear shirts; women wear slacks and loose tops. Here in the United States, the difference in dress is as great, though the severely formal Italian mode becomes dressy casual, and the utter freedom and comfort of the Castillos becomes stylishly casual.

I have only displayed the tip of the iceberg. The differences between the two families are massive, and are evident in philosophies, political bents, leisure activities, values and many other areas. I believe I have described enough, however, to suggest how great the differences in one family can be.

THE EXPLANATORY/ANALYTIC ESSAY

An *explanatory* essay question calls for the writer to explain current issues and ideas, controversies, difficulties, or opinions. A typical question of this type is the following:

> Charges for public services have skyrocketed in recent years. As a result, the public is being forced to dole out a greater and greater percentage of its expendable income for sales taxes, gasoline taxes, public university tuition, smog inspection, transportation levies, and state, federal, and local income taxes, to name a few. Services that used to be free, ambulance transportation, police calls, weed clearance, street sweeping, street parking, garbage collection, for example, are now billed. What impact has the new "pay as you go" society had on you? What specific changes would you like to make?

A more complex dimension is added to such a question when the student is asked to *analyze* such material—that is, to break it into its component parts and with these parts perform a task such as comparing them, evaluating them, or characterizing them in some way.

- **Technical analysis** answers the question, "How is it put together?" and almost always occurs with functional analysis.
- **Functional analysis** answers the question, "How does it work?"
- **Process analysis** answers the question, "How is it done?"
- **Causal analysis** answers the question, "What caused it?"
- **Qualitative analysis** answers the questions, "How good, important, or true is it?" Whatever the type of analysis, you can be sure that the question will call for an *explosion* or *segmentation* of a single item or idea into its elements. Take the following explanatory/analytic question:

> Some people feel the world is advancing too fast and that "modern is not always better." Choose some recent (within 50 years) technological invention or discovery and show that it has some negative spinoffs. Explain how the negative impact of the invention or discovery has affected you and your life. What are the long-term effects of the innovation on the world?

Sample essay beginning:
> The invention of the computer took place about fifty years ago, and, since that time, it has brought the human population of the world untold advantages. Computers keep our bank accounts, and issue our pay checks. Computers run our airlines and practically manufacture products like toasters, washing machines, and automobiles. Without computers, this country could not have sent missions to the moon, and without them, we could not perform open-heart surgery, unravel the mysteries of DNA, or watch an event live from the other side of the globe. However, the computerization of human life on earth has so quickened every transaction and so ruthlessly made every person accountable so frequently, that it has taken a toll of another sort, a toll on the minds and spirits of individuals like you and me.

(The writer can now explain how the quickening of transactions and imposition of frequent accountability is taking a toll on our minds and spirits. One way of developing these ideas is to write a paragraph about the *quickened transactions* and another about the *frequent accountability*. The reader should always maintain the supremacy of the pregnant sentence (discussed in Chapter 3) at the end of the paragraph: "the computerization of man's life...has taken a toll." He should also remember that the question calls for an analysis of the word *computerization*, that is, a separation of the word into all of its aspects. In this paper, the writer is locked onto negative aspects by the topic. A concluding paragraph might issue some hope for the negative state of affairs.

Sometimes explanatory/analytic questions take the form of a problem to be solved or a judgment to be made. Take the following example involving your assessment of information in a table. Although such table questions have diminished in recent graduate writing exams, you may encounter one nonetheless, and you must be cautious. You will be tempted to simply reproduce the statistics from the table into your sentences, but in so doing you may risk lowering your score. You will achieve a better result to use personal examples of people you know whose situations mirror or parallel the ones in the table. Then you can discuss what happened to them, and evaluate the consequences.

Directions: You will have a total of 60 minutes to respond to the topic below. You will be given 5 minutes to plan your essay, 40 minutes to write it, and 15 minutes to review, edit, and complete your essay. The above times will be announced by the proctor.

You will not be allowed to leave early.

Express your thoughts carefully, logically, and effectively. Provide examples and evidence to support your ideas.

You have just completed three job interviews and compiled the table of information below detailing the job offers you have received:

Aspect to Consider	Job A	Job B	Job C
Annual Salary	$37,000	$26,000	$20,000
Automobile provided?	no	yes	yes
Location	New York, NY	Aspen, CO	Portland, ME
Apartment rent per month	$1400	$900	$600
Number of employees in company	2800	150	19

- Based on the above data, which job would you choose? Why?
- What other aspects of the job or considerations not shown would be important to you in making this decision?

You may use this timetable to outline your thoughts:
- 5 minutes to plan
- 40 minutes to write your essay
- 15 minutes to review, edit, and complete

Here is a question and complete essay in the explanatory/analytic mode.

> We all attempt to make a change for the better at some time in our lives. In fact, all progress made on this planet has been the result of humanity's quest for a better life. Think of a major "change for the better" that you experienced or witnessed in your lifetime, a significant change involving several stages or steps over a period of time. Identify the change, discuss each of its steps, and the effects each step had on you or the principals involved. Be sure to explain how the final outcome was a change for the better.

Student response:

Kadan is a small town in Northern Czechoslovakia. It was established in the thirteenth century when King, and also Emperor, Charles IV was traveling through Czech country looking for a piece of beautiful land. I had the good fortune to live in Kadan for twelve years. During those twelve years, I witnessed major changes that were made in the town, most of which affected me profoundly.

I was six years old when my family moved to Kadan. My first impression of the place was one of crushing disappointment. All I could see were several old historical buildings, dingy houses, various churches, and castles in very deteriorated condition. It was like a bad dream. I could not picture myself living and growing up in the middle of this town. There were about 10 apartment houses that made up a very large complex. All of them looked exactly the same. It reminded me of boxes that were put together to make a discouraging impression for immigrants coming to town.

The second day after our arrival, we went to see the town. It took us no time to find the central area with an old town hall and a monument to a WWI soldier in the middle of the square. There were not many shops. I remember seeing a police station, an elementary school, a fire station, a few pubs, a very old and unkempt movie theater, and a nondescript hospital.

Without a smile on our faces, my brother and I accepted the reality and started attending elementary school the following Monday. We settled down to routine work in a few days. During the third week or so, we returned home to find a massive construction project beginning right next to our apartment house. Within a couple of months, a beautiful sports complex was completed. We were able to play tennis whenever we wanted, or go swimming all year long. I developed skill at both sports, and won several championships in swimming. My self-confidence began to rise, and I saw life as positive and good.

It did not even take one more year for Kadan to build a truly beautiful hospital with a clean brick and stainless steel design, two more complexes of apartments in more attractive buildings, and a huge shopping center. Life in the town became more enjoyable. The new additions brought jobs, opportunities, and variety to our lives.

A year or so later, a committee made up of well-known architects and other experts evaluated the old historical center of the town. Consequently, most of the buildings were reconstructed from top to bottom, and afterwards, the town center was an incredibly beautiful sight to behold. The committee converted one part of the main castle to a gallery and museum. We people in the town became very interested in the history of our town, and began to take great pride in this captivating place we inhabited.

During the next ten years, Kadan became the most beautiful town in Czechoslovakia, and the most historically exciting. Three new secondary schools were built, and became so popular that students attended from all over the world. A magnificent Greek theater was carved out of a hillside near the town center; within a year, the town was treated to a stunning series of concerts and plays by the world's greatest playwrights and composers. Again, I personally benefited from this innovation. Directly because of the inspiration I received from those wonderful evenings, I became a humanities major and even took up acting.

In the summer months, Kadan was full of tourists and visitors. Parks, tennis courts, and playgrounds were crowded, and it was difficult to eat in any of the wonderful restaurants without a reservation. I could not believe that this was the same bleak town I had moved to just a few years earlier. Suddenly there were so many nice and fascinating places to go, and so many rich and historical treasures to study. The inhabitants of Kadan are proud of their town, and they take good care of it. It is now full of flowers, little parks, and trees. It seems we have all been transformed by the physical changes made in the town.

EVALUATION OF ESSAY

This well-organized, well-written essay fulfills in detail the prompt requirement to write analytically about the progressive changes that took place, in this case in the Czechoslovakian town of Kadan. The writer is careful to explain the beneficial effect of each change, not only on the people of the town, but on the writer herself, as well as long-term effects of the change. In doing so, the writer writes *analytically*. The essay is unusually long for a student response in a 60-minute writing where some of the available time had to be spent on prewriting and organization. Naturally, good writers have more to say, and it is easy to say more when you are familiar with your examples (from personal experience) and interested in them. An average student has only time for about six completely developed paragraphs in a 60-minute writing, whereas the eight paragraphs above represent an unusually fluent student. All writers can learn from such good examples, however.

THE ARGUMENT/PERSUASION ESSAY

An argument essay is an appeal to logic and reason; a persuasion paper is an appeal to emotions or ethics. Very seldom, however, does a writer use solely one or the other when he or she is attempting to persuade the reader to embrace a point of view. In the argument/persuasion paper, the writer hopes to *convince* the reader and attempts to do so through a series of steps:

1. Gain the reader's attention.
2. Outline the problem or situation.
3. Anticipate or recognize opposing points of view.
4. Appeal to both reason and emotion in presenting strong, factual data that will sway the reader to your side.

Keep in mind that the prompts that accompany argument/persuasion topics might alter your overall plan.

Here is an example of an argument/persuasion topic:

> Increasingly, the government is backing away from social programs and government sponsored enterprises. There are many voices in the Republican right who are adamant in their opposition to a state-supported university system, arguing, among many other points, that the system is plainly not economically feasible. Indeed, the State of California seems to be bowing under the weight of too many social programs, and may soon have to decide where to make massive cuts. We may be witnessing the beginning of the end of public university education as we have known it in California.
>
> Support one side of this pertinent issue, arguing convincingly by presenting as many strong points as possible. Be sure to anticipate an opposing point of view by countering some of those arguments in your own paper.

Sample essay beginning:

    To reduce or discontinue affordable public university education is to end life as we have known and lived it in California. The economic ramifications alone are staggering, so pervasive have the UC and CSU systems become in the workforce of our state. The engines that have produced generation after generation of our most productive and talented citizens cannot be replicated or offset easily. Where will our lawyers, doctors, business executives, teachers, nurses, health care professionals, or scientists come from? How will our literary traditions, research practices, humanities, business schools fare in the meanwhile? Like the fine state mental health system that was phased out by Governor Reagan in the 1970s, the higher education system could very well become a faint shadow of itself.

(The writer would proceed by developing the body of this essay, with paragraphs that detail, substantiate, and add to the general points made above. The writer would also answer some of the countering arguments that he or she assumes might occur to the readers, and then close with a strong appeal for support in the final paragraph.)

Here is another argument/persuasion topic:

> How many times have you heard the statement, "There ought to be a law!" Describe a contemporary problem in society, politics, or the workplace that could be solved by a new law. Explain what the law should accomplish and how it would be beneficial. Persuade your reader that your point of view is correct.

Sample essay beginning:

    There ought to be a law against any kind of disturbance of a person's privacy or leisure time. My wife and I work hard for long hours and our times together, when we can relax and regenerate our energy, are not only important to us, but essential. Yet, we find there are many interruptions and intrusions into our private time. The phone rings constantly. Because we have family, we must answer it, often to hear a sales or charity pitch. I have found that the violations of our leisure time are always one of three kinds: (1) the telephone, (2) the doorbell, and (3) the call from work.

(Obviously, the writer has designed his essay in this short beginning. He will have three developmental paragraphs expanding upon the three intrusions into his personal time, and then conclude with a paragraph or two that satisfy the three points requested in the prompt, an explanation of the law he proposes, ways it would benefit the community, and reasons why we should all agree.)

Here is a complete argument/persuasion paper.

> All fields of study are occasionally enlivened by controversies within their ranks. Medicine has been shaken by formidable disagreements on universal health coverage, abortion, the clinical definition of death, and many more. In literary fields, scholars sometimes disagree vehemently on issues such as the status of authors, or critical interpretations of a work or passage. Historians have argued mightily about "tilted" history books that emphasize, for example, a Western interpretation of the age of exploration. Identify a controversy in your field of study or one with which you are familiar. Represent both sides of the controversy with some balance, if feasible, and then argue for the position you embrace.

Student response:

    I am a Public Health major. When I graduate, I hope to work with the Food and Drug Administration in Washington, D.C., where I was assigned as a Mentor Scholar last summer. An interesting aspect of my chosen profession is the controversy it has always seemed to attract. The current flaps in the Administration involve such issues as the early release of untested drugs, the safety of breast implants, the misleading labeling of foods, and the morality of early pregnancy termination through drugs. One health issue that I have done a little research on involves the irradiation, or "nuking," as the opponents of the process say, of food. Irradiation is a procedure that has been used for years in the processing of seeds, spices, edible herbs, and beans. Usually foods are placed on a conveyor belt, which travels into a chamber that is protected by thick concrete walls, and then bombarded with gamma rays from a radioactive source. Irradiation kills the insects, molds, and bacteria, allowing fruits and vegetables to stay fresh for several weeks. Farmers are then able to sell fresh food in more distant markets. More important, fruits and vegetables in the market remain fresh and crisp.

    The official position of the government is that irradiation of food on its way to market is a safe and efficient way to retard spoilage and kill organisms that cause illnesses like salmonella and diarrhea. Many food processors and consumer health organizations agree, viewing radiation as a process as necessary and important for food as pasteurization is for milk. The FDA approved irradiation only after hundreds upon hundreds of studies and experiments conclusively declared the technology safe. Researchers and scientists at most major universities with food institutes also consider the process safe and necessary.

    Opponents argue that "zapping the food supply" causes many more problems than it solves. They believe that it robs food of some of its nutritional value. More important, they argue that it requires the use of dangerous nuclear material which, in turn, increases the risk of cancer, sterility, birth defects, and other maladies. I must admit that some opponents of the new technology simply want to wait until more testing has proven conclusively that it is safe. In fact, several states have temporarily banned irradiated produce. Anti-nuclear groups are often behind the anti-irradiation movement and are usually the ones picketing and conducting sit-ins wherever irradiation threatens to spring up. Their rhetoric has spawned a consumer wariness about irradiated foods, and most retail food chains will not sell irradiated foods as a result.

    Having read many of the studies done on irradiated produce and meats, I believe the process to be safe. We have seen serious health problems caused by unclean food, like salmonella poisoning from infected chicken, stomach infections caused by amoeba, and deaths resulting from botulism, all of which would be prevented by the irradiation process. Most of the time, those people protesting irradiation fly in the face of studies which prove their claims to be unfounded. Almost none of them have scientific or medical training. I see nothing wrong with more studies, but I believe we should not listen to emotional rhetoric not based on scientific evidence.

EVALUATION OF ESSAY

> This is a well-organized, well-written answer to the question, adequately covering both sides of the argument. The writer convincingly takes a position, namely that irradiation is safe, and supplies solid details to substantiate that position. There are few technical errors. The writer's main task is to analyze the term *irradiation*, that is, to break it into components and then organize a pro and con discussion based on the components, a task he has done well. The authoritative "voice" of the writer helps unify the paper.

LENGTH OF PROMPT

Some essay assignments are longer than others. Often, they are written with the intention of helping the student understand exactly what is required. Here are some examples:

Short:

> How well did your elementary and high school teachers prepare you for the efforts you are now making in college? Discuss how your previous experience or schooling was helpful and how it could have been more helpful.

As this one does, most short prompts give you freedom to design the structure of your essay. Note that, as short as it is, the assignment spells out specific content that the exam readers will expect to see in the paper.

Medium:

Please read the following quotations:
"How sweet and gracious, even in common speech,
Is that fine sense which men call courtesy?"

"Of courtesy, it is much less
Than courage of heart or holiness,
Yet in my walks it seems to me
That the Grace of God is in courtesy."

> *Courtesy* is an interesting word. It is derived from the word *heart* and has suggested admirable qualities in a person: forbearance, restraint, dignity, and charity. Yet, throughout time, courtesy has sometimes been suspected of masking sinister or dishonest intentions. Compare the two quotations above. How do you believe each of the speakers would define courtesy? How do you define courtesy? How important is courtesy in your mode of behavior? Are there times when you find courtesy would be embarrassing to you? Is courtesy "in" in the social world of 1998? Are there times you have seen courtesy used to mask other intentions?

The preceding prompt contains several specific tasks that you are to do as you write your essay. Read the prompt five or six times. Be sure to cover each one of the points it requires.

This question points up the fact that longer prompts require extra vigilance on the part of the persons being tested.

Long:

Please read and study the following quotation:

> Ask any two persons—anytime, anywhere—to give you their definitions of *science fiction* and you will have two different answers. Read any six books on the subject and you have six more versions of what the term means.
> It is not our intention to impose upon you, or even to suggest, our choice in this matter; rather it is our hope that this book will enable you to formulate a

definition of your own. When you can explain clearly what science fiction means *to you*, this book will have served its purpose.

In the past, this form of literature—whether in books or magazines—was published under such titles as *Travel Adventures, Wonder Stories, Fantastic Tales, Mysteries of the Universe,* etc. It took such garish "headlines" to draw public attention to the nature of the books' contents.

Hugo Gernsback, a New York magazine publisher and one of the great pioneers in the field we are exploring here, provided the much-needed common denominator by coining the magic name *Science Fiction* in 1929.

Instantly and universally, science fiction was defined and accepted as a form of literature distinct and apart from all others, a form which imposed on the writer none of those shackles that confine traditional writing to the limits of rules and precedents.

Comfortably settled under the aegis of its brand-new generic name, science fiction prospered in spite of a world-wide depression and World War II. Other media of entertainment contributed their shares: the movies gave us Boris Karloff as Frankenstein's monster and Fredric March as Dr. Jekyll. In 1938 a science fiction radio program threw the East Coast of the United States into a panic.

Now that we have a rough sketch of its present structural form, what of the basic elements of science fiction; how and when did it begin?

All creatures in the animal kingdom have the instincts of curiosity and fear. Man alone was endowed with imagination, a fact [that] was bound to complicate matters for him; whereas a fox, let us say, was able to shrug off the mysteries of the heavens and such whims of nature as lightning and earthquakes, Man demanded an explanation...

And so began the myths, the ancient creeds, witchcraft, astrology, the fantastic tales of wanderings into the unknown reaches of space and time, the distortions of the mental and physical capabilities of man himself. Evidently, "explanations" were not enough: Man developed a thirst for something *beyond* the ever-growing knowledge brought to him by concrete scientific research. The French call this thirst *le culte du merveilleux*. We call it science fiction.

To keep ahead of reality as he must, the science fiction writer has had to do some fast thinking: in the span of about thirty years, true science has given us the atomic and hydrogen bombs, coast-to-coast television, and jet engine, intercontinental ballistic missiles, Sputnik I, two Navy submarines under the North Pole, John Glenn in orbit, the first human heart transplant, Neil Armstrong and Ed Aldrin on the moon.

You will determine, in the course of your study, how well contemporary science fiction has met the challenge of reality. Somewhat to your surprise, you will learn that it could not have done so without your help. We are referring to the tacit understanding between the writer and you, the reader: your willingness to accept the unbelievable if, by doing so, you are entertained, surprised, mystified, even frightened. There will be other, more lasting rewards. You will gather much valid technological information; your imagination will be challenged by the presentation of actual problems of which you were not aware, and you may be tempted to solve them. Now and then, a story will lead you to serious thoughts about the future—yours, and that of all of us. And who knows?...*You* may find some of the answers.

Assignment: The passage above, written in 1976, is an introduction to a collection of science fiction stories. Even though it is more than twenty years old, the selection is dated in several areas. Write a well-organized essay in which you explain where it is dated and present new information that brings it up to date.

Much of the time, as in this essay question, a long prompt becomes a source of material and ideas that you use in writing the paper. It helps, in such a case, to read the essay assignment *before* you read the informative material. When you have a long prompt, remember to skip down the page and read the assignment at its conclusion *before* you read the passage.

3 How to Write an Impromptu Essay

On-the-spot essays differ considerably from the papers you write at home, revise and proofread several times, and then turn in to your professor. In fact, by the time you write your final version of an at-home paper, you are actually *rewriting* it, going back to be sure it meets the basic standards of an essay:

I. A clearly evident, three-part structure:
   A. An *introduction* that gives a general answer to the question posed as well as a skeletal plan of the whole paper;
   B. A *body* that strengthens or develops the answer, providing details and supporting points that develop the plan blocked out in the introduction;
   C. An analysis that brings together the ideas and explains their significance relative to the essay prompt. The analysis section also assesses advantages and disadvantages of the views propounded in the essay, and it builds toward an application or principle that can be identified in the conclusion;
   D. A *conclusion* that brings the essay to a close by restating your main points or concluding in some other way.
II. A comprehensive, complete treatment of the subject, with many concrete supporting details.
III. A well-written paper that presents one distinct idea.
IV. A paper free of writing errors.

These standards are quite difficult to meet if you are writing an in-class, timed essay; fortunately, you can be sure that the professors who grade the papers know that. They *do* expect you to have a rough structure, however, a *beginning*, a *middle* and an *end*. Additionally, they expect your paper to have *unity*, meaning a distinct idea to which everything logically relates, as well as *coherence*, a logical and understandable flow of ideas. In other words, they expect a straightforward, sharp, detailed statement from you. In many ways, the on-the-spot essay that you are expected to write is more like a speech than the formal at-home essay, and it is unlikely your professors will grade you down if you are somewhat informal and conversational in writing it, although you should avoid colloquial or careless usage.

WHERE DO I BEGIN?

Most GWAR essay formats incorporate planning time into the prompt: "You have five to ten minutes to plan and write an essay on the following topic. . . ." In some cases the proctors of the exam will not let you begin writing during this planning stage, so you must use that time wisely. Of all the strategies recommended for prewriting, the most successful and time-efficient centers on the process of immediately choosing examples to fit the essay question. In other words, the very first thing you should do in the planning stages is select interesting examples from your background or others' background that relate to the topic. In the preplanning stage, sketch these examples/illustrations into fuller details and sequence them according to the question. Jot these sequenced ideas down in key words on your scratch paper. The best sequence, of course, is one that arranges your examples from your least important or interesting to the most important or interesting. In this way, you ensure that the readers/scorers have something to look forward to. At the end of this process of selecting applicable examples, you will wish to formulate or revise your thesis (or argument) that can be expressed succinctly in one sentence.

Consider the following topic:

> Every age is represented by objects, ideas, symbols, events, and people. If your community was burying a time capsule containing such items, or news clippings of events and people, which three from our modern age would you select and why?

A student, Mark, reported the following experience wrestling with this topic.

> I first tried to think of a possible thesis statement, but ended up only recycling the prompt: "Certain objects are symbolic of our age, as are certain people, etc." I realized that to operate in this manner was wasting my prewriting time and getting me nowhere. So I decided to leave my thesis until later, and tried to think of the items I would include. I wanted my family journal, I wanted information about the impending destruction of the ocean's ecosystem, and I wanted to include CD ROM disks containing the knowledge that human beings have gained so far. In these objects I could preserve my family history, provide the roots of a severe problem facing us human beings today, and preserve what we had positively accomplished. Then I started jotting down details in key words expanding my items into information I was familiar with. Once the proctor said I could start writing, I knew what my thesis was going to be: "The necessary objects to be included in a time capsule should serve the individual, the community, and the world, creating a synthesis of personal preferences harmonized with local and global ones. Therefore, in my case, the best objects for inclusion in a time capsule include . . ." and I listed my three items in order of most selfish to least selfish. I found it quite time effective to think of my concrete examples first, and then ask myself how to introduce these examples with my thesis second.

Mark's system above is the most efficient and specific way to work. It prevents you from re-phrasing the question; it prevents you from overgeneralizing without referring to specifics; and it outlines the initial structure of your essay.

THE PREGNANT SENTENCE

Since students over the years often learn from their teachers to try and write or compose their thesis sentences first, they may find it more comfortable to create the large-scale argument before detailing their examples. Or, in the prewriting stage, they may find it helpful to list where the essay has to go first. At some point, however, the main idea of your essay must be expressed in one sentence. It must be a sentence, because only a sentence is able to express an *idea*. Such a sentence is termed a *pregnant sentence* as it carries the idea that you will be developing in your essay. Once you write your pregnant sentence, everything you write must flow derivatively from it, and from it alone.

Take the following topic:

> "The best things in life are free." In a busy world like ours, people tend to overlook the value of commonplace objects, relationships, pets, possessions, or other aspects of life. Write a well-organized essay about something that you consider very valuable though it is usually taken for granted. Be sure to explain in detail why you believe your subject is valuable.

One of my students, Lisa, likes dogs and knows a little about them. When she read the question, she decided to try dogs as a topic. First, she had to transform the topic into a pregnant sentence so that her essay would have an underlying idea. She thought for a while, and then scribbled on a scrap of paper:

Dogs...what value?
  What do they do for us?
  • police dogs
  • guide dogs
  • sniffers
  • protect our homes
  • companions and pets
  • save lives

How to Write an Impromptu Essay 25

THE FAR SIDE By GARY LARSON

© 1991 UNIVERSAL PRESS SYNDICATE
Reprinted with permission. All rights reserved.

"Well, this is just going from bad to worse."

At this point, Lisa was ready to write her pregnant sentence.

> Dogs are a valuable asset to our society.

She then performed the "content" test by asking, "*how or in what way* are dogs a valuable asset to our society?" Here is what she came up with.

> 1. They can be taught to perform jobs.
> 2. They protect you and your property.
> 3. They give pleasure and companionship.

There seems a good deal to say about the pregnant sentence *Dogs are a valuable asset to our society*. Notice that each sentence directly answers the test question. There are no sentences that are vaguely and aimlessly related to the pregnant sentence like, "I had a miniature collie once," or "Dogs differ from cats in their attentiveness to their owners."

Lisa also thought of the following sentences:

> 4. They are employed in extensive medical research.
> 5. Breeding and showing dogs is a significant business.

The previous two sentences do meet the test. They answer the question, "How or in what way are dogs a valuable asset to our society?" However, she decided that they were a trifle off topic, because they differ from the others in the impersonal way the dogs are treated in research and breeding. She kept them in mind, anyway, in case she ran a little short later on.

The next step for Lisa was to write three or so sentences *that are directly derived from* each of the second-level sentences. Again, it is very important that you write *sentences* so that you remain in the realm of *ideas*, not topics. And again, it is very important that each of these second-level sentences do not wander away from the idea being developed.

> Dogs are a valuable asset to our society.
> 1. They can be taught to perform jobs.
>   A. Dogs are trained to be police dogs and professional watch dogs.
>   B. Dogs are used to assist the handicapped.
>   C. Dogs are used to detect drugs and explosives.
> 2. They protect you and your property.
>   A. Barking dogs will usually deter an intruder from entering your home.
>   B. Dogs will alert you of a presence near their home.
>   C. If a stranger enters a person's home, many dogs will act aggressively toward the intruder.
> 3. Dogs are loyal companions.
>   A. Dogs have given their lives to protect police officers.
>   B. Dogs remain faithful to their friend regardless of the treatment they are given.
>   C. Dogs truly are man's best friend.

While she was jotting down this little outline, Lisa was accomplishing two essential preparatory tasks; first, she was planning her entire essay, and second, she was checking to see if her pregnant sentence, or topic, had enough substance to be developed into a full essay. It may seem a time-consuming exercise, but notice that her essay is all but written now. As she wrote the essay, Lisa made several impromptu additions and changes, as you will see in the following versions.

Lisa's essay:

THE VALUE OF DOGS TO SOCIETY

The term "dumb animal" perplexes me, especially when it is applied to our canine friends. I have always considered dogs a valuable asset to society. They are trained to perform jobs to assist people, they protect their owners and their owners' possessions, and they are great companions. I strongly believe that dogs are a valuable asset to society and that a world without dogs would be a lesser place.

The jobs that dogs perform to assist their masters are often important jobs, such as police work. When the day is done, these same dogs are the family pet, gentle and loving to children and other family members. Who can discredit dogs that are the eyes of the blind or the ears of the deaf? Consider airport customs dogs who detect drugs. In return for such valuable work, a dog requires little.

After writing the preceding two paragraphs, Lisa felt she had a good start. She had established a distinct idea in the first paragraph, and written one of the three paragraphs that will comprise the middle or generative part of her essay. Something was not right, however. Lisa realized that she was not developing enough of a statement, and that the work she was writing would sound sparse and abbreviated, a chronic problem she has had with her writing throughout her years in school. However, she had to be careful at this point. If she added sentences carelessly, she would destroy the unity of her essay, that is, the unimpeded and undeviated flow of specific details that strengthens and enriches the single idea declared in the pregnant sentence, *Dogs are a valuable asset to our society*. To avoid disturbing the unity she had achieved, she decided to rewrite her second paragraph, building it *from the inside*, that is generating content by becoming more specific about what she had already written, making the idea more clear and meaningful rather than adding new and competing ideas.

Here is her final version. The italicized portions of the second paragraph are what she added. As she wrote the rest of the essay, she continued to add layers of concrete and specific modification to her sentences.

THE VALUE OF DOGS TO SOCIETY

The term "dumb animal" perplexes me, especially when it is applied to our canine friends. I have always considered dogs a valuable asset to society. They are trained to perform jobs to assist people, they protect their owners and their owners' possessions, and they are great companions. I strongly believe that dogs are a valuable asset to society and that a world without dogs would be a lesser place.

The jobs that dogs perform to assist their masters are often important jobs, such as police work, *search and rescue duty, and the control of herd animals. Possessing a keen sense of duty, police dogs function as partners to police officers, and frequently find and subdue armed criminals. In addition, if an officer is ever confronted by a threatening or unruly group of people, a police dog can keep them at a distance.* Yet when the day is done, these same dogs are the family pet, gentle and loving to children and other family members. Who can discredit dogs that are the eyes of the blind or the ears of the deaf? Consider airport customs dogs who, *employing their vastly superior sense of smell*, detect drugs *and explosives in mountains of luggage*. In return for such valuable work, a dog requires *nothing more than some kibbles and a scratch under the ears or a "Good dog!"*

Even in the ways we entertain ourselves, dogs play a significant role. When I lived in New York, I used to attend greyhound races with my father and uncle in Flushing. What a thrill it was to walk through the prep areas, choose a dog I thought was going to win, and then see him whip over the finish line a body length ahead of his competitors. In racing one really sees the difference breeding can make in the development of a dog, most of the winners being related to past champions. Breeding also figures importantly in the bloodlines of hunting dogs and show dogs.

How many of us know of people, perhaps elderly people, who live with a dog and consider the dog a stable and positive part of their lives? Many studies have proven that dogs have beneficial effects upon the health or feelings of well-being of their elderly owners. Their beneficial effects range from lowering the heart rate of their owners to giving them a purpose for living. Dogs in such circumstances are saving lives as surely as the legendary Saint Bernard who traveled frigid alpine trails with a cask of rum under his neck.

Personally, I feel safe in my own home, knowing my Labrador will alert me to an unknown intruder, and that an unknown intruder will be wary of my Labrador. Instinctively territorial in nature, it's no wonder dogs make such effective guards.

The loyalty of this animal astounds me. Every day, police dogs risk their lives to maintain the safety of their human partners. This loyalty is not reserved for loving masters either. A dog will love you regardless of ill treatment, abuse, or neglect. I know I do not stand alone in my one-sided opinion of dogs. Somewhere along the line someone called dogs "man's best friend." I am inclined to agree.

Now let's trace the development of a more complex essay. Here is the assignment:

Please read and think about the following two quotations:

(A) "The created world is but a small parenthesis in eternity. I count it not an inn, but a hospital; and a place not to live, but to die in. Were the happiness of the next world as closely apprehended as the felicities of this, it would be a martyrdom to live."

(B) "I feel no need for any faith than my faith in human beings. Like Confucius of old, I am so absorbed in the wonder of earth and the life upon it that I cannot think of heaven and the angels. I have enough for this life. If there is no other life, then this one has been enough to make it worth being born, myself, a human being."

It is evident that both authors express views concerning life on earth. Compare and contrast the quotations, explaining, first, what you believe each author means, second, how each view is likely to have been reflected in the lifestyle of the person quoted, and, finally, what you personally feel to be the most valid of the two statements. Be sure to give reasons for your assessment.

Right at the outset, you need to be clear about one thing. When you write a comparison/contrast essay, you are really writing two separate essays and then juxtaposing them. Furthermore, you should be aware that this is a prestructured question. You are asked to:

1. Compare and contrast the quotations, explaining:
   A. What you believe each author means.
   B. How each view is likely to be reflected in the lifestyle of the person quoted.
   C. Which of the two statements you feel is valid, giving reasons for your assessment.

As discussed in Chapter 2, remember that there are two ways to organize a comparison/contrast essay, the *point-by-point pattern* or the *block pattern*. David, the student who wrote the sample essay *below*, chose to organize his answers by means of the block style.

David decided to summarize in his own words the views of each author—which he felt would be sufficient to function as a pregnant sentence or thesis for each. Then he charted his impressions of each author and reconciliations of their views with his views.

Here is how he summarized each author's view and created possible pregnant sentences/theses:

Author A believes that life on earth is subordinate to the afterlife.	Author B believes that life on earth with other human beings is worthy enough to justify human existence.

Here are David's impressions charted on his sample scratch sheet:

Author A and paragraph 1	Author B and paragraph 1
1. Old-fashioned language—Middle Ages 2. Christian philosophy of Heaven 3. Life on earth unimportant 4. Influenced by church in pre-science age	1. 20th century language 2. Doubts Heaven 3. High value on life now 4. Influenced by industrial age
paragraph 2	paragraph 2
1. The way life was to author A = anti-material 2. Lived by faith and Christian values 3. Rationale pointed to a day of judgment	1. Loved human contact and travel 2. Loved variety of humanity 3. Lived in the miracle of "now"
Reconcile in paragraph 3 and my view	Reconcile in paragraph 3 and my view
1. I am a member of a religion also 2. I have been taught about an afterlife 3. The afterlife provides a banked security	1. I celebrate life 2. I want to teach music 3. This humanity has done a lot. DILEMMA!

David's essay:

The authors of the two statements have very different views about man's place on earth. The first believes that one's worldly existence is only a brief preparation for eternal life, and that all aspects of life on earth are therefore subordinate to life after death. The second, on the other hand, emphasizes his faith in human beings, and believes his life on earth justifies his existence. I find myself unable to fall into the camp of either one.

The very language used by the first author indicates that he must have lived some time ago, perhaps during the Middle Ages, the "Age of Faith" when virtually all the avenues by which people speak and share ideas were informed and controlled by Christian philosophy. Whatever the reasons, there is no doubt that he believes life on this planet to be infinitely less important than the life that follows. The second author, on the other hand, expresses an uncertainty about even the existence of a second life. He (or she), instead, places a very high value on "the wonder of earth and life upon it." Again, the language used in the statements gives us some data. The second author seems to have lived in this century, and probably has been influenced by all that has happened between the Middle Ages and the twentieth century: the Renaissance, with its reaffirmation in mankind, the industrial age, the rise of science and the accompanying miracles of the twentieth century. How much more the second author had to rely on in his statement that life on earth was enough!

A life as subordinated as that of the first author must have been reflective and meditative, shunning material possessions and pleasures. It is probable that such a person limited his acquisition of material goods, and lived in modest housing. He or she must have treated other people according to the requirements of the faith, which almost surely was Christian, and which demanded charity, patience, virtue, and the other requirements of the ten commandments. It is sufficient to say, though, that the author's life was one of care and caution, because it assumed a forthcoming judgment and day of atonement. The second author loved human contact, and was innately interested in accounts and anecdotes about human beings. He or she probably traveled, given the awe expressed in the statement about the wonder of earth and life. The author also suggests a feeling of pride in being a human being in these times. There is no doubt that such views were expressed by a person who studied life and humanity, an alive and appreciative and enthusiastic person, fully immersed in life itself, who must have traveled and entertained and probably wrote books or poetry.

    I am a member of an established religion. All my life, I have been taught that this life is a prelude to an even more glorious one that will be everlasting. I am not inclined to deny such a belief; it is like money in the bank to me, it does provide solace in my private moments, and it does provide a rationale for hope and security in a very frightening world. However, like the second author, I, too, feel like celebrating life. Soon I will graduate, and will, I hope, be teaching music at the university level sometime soon. What I see in the world around me, and what I have learned about mankind and his brief span on this earth is staggering to me. I am not likely to subordinate this great human race to anything else. Perhaps the years ahead will help me to resolve my dilemma.

4 How Your Essay Will Be Scored

WHAT YOU NEED TO KNOW ABOUT HOLISTIC SCORING

Understanding the full politics of holistic scoring differs little from understanding the politics of any relationship between a writer and readers. Knowing what happens to your essay after you write it and knowing how it will be scored will establish for you a mission. You will see why you must replace distracting and time-wasting habits with the immediacy of following the advice offered later in this chapter—in order to give the readers exactly what they are looking for to pass your essay with a high score. *Because that's what they want. They want you to pass and pass well.*

So let's follow your essay after you finish it and it goes through a possible scoring procedure.

First, when time is called, the proctors collect your exams and put them in a big pile. Next, these piles go to the testing office where they are cross-checked against the master list of students who signed up for the essay. The testing coordinator then has a week to set dates for the chief readers and scorers for the scoring process. The coordinator must choose from senior and proven faculty from **any** discipline who volunteered to serve at that particular time. (How faculty are "proven" we'll discuss shortly.) Once the chief readers have been selected, these meet to select preliminary range-finder faculty from an "approved" list. It is the job of the chief readers and these range finders to go through that pile of essays looking for samples that represent the possible range of scores of the scoring guide (see the next section for a representative scoring guide). The chief readers and the range finders negotiate until they can agree on sample essays from the large pile that illustrate a 6 or particularly good essay, a 5 or good essay, a 4 or adequate essay, a 3 or unsatisfactory essay, a 2 or weak essay, or a 1, an essay totally inadequate at any college level.

They go to this trouble for real reasons. Since each essay test question has its own issues of phrasing, effectiveness, and populations that take the test, the chief readers and range-finding faculty, therefore, preview the test to give the eventual faculty who score the test a sampling of the kinds of essays to expect. Also, the eventual faculty who score the test may not have scored any essays since the last exam, and some of the faculty may be new volunteers to the process. All of these faculty must be trained or "retrained" for the conditions of the latest exam.

Once the chief readers and range-finding faculty have selected the sample essays and faculty who will score, the actual day of scoring arrives. The chief readers remind the scoring faculty of the university scoring guide and the chancellor's office mandate that GWAR's must be implemented and scored. Then the chief readers pass around the *sample* student essays, unscored, and the scoring faculty must score each of the samples according to the university-established scoring guide. (Personal scoring systems are unacceptable.)

Afterward, the chief readers poll the faculty on their scores, and all discuss each sample essay and the "recommended" scores. In this way faculty are gently brought in line with the university standards for passing the GWAR. The benefits of this system for students should be clear. If any individual faculty member arrives to the scoring in an unpleasant mood, or fresh from applying singular grading standards in a specific class, then the sample essay scoring procedure should serve to adjust the faculty member's individual system with a mind to the whole.

Other issues relevant to your performance mission may be less obvious, however, including how and why faculty are selected to serve in the scoring process. Of course, the selection process varies between institutions, since some of the CSUs are so small that any and all interested faculty must serve, whereas at larger institutions it is both time and cost effective to have highly efficient and accurate faculty score a large number of essays. Usually faculty are selected because they combine a high speed of reading with high accuracy of scoring.

Accuracy of scoring is paramount in the holistic process. It is unacceptable for scorers representing university standards to differ from their colleagues on the score of any single essay beyond a tolerable divergence—beyond **ONE** point or the equivalent of 17 percent on a six-point scale. To put it simply, if one scorer gives your essay a 5 and another a 3, then one is, or both of these scorers are, <u>wrong</u> regarding the actual score of your essay. Once an essay has received a discrepant score, the faculty involved are tracked and the discrepancy is noted. (That discrepant essay must be read and scored *another* time, by the chief reader finally, to resolve the gap in scores.) Once faculty demonstrate discrepancy rates of 6 percent or more of their total number of essays read, they become inefficient in the scoring process. Accurate faculty with low to nil discrepancy rates, and reasonably high but safe reading speeds, serve all components of the process. Thus develops the idea of "approved" scorers. These approved scorers comprise the readers that represent **your** interests, in light of the university standards. They are your audience.

Meanwhile, what determines a sufficient reading rate for approved scorers directly relates to your performance mission. The average reader/scorer should read approximately 140 essays in a six-hour period, with breaks and sub-training routines included in the total time. Some read faster, some slower, resulting in the average expectation.

What this means for you, the student, is quite important. Each scorer who reads your essay is reading anywhere from 100 essays to 300 essays in the same scoring period. With so many essays to read, they might be tempted to read only key parts of your essay, but which ones? They can't just read the introduction, because it is well known that students sometimes start slow and get better. Also, some student essays start well and sound great, but after a paragraph they go nowhere and cannot develop the initial ideas, in which case the scorer needs to read the whole essay. Nor does it help the reader to skip the introduction and pass onto the last part of the essay, because some students with sharply insightful and analytical minds can fully evolve an argument and point, extrapolating far beyond the initial scope of the question. In such a case the last part of the paper, if read alone, may at first glance appear to have nothing to do with the initial topic or point. The student's careful sequence needs respect.

To put it briefly, faculty face the burden of many papers that must be read entirely, all on the *same* topic.

Anywhere from 500 to 2000 students write on the same day you do. Each of these essays has to be read two or three times, depending on how many scorers must contribute to your final total score (your final possible total score, 12 out of 12, or 18 out of 18).

WHAT THIS ALL MEANS TO YOU

1. You must answer the full question.
2. You must reveal a clear organization.
3. You must use university-level language.
4. You must reduce errors you tend to make and avoid mechanical errors.
5. It helps to write legibly, with so many hand-written essays being scored. (Pencil is often OK.)
6. Use your allotted time carefully.
7. You must strive to be unique by selecting specific examples and developing the topic in a way you find interesting.
8. If you get a chance, ensure that your thesis has some objectivity and applies to all readers (not just to yourself)

Most of the schools grade the essays *holistically*, that is, with a single score for overall impression and quality. Each essay is scored by two readers in most cases, each of whom assigns a score of 1 to 6. On this scale alone, the grades 3.5–6.0 are passing grades. Thus, a student must have a grade of 7–12 to pass the exam, depending on the school. However, the scale is sometimes combined with other factors, such as scores on an objective test or required courses. At least two schools employ scales of 1–4 instead of 1–6. The grading criteria change each year as schools refine and adjust their scoring formulae. Be sure to check the current brochure or bulletin concerning the exam at your school.

Typically, all of the papers from a single test are read and scored at the same time by a group of English instructors as well as instructors from other disciplines. In most cases, the scorers are regular readers of these essays. New readers are trained at special sessions prior to the reading where sample papers are read and discussed, and criteria are established. Studies have shown holistic grading to be remarkably accurate.

REPRESENTATIVE SCORING GUIDE

Passing

6 — Particularly Good

A paper in this category contains a clear and direct response to the question asked and develops that response through a sequence of reasonably organized paragraphs. It will be nearly free from errors in mechanics, usage, and sentence structure, and there will be evidence of superior ability to use the language. In all regards, this paper is an excellent response to the question. The paper will have a consistent, authoritative "voice," and it will have original, lively, and interesting ideas.

5 — Good

A paper in this category may execute the assignment less completely than a 6 paper does, but the writer will demonstrate a clear understanding of the writing task. Although the paper may have minor weaknesses in paragraphing, it will contain evidence of the writer's ability to organize information into coherent and unified paragraphs which display specific and detailed development. The essay will be largely free from serious errors and will be generally clear and well written.

4 — Adequate

A paper in this category will have a discernible plan with a beginning, middle, and end and will complete at least the basic tasks of the assignment. There may be somewhat ambiguous and imperfect reasoning, and ideas may be repeated rather than developed. But it will be organized and paragraphed well enough to allow the reader to understand the point of the discussion with relative ease. It may contain errors, but not enough to continually distract the reader from the content.

Not Passing

3 — Unsatisfactory

A paper will fall into this category if it shows serious difficulty completing or satisfying the tasks of the assignment; if it lacks an overall plan with a beginning, middle, and end; if key ideas in paragraphs lack development or illustration; or if errors in word choice, sentence structure, and mechanics seriously interfere with readability. Paragraphs may be somewhat disorganized, but the total effect will not be chaotic. The writer's control of language may be uncertain.

2 — Weak

A paper in this category may fail to complete the assignment, that is, requirements set forth by the question may be ignored or misinterpreted. The writer may substitute narration for expository discussion. The paper may contain one or more of the following defects: serious errors in reasoning; little or no development or support of ideas; few or no

1
Totally Inadequate

connections between ideas. Serious and frequent errors in word choice, sentence structure, or mechanics may interfere with readability.

This category is reserved for the paper that is plainly incomprehensible due to a combination of errors in sentence structure, organization, and mechanics. The ideas are confused, and the writer may depend upon narrative rather than an exploration or analysis of ideas. A paper may also receive a 1 for failing to deal with the topic.

0
Not Accepted

Some schools reserve this score for blank or nearly blank test papers, or essays that are completely off the topic.

In other words, to do well on this test you must use the six strategies that follow to fulfill the exam's criteria.

I. ANSWER THE QUESTION, FULLY AND COMPLETELY

You need to read the prompt or question carefully, and make sure to address all the tasks it assigns. If it asks you to describe a series of actions, and *then explain why each one is important*, be sure to do just that. If it asks you to *analyze* the parking problem at your school, be sure to break the parking problem into components and to discuss and evaluate each one. If it requires that you identify certain changes on your campus that you would make and then *explain* what results you would expect from these changes, be sure you respond to that need with plenty of concrete details, specific facts, anecdotes, references.

II. BE ORGANIZED

Remember the old saw that an essay must have a beginning, a middle, and an end. It's not really an old saw; it's an essential—a necessity. All good essays have such a structure, but the *really* good ones do more with that structure.

The beginning paragraph, for example, is not just a general statement that needs development in the subsequent paragraphs. It is a rich, informative, expansive statement itself that hints of a promising development in the body of the essay.

The middle, or developmental, paragraphs do not merely give adequate specifics about the topic, they go into minute detail. They carry out a finer and finer, more concrete, and more fundamental exploration of their subject.

The concluding paragraph is not just a brief recapitulation of the general statement in the beginning paragraph, but rather a comment that "puts the hat" on the essay, and perhaps offers a fresh and provocative parting thought.

Examples of inadequate, adequate, and particularly good paragraph development are given at the end of this chapter. Study them carefully. Notice the great difference between a paragraph with generalities alone and one with fine supporting detail.

III. USE COLLEGE-LEVEL LANGUAGE

There is only one way to write. You are expected to use the English language as an educated, discriminating, intelligent student would. That does not mean you have to write with a flourish or with a stylistic flair, or, for that matter, any way that is not natural to you. It *does* mean you need to use standard American English that is sharp, professional, informative, businesslike, clear, and direct.

IV. AVOID ERRORS IN MECHANICS, USAGE, AND SENTENCE STRUCTURE

Mechanics refers to rules of punctuation, capitalization, spelling, paragraphing, format, and the like. If you are weak in this area, be sure to read Chapter 10, English Review and Practice, take all of its practice tests, and complete all of the model tests in the last section of this guide, studying the answers and explanations of each one. True, it is not exciting to learn that you need to put a comma before a conjunction that joins two equal clauses. However, not to have that comma in your own writing is an error in mechanics that most educated people will spot immediately. *Usage* regards English grammar and the knowledge and understanding of verbs, the principal parts of verbs, adverbs, adjectives, subject-verb agreement, pronoun-antecedent agreement, and the proper use of connectives. *Sentence Structure* deals with the nature of the sentence, including the relationship between clauses, the correct use and placement of modifiers, parallelism, and consistency in point of view and tense. All aspects of grammar, usage, and sentence structure are discussed in Chapter 10 as well, and drilled in the practice and model tests. Chart and reduce your personal error areas.

V. WRITE LEGIBLY

There is no point in writing an essay if no one can read it. The instructors who read your paper will be reading large numbers of papers and have little patience with script they simply cannot make out. Illegibility can and does flunk papers!

VI. PLAN AND USE YOUR ALLOTTED TIME CAREFULLY

Remember to use 10 to 20 percent of your time on prewriting and planning, and another 20 percent at the end of the writing period on proofreading alone. Proofreading does not mean "copying"; in fact, if you have an hour or less to write, you will not have time to copy. If you have "copyosis," a need to make a fresh copy of anything you turn in to your instructor, practice the avoidance of that, in this case, destructive little habit as you write your practice essays. Proofreading means a careful, intense, swift rereading of your essay to see that it makes good sense, it includes everything the assignment calls for, and it does not have any grievous errors. If you make changes, make them neatly, perhaps with an erasable pen. No exam reader will fail a paper because the author has corrected an error.

Here is a sample time breakdown for a one-hour topic:

First five minutes—say 9:05 AM to 9:10 AM	Recall or select interesting examples and concrete details to fit the GWAR topic. Jot these as key words.
Next minute—9:10 to 9:11	Sequence or number those examples from least to most interesting.
Next two minutes—9:11 to 9:13	Ask yourself how your examples are significant and relevant to the GWAR topic. Jot these thoughts as key words also.
Next two minutes—9:13 to 9:15	Compose your thesis or pregnant sentence. This sentence represents your opinion, combining references to your examples and how they are significant to the overall topic.
Next forty minutes—9:15 to 9:55	Write your essay out. IF you have time, add a second-to-last paragraph before the closer, discussing significance and applicability of your examples. Attempt to include analysis.
Next five minutes—9:55 to 10:00	Add a closing paragraph that unifies your ideas into a principle or recommendation.
Last five to ten minutes—10:00 to 10:05	Proofread for your personal error areas.

Here's a sample essay topic:

> Essay Assignment: Tell us about your major. Describe the life and activities of a typical major in your field. Explain why you chose that major, in turn giving us some evaluation of the reasons themselves.

PREWRITING CONSIDERATIONS

This essay assignment must be answered by all students, although some actually taking the exam might think, "I haven't chosen a major yet." Although GWAR questions such as these are intended for students facing graduation who have already finished most of their major and graduation requirements, it is possible that first- and second-year students who haven't chosen majors yet may be attempting the exam. For those students it is important to realize they must take and answer the test in good faith. To think "I haven't chosen a major yet" is unnecessarily self-defeating. It is better to think "I need to write an essay on this topic, and though I haven't chosen a major yet, I'm **thinking of choosing** (say) Marine Biology, Physics, or Business. Why would I choose this major and what are the typical duties and services of an expert in this field?" You will achieve a further advantage to think of examples of people you are familiar with who are successful in your considered field. They will provide you with supporting examples for your essay.

Here follow sample paragraphs of responses at different levels of expertise. The italicized words represent added material elevating the level of the response.

Barely Adequate Introductory Paragraph

I determined to become an M.D. and so chose a pre-med major in college because of family precedence, aptitude scores, and a desire to do some good. A pre-med major is a good deal of work, as you will see.

> This paragraph lacks concrete detail, has a minimal argument, and lacks objectivity.

Adequate Introductory Paragraph

In my senior year of high school, I determined to become an M.D. and so chose a pre-med major in college. I chose this major for three reasons: family precedence, aptitude scores, and a desire to do some good *in the world*. A pre-med major is a good deal of work *because most of the courses are difficult science courses*.

> This paragraph offers more detail, intensifies the argument, and suggests applicability.

Particularly Good Introductory Paragraph

In my senior year of high school, I determined to become an M.D. and so chose a pre-med major in college, *a course of study that I have found to be rigorous, with most of its requirements consisting of chemistry, molecular biology, anatomy, physiology, microbiology, and physics courses.* I determined to become an M.D. *because my family history demands it. My grandfather, mother, father, and three uncles are doctors now, and my sister and three cousins attend medical school. In addition*, the two major aptitude tests *I took in my junior and senior high school years* both indicated *to the 90th percentile that I was well suited for medical science, both in academic inclination and temperament*. Finally, I chose to be an M.D. because I want to do some good in the world, *and the medical field, I believe, gives a person many different opportunities to make a difference in the world. These reasons for my choice of career may seem fortuitous at first glance, but they did take a great deal of thought and self-evaluation.*

> This paragraph concretizes the detail, specifies the rationale, and considers its own limitation.

It is important to note that good first paragraphs should include a certain amount of objectivity, and in consideration, given time, a student writer should reduce any language in the introduction that makes the thesis appear self-centered, and give it more applicability to a "generalized" readership. With time and practice it gets easier to convert such paragraphs into objective language. Below is the particularly good paragraph from above revised to sound more objective.

Particularly Good Introductory Paragraph Revised to Be More Objective

In their senior year of high school, students should select a possible major for college, and one of the best is the pre-med major, a rigorous course of study with most of its requirements consisting of chemistry, molecular biology, anatomy, physiology, microbiology, and physics courses. In my case, my family history demanded that I become an M.D. My grandfather, mother, father, and three uncles all work as doctors now, and my sister and three cousins attend medical school. In addition, the two major aptitude tests I took in my junior and senior high years both indicated to the 90th percentile that I should be well-suited for medical science, both in academic inclination and temperament. I chose to become an M.D. in order to do some good in the world. The medical field presents various opportunities to make a difference. And though these reasons seem to derive from my fortunate family history, they still needed thought and evaluation to implement.

> This paragraph reduces the self-centered nature of the thesis, focuses the personal background with the reader in mind, admits its limitations, and suggests applicability. Admittedly, it is difficult in a timed, impromptu essay to achieve a balanced introduction, but if you read the last two models closely a couple of times, you will hear the difference in tone that makes the final model more elegant.

Here follow sample supporting paragraphs.

Barely Adequate Supporting Paragraph 1

First of all, you have to complete a good deal of high-level mathematics courses at the high-school and early college levels. In addition, you are expected to complete biology, microbiology, physics, anatomy, physiology, and chemistry courses. These courses require much dedication and many late nights to complete with an acceptable grade. In addition, a pre-med student in college spends some "shadowing" or mentor time in a hospital or laboratory. There, you learn something about life as a medic.

Adequate Supporting Paragraph 1

First of all, you have to complete a good deal of high-level mathematics courses at the high-school and early college levels, *among them calculus, differential calculus, mathematical analysis, and medical statistics*. In addition, you are expected to complete biology, microbiology, physics, anatomy, physiology, and chemistry courses. These courses require much dedication and many late nights to complete with an acceptable grade. In addition, a pre-med student in college spends some "shadowing" or mentor time in a hospital or laboratory. There, you learn something about life as a medic, *and you even meet some medical "contacts" that could hold you in good stead later on*.

Particularly Good Supporting Paragraph 1

To be a pre-med student today means to be dedicating yourself to the medical profession at an early age. Even as a sophomore, a pre-med student spends time in a "shadowing" or mentoring capacity in a hospital or *medical* laboratory. There, you begin to learn something about the life of a medic, and you even meet some medical contacts that could hold you in good stead later on. *My experiences were in Freeman Memorial Hospital in Burbank and in the Merck Laboratories in Glendale. At the Hospital, I "shadowed" Dr. Myron Levitt, a Cardiac Surgeon who specialized in pacemaker and fibrillator implants, actually being allowed to "suit up" and observe two open-heart procedures. At the Laboratories, I was a mentor working in the outpatient research section interviewing patients about side effects of the drugs they were taking.*

Barely Adequate Supporting Paragraph 2

My grandfather, father and mother, and three uncles are doctors now, and my sister and three cousins are in medical school. Medicine seems to dominate every family get-together. At every Christmas or Thanksgiving dinner we have what amounts to a bull-session on medicine. Everytime anyone is sick in our large family, there are phone calls criss-crossing the city as the right family expert is consulted. Our family is really a medical clan.

Adequate Supporting Paragraph 2

My grandfather, father and mother, and three uncles are doctors now, and my sister and three cousins are in medical school. Medicine seems to dominate every family get-together. At every Christmas or Thanksgiving dinner we have what amounts to a bull- session on medicine. Everytime anyone is sick in our large family, there are phone calls criss-crossing the city as the right family expert is consulted. Our family is really a medical clan. *My grandfather practiced medicine in Lausanne, Switzerland, my father in the USC Medical Center, and my mother in the Kaiser Sunset Family Ward. My Uncle Charles on my mother's side is an anesthesiologist, and both of my other uncles, my father's brothers, are cardiac surgeons at large hospitals in Buffalo and Philadelphia.*

Particularly Good Supporting Paragraph 2

My grandfather practiced medicine in Lausanne, Switzerland, *at the Academie des Medecines, a well-known research hospital specializing in the regeneration of crucial body cells like pancreatic and pituitary cells*. My father *was in charge of the Women's Hospital* in the USC Medical Center, *a place where much research is done on subdermal injections of drugs and other medications directly on the spinal cord*, and my mother runs the Family Ward, *meaning obstetrics*, in the Kaiser Sunset *Facility located in Hollywood*. My Uncle Charles on my mother's side is an anesthesiologist *at St. John's Hospital in Santa Monica, a wonderful facility that has one of the most advanced pain clinics in the nation*, and both of my other uncles, my father's brothers, are cardiac surgeons at large hospitals, *Uncle Phil at Sullivan Municipal Hospital in Buffalo where he is a family practice physician, and Uncle Eddie at Kaiser Permanente Hospital* in Philadelphia *where he does routine surgery. There is no doubt in my mind that such a distinguished family history in medicine created a subconscious compunction in my mind to study medicine. I have at times wondered whether a need to follow my family's professional traditions was a rational and aware kind of behavior and have decided that it is not. Accordingly, I have taken pains to see that I am making the right career choice independently of my desires to remain "in the family."*

We have used the first three paragraphs of this model essay, which appears in its entirety in Chapter 6, to demonstrate how deeper levels of specificity within paragraphs are what make competent writing. Note that the material added in these paragraphs *is not new material*, but rather finer, more concrete, more discerning detail *that comes from an inward exploration* of the key supporting points.

A Final Word About Examples

Since, by the nature of essay test questions discussed earlier, you are expected to offer some exemplification, you may be tempted to feel that you "don't have any experience to draw on to provide exemplification" for a specific prompt. Put this thought aside if you can. Realize that experience and examples can come from reading, texts you are familiar with, the experiences of friends you've heard about, interviews from magazines, newspapers, and talk shows, film, and almost anywhere. Often test designers who create prompts that ask for personal experience will accept your relating experiences of others or examples from other sources. Be sure to add as much detail to your examples as possible within the time limit.

One Type of Procedure for Ensuring a High Quality Response on a One-Hour GWAR

You have 10 to 15 minutes to plan, and 45 to 50 minutes to edit. One-page essays of medium-sized handwriting rarely, if ever, pass. One-and-a-half-page essays rarely pass. Two-page essays seldom pass. Most passing essays reach the three- to four-page range, single-spaced. So, follow these steps to use your time wisely. Steps 1 through 3 below fill your planning time. Steps 4, 5, and 6 use about 32 minutes. Steps 7, 8, and 9 use your remaining time.

1. Read the question and its tasks/prompts carefully, jotting down references to possible examples with details you can use to illustrate your answer. Also, add thoughts in key words that address each of the tasks.
2. Outline these key words and references in a sequence of least important to most important, or list them chronologically, or arrange the sequence from simpler examples and thoughts to more complex ones.
3. Compose a pregnant sentence or thesis that unites (a) your opinion about the GWAR topic with (b) your forthcoming examples, and (c) how—and why—these are significant. Jot down this "working" thesis on your scratch sheet.
4. (Optional) As soon as you are able to write, skip five lines for your first paragraph, in other words, skip writing your thesis/pregnant sentence. The best thing to do is come back and fill this first paragraph in later after you finish the body and analysis of your paper. Though you've written a thesis you can consult on your scratch sheet, you will probably want the option to change it as you develop your essay.
5. Start paragraphs two, three, and four, the body of your essay, following your sequence and adding details to the examples you selected in the planning stage. As you finish each paragraph of the body, add a last sentence to each paragraph, assessing the significance of the example in that paragraph and how it relates to the GWAR topic and prompts/tasks. This step ensures unity and coherence. Check your time, allowing about eight minutes per paragraph.
6. Once the body of the essay is finished, add a further paragraph bringing together all of your ideas into an application. How would you apply your ideas? How are they useful? What principles have you identified? In what ways do your ideas solve issues current to general ones readers confront every day? What are the advantages and disadvantages of your views relative to your audience? Answers to these questions relative to the tasks and prompts of the topic will add a level of depth to your response. This second-to-last paragraph also requires about eight minutes.
7. Go back to the beginning of your essay and compose a thesis/pregnant sentence that states your opinion and leads the readers to all of your ideas you just finished.
8. Go to the end of your essay and add a closing paragraph, a recommendation derived from your essay.
9. Reread your essay checking for transitions, end-of-paragraph assessment sentences, and your own personal error areas. Check each paragraph for relevance to the overall GWAR topic and prompts.

Total time? Sixty minutes. The hour format makes it hard to write much more than four to five fully developed body and analytical paragraphs and a thesis and the closer which should not be longer than three sentences each on average. Most of your writing is in the body and analysis.

5 Thirteen Mistakes That Fail Tests

MORE ON HOLISTIC SCORING (ADDRESSING THE READERS)

A very real phenomenon takes place during a holistic scoring: after a while readers get tired of scoring essays on the same topic. It's human nature and almost impossible to fight. When the readers (and the essays) are fresh, they approach the task with enthusiasm and interest. The students' ideas look good, and the readers enjoy engaging the active minds behind the responses. But soon the essays bunch toward the median as their writers' responses get more and more stereotyped. At this moment in the scoring process comes the dangerous time. As readers get saturated with similar responses, their levels of enthusiasm drop, to be replaced with encroaching feelings of irritation and boredom. Chief readers responsible for the morale in the room combat the eventual downturn by providing frequent breaks, and often implement a refreshing range-finder session in the afternoon to reintroduce scorers to the rubric (See Chapter 4). But more discrepancies occur in the afternoon, and the scores tend toward the lower range of passing, if extraordinary steps aren't followed.

For you, the student writer, the message is clear. You must understand the give-and-take relationship between yourself and the readers in the room, and to ensure that your essay receives a high score you must offer that something extra in your essay that raises it above the stereotypical response. You cannot predetermine where in the stack of essays your essay will fall, and even if you could, at some stage in the process your essay will appear later in the afternoon for at least one of the scorers.

Therefore, if you approach the writing as a boring task you must get over with as quickly as possible, your language and lack of concrete examples will represent your attitude, and you will risk a no pass. But if you approach the writing with the attitude that the scorer is another human being, like yourself, with a duty to perform, with a sense of humor, a desire to be informed, and an engaging interest in students, you can uplift your answer beyond the average.

Walk in on the day of the exam with the attitude of enjoying a polite, intelligent discussion (almost as if over a cup of coffee)—albeit written and one-sided—with a faculty member, a person you've never met. Under those circumstances, if you adhere to the courtesies of social conversation, you should do quite well and avoid the mistakes detailed below.

In our years of grading writing proficiency examinations, as well as from conversations with colleagues about scoring such essays, we have always been perplexed by the predictable state of approximately 10 to 15 percent of the papers turned in. These papers unnecessarily fall below minimum standards—without a fight. Their authors commit errors or mental lapses that their prose indicates they can avoid. While their writing is clear and direct, and while their ideas are focused and right on target, their errors suggest they do not care. Scorers know that they do care, but that they experience these major lapses because of stress, depression, anxiety, or insecurity. This chapter details the weights of certain errors and then expands on how to correct those errors.

WEIGHTS OF SPECIFIC ERRORS ACCORDING TO THE HOLISTIC SCORING PROCESS

Certain errors will cause your essay to receive a no-pass on the global scale; and certain errors will cause you to receive a no-pass on the sentence scale. Other kinds of errors are often harmless by themselves, such as single errors repeated, like misspelling "their," for example.

The single most grievous error on the large scale is the off-topic essay. A fluent and sophisticated essay will receive a no-passing score if it is off-topic. If holistic scorers accepted and passed off-topic essays, what would prevent dishonest students from memorizing "canned" essays? No, the writing must comprehensively and accurately cover the prompts and tasks.

The second most grievous error on the large scale is lack of exemplification and detail. A fluent and sophisticated essay that addresses the topic might pass, if it is fully analytical and operating in an abstract but intelligent mode. That kind of writing is rare and hard to accomplish, however. By contrast, a fluent essay, with reasonably good grammatical and punctuation skills, might not pass if it offers no examples to support its claims. Competent essays back up all statements regarding the prompt with specific examples and details from their writers' background, others' background, reading, films, interviews, and so on.

Beyond these omissions, losing track of the topic, even while giving examples, can hurt your score, as can ongoing grammatical and punctuation errors of varying types. Writing ongoing transitions and assessments of examples, with an eye on the overall topic, will help you stay on track.

At the sentence level, three types of errors will damage your score. The first relates to knowledge of what a sentence is. A sentence is basically a subject-verb marriage. A subject floating by itself (i.e., Africa.) is not a sentence, even if it has a period after it, nor is a verb floating by itself (i.e., awaits.), even if it has a period. (Attempting to use sentence pieces like these often fails in communication, since such pieces lack transition and relevance to idea development. These kinds of pieces are called fragments of sentences.)

In English, complete sentences require a "something," or a subject, which "acts" or "does." (This action or doing equates to the verb portion of a complete sentence, which, with all of its parts, is also called a predicate.) This knowledge about the fundamental building block of English prose leads us to the secret of English:

> Punctuation serves readers by indicating the locations of subjects and verbs in sentences and where complete sentence ideas known as "independent clauses" start and end.

"Africa awaits." is both a complete sentence and can be an independent clause: it can stand as a sentence as it does here, by itself. Not all verbs, strangely enough, are sufficient to bring independence to a subject, and therefore these special kinds of verbs are insufficient for creating complete sentences. As an example, the phrase "Africa offers . . ." is not complete, even though it has both subject and verb, and thus cannot stand by itself. The verb *offers* needs a finishing object like "a great vacation experience."

Students must understand the principles above and know where sentences begin and end in order to pass the GWAR essay requirement. Also, to pass, you must have progressed beyond writing only simple sentences; you must have learned to coordinate successfully—to link independent clauses with "for," "and," "nor," "but," "or," "yet," and "so" (the conjunctions): "Africa offers a great vacation experience, *but* it will cost you at least two thousand dollars to get there." To evolve further, you must learn subordination, the art of compressing ideas without relying on the conjunctions.

If you do not know what is wrong with the following line, you are not ready to pass the GWAR, and you must get help today: "Africa offers a great vacation experience it has places like Cairo, Tunisia, and Sudan." It only takes a few fused sentences and/or comma splices to damage your writing effort. (See the English review section in this manual.)

The second kind of sentence-level error that costs you points involves subject-verb agreement. Subjects have number, singular or plural, and some subjects can be singular in some contexts and plural in others. Therefore, the verb must indicate whether the subject is singular or plural. Most languages attempt to deal with subject number in certain ways, and most speakers of those languages have not attained proficiency until they can demonstrate mastery over subject and verb agreement. For the world over, mastery of this element of language is paramount. Holistic scorers of the GWAR cannot pass an essay with errors in subject-verb agreement.

Similarly, writers must master verb tense. English has four basic time periods, the past perfect, the direct past, the present, and the future, and then compulsory perfections of the present and future, discussed in this chapter and in the review of English. If a writer cannot manage the time periods of events as they interrelate with each other and with current events, that writer will not pass the GWAR essay requirement. If you are an ESL student, you must practice these elements of English to increase your competitiveness on the exam.

Students often worry about spelling, perhaps because they believe that accurate spelling measures writing competence. The truth is that inaccurate spellers can write brilliant essays. But good spellers possess good memories, which they also use to apply their learned writing skills. You <u>can</u> make spelling errors and pass—provided that the rest of your essay is competent, coherent, avoids the errors outlined in this manual, and addresses the prompt. But you should be fairly warned. Experienced holistic scorers recognize the difference between a competent essay with inaccurate spelling, and bad spelling that is one of the indicators of an incompetent essay.

Certain people prone to misspelling words, such as dyslexics, for example, can write fluent essays and even invert word order. You might have a question about what happens in their cases. Experienced holistic scorers—often, though not all of the time—recognize the kinds of errors dyslexics can make, and can score the essay fairly. But if you are dyslexic and know it, you should sign up with your local Disabled Students Services Center, get tested, and apply for special consideration on the GWAR exam. Most CSU's offer key disabled student services, including help with exams. Similarly, if, as far as you know, you are not dyslexic, but have a tendency to misspell common small and larger words, invert letters and words, and experience trouble processing written text (or verbal instructions), then you also should interview with a reading or disabled student specialist at your local tutoring center and get tested. Programs and tools exist for dyslexics that can make their lives immensely easier.

Finally, a very subtle aspect of writing can lower your score, and that is the over-reliance on low-level verb words. If you have self-tested your writing with sample essays, count the number of times you use such verbs as (in any tense) "be," "is," "get," "say," "think," "talk," "make," "do," and "go." If your entire verb vocabulary consists of these verbs in their various tenses ("is," "are," "went," "got," "did," "were," "had been"), then your essay will probably never rise above the average score. Holistic scorers won't consciously downgrade the score of an essay if all of its verbs are low level like these, but they will recognize that the scope of vocabulary (especially of the action words) is limited, thus limiting the conditions of movement and action and time that apply to subjects in sentences. A good verb conveys implied detail: "pondered," "will acknowledge," "had earned," "provided," "solders," all create images that readers associate with actions, providing implicit details. The low-level verbs we have discussed above have no specific images associated with any of them. If you have time, upgrade your verb vocabulary, and write in an active voice, as discussed in this chapter.

Now you know some of the error areas that holistic scorers track, as well as skills they reward.

Here follow the mistakes that lead to these types of errors, arranged according to the relative magnitude of damage they do to a paper's score, from high damage to low.

1. NOTHING TO SAY

A certain percentage of essays are too short to represent a substantial, university-level timed writing, though these essays are often neat. The student seems to have drawn a blank, and can think of nothing more to say than a direct rephrasing of the essay question itself. Some students find a way to put into their own words the text of the question, and after some brief generalizing, close by summing up the question, as if repeating the thesis. Unfortunately, scorers can detect a simple paraphrase of the prompt. Perhaps, the student froze.

To overcome this type of anxiety you can prepare mentally for the test by expecting to generate examples to fit the prompt. You can achieve a state of mental readiness by thinking "Example." When in doubt give sufficient detailed examples, and then evaluate their significance to the topic.

Remember, for an hour-long writing, a one-page essay will not pass. Only five in a hundred two-page essays will pass. Aim at three to four pages of medium-sized handwriting when you plan your essay and concentrate on an organized sequence of examples. If your will fails you, try to keep in mind that passing the GWAR will move you directly toward your diploma.

Finding a Topic to Write About

After reading the essay question and prompts, most of the time you still have the job of choosing a topic. Keep in mind that a writing proficiency examination differs somewhat from other writing you are called on to do in that it measures *writing proficiency*. Readers will be looking at your prose to see if you can organize a topic, supply adequate details, and generally write well. You do not need to think up a remarkable and innovative thesis to perform well. All you need to do is remain honest and direct about your examples and how they apply. Be cautious, however, about confusing the "courtesy" discussed above with a lack of directness. Sometimes, student writers want to show how much respect they have for others' opinions and end up reducing the strength of their arguments. They add "I think" or "I believe" to their argumentative statements in their thesis paragraphs, or at the outset they over-negotiate their point. The true time to negotiate the point occurs later, after all of the examples have been presented and evaluated. Then you can discuss the advantages and disadvantages of your overall presentation. Initially, however, your readers expect a bold and direct opening.

Take your firm stand as you plan your essay. Your readers want to hear a controlling "voice" in your paper. Put your thesis statement in your first paragraph, and hide nothing. Your beginning should tell the reader what to expect and where this essay will be going. Look at the following beginning paragraph:

> I realized when I was assigned a post in Yarmouth, Maine that I would miss New York City. Little did I realize, however, that I would be so fundamentally affected by my move. Fortunately, I emerged from the whole experience much better off than when I started.

Notice that the whole essay is planned in the preceding short beginning paragraph and now only requires detailed and careful development.

Also, the writer could have implemented a little more objectivity and boldness by leading in with the following improvement:

A move from one location to another, though risky, brings unexpected benefits. I realized...

And then ending with

I earned more money, visited beautiful countryside, and, best of all, made a lifelong friend.

to <u>specify</u> the advantages of the move.

2. ALMOST BUT NOT QUITE

The student writes well, with attention to detail and supporting material. Unfortunately, though, this student did not read the question carefully and left out one of its main components. For example, once I administered a test with the following topic:

> Discuss a specific success or failure that taught you something important. Do not merely tell a story, but explain in detail how your experience affected your subsequent attitudes and actions.

One of the best writers in the group composed an excellent essay about her experiences as a Peace Corps volunteer, concentrating on the success she had enjoyed helping the rural farmers in El Salvador build a corn silo. Unfortunately, she did not complete the second part of the question, namely explaining how that experience affected her attitudes and actions. She explained to me later that she felt she had really "aced" the question, and had clearly demonstrated writing proficiency. I reminded her that she had missed perhaps 30 percent of the question, and had possibly demonstrated a carelessness in reading.

Always read the question more than once. Make a point to answer all parts. Plan to provide examples for each part. Reread the question as you write.

3. WITHOUT PERCEPTIBLE DIRECTION OR PURPOSE

The phrase "without direction or purpose" may be a little harsh, but it does come to mind for a grader reading a paper without unity or coherence, that is, a paper that lacks proper arrangement or sequence of ideas. The ideas are usually there, but they are so misplaced that they are not available to the reader on a first perusal of the paper. Usually the questions students face on these extemporaneous essay tests are clearly posed and direct. They have to be, because the test must be understood by a vast number of very different constituents, some of whom write English as a second language. As Henry James said to his brother, "For God's sake, William, just say it!" Have a good general point to every paragraph, and then support that general point with cogent and direct data. (See the Pregnant Sentence, Chapter 3.)

Think, ahead of time, about the qualities of unity and coherence in written work. Be sure the concepts are clear in your mind; do not neglect them when you write your essay.

A. Lack of Unity

Every point you bring up in an essay needs to contribute to a *single* idea or thesis. A paragraph is unified when each sentence contributes to developing a central thought. Each single thought developed in each paragraph must contribute, in turn, to the single idea that unifies the essay.

If you are writing a paragraph in which you argue that fast food is nutritious, you must discuss *how* or *in what way* fast food is nutritious in virtually everything you say. You can say that fish and chips contains protein and niacin, you can say that potatoes contribute needed fiber, and you can say that pizza contains cheese rich in protein and calcium. You cannot discuss the fact that McDonald's outlets are more numerous than Jack-in-the-Box outlets, or the fact that your brother works at Carl's Jr. The key to avoiding papers that are disconnected is to concentrate on a single point. Use the pregnant sentence method of development. If you need to add more to what you have written, add it by *becoming more detailed, concrete, and specific about what you have already said* rather than by adding new and disparate thoughts.

Suppose, in other words, that you are writing an essay about the fact that classes fill too quickly during registration and you find yourself without a great deal to say. Try explaining more and more *minute* portions of the problem; go into your subject more and more. Put on microscopic glasses and dive into the inner world of your main idea. Describe how students camp on the doorstep of the registrar's office at five in the morning in order to have a chance to sign up for a class they need, or that more and more instructors are continually lobbied for add-ons, even during the previous semester, or that many students spend five years in college because they cannot sign up for the classes they need, or that some students have to drive to three different schools to have a full schedule, or that students on various types of aid must have twelve units, or that some infrequently offered requirements fill up so quickly that it is conceivable that some majors may never finish college. Observations such as these are the fine details that make a point dramatic and important because they all converge in the pregnant sentence that lies at the heart of your statement. By adding assessment sentences relating your examples to the topic you can increase unity.

B. Lack of Coherence

Coherence is the quality of sticking together—that is, of ideas sticking together in a composition. One sentence should lead naturally to the next, and each new idea should evolve from a previous one. Without a logical progression of ideas, an essay becomes *incoherent*, a word that has become synonymous with not understandable. A writer achieves coherence by being careful how he or she arranges a string of ideas. They have to be in a sensible order. If you are discussing events or actions, they must be in *chronological* order. If you are explaining the negative effect of a recession on universities, let us say, you might plan and write in *order of importance* as your arrangement scheme. Often the movement within a composition or paragraph is from *general to specific*. If you are describing something, usually you describe it in *spatial order*. There are many other arrangement plans, such as *problem-solution, question-answer, topic-illustration*. None are difficult to use; the trick is to be sure to use a plan consistently that is clear to you, the writer, and that is appropriate for the topic being developed. Make sure you know what you want to say and what sequence you want to follow. Take the trouble to phrase each sentence so that it flows grammatically and logically from what you have written before.

Acquire the art of using transitional devices, which are essential in achieving coherence. Some of the important ones are the use of pronouns, the repetition of key words or ideas, the use of conjunctions and other transitional expressions like the following:

To signal additions
also, and, besides, equally important, first, second, third (etc.), further, furthermore, in addition, too, next

To signal similarities
likewise, in the same manner, each in its turn, similarly

To signal differences
but, in contrast, however, on the other hand, on the contrary

To signal examples or intensity
after all, even, for example, for instance, indeed, in fact, it is true, specifically, that is, to illustrate, truly

To signal place
above, adjacent to, below, elsewhere, nearby, on the other side, opposite to, to the left

To signal time
after a while, before, during, earlier, finally, first, immediately, later, simultaneously, when, then, while, subsequently, as long as, at length, at that time, at last

4. MAJOR SENTENCE ERRORS

It is safe to say that everyone is expected to write complete sentences when he or she takes the writing proficiency test, and that there are no gray areas where run-on or fragmented sentences are acceptable. If you have a tendency to make sentence errors in your writing, that is, *fragments, comma splices*, or *fused sentences*, you need to take steps to rid your writing of such errors before you take the test. If you are not sure if you make such errors, visit your campus tutorial or writing lab and ask if someone there will evaluate your writing. Most tutorial centers and writing clinics have a number of computer-aided instructional programs that do wonders for students who are not clear in their minds what a sentence really is. Do not attempt to avoid sentence errors by writing primer-style sentences. Essays that begin, "I believe a good education is important. I believe men and women should have it. A good education is what makes a good life..." will, at the least, be graded down as lower-than-college-level writing. (The English review section of this manual will help.)

Take the time to rid your writing of fundamental sentence errors *before* you hazard this examination.

The lone or infrequent occurrence of the errors that are discussed from here on is no longer in the "gross" category and is less damaging to a student's score than the faults described up to this point. However, you can be sure that the errors will be noticed, and, if they (or combinations of them) occur with frequency, they will cause a student to lose credit and possibly even fail the examination.

5. "BERMUDA TRIANGLE" ERRORS

I have found that many students have their own custom Bermuda Triangle when it comes to writing, their own set of grammatical or writing problems that never ceases to make them nervous when they enter those waters. Jim, for example, never quite knew how to use cases. He seemed to believe that the use of the pronoun *me* was always wrong, so wrong, that whenever he said or wrote it, he would sound really bad. He would write, "The coach gave Phil Lozano and *I* three days to straighten out." (Just to keep the record straight, he should have written the objective form of the pronoun, *me*, because it is receiving action). Another student, Ed, always became befuddled when he used gerund phrases with a possessive pronoun. He would say, "Me staying out late with my buddies is all right with my girlfriend." (He should have said, "*My* staying out late with my buddies is all right with my girlfriend.") Many students say that some teacher in their past strongly warned them not to write in the first person, *I*. (The truth is there is nothing wrong with using the first person as your point-of-view; in fact, most of the questions asked on a timed writing test deal with personal reminiscence and experience and require a first-person response.) What most students remember having been told about the pronoun *I* is that it should not be used in severely *formal, elevated* discourse, and it should not be mixed with an already-established third-person (*he, she,* or *it*) point of view.

If, like many students, you feel nervous when you write, perhaps it is because you have a few *areas* in writing that bother you, and you write perfectly well otherwise. For example, do you have problems with the use of the nominative and objective case? Are you frequently unsure of *who-whom*, or *I-me* options? My advice to you is that you think a bit about your rough areas (we all have them), *trap* or *isolate* them, and then complete the relatively minor job of studying and memorizing that will rid you of the problem for good. The English review in Chapter 10 includes many practice and summary tests. If you need further help identifying your errors, there are many good diagnostic English surveys. Check with your counselor or tutoring lab.

6. ERRORS IN PREDICATION OR MIXED SENTENCES

Predication refers to the process of joining the *naming* part of the sentence (the *subject*) to the *doing* or *describing* part of a sentence (the *predicate*). Mixed sentences occur when the writer equates unlike constructions or ideas. Look at the following incorrect examples.
Mixed:
By working at such technical plants as Lockheed and Bendix gives the engineering students insight into what will be expected of them. (*By working* does not give them insight; *working* does.)
Corrected:
Working at such technical plants as Lockheed and Bendix gives the engineering students insight into what will be expected of them.
Mixed:
Among those who take the writing examination, they do not all have to take it again. (The modifying phrase beginning with *Among* requires a subject that gives an amount, such as *sixty percent* or *many*, not the general *they*).
Corrected:
More than three-quarters of those who take the writing examination do not have to take it again.
Mixed:
A writing proficiency examination is when you write an essay right on the spot. (Written definitions require nouns or noun clauses on both sides of *be*).
Corrected:
A writing proficiency examination is writing an essay on the spot.
Mixed:
The reason I decided to buy an American car is because I felt sorry for American auto workers. (The words *reason* and *because* both imply the same thing, namely, *purpose*.)
Corrected:
I decided to buy an American car because I felt sorry for American auto workers.

Be sure that all parts of your sentences, particularly the subjects and predicates, fit together grammatically and logically.

7. SUBJECT-VERB AGREEMENT ERRORS

Nouns, verbs, and pronouns often have endings or special forms that signal *number*, that is, whether or not the word is singular or plural; it is a principle that a verb always agrees in number with its subject.
Singular: The *cat* in the alley *looks* hungry.
Plural: The *cats* in the alley *look* hungry.
Make sure a pronoun agrees in number with the noun it is taking the place of, its *antecedent*.
Singular: A teenage *girl* has *her* own language.
Plural: Teenage *girls* have *their* own language.
Sentences that are uncomplicated, such as those above, do not present problems for most writers. It is in sentences where words or groups of words come between the subject and verb that students are tripped up. Here are some guidelines to help you avoid the problem.

1. **Be sure of the number of the subject.** Sometimes it is not so easy a matter to decide. Collective nouns such as *class, herd, audience, half, part, crowd*, and *most* can be either singular or plural, since they can refer either to a collective unit or to separate entities. Take the following examples (all correct):
   - Half of the class are failing.
   - Half of the class is devoted to the study of torts.
   - Part of the herd are suffering from heat exhaustion.
   - Part of the herd is going to be sold to the Triangle Ranch.
   - Half of the crowd are buying popcorn, souvenirs, and the like.
   - Half of the crowd is doing the wave.

2. **Be sure the verb agrees with the subject,** even though the normal word order is inverted, as in questions or expletive constructions (*there is* or *there are*). Here are some examples (all correct):
   - Is the AIDS virus harmless or contagious?
   - Are Beatrice and Ed really married?
   - Is the *Citizens versus the City of San Jose* trial over yet?
   - There are, after the appeal has been heard, two directions we can take.
   - After many arguments and separations, there is negotiation in the air.

3. **Be sure subjects and verbs agree,** even when other words come between them. Here are examples (all correct):
   - A slew of new IRS regulations and restrictions bewilders taxpayers every year.
   - The violations made by the Meat Packing Union are staggering in number.
   - One of my sons is a soldier.

8. DANGLING OR MISPLACED MODIFIER

The arrangement of words in sentences usually tells the reader how the words are related. Sometimes, however, a sentence is confused if the reader cannot connect modifiers to the words they describe.

To avoid confusion or ambiguity, place the modifying words, phrases, or clauses near the words they modify.
Confusing: The electric pencil sharpener needs repair in the mail room.
Correct: The electric pencil sharpener *in the mail room* needs repair.
Confusing: He packed all of the books and fine photographs into his van, which he was donating to the library.
Correct: He packed all of the books and fine photographs *which he was donating to the library* into his van.
Confusing: In designing the new science building, a venting system was overlooked.
Correct: In designing the new science building, *the architects overlooked the venting system*.

If you concentrate on keeping one idea in the paragraph as the main subject word and making sure that all modifiers apply to that word, you can avoid this type of error.

9. MISUSE OR OVERUSE OF SEMICOLON

The semicolon can be used as a "weak period" to separate closely related sentences. It cannot be used to separate a subordinate clause or a phrase from the main sentence.

Wrong: According to the Labor Bureau; more women are working today than ever.
Revised: According to the Labor Bureau, more women are working today than ever.
   The semicolon cannot be used to introduce a series:
Wrong: Most instructors have heard the standard reasons for not finishing a paper on time; a death in the family, illness, a sudden rush at the workplace.
Revised: Most instructors have heard the standard reasons for not finishing a paper on time: a death in the family, illness, a sudden rush at the workplace.
   Overuse of the semicolon leads to over-coordinated sentences and ideas. *Use the semicolon only to join coordinated elements. Avoid using it too often; instead, use the principles of subordination.*

10. PROBLEMS WITH VERB TENSE

The choice of the appropriate tense usually presents few problems in papers of students who are native speakers of English. Those problems that do occur usually involve the use of the present tense in a special sense or uses of the perfect tenses.
   The present tense generally signifies action at the time the subject is speaking, as in *Fritz knows the answer* or *I am making your eggs right this moment*. It is also used in a few special cases.
To indicate recurring or habitual action
The college police generally *use* common sense.
The train in Switzerland always *runs* on time.
To state a universal or timeless or general truth
The sun *is* the source of all energy.
The early bird *gets* the worm.
To discuss or recapitulate action occurring in literature, plays, film.
In *Wuthering Heights*, Heathcliff really *loves* Catherine Earnshaw.
In the Old Testament, Abraham *prepares* to sacrifice his only begotten son, Isaac.
To indicate future time
Remember that Spring Break *comes* early this year.
   The perfect tenses all use the helping verb *has/have/had* in their formation in conjunction with the past principle of the verb. Students sometimes err writing the past participle. (See also pages 159–163)

Infinitive	Present Tense	Past Tense	Past Perfect Participle
to arise	arise	arose	arisen
to bid	bid	bid	bid
to choose	choose	chose	chose
to speak	speak	spoke	spoken
to sink	sink	sank	sunk
to drive	drive	drove	driven
to ride	ride	rode	ridden
to hang (suspend)	hang	hung	hung
to hang (execute)	hang	hanged	hanged
to tear	tear	tore	torn
to wear	wear	wore	worn
to shake	shake	shook	shaken
to stand	stand	stood	stood
to steal	steal	stole	stolen
to spring	spring	sprang	sprung
to swim	swim	swam	swum
to throw	throw	threw	thrown
to go	go	went	gone
to drink	drink	drank	drunk
to sit	sit	sat	sat
to set	set	set	set

If you have had trouble with verb forms in the past, practice the use of these forms, particularly in forming perfect tenses, because that process is where most students make verb errors. A good way to practice is to spend some time forming perfect tenses for each of the verbs listed using the following models:

PRESENT PERFECT TENSE

Person	Helping Verb	Past Participle
Singular		
1 I	have	_____
2 you	have	_____
3 he, she, it	has	_____
Plural		
1 we	have	_____
2 you	have	_____
3 they	have	_____

PAST PERFECT TENSE

Person	Helping Verb	Past Participle
Singular		
1 I	had	_____
2 you	had	_____
3 he, she, it	had	_____
Plural		
1 we	had	_____
2 you	had	_____
3 they	had	_____

FUTURE PERFECT TENSE

Person	Helping Verb	Past Participle
Singular		
1 I	shall have	_____
2 you	will have	_____
3 he, she, it	will have	_____
Plural		
1 we	shall have	_____
2 you	will have	_____
3 they	will have	_____

Take the time to use proper verb forms in all your writing.

11. THOUGHTLESS USE OF THE PASSIVE VOICE

Writers should concentrate on forming active-voice sentences, as opposed to passive-voice ones. The discussion below will help you recognize the difference.

Action verbs have two voices, the *active voice* and the *passive voice*. Through the use of voices, verbs that take objects (transitive verbs) can show whether their subjects are acting or acted upon.

In the active voice, the subject *does* the action:
   Harvey started the engine.
   The professor coordinated the writing program.
   Elizabeth earned a degree in health sciences.

In the passive voice, the subject *receives* the action:
   The writing test is taken by 3,500 students every year.
   The engine is started many times a day.
   The term paper was written by Norma Garza.

To form the passive voice, the writer employs the verb *to be* as a helping verb, adding it to the past participle of the main verb.

PASSIVE CONJUGATION OF THE VERB *TO GIVE*, 3RD PERSON SINGULAR

Passive Voice	Helping Verb To Be	Past Participle of Main Verb
Present Tense:	he is	given
Past Tense:	he was	given
Future Tense:	he will be	given
Present Perfect Tense:	he has been	given
Past Perfect Tense:	he had been	given
Future Perfect Tense:	he will have been	given

To change a verb from the passive to the active voice, we convert the verb's subject into an object and replace the verb with the appropriate direct tense:

> Passive: Phil *was given* a plaque by the senior class.
> Active: The senior class *gave* Phil a plaque.
> Passive: The ruling about the deductibility of loan costs *was changed* by the IRS.
> Active: The IRS *changed* the ruling about the deductibility of loan costs.

Notice how the passive voice sentences seem to lack punch, and how they are wordier than the active versions. Because the passive leaves out or de-emphasizes the *actor* (the performer of the verb's action), it is often ambiguous or confusing or deliberately screening the actor.

> Weak Passive: The writing test is considered by the students to be difficult because they are not given adequate time to rewrite and proofread their work.
> Strong Active: The students consider the writing test difficult because it gives them inadequate time to rewrite and proofread their work.

The passive voice is appropriate in two contexts: when the receiver of the action is more important than the doer, or when the doer is unknown and when you want to keep the receiver of the action first in your sentences in a paragraph.

> The vice-president was murdered this afternoon.
> (The murderer is presumably unknown, and the vice president's death is the important point).
> On the first trial, ethyl alcohol was added to the gasoline.
> (The person who added the alcohol is incidental to the fact that it was added. The passive voice is used frequently in scientific writing.)

Prefer the active voice to the passive voice, except when the doer of the action is unknown or unimportant.

12. INEFFECTIVE COORDINATION AND SUBORDINATION

Establishing understandable and coherent relationships between ideas is the main function of subordination and coordination.

To *subordinate* is to "move to a lower structural rank." The italicized passages in the following sentence are subordinated.

> *When the oxygen gas in the bloodstream drops to the .06 level,* the surgeon must decide whether or not to go in again, *the risks of open-heart surgery vying in his mind with the risks of heart failure.*

Although the ideas carried in the grammatically subordinate structures are very important, subordinating them emphasizes the main clause and establishes their relationship to the ideas carried in the main clause. The sentence has one point, and that one point is given weight and importance by the subordinated ideas. One of the marks of a seasoned writer is the ability to subordinate skillfully.

To *coordinate* is to "make equal in structural rank." The italicized passages in the following sentence are coordinated.

> *The precious oil we burn is finite,* but *trees and their derivatives alcohol and methane are self-renewing.*

> **WAYS TO COORDINATE AND SUBORDINATE IDEAS IN THE SENTENCE**
>
> Use *coordination* to link ideas of equal weight.
> 1. Join main clauses with a comma and a coordinating conjunction (*and, but, for, or, yet, so*):
>   The Gulf War liberated Kuwait, *and* it lifted the hearts of millions of Americans.
> 2. Join main clauses with a semicolon alone or a semicolon used with a conjunctive adverb (*although, nevertheless, therefore, however, consequently,* etc.):
>   He was very aware of the dangers of smoking; *nevertheless* he continued to smoke two packs a day.
> 3. Within clauses, connect words and phrases with coordinating conjunctions (*and, but, or, nor*):
>   The trombones *and* trumpets became louder, *and* the whole crescendo of the orchestra and chorus shook the building.
>
> Use *subordination* to position ideas logically and unambiguously:
> 1. Subordinate a clause by beginning it with a subordinating conjunction (*if, unless, before, after, since, when, because, as, how, if,* etc.):
>   *Before inflation consumes our collective savings and our retirement systems*, we must lower the national debt.
> 2. Use relative pronouns (*who, that, which, what*) to subordinate clauses that are more logically adjective or noun clauses:
>   The Arab leader *who attracted the most attention in 1991 was* Saddam Hussein.
> 3. Use a phrase to carry a subordinate idea:
>   *Between the compressor and the fan* lies the master cylinder. (prepositional phrase)
>   The window *broken by the fury of the hurricane* allowed enough water in *to destroy the contents of the room*. (Participial phrase; infinitive phrase)
>   My son, *a soldier with the 3rd Armored Division*, spent several weeks in Iraq. (appositive or inserted descriptive phrase)
> 4. Use a simple modifier:
>   The reason *sprawling* Los Angeles is *not attractive* as a city is that *greedy* builders put up *relatively cheap* and *architecturally incompatible* structures.

Use coordination to link equal words and ideas. Use subordination to de-emphasize ideas less important than the main idea. In your essays mix both techniques.

13. ERRORS IN PARALLELISM

One of the most important "rules" in English is called the "Parallel Rule." College-educated writers must not make errors in application of the Parallel Rule. If they do so they disintegrate their internal sentence logic.

> Parallel Rule: Whenever you have *two or more* repeating units of any kind in a sentence, they must be in exactly the same shape and form.

For example, whenever we list two or more words in a series, we make sure they are identical parts of speech.

George, Fred, and *Pete* went hunting on Monday.
I enjoy most nuts, but particularly *peanuts, walnuts,* and *chestnuts.*

But suppose they are not identical:

The campers ate a hearty meal of *tuna sandwiches, scrumptious,* and *swallowed.*

The sentence has become nonsensical because it attempts to parallel a noun, an adjective, and a verb. Nouns are used with other nouns, verbs with other verbs of the same tense, adverbs with other adverbs, and so on. Parallelism is essential in writing because readers of English expect balance and symmetry in any coordinate sequence.

Awkward:	As a lecturer, he was rude, with intimidating gestures, and he calls some students names.
Parallel:	As a lecturer, he was rude, intimidating, and insulting.
Awkward:	His wife gave him a day runner with a calculator and even including a digital watch and a radio.
Parallel:	His wife gave him a day runner with a calculator, a digital watch, and even a radio.

Sometimes the parallel structure simply needs to be pointed up by the repetition of a strategic word or words.

Awkward:	The Reverend Taylor wanted the church elders <u>to establish</u> liaisons with local business organizations, <u>offering</u> the resources of the church to the chamber of commerce, and <u>to schedule</u> arts and hobby classes that were desired by everyone. (The underlined parts don't match.)
Parallel:	The Reverend Taylor wanted the church elders *to* establish liaisons with local business organizations, *to* offer the resources of the church to the chamber of commerce, and *to* schedule arts and hobby classes that were desired by everyone. (The verb forms now match.)
Awkward:	The keynote speech was interminable, repetitious, and could not easily be heard.
Parallel:	The keynote speech was interminable, repetitious, and inaudible.

Errors in parallelism are often made after correlatives (*either-or, neither-nor, whether-or, both- and, not only-but also*).

Awkward:	Modern classical music is neither <u>inspiring</u> nor <u>did I find</u> it intellectually fulfilling. (An adjective in attempted parallel with a verb clause.)
Parallel:	Modern classical music is neither <u>inspiring</u> nor <u>fulfilling</u>. (Two parallel adjectives.)
Awkward:	Not only are the gang members <u>spraying graffiti</u> all over the brick walls of the campus but also <u>in adjacent residential neighborhoods</u>. (A verb clause in attempted parallel with a prepositional phrase.)
Parallel:	Not only are the gang members <u>spraying</u> graffiti all over the brick wall of the campus, but they are also <u>spraying</u> in adjacent neighborhoods. (Two parallel clauses.)

Maintain parallelism in sentences that require two or more equal grammatical units.

6 Representative Essays

The following essays are student papers that are likely to pass the writing proficiency test at any university, in my opinion, though they vary considerably in quality.

PERSONAL EXPERIENCE

Essay 1

> Many great stories are based on the events surrounding a natural disaster such as an earthquake, flood, volcanic eruption, tornado, hurricane, tidal wave. To be sure, many human beings live these dramas daily. What disaster is likely to hit your home? How have you, or how *should* you be prepared for such a disaster? What kinds of problems are you liable to encounter in the event of such an occurrence? (One Hour)

Being aware how many faults lie below us in California makes one realize that earthquakes are a possibility in our lives every living moment we stay in California. California is part of two enormous geologic plates, the Pacific Rim Plate and the Continental Plate. In reality, that means we have two very active forces hitting against each other just beneath us. The last big earthquake we had in this area was the Sylmar earthquake of 1971 which was the result of movement in a fault that had not been active since before the Ice Age and that scientists had labeled extinct.

Being prepared for an earthquake ahead of time can mean the difference between survival with minimum consequences and personal injury, damage, and loss. Preparation means stocking up on essential survival items, taking some important precautions in your home and place of business, and preparing to cope with the psychological trauma a really bad temblor can cause.

To be prepared for an earthquake, a person needs to store a minimum of two weeks of supplies. In a big quake, *all* services and supply lines are inactive and non-functioning. Even gas pumps in gas stations will be out, because there will be no electricity for weeks. Water is the first essential. It may be needed to put fires out, for fires are an ever-present consequence of earthquakes. It may be needed to clean up dangerous spills. If people are hurt, water will be needed to wash their wounds. And, of course, water is personally needed to drink and clean up. Wise people have a water flow tank to store their emergency water supply, that is, a tank of a thousand gallons or so that is part of the normal circulating flow of water to your home and so does not need changing at regular intervals. Otherwise, the swimming pool or hot water tank can be considered a source. At the very least, all families in California should store 25 gallons of water for every person in their family. Canned, freeze dried, MRE paks, and so on is an essential as well, at least enough food to last two weeks. Flashlights and radios with storage-tolerant batteries are an absolute necessity. Blankets, medical supplies, extra shoes, clothing, pet food if necessary, and money are also essentials to store away, money because cash is king in a natural disaster which will probably be the only tender accepted. Your car should also have a

53

few essential supplies, particularly water, a flashlight, and a radio in case you are caught far from home.

To physically prepare your home for an earthquake, you need to walk around it and visualize what will move if the house shakes violently. Tie down water heaters with steel straps, anchor large pieces of furniture like clocks or curio cabinets with straps at their tops (most of the time you can do so invisibly). Buy safety latches for cabinets, so they will not open when the shaking starts. At all times be ready to turn off gas and water supplies to the house.

To be psychologically prepared for an earthquake, you need to realize that a large quake has many aftershocks, themselves as strong as regular earthquakes. An earthquake is a profoundly frightening experience. Many people feel an immense malevolence is part of their life after such an experience. Psychiatrists tell us that sharing worries and fears with people around you is one of the best available ways of handling such feelings of anxiety, and, later on, to attend group therapy.

A natural disaster can be a major life shock. A wise and prudent person will try to stave off as much of the pain as possible by taking reasonable precautions.

Score 10 (out of 12).

Essay 2

At some time during our lives, almost all of us have experienced a failure which provided the background for later success, or we have observed others who turned failure into later successes. Describe a failure that you experienced or that you observed which provided the basis for later success. Explain how the failure provided the basis for later success. (One Hour)

Failure is a crucial aspect of human development—a cause for reflection, analysis, and reevaluation. My life mirrors these stages of failure/success/reflection. But perhaps the most thought-provoking failure was one that triggered a particularly deep reaction.

When I was sixteen I was hired by the West Irvine County Community Recreation Centers. During the summers, I was to spend time either at the day camps in the Irvine area or at the resident camps in the local mountains. It was at one of these mountain resident camps that I experienced my "failure."

My "cabin" consisted of a group of eleven boys between the ages of eight and ten. Most of them came from lower-middle class families; moreover, they reflected diverse cultural backgrounds. By contrast, the boy this essay centers on came from an upper-class family. Wesley owned matching luggage, the top of the line fifty-dollar Mag flashlight, and his own basket of "Goodies" to tide him through the rigors of camping.

However, it seemed that Wesley had not profited from his rich background. His behavior was unruly, his attitude towards those less fortunate rude and nasty. He cursed, fought, and kicked people and showed his intolerance with other physical abuses. He failed to interact with the other boys, except to harass them if they touched his belongings or smiled at him in the wrong way. It seemed to be part of my ongoing job to discipline Wesley, but after my frequent interventions I continued to feel something was amiss.

My assessment proved quite superficial. I had simply determined that Wesley was a "spoiled" rich kid. How wrong I was became clear after the final confrontation—where he demonstrated some particularly intolerable behavior that required me to report the misconduct to the director. My intention was to get rid of this little hellion; his was to inflict as much damage to my shins as possible en route to the director's cabin.

When Wesley's mother arrived later that day, I was summoned to give my list of grievances. After I had done so, his mother asked Wesley to leave the room. She spoke, and at that point I discovered part of my failure. Wesley's father had died suddenly two weeks prior to the start of camp; his mother, on the verge of a breakdown, had reasoned that camping might take Wesley's mind off of his father's death.

What I began to understand was Wesley's sense of abandonment—first by his father's death, and second, by his mother's sending him away to camp. Quite naturally, he had begun building defenses against any more such "desertions" by not permitting anyone to get close to him. That getting close to him should have been part of my job. My failure resulted from my not attempting to communicate with Wesley, not encouraging him to share his feelings. I had countered his "withdrawal" by hostility with the formation of shallow stereotypes about a rich spoiled kid.

The success I gleaned from this experience proved to be more important that any material "success." That little boy changed forever my methods of judging and labeling people. My greatest failure was my inability and/or unwillingness to understand and acknowledge this child's pain. Now when I see a person in pain or hear an unspoken call for help, I am better equipped to recognize it. My failure to help one person has led me toward success as an individual who helps people in mental anguish. I cannot honestly say that my experience with that one little boy shaped my whole life, but I must tell you that my chosen major is psychology and my career goals involve counseling and guidance. Then again, perhaps it did shape my life.

Score 11 or 12.

Essay 3

According to some expert psychologists, when children call each other names, irreparable psychological harm can result. According to others, the name-calling phase amounts to a toughening-up process that prepares young people for the eventual knocks they will receive in adult life. Which view do you support and why? (One Hour)

Name calling is always wrong and always causes harm. It is the duty of adults who are responsible for the education and upbringing of their children or students to teach their charges why name-calling, teasing, or any kind of labeling leads to long-range damage. I learned to think carefully when it comes to labeling people, and my experience with Scott validates my view.

I attended Foster elementary school in Lakewood, California with Scott. He had brown hair, a round face, a round body, and a great sense of fun. In third grade, during recess, the two of us played handball, swung on the monkey bars, enjoyed kick-ball, and during lunch sat together in the cafeteria eating cheese macaroni and laughing—because we were friends. Other kids, boys and girls alike, with names like Cindy, Garrot, Tom, and Susan, never called Scott by his given and rightful name. Instead, they said things to him like, "Hey, Tug-Boat, what are you doing? Sinking?" Or "Chubby boy, come here chubby boy, hey look everybody, it's chubby boy." Or they said, "Run!! It's the Blob, the Blob." As a result Scott felt sad and depressed, as he often confided to me. Once he ran into the library, to find a corner where he could cry. When I found him, he sat without responding to me, staring at nothing, making no move, showing no sign that he heard me asking for him to ignore those kids. It was clear to me that their words were provoking in him a self-hatred for something he couldn't control, and an outward hatred for those other children.

I could never figure why the teachers, the coaches, and the other adults in the school didn't step in and correct those kids, and so I felt a strange kind of duty to defend him. Unfortunately, there was only so much I could do. Yelling "Leave him alone," or "Look at yourself!" didn't accomplish much. I even heard names directed at myself for taking his side. They called me "Fat-boy lover," "Whale-lover," or they'd tease me and say, "Hey, it's fat-boy's girl friend. Nah nah nah nah." I never let them bother me, since Scott was my friend, and nobody was going to get away with calling him "harmless" names while I was around. Still, Scott's morale faded ever more each day, and he never seemed to develop the toughness that some children acquire in the heat of name-calling. When I asked him, "Why not just dish it back?" He answered, "If it hurts me, won't it hurt them too? Why should I play this kind of game?" Scott was someone that the other kids never understood they should admire. He was smart. But we were all children in over our heads. We were children without the wisdom to solve our heartaches. And the other children were allowed to get away with mental cruelty. All of this proceeded under the "watchful" eyes of our teachers and coaches.

Summer came and went, and when we started fourth grade, all of the kids returned—except for Scott. I looked for him at recess, and during reading time, coloring, and lunch. In the cafeteria I overheard some of the other boys saying, "Did you guys know the Scott-meister moved away?" Another answered, "Isn't that great! He was too fat and ugly to come to this school anyway." Their evil spirit remained, even in Scott's absence, showing, of course, the lack of civilizing parental influence. After I asked one of the teachers, Mrs. Lincoln, what happened to Scott, she told me, "His parents placed him in a special school." I hoped at that time that his parents had placed him in a school where he could be enjoyed for his mind and fun. Perhaps it hadn't been too late for Scott's parents to do something to move Scott in a positive direction.

Many years later, after I started my university work, I read an article in the paper about a computer hacker convicted for hate crimes over the Internet. As you can guess, I was surprised to see Scott's picture as an adult and his name right in the *Los Angeles Times*. I knew exactly why he had ended up where he did. The seeds of hate had been planted by those children in elementary school, and the hatred had grown, warping and distorting Scott's soul, until his desire for revenge against the world had overcome his natural intelligence and sense of fun. Childhood's seeds of hate had grown into adult evil and inhumanity. There's not much difference at the childhood scale when one child calls another names, and the adult scale where the population of one country calls the population of another "inferior." Or within a country, one racial group disdains another as "less evolved or less intelligent." Unfortunately, only adults have a clear view of the adult world, and they are the only ones who can see the direction of mental cruelty which—unchecked—invariably results in physical cruelty and barbarism. Therefore, every adult owes it to herself and her children to teach all children in her care about the dangers of name-calling and labeling.

If anyone intends to have children one day, or become a teacher or coach, that person will have to solve this inevitable issue, and only with careful ongoing communication with and monitoring of her children will she preserve human self-esteem, courage, and civilization.

Score 11.

Essay 4

Write an essay in which you describe a journey that was particularly unforgettable or momentous in your life. Explain why you feel this journey is a memorable one. (40 Minutes)

Night of the Dead in Janitzio

Five years ago, I had a journey that was transcendental in my life. I went to Janitzio, Mexico, just to spend one night and celebrate the traditional "Night of the Dead." This trip gave me experiences that changed my life in a positive way.

This journey helped me to have a better friendship with my classmates. I was at the University and the journey was the first I shared with my classmates. After we went to Janitzio, we became close friends with each other and started study groups which lasted throughout college. Later, we organized more trips, to Guanajuato, Aguascalientes, Monterrey, Mazatlan, Puerto Vallarta, and Mexico City. The friends I made on those journeys are lifelong friends; I still maintain contact with each of those close friends.

The "Night of the Dead" in Janitzio was a fascinating trip where I could learn more about the traditions of my country, Mexico. Janitzio is a little town on an island on Patzcuaro Lake where only the natives are allowed to live. They have to live by rigid rules; they all must be fishermen, and they all must marry someone who lives on their island. The most important event in Janitzio is the second day of November when all of the natives honor their dead relatives. They have a festival in the town's central pantheon with flowers, food, music, and thousands of candles. They also dance on the dock of the island and organize a parade with their canoes and hundreds of torches on the lake.

I felt I changed after participating in the "Night of the Dead" celebration. I thought a great deal about death. When I witnessed the great celebration in the pantheon and saw the natives singing beautiful, moving songs, and carrying flowers and food for their dead relatives, I understood that we do not really die if someone who loves us remains, because we continue to live in the minds and hearts of such people. The love that we had for them and the love they still carry for us is the same love, and it still lives.

My trip to Janitzio was the beginning of many changes that have transformed and enriched my conception of who I am, what I have, and who I am going to be after I die.

> Score 9 or 10.

COMPARISON/CONTRAST

Essay 1

> Please read the following quotation:
> "The modern world rewards constancy and uniformity among men and women, because the industrial world depends upon fixed patterns and repeated cycles of desire."
> The point of the quotation, that artificial means are forcing mankind into patterns of sameness is undeniably true. Yet, the human being has an indomitable spirit of independence and freedom. Compare someone you know well who typifies the point of the quotation, that is, whose life is being driven to conformity with another person you know well who is just the opposite, who, in fact, is the antithesis or opposite of conformity. Try to explain why each person has adopted his or her pattern of behavior. (One Hour)

My roommate, Chuck, is a basic, block pattern freak. He reminds me more of a droid than a human being. He arises each morning at 5:30 a.m., and goes jogging for an hour. Precisely at 6:38 a.m., I wake up to the sound of the shower (next to my bed) being turned on. He showers, shaves, dresses, and leaves in time for breakfast at Denny's at 7:05 a.m. sharp. He attends his morning classes and then goes to work at the Wherehouse in West Hollywood. I understand he is a whiz at putting tapes and CD's in their correct cubbyholes. On Friday and Saturday evenings at exactly 7:30 p.m., Chuck leaves on his way to meet his girl Ramona, another droid, I believe, only more severe. Chuck and I have talked about his basic-pattern lifestyle. He tells me that it does not bother him to repeat a routine; in fact, he becomes very anxious and frazzled if his actions are not according to an established pattern. Chuck never enjoys a vacation for that reason, or even a serendipitous afternoon at the Huntington Library or at a baseball game. I met Chuck's mother once. She also is an android. She couldn't stand our apartment and kept sniffing the air. I have a feeling that she breast fed Chuck according to a stopwatch-accurate schedule, and that, partially at least, explains why he is the way he is.

My brother Ernie is a street person. He usually sleeps on an old couch in an alley near Union Station downtown. He enjoys walking around on a sunny morning, pushing his shopping cart loaded with a sleeping bag, clothes, and other scraps and pieces that he just wants to keep. My mother has told Ernie for years that she has a clean room with its own bathroom and shower for him, as well as an allowance of $200 a month, whenever he wants it. He doesn't want it. He once told me that staying with anyone who is pampering him is like a slow suffocation, he has to leave. He is not a drunk, as most of our friends and family believe, and he only takes drugs once in awhile, and then only marijuana. He behaves the way he does because it is *his* behavior, and that fact means everything to him. Why does someone grow up with that stubborn kind of personality? It's hard to determine. I grew up in the same house, and I am much more together. Of course, Ernie is older, and had to deal with my father, who was a drunk and very abusive toward Ernie. He died just before I was born.

The two people, Chuck and Ernie, are so different that I have trouble trying to equate them for comparison. I can say that I feel much more comfortable with Ernie, and not because he's my brother, either. Ernie has human weaknesses and hopes and dreams. He will probably be found dead of exposure some cold, rainy morning, but he still talks of making it, "big!" I have no such sympathy with Chuck. He is Mr. Business, "That's the way it is." He will be a clinically sanitized success in life. He and Ramona will get married, and, at a socially correct measure of time from their wedding night, give birth to a perfect baby of 6.8 pounds. They will live in the suburbs, and have a condominium with three bedrooms, one of which has an exercycle in it. Somehow, I believe there's more to life. And somehow, I feel Ernie knows more about what it is.

Though this paper lacks a sharp thesis and final application of principle, it would score 10 for details.

Essay 2

Write a well-organized essay in which you identify two people you are familiar with—instructors, friends, boyfriends, girlfriends, neighbors, teammates—who were so different from each other, that one succeeded and the other did not; that is, one worked to success, productivity, a positive outcome, and the other worked to lack of success and a negative outcome. Be sure to tell us why you feel one achieved the positive results and why the other did not. (One Hour)

This is an essay about two teachers I have had. One was Mr. Godsey, my high-school algebra teacher, who taught so skillfully and with such a respect for his own subject, that I was transformed into a mathematics major even though I had formerly been afraid to count above the number twelve most of my life. The other is an upper-division college instructor, Dr. Milo Farashi, with whom I am presently taking organic chemistry, and because of whom I will probably change my major from mathematics to liberal studies. Both are obviously well-prepared, well-respected personalities in their subject areas; however, the manner in which they address their students makes all the difference. Mr. Godsey builds scholars as well as math science enrollment; Dr. Farashi tears them down. Mr. Godsey has truly varied, relevant ways of putting across the subject; Dr. Farashi does not put the subject across at all. Mr. Godsey is a school-wide personality who augments life at Encino High School for every student; Dr. Farashi teaches his one class, period.

The first week I was a student in high-school algebra, it was obvious that I was likely to have trouble with the subject. I had failed two quizzes and I was mixed up during class discussions. I stopped to talk to Mr. Godsey after class at the suggestion of my mother, who was concerned because I was unable to sleep, and because I was making a "thing" of math again, as I had before with disastrous consequences. Mr. Godsey sat down with me and gave me a pep talk. He told me I was as capable as anyone and that I am creating my own confusion. He made arrangements to sit down with me *every afternoon* for fifteen minutes. Also, he invited me to eat lunch in his room at noon, where he eats his own packed lunch and invites any student to join him who has any problem of any sort in math. I spent every lunch period with him, as well as a session at the end of every day. By the end of that semester, I was really good in algebra. Far different is the experience I had with Dr. Farashi early this semester when I was having problems with lipid formulae. I said, "Dr. Farashi, I'm having trouble understanding this formula; I've gone over it twenty times, and it never computes. Do you think you can tell me what I'm doing wrong?" I'll never forget his answer. He said, "The main thing you're doing wrong is taking this class. This is the big leagues, honey. This class isn't for the cheerleading crowd." With those words he left the room.

Mr. Godsey's methods of teaching are something to remember. He is conspicuously *interesting*, and he achieves that quality by working hard. He'll arrange a field trip to the filtration plant when the class is working on word problems involving acre feet. He'll set up model cars in the football field when he assigns distance-time problems, and he'll make huge charts involving real problems involving members of the class when he assigns budget problems. He invited an astronaut to talk to his students when they were dealing with telemetric formulae, and he took his class to the observatory when they discussed celestial navigation and star plotting.

In stark and very unpleasant contrast, Dr. Farashi stands in front of the class glowering, unless he is lecturing. His version of lecturing is reading from sheets of yellow paper. He does not encourage questions. If a student insists on asking a question, he treats that student as if he were trying to disrupt the class, and is very sarcastic with him.

Mr. Godsey is very active in all aspects of life at Encino High School. He is a sponsor of several clubs in addition to the Math Club, namely the Chess Club, Photography Club, Computer Club, and Ski Club. As Ski Club sponsor, he spends six weekends a year on Ski Club outings with the members. He is also Medallion (honor society) sponsor and cross country track coach in the fall. Each of these jobs he does with real distinction, and the distinction is always excellence. He has a knack of making every student in every class or organization he is connected with, gain something significant from that relationship. On the other hand, other than his involvement with the chemistry class, Dr. Farashi's connections with the college are nonexistent. In fact, a story appeared in the campus newspaper last year about the fact that the college administration tried to force him to become a mentor for a chemistry student. Dr. Farashi sued the university on the basis that the request was unrelated to teaching and won.

I think it's a real shame that there can be such an enormous distance between two publicly paid instructors in what they deliver.

Score 10 or 11.

EXPLANATORY/ANALYTIC

Essay 1

> It is a great source of satisfaction to a craftsman or anyone who completes a project or undertaking to do it efficiently, without wasted time or motion. Describe a process you or someone close to you completed that was done in a manner you consider particularly professional, or efficient, or well done. Be sure to give reasons for each step of the process, and explain why you think each one is important. (One Hour)

I would like to explain a process by which some doctors in Kaiser Permanente Hospital in Woodland Hills helped me to breathe normally again. My problems began during the last week of October, 1987, when I found I could barely breathe. Dr. Norman Mundsack, who was the first to see me in the emergency room, noted that my face was gray, my breathing was shallow, and that my EKG and monitor display indicated a significantly reduced blood flow from my left ventricle. He prescribed Lasix, a diuretic, to improve the ability of the kidney to eliminate the excess fluids that were building up throughout my body tissues, particularly my lungs, and digitalis, a drug which strengthens ventricular contractions and corrects irregular heartbeats. This immediate treatment was important, because it enabled my breathing and circulation to stabilize so that the doctors had time to perform more exhaustive diagnostic tests.

The first of these was given the next morning in the hospital's heart clinic. It is called an echo test and works by showing a sonar picture of the inside of your heart on a television screen. I was able to watch the screen myself and was very impressed when I saw my own mitral valve open and close like a little parachute, and my own left ventricle squeeze blood into the aorta on its way to the lungs. The cardiologist, Dr. Robyn Adare, saw a great deal more, a massive leak in my mitral valve that prevented the ventricle from building up enough pressure when it contracted. This echo test was very important, because it gave more evidence to the doctors that I needed to undertake the next test, which carried some risks, the angiogram.

In taking the angiogram, or "picture of the blood vessels," the doctors snake one or two catheters through your veins to the heart itself. The catheters permit them to release dyes and measure pressure changes in the heart with some accuracy. The angiogram, if their findings are positive, ascertain the preliminary diagnosis and give the doctors the final authority to prescribe open-heart surgery.

In the open-heart surgery, the doctors first split apart my sternum or breastbone, right down the middle. They then cut through the pericardium or covering of the heart, and exposed the heart itself. Then they connected a heart-lung machine to my circulatory system. Without the heart-lung machine, they would not be able to stop the heart and cut into it to make repairs.

Once they exposed the left atrium, the surgeons made a final diagnosis of the problem by observing and touching the mitral valve. Their judgment was that it could not be repaired surgically, and that it had to be replaced by a caged-ball valve. They removed the old valve and sutured in the artificial valve. The new valve would stop the leakage and allow the blood to flow with normal pressure throughout the body so that fluids would not build up, and enough oxygen would be delivered to all the tissues of the body.

Obviously, I admire all of the doctors who completed this medical procedure because they improved my quality of life and gave me many more years to live. However, it was clear during the whole lengthy process, from my preliminary diagnosis in the e.r. to the day I was wheeled out of intensive care, that I was in the hands of a sharp, professional outfit that knew exactly what needed to be done. I feel, as well, that I myself was part of a process that improves with each new patient, because each patient is observed and studied carefully.

Score 10.

Essay 2

> Essay Assignment:
> Tell us about your major. Describe the life and activities of a typical major in your field. Explain why you chose that major, in turn giving us some evaluation of the reasons themselves. (One Hour)

Note that the three following essays are the finished versions of the essays used in Chapter 4 to illustrate levels of detail.

Barely Adequate Essay

I determined to become an M.D. and so chose a pre-med major in college because of family precedence, aptitude scores, and a desire to do some good. A pre-med major is a good deal of work, as you will see.

First of all, you have to complete a good deal of high-level mathematics courses at the high-school and early college levels. In addition, you are expected to complete biology, microbiology, physics, anatomy, physiology, and chemistry courses. These courses require much dedication and many late nights to complete with an acceptable grade. In addition, a pre-med student in college spends some "shadowing" or mentor time in a hospital or laboratory. There, you learn something about life as a medic.

My grandfather, father and mother, and three uncles are doctors now, and my sister and three cousins are in medical school. Medicine seems to dominate every family get-together. At every Christmas or Thanksgiving dinner we have what amounts to a bull-session on medicine. Every time anyone is sick in our large family, there are phone calls criss-crossing the city as the right family expert is consulted. Our family is really a medical clan.

In high school, I took two general aptitude tests with private companies. Both tests indicated that my skills all were in the physical sciences, specifically medicine; for this reason, I took a math-science program designed for pre-med majors. I realize that we cannot trust such general interest surveys totally. However, in my case, I believe the results parallel other aspects of my schooling that point to medicine.

I want to do some good in the world. I intend to join the Peace Corps and would like to be matched at the USC Medical Center where most of the clients are very needy. I am very genuine about that desire.

Adequate Essay

In my senior year of high school, I determined to become an M.D. and so chose a pre-med major in college. I chose this major for three reasons: family precedence, aptitude scores, and a desire to do some good in the world. A pre-med major is a good deal of work because most of the courses are difficult science courses.

First of all, you have to complete a good deal of high-level mathematics courses at the high-school and early college levels, among them calculus, differential calculus, mathematical analysis, and medical statistics. In addition, you are expected to complete biology, microbiology, physics, anatomy, physiology, and chemistry courses. These courses require much dedication and many late nights to complete with an acceptable grade. In addition, a pre-med student in college spends some "shadowing" or mentor time in a hospital or laboratory. There, you learn something about life as a medic, and you even meet some medical "contacts" that could hold you in good stead later on.

My grandfather, father and mother, and three uncles are doctors now, and my sister and three cousins are in medical school. My grandfather practiced medicine in Lausanne, Switzerland, my father in the USC Medical Center, and my mother in the Kaiser Sunset Family Ward. My Uncle Charles on my mother's side is an anesthesiologist, and both of my other uncles, my father's brothers, are cardiac surgeons at large hospitals in Buffalo and Philadelphia.

While I was in high school, I tool a general aptitude test at a private educational research company considered the best around, as well as the Bradley Inventory, considered the most accurate test of its kind. The results of both tests were very pointed; they indicated that my interests and abilities all lay in the physical and numerical sciences, specifically medicine. As a result, I committed myself to courses compatible with a pre-med major in college. I realize that we cannot trust such general interest surveys totally; however, in my case, I believe the results parallel other aspects of my schooling.

The third reason I chose the medical field as a career is to do some good in the world. I have already applied to the Peace Corps; I also hope to be matched at the USC Medical Center for my internship, a medical center where most of the clients are very deprived and where there seems to be such a need for doctors who care. I have been very lucky and I sincerely want to give something back.

The medical field has been criticized heavily over the past few years, in many ways justly. I hope I am able to perform my professional duties in such a manner that I am able to reverse that tide. At least that is my intention.

Particularly Good Essay

In my senior year of high school, I determined to become an M.D. and so chose a pre-med major in college, a course of study that I have found to be rigorous, most of its requirements consisting of chemistry, molecular biology, anatomy, physiology, microbiology, and physics courses. I determined to become an M.D. because my family history almost demands it. My grandfather, mother, father, and three uncles are doctors now, and my sister and three cousins are in medical school. In addition, the two major aptitude tests I took in my junior and senior high school years both indicated to a high degree that I was well suited for medical science, both in academic inclination and temperament. Finally, I chose to be an M.D. because I want to do some good in the world, and the medical field, I believe, gives a person many different opportunities to make a difference in the world. These reasons for my choice of career may seem fortuitous at first glance, but they did take a great deal of thought and self-evaluation.

To be a pre-med student today means to be dedicating yourself to the medical profession at an early age. Even as a sophomore, a pre-med student spends time in a "shadowing" or mentoring capacity in a hospital or medical laboratory. There, you begin to learn something about the life of a medic, and you even meet some medical contacts that could hold you in good stead later on. My experiences were in Freeman Memorial Hospital in Burbank and in the Merck Laboratories in Glendale. At the Hospital, I "shadowed" Dr. Myron Levitt, a Cardiac Surgeon who specialized in pacemaker and fibrillator implants, actually being allowed to "suit up" and observe two open-heart procedures. At the Laboratories, I was a mentor working in the outpatient research section interviewing patients about side effects of the drugs they were taking.

My grandfather practiced medicine in Lausanne, Switzerland, at the Academie des Medecines, a well-known hospital specializing in the regeneration of crucial body cells like pancreatic and pituitary cells. My father was in charge of the Women's Hospital in the USC Medical Center, a place where much research is done on subdermal injections of drugs and other medications directly on the spinal cord, and my mother runs the Family Ward, meaning obstetrics, in the Kaiser Sunset Facility located in Hollywood. My Uncle Charles on my mother's side is an anesthesiologist at St. John's Hospital in Santa Monica, a wonderful facility that has one of the most advanced pain clinics in the nation, and both of my other uncles, my father's brothers, are cardiac surgeons at large hospitals, Uncle Phil at Sullivan Municipal Hospital in Buffalo where he is a family practice physician, and Uncle Eddie at Kaiser Permanente Hospital in Philadelphia where he does routine surgery. There is no doubt in my mind that such a distinguished family history in medicine created a subconscious compunction in my mind to study medicine. I have at times wondered whether a need to follow my family's professional traditions was a rational and aware kind of behavior and have decided that it is not. Accordingly, I have taken pains to see that I am making the right career choice independently of my desires to remain "in the family."

While I was a high-school sophomore, I took a general aptitude test at a private educational research company that my parents knew of, an expensive three-hour survey that was considered the best around. The results of that test were very pointed; they indicated that my interests and inclinations, as well as abilities, all lay in the physical and numerical sciences, specifically medicine. As a result, I committed my course of study to high-level math-science that would enable me to declare a pre-med major as soon as I hit college. During my junior year, all members of the honor society were treated to another highly respected aptitude survey, the Bradley Inventory, considered the most accurate test of its kind. The results of this test again verified my predilection for math and the sciences, but this time I showed an inclination toward the life sciences as well. I realize that we cannot trust such general interest surveys totally; I'm sure that they have been inaccurate at times. However, in my case, I believe the results parallel other aspects of my schooling, my grades in the sciences, for example, and my enthusiasm for all mathematics courses, as well as my success in subsequent years as a pre-med major. For these reasons, I believe our reliance on the formal aptitude tests was wise.

The third reason I chose the medical field as a career is to do some good in the world. Certainly, I could accomplish the same end in other ways and with a different major, but I have come to believe that I am good at my field, and so I am choosing my strongest suit. I have already applied to the Peace Corps for membership once I have completed my intern year. In addition, I hope to be matched at the USC Medical Center where most of the clients are very deprived non-citizens, street people, and hopeless alcoholics, and, consequently, where there seems to be such a need for doctors who have compassion. The only evaluative comment I can make about this third reason for my choice of major is that I am very genuine about it. I have been very lucky, born into a family with the means and tendency to make life very good and rewarding for me. I sincerely want to give something back.

The medical field has been criticized heavily over the past few years, in many ways justly. I hope I am able to perform my professional duties in such a manner that I am able to reverse that tide. At least that is my intention. One way to start is to care about people, not money; and to care and actively become involved with the profession, its reputation, its weaknesses. I want to be the kind of doctor who is a credit to that profession.

Score 12.
NOTE: This amount of content in one hour *is* extraordinary. It helps to be familiar with an experience.

ARGUMENT/PERSUASION

Essay 1

The nation of China has been severely criticized in recent years for its forced sterilization policies. Married couples are permitted by the government to have one child only; if they break the law and give birth to a second child, they are punished by the government, and chastised and ostracized by their own townspeople.

Such treatment of human beings is unacceptable by most moralists in the Western world. Yet, no one can deny that China has cut its population growth dramatically, a truly enormous undertaking given China's size. Nor can anyone deny that the world's capacity to maintain life is now being threatened by out-of-control population growth. Virtually all of the world's environmental troubles, from the destruction of the South American rain forest to the depletion of the ozone layer, from the starving children in Bangladesh to global warming, from pollution of the planet's air and water to the extinction of animal life, all are related to excess population.

Write an essay in which you defend or attack China's position regarding birth control. Be sure to anticipate arguments that might be used to counter your point of view by bringing them up and countering them in your own essay. (80 Minutes)

I definitely feel that China has broken some moral laws in the way it has trampled on the rights of its own citizens. However, I also feel that the head-in-the-sand attitude of most Western nations toward environmental danger signals, pollution, global warming, the hole in the ozone layer, the permanent loss of wildlife, and many other signs that man is rapidly driving himself to extinction is more irresponsible and immoral than what China has done. Let us limit our argument to one segment of the Western world, namely, the United States.

In spite of several prominent national organizations and on-going campaigns to promote environmental concerns, there is no national program in the United States, for example, to reduce population. Why? The answer is obvious. Growth of population means growth in the economy, and the economy is king.

Acid rain has been on my mind for years now, mainly because a large part of my family is from Canada, and I have been kidded and chided by them my whole life because the U.S. government is so dragging its feet on acid rain legislation. I must ask why the government is so slow on such an environmentally sensitive issue. No one doubts that the water of the St. Lawrence river and many estuaries deriving from Canada is undrinkable, and that trees and wildlife reveal new evidence each year that acid rain is slowly stripping the earth of life. The same can be said for the quality of the air in cities like Los Angeles, Detroit, and many other places. People are dying earlier because of the air, and trees are turning brown.

And then there is the truly astounding fact that the government for forty years now has virtually ignored the field of energy alternatives, except for laws mandating automobile efficiency and some grants to aid the development of alternative energy sources. Now such funding is drying up, however, and even automobile efficiency is being put on a back burner.

One hears every once in a while of great strides being made by private entrepreneurs in methane production (as an alternative to gasoline), electric car design, wind, solar, tidal energy, heat retentive homes, super-efficient cars and appliances, but they are only echoes in the wind. Big industry, capital, and government are not interested.

American public assistance regulations and social security laws not only encourage, they compel low-income, low-education women to give birth to five or six children and live on welfare. Not only that, government officials and lawmakers, fully aware of the problem, allow many thousands of new women each year to elect the lifestyle.

So, if the purpose of this essay question is to ask me if I believe that China is wrong in mistreating people who have more than one child, the answer is yes, I am very much against the brutal treatment of people and the suppression of their human rights. However, that answer is too simple. I am also contemptuous of governments, like the U.S. government, who flatly turn away from their obligations as leaders to at least try to handle some of the pressing problems of an overpopulated, overconsumptive, overpolluting, unprincipled world out of control.

Score 9.

Essay 2

Consider the following quotations regarding capital punishment:

"The only way to break the chain of violent reaction is to practice nonviolence as individuals and collectively through our laws and institutions. Can we expect a decent society if the state is allowed to kill its own people?"

—Coretta Scott King

"To be effective, punishment must fit the crime, and the punishment must be certain and swift."

—Cesare Beccaria

Write a well-constructed paper in which you argue for or against capital punishment, making sure to acknowledge and counter some of the stronger opposing views. (One Hour)

I am only 22 years old, but I feel the controversy about capital punishment has been with me all my life. Even in the sixth grade, I remember arguing the issue in class and even taking part in a class vote on the controversy. So, like most of my peers, I have an opinion about the issue. My opinion is very one-sided because, like everyone else in the United States, I have watched every day the increasing murder rate on our streets, in our neighborhoods, and in our homes. My opinion is very simple: death to the killers.

Since the Vietnam War, crime has been increasing in the United States. Mass murders are almost common now, and the daily death of skid-row drunks, young women who are also rape victims, gang members or anyone within fifty feet of them, robbery victims, all-night store clerks, competing lover, you name it, has made life in the U.S.A. much less safe and pleasant. Before we make social or economic progress in this country, we must suppress crime. We need to give a rest to the notion that crime, especially violent crime, is the result of need on the part of starving people. Study after study has shown that poverty is not the cause of crime, but is more often the reason for spectacular feats of recovery, retraining, regeneration within the family. The fact is that most criminals commit their crime because they choose to do so; in their setting and lifestyles, there are always alternatives for them, but they choose crime.

The broadening of suspects' rights under the Warren Court have resulted in a series of convictions and sentences that are so compromised and light that they do not discourage even the convict himself from resuming a criminal career.

Thus we have arrived at a need for clear punishment, and, since violent crime has become such a prominent concern to us, we must include capital punishment. Kidnapping was at epidemic levels until it was made punishable by death. Then it almost disappeared. The same is likely to happen with killing if we ever enact a system where justice is certain and swift.

There are those who say that the death penalty is not an effective deterrent, but they have no convincing proof. In fact, they have pretty much had their way over the past twenty-five years, with the number of executions across the country reduced to three or four. What has been the result? An overwhelming explosion in the homicide rate. Opponents of the death penalty, by their very effective campaign, have doomed thousands of innocent people to death. These people talk about a "bloodbath" if executions resume in large numbers, but they say nothing (and possibly feel nothing) about the "bloodbath" happening now, daily, hourly, in our streets and in our homes. The *Los Angeles Times* this morning published a chilling statistic; in 1991, in Los Angeles City alone, 2340 people were slaughtered, most of them innocent victims.

For years, innocent people have lived with the fear of death, reinforced each day in the news. It is time for potential killers to live with the same fear.

Score 10.

Essay 3

Identify some aspect of your work or college or neighborhood that you feel should be changed. Argue for that change, making sure to present some convincing facts and ideas. Present at least *one* opposing argument along with your counterpoint to that argument. (One Hour)

Working as a teaching assistant has some advantages. Since I started, working as a TA has helped me develop many skills which will help me to become a better teacher. But, because the Los Angeles Unified School District does not offer the assistants benefits, guaranteed hours, or job security, I feel we must form a union. The job we perform is an important one. Most teaching assistants are bilingual, and help to form a bridge between the students, who do not speak English, and the teachers, most of whom speak only English. Important threads of rapport form in every classroom between the students and the aide, and between the teacher and the aide. There is a working relationship which results and which will remain only with a stable staff, that is, employees who persevere over several years. However, with low pay and no benefits, it is difficult or impossible for all but a few aides to stay on the job for very long. It is a "pin money" job, though its responsibilities are career caliber.

The District employs thousands of people. The largest group of workers are the teachers. These employees have benefits. On the other hand, the second largest group of workers in the Los Angeles District, namely 10,000 teaching assistants, 70% of whom are bilingual, receive no benefits, no vacation, no sick or holiday pay, no medical or dental coverage. The District knows that, without teaching assistants, the schools would not be able to operate, though the District will not acknowledge the assistants as a unionized group, and is avoiding the cost of paying benefits.

The TA's are hired to work an average of three hours a day. Part of their job is to teach reading, math, and science to groups of students. In fact, where a bilingual TA is assisting a monolingual teacher in a totally Spanish-speaking class, the TA does pretty much all of the teaching, if the truth were known. For this reason alone, we deserve better treatment from the District.

The number of teachers is steadily decreasing, and class size is steadily inclining upward. Not all students get help from their teachers. There are approximately 38 students per class now, and one teacher alone cannot devote enough of her time to individual pupils who need attention or nurturing. A TA goes a long way to help this unacceptable situation.

TA's need to help themselves. They need to form a solid union, and then threaten to strike. Then, and only then will we receive the pay raise and benefits that will stabilize our working relationship with the students and teachers. There are those who look back to the past and say, "Why do we need TA's anyway? We didn't have them years ago, and the schools were great." My answer to them is very simple. That was years ago when everyone was white and English speaking. Now you have a District that is 65% Hispanic and speaks only Spanish, and another 7% that is Chinese and speaks only Mandarin or Cantonese. The aides are very essential. What will all those English-speaking teachers do with whole classrooms full of students who don't speak their language?

Score 10.

# 7 Essay-Writing Practice

Practice writing essays of the type you are likely to be assigned. Listed below are topics for each of the four essay types discussed in Chapter 2—namely

1. Personal experience
2. Comparison/contrast
3. Explanatory/analytic
4. Argument/persuasion

Make an appointment with and bring your practice essays to an experienced holistic scorer on your campus. Also, your university's testing center will have additional sample topics.

PERSONAL-EXPERIENCE TOPICS

1. One of the final requirements in the process of becoming an Eagle Scout is to do one hundred hours of community service. Sometimes courts punish individuals convicted of lesser crimes by requiring that they do a fixed number of hours of community service. Also, often one can see businessmen and business organizations, actors, fraternities, and sororities performing community service as an expression of simple good will. Whatever the reason, suppose you had to complete one hundred hours of community service. What acts and services would you choose to perform for your community? Be sure to explain why you would choose them, and what difference you think you might make.   (1 hour)

2. If you could live your life over again, what changes would you make in choices and behavior? Be sure to explain why you would make such changes, and what the results might be in your present circumstances.   (1 hour)

3. Given the nature of the world today, as well as the liabilities that seem to face the next generation in such arenas as the economy, the world food supply, the environment, crime, education, morality, and others, what values and talents would you most want to impart to your children?   (1 hour)

Note

  Values = intrinsically valuable principles or qualities
  Talent   = the abilities, powers, and gifts bestowed upon a person

4. People sometimes change long-held sentiments or opinions because of chance incidents that occur in their lives, lifestyle changes, new acquaintances, or some other incitement. Write an essay about a fundamental change in a sentiment or opinion of yours or of someone close to you. Describe what prompted the change, and, if possible, explain some long-term reasons why the change occurred. Describe the opinions held before and after the change, and explain how the change affected your or the subject's pattern of behavior.   (1 hour)

5. Being a part of a group is very important to many people; in fact, for some it is essential for survival. There are many other positive consequences of group membership; belonging provides protection, social release, and a feeling of strength. But there are negative effects of belonging to groups as well if they are groups like gangs, skinheads, the KKK, the Red Guards, or any other hate groups. Argue for or against the importance of belonging to a group.   (1 hour)

6. Not a day goes by that most of us are not given service of one sort or another, in purchasing an item at the store, having our car repaired, our teeth cleaned, our dinner served, our lawn mowed, our streets kept safe by the police, or our appendices removed by a surgeon. Write a well-crafted essay about the best service you have received. Explain why the event remains lodged in your memory. (1 hour)

7. Describe an incident in which you or someone close to you was cut from a team or rejected in some manner from a group or activity. Be sure to explain the logic behind the reasons for the initial rejection, the reasons you feel the refusal was just or unjust, and the long-term effect of the incident. (45 minutes)

8. There are very few truly solitary individuals today, so insistently are group activities woven into the patterns of American society. Describe some groups you have been a part of, explaining which you wished you had never joined, and which have had a positive influence on your life. Do not merely list the groups. Be sure to describe them specifically, explaining *what you did* in each group and why you consider each group a good or bad influence. (1 hour)

9. Identify a person outside your family who has had a measurable influence on your life. Describe the person and the influence he or she generated, the means by which the possible changes came about, and the difference the influence has made in your life. (45 minutes)

10. How well did your elementary or high school teachers prepare you for the efforts you are now making in college? Discuss how your previous experience or schooling was helpful and how it could have been more helpful. (1 hour)

11. Describe your major in some detail. Portray the life and activities of a typical major in your field. Explain why you chose that major, in turn giving us some evaluation of the reasons themselves. (45 minutes)

12. Discuss a specific success or failure that taught you something important. Do not merely tell a story, but explain in detail how your experience affected your subsequent attitudes and actions. (1 hour)

COMPARISON/CONTRAST TOPICS

1. Bert and Ernie, from the muppet series "Sesame Street" are best friends. Yet, they are complete opposites; Ernie is messy, disorganized, outgoing, and hip, whereas Bert is neat, organized, reserved, and square. Think of someone you know well who might be characterized as your best friend. Compare *and* contrast your personality with his or hers. Explain what makes you such good friends. (80 minutes)

2. Compare and contrast two different families that you know well but find very different from one another. Be sure to establish the basis of your comparison early in your essay (personalities, lifestyles, activities, talents, etc.). Explain which living style you prefer and why. (1 hour)

3. Often students of different nationalities, cultures, or backgrounds will utilize completely different study habits to succeed academically. Pick two students of your acquaintance and compare and contrast their study techniques. In what ways were their eventual results similar and different? What kinds of conclusions can you draw? Can you derive a successful set of strategies from such examples? (1 hour)

4. Write a well-organized essay in which you identify two people you are familiar with—instructors, friends, boyfriends, girlfriends, neighbors, teammates—who were so different from each other that one succeeded and the other did not; that is, one achieved success, productivity, a positive outcome, and the other found a lack of success and a negative outcome. Be sure to tell us why you feel one achieved the positive results and why the other did not. (80 minutes)

5. Dreams are but the touchstones of our characters.

—*Henry David Thoreau*

(A touchstone is a hard, flintlike stone that for centuries was used to test the authenticity of gold or silver. Now, the word *touchstone* has come to mean any criterion or test used to measure the quality of a thing.)

In a well-structured essay, describe a dream you or someone you know well attempted to fulfill, only to discover that the dream did not match the reality, once it was achieved. Compare and contrast the dream with its own fulfillment. Show in what ways your life was changed because of your discovery. (80 minutes)

6. Please read and give some thought to the following two quotations:
   A. There's one born every moment.   —*P. T. Barnum*
   B. You can fool all of the people some of the time, and you can fool some of the people all of the time, but you can't fool all of the people all of the time.
                                   —*A. Lincoln*

   Write an essay on the two statements above in three parts as follows:
   (1) Compare the statements. Explain what they have in common and how they overlap.
   (2) Contrast the statements. Explain how they differ.
   (3) Explain what your position might be regarding the two statements by choosing one or describing the favorable and unfavorable aspects of each. Support your view with examples from your personal experience. (80 minutes)

7. Computer experts have asserted that the true Age of Computerization has not yet arrived, that, in fact, second-generation computers are about to invade every habit and every process in which humanity engages. In the near future, there will be no way to avoid "ubiquitous computers" in daily living.
   Compare and contrast the negative and positive effects of computer use as you know it to exist now. Illustrate your discussion with specific anecdotes and illustrations from your own experience. (1 hour)

8. Examine both sides of a controversial issue such as AIDS testing, condom distribution in public schools, the outlawing of guns, or abortion. Compare and contrast arguments on both sides of the topic, explaining how slogans used with either side ("Guns don't kill; people do!"; "Abortion is murder!") can distort the issue by oversimplifying it. Compare and contrast the assumptions and logic that lie behind each slogan. (1 hour)

9. Compare and contrast a place, a room, a school, a town that you knew both as a child and, now, as an adult. Explain your vision of the way it used to be, and the way it is now. What have you learned about the place as a result of this comparison and contrast? (1 hour)

EXPLANATORY/ANALYTIC TOPICS

1. Please read and think about the following two quotations:
   A. At thirty, man suspects himself a fool;
      Knows it at forty, and reforms his plan;
      At fifty chides his infamous delay,
      Pushes his prudent purpose to resolve;
      In all the magnanimity of thought
      Resolves, and reresolves; then dies the same.   *Edward Young,* 1758

   B. From birth to age eighteen, a girl needs
      good parents. From eighteen to thirty-
      five, she needs good looks. From thirty-
      five to fifty-five she needs a good personality.
      From fifty-five on, she needs good cash.   *Sophie Tucker,* 1953

   Write an essay on the above two statements in three parts as follows:
   (1) Compare the statements. Explain what the two statements have in common, and how they overlap.
   (2) Contrast the statements, explaining in what ways they differ.
   (3) Both quotations are observations about stages of life. Which one do you find the most meaningful? Why? Support your position with examples from your own perception or experience. (1 hour)

2. Discuss the profession or career you expect to embark upon during the next few years. What exactly will you be doing? Why did you choose it? What are its advantages and disadvantages? What is the prognosis of that field or career in tomorrow's world? What chances of advancement does it give you? (45 minutes)

3. Subtle, unspoken "messages" are all around us, woven into our daily life. For example, we live in a high-security, low-trust society. When we buy gas, we have to pay in advance at burglar-proof, bulletproof cubicles. There are TV monitors in every retail store, burglar alarms in every home, antitheft tags on store merchandise everywhere. What are we to believe but that around us are thieves; none of us can be trusted. Identify a "message" that you have received from your observations of the world around you. Describe the events or observations that prompted the message, the reasons those events came about, and your opinion about the quality or justifiability of those reasons. What is the overall effect of the "message" on you? (1 hour)

4. Please note this statement:

"We must live in the present. If we dwell on the past, we will lose the present."

To what extent and in what ways do you agree or disagree with the statement? Explain and illustrate your answer with observations and experience. (1 hour)

5. Please read the following quotation:

> It is art that *makes* life, makes interest, makes importance, for our consideration and application of these things, and I know of no substitute whatever for the force and beauty of its process. —*Henry James*

Identify a work of art, a fine movie, a play, a novel that caused you to feel or become important, at least more so than you felt before. Explain how the work caused you to feel different about yourself, and how your feeling was reflected in behavior. Specify what in the work enabled you to reach a new understanding of yourself. (1 hour)

6. Please read the following lines:

> If I had peace to sit and sing,
> Then I could make a lovely thing... —*Anna Wickham*

Avocations and hobbies can be rewarding to oneself and others. Identify a hobby, community activity, school involvement, sport, or volunteer project that you have observed closely or participated in that proves that spare time may well be spent. Describe the specific steps in the process, making sure to explain how each step is essential or desirable. Explain how you and others benefited from the activity. (1 hour)

7. Note the following quotation:

> All that is necessary for the triumph of evil is that good men do nothing. —*E. Burke*

To what extent and in what ways do you agree or disagree with this statement? Explain and illustrate your answer from history, literature, and the observation of the world around you. (1 hour)

8. At times we all purchase or acquire something that requires a selection of a number of options. Explain what criteria and standards you applied in the purchase of a home, car, boat, or in the selection of a school, vacation spot, or apartment, or other item. Explain why you chose each and why each is important. (1 hour)

Sometimes explanatory/analytic questions take the form of a problem to be solved or a judgment to be made. Take the following example:

DIRECTIONS: You will have a total of 60 minutes to respond to the topic below. You will be given 5 minutes to plan your essay, 40 minutes to write it, and 15 minutes to review, edit, and complete your essay. The above times will be announced by the proctor.

You will not be allowed to leave early.

Express your thoughts carefully, logically, and effectively. Provide examples and evidence to support your ideas.

9. We all attempt to make a change for the better at some time in our lives. In fact, all progress made on this planet has been the result of humanity's quest for a better life. Think of a major "change for the better" that you experienced or witnessed in your

lifetime, a significant change involving several stages or steps over a period of time. Identify the change, discuss each of its steps, and the effects each step had on you or the principals involved. Be sure to explain how the final outcome was a change for the better. (1 hour)

10. Some people feel the world is advancing too fast and that "modern is not always better." Choose some recent (within 50 years) technological invention or discovery and show that it has some negative spin-offs. Explain how the negative impact of the invention or discovery has affected you and your life. What are the long-term effects of the innovation on the world? (1 hour)

11. The drive for racial equality has been a major fact of the last two decades. Virtually no public institution and few private ones have been unaffected by affirmative action laws and regulations. Explain ways in which your workplace and/or community has been changed by such human rights regulations. (1 hour)

You have just completed three job interviews and compiled the table of information below detailing the job offers you have received:

Aspect to Consider	Job A	Job B	Job C
Annual Salary	$17,000	$23,000	$24,000
Automobile provided?	no	yes	no
Location	Santa Fe, NM	Florence, Italy	Chicago, IL
Apartment rent per month	900	800	1000
Number of employees in company	22	51	2219

- Based on the above data, which job would you choose? Why?
- What other aspects of the job or considerations not shown would be important to you in making this decision?

In outlining your thoughts, give yourself:
- 5 minutes to plan
- 40 minutes to write your essay
- 15 minutes to review, edit, and complete

(60 minutes)

ARGUMENT/PERSUASION TOPICS

1. We live in volatile times. Every week, fundamental changes are taking place in once-immovable institutions and traditions. Argue for or against a major change in one of our long-standing traditions or institutions, such as public support for schools, universal health care, the ownership of guns, private insurance, etc. Be sure to give ample reasons why you believe the change you suggest should be made. Explain what is wrong with the old way and why your change will be more beneficial.

2. Read the following quotation:

   Ah, love, let us be true
   To one another! for the world, which seems
   To lie before us like a land of dreams,
   So various, so beautiful, so new,
   Hath really neither joy, nor love, nor light,
   Nor certitude, nor peace, nor help for pain;
   And we are here as on a darkling plain
   Swept with confused alarms of struggle and flight,
   Where ignorant armies clash by night.   —*Matthew Arnold*

   Do you have as dark a view of your future as Arnold had of his? Argue whether or not we should be optimistic about our next fifty years or pessimistic. Give ample reasons for your view. Anticipate several counter-arguments by addressing them in your paper.

3. During the Persian Gulf War, news organizations complained vehemently that their access to the war and its stories was so limited and curtailed as to be repressive. Yet, the military command stated that it withheld only information that would compromise the safety of their men. In a carefully designed essay, argue for or against the kind of "news management" that the Pentagon exercised. What are the advantages and disadvantages of such control?

4. Universal military training has been discussed for over a century as a means of instilling discipline and moral toughness in the youth of America. In spite of the waning of the cold war and the "disappearance" of most of our enemies in the world, the topic is still being discussed from time to time. Argue for or against universal military training for all citizens eighteen years old. Explain why you believe your arguments are correct.

5. All fields of study are occasionally enlivened by controversies within their ranks. Medicine has been shaken by formidable disagreements on universal health coverage, abortion, the clinical definition of death, and many more. In literary fields, scholars sometimes disagree vehemently on issues such as the status of authors, or critical interpretations of a work or passage. Historians have argued mightily about "tilted" history books that emphasize, for example, a Western assessment of the age of exploration. Identify a controversy in your field of study or one with which you are familiar. Represent both sides of the controversy with some balance, if feasible, and then argue for the position you embrace.

6. How many times have you heard the statement, "There ought to be a law!" Describe a contemporary problem in society, politics, or the workplace that could be solved by a new law. Explain what the law should accomplish and how it would be beneficial. Persuade your reader that your point of view is correct.

7. A prevalent note is heard today from individuals and organizations who feel that big government is too big, that it is, in fact, strangling individuals and businesses with regulations, accountability, and restrictions. Take a position on this issue, and argue for that position with personal references to your own experience. Be sure to represent the opposing point of view, and then answer that opinion with a counter-argument.

8. A "Buy American" wave of sentiment sweeps the United States every few years. Countries like Japan, China, and the oil producing nations of the Persian Gulf are vilified for their selfishness, and Americans are asked to buy American products only. Argue for or against this protectionist view. Catalogue which foreign-made products you have purchased in the past, and explain how you will fare buying American versions.

9. There is no doubt that America is a melting pot; by the same token, there is no doubt that most members of specific races and nationalities strive their whole lives to maintain a link with their true ethnic identity and culture. The two impulses are not always compatible. Often, success is interpreted as total immersion in and assimilation by the new culture. Argue for a lifestyle that emphasizes the maintenance of cultural ties, or a lifestyle that emphasizes success and assimilation, using your own experience as a source of examples and illustrative anecdotes. Anticipate opposing arguments and answer them in your essay.

10. Women's rights organizations speak frequently of the need for women to change their stereotype. There are also those who argue that men need to be liberated from their role in society as well. Write an effective argument/persuasion paper in which you convince the reader of one position or the other.

ESSAY BASED ON READING

Occasionally, essay questions are assigned that have as their basis a reading, usually an essay. Here is an example.

You will have a total of one hour and forty minutes to complete this assignment. Spend no more than forty minutes reading the essay "Mankind's Better Moments" by Barbara Tuchman (following). Spend the remaining hour writing a carefully designed essay on the assigned topic, which follows the reading.

MANKIND'S BETTER MOMENTS

In this troubled world of ours, pessimism seems to have won the day. But we would do well to recall some of the positive and even admirable capacities of the human race. We hear very little of them lately.

Ours is not a time of self-esteem or self-confidence as was, for instance, the 19th Century, whose self-esteem may be seen oozing from its portraits. Victorians, especially the men, pictured themselves as erect, noble and splendidly handsome. Our self-image looks more like Woody Allen or a character from Samuel Beckett. Amid a mass of worldwide troubles and a poor record for the 20th Century, we see our species—with cause—as functioning very badly, as blunderers when not knaves, as violent, ignoble, corrupt, inept, incapable of mastering the forces that threaten us, weakly subject to our worst instincts; in short, decadent.

The catalogue is familiar and valid but it is growing tiresome. A study of history reminds one that mankind has its ups and downs and during the ups has accomplished many brave and beautiful things, exerted stupendous endeavors, explored and conquered oceans and wildernesses, achieved marvels of beauty in the creative arts and marvels of science and social progress, loved liberty with a passion that throughout history has led men to fight and die for it over and over again, pursued knowledge, exercised reason, enjoyed laughter and pleasures, played games with zest, shown courage, heroism, altruism, honor and decency; experienced love, known comfort, contentment, and, occasionally, happiness. All these qualities have been part of human experience and if they have not had as important notice as the negatives nor exerted as wide and persistent an influence as the evils we do, they nevertheless deserve attention, for they currently are all but forgotten.

Among the great endeavors, we have in our time carried men to the moon and brought them back safely—surely one of the most remarkable achievements in history. Some may disapprove of the effort as unproductive, as too costly, and a wrong choice of priorities in relation to greater needs, all of which may be true but does not, as I see it, diminish the achievement. If you look carefully, all positives have a negative underside, sometimes more, sometimes less, and not all admirable endeavors have admirable motives.

Great endeavor requires vision and some kind of compelling impulse, as in the case of the Gothic cathedrals of the Middle Ages. The architectural explosion that produced this multitude of soaring vaults, arched, ribbed, pierced with jeweled light, studded with thousands of figures of the stone-carvers' art, represents in size, splendor and numbers one of the great, permanent artistic achievements of human hands.

What accounts for it? Not religious fervor alone. Although a cathedral was the diocesan seat of a bishop, the decision to build did not come from the Catholic Church alone, which by itself could not finance the operation, but from the whole community. Only the common will shared by nobles, merchants, guilds, artisans, and commissioners in general could command the resources and labor to sustain such an undertaking. Each group contributed donations, especially the magnates of commerce who felt relieved thereby from the guilt of money-making. Collections were made from the public in towns and countryside, and indulgences granted in return for gifts. Voluntary work programs involved all classes. "Who has ever seen or heard tell in times past," wrote an observer, "that powerful princes of the world, that men brought up in honors and wealth, that nobles—men and women—have bent their haughty necks to the harness of carts and like beasts of burden have dragged to the abode of Christ these wagons loaded with wines, grains, oil, stones, timber and all that is necessary for the construction of the church?"

The higher and lighter grew the buildings and slenderer the columns, the more new expedients and techniques had to be devised to hold them up. Buttresses flew like angels' wings against the exterior. It was a period of innovation and audacity. In a single century, from 1170 to 1260, 600 cathedrals and major churches were built in France alone. In England in that period, the cathedral of Salisbury with the tallest spire in the country was completed in thirty-eight years. The spire of Freiburg in Germany was constructed entirely of filigree in stone as if spun by some supernatural spider. In the Sainte

Chapelle in Paris the fifteen miraculous windows swallow the walls; they have become the whole.

Explanations of the extraordinary burst that produced the cathedrals are several. Art historians will tell you that it was the invention of the ribbed vault, permitting subdivision, independence of parts, replacement of solid walls by columns, multiplication of windows and all the extrapolations that followed. But this does not explain the energies that took hold of and developed the rib. Religious historians say these were the product of an age of faith that believed that with God's favor anything was possible. In fact, it was not a period of untroubled faith but of heresies and Inquisition. Rather, one can only say that conditions were right. Social order under monarchy and the towns was replacing the anarchy of the barons so that existence was no longer merely a struggle to stay alive but allowed a surplus of goods and energies and greater opportunity for mutual effort. Banking and commerce were producing capital, roads making possible wheeled transport, universities nourishing ideas and communications. It was one of history's high tides, an age of vigor, confidence and forces converging to quicken the blood.

Even when the general tide was low, a particular group of doers could emerge in exploits that still inspire awe. What of the founding of our own country? We take the Mayflower for granted, yet think of the boldness, the enterprise, the determined independence, the sheer grit it took to leave the known and set out across the sea for the unknown where no houses or food, no stores, no cleared land, no crops or livestock, none of the equipment or settlement of organized living awaited.

Equally bold was the enterprise of the French in the northern forests who throughout the 17th Century explored and opened the land from the St. Lawrence to the Mississippi, from the Great Lakes to the Gulf of Mexico. They came not for liberty like the Pilgrims, but for gain and dominion, and rarely in history have men willingly embraced such hardship, such daunting adventure and persisted with tenacity and endurance.

Happily, man has a capacity for pleasure too, and in contriving ways to entertain and amuse himself, has created brilliance and delight. Pageants, carnivals, festivals, fireworks, music, dancing and drama, parties and picnics, sports and games, the comic spirit and its gift of laughter, all the range of enjoyment from grand ceremonial to the quiet solitude of a day's fishing has helped to balance the world's infelicity. Homo ludens, man at play, is surely as significant a figure as man at war or at work. No matter what else is happening, the newspapers today give more space to the sports pages than to any other single activity. (I do not cite this as necessarily admirable, merely indicative.) In human activity the invention of the ball may be said to rank with the invention of the wheel. Imagine America without baseball, Europe without soccer, England without cricket, the Italians without bocci, China without ping pong and tennis for no one.

But mankind's most enduring achievement is art. At its best, it reveals the nobility that coexists in human nature along with flaws and evils, and the beauty and truth it can perceive. Whether in music or architecture, literature, painting or sculpture, art opens our eyes and ears and feelings to something beyond ourselves, something we cannot experience without the artist's vision and the genius of his craft. The placing of Greek temples like the Temple of Poseidon on the promontory at Sunion outlined against the piercing blue of the Aegean Sea, Poseidon's home; the majesty of Michaelangelo's sculptured figures in stone; Shakespeare's command of language and knowledge of the human soul; the intricate order of Bach, the enchantment of Mozart; the purity of Chinese monochrome pottery with the lovely names—celadon, oxblood, peach blossom, claire de lune; the exuberance of Tiepolo's ceiling where, without the picture frames to limit movement, a whole world in exquisitely beautiful colors lives and moves in the sky; the prose and poetry of all the writers from Homer to Cervantes to Jane Austen and John Keats to Dostoevsky and Chekov—who made all these things? We—our species—did.

If we have lost beauty and elegance in the modern world, we have gained much, through science and technology and democratic pressures in the material well-being of the masses. The change in the lives of, and society's attitude toward, the working class marks the great divide between the modern world and the old regime.

It is true, of course, that the underside of the scientific progress is prominent and dark. The weaponry of war in its ever-widening capacity to kill is an obvious negative, and who is prepared to state with confidence that the overall effect of the automobile, airplane, telephone, television, and computer has been on balance beneficient?

Pursuit of knowledge for its own sake has been a more certain good. There was a springtime in the 18th Century when, through knowledge and reason, everything seemed possible; when reason was expected to break through religious dogma like the sun breaking through fog, and man armed with knowledge and reason would be able to at last control his own fate and construct a good society. The theory that because it exists, this is the best of all possible worlds, spread outward from Leibniz; the word "optimism" was used for the first time in 1737.

What a burst of intellectual energies shook these decades! In the 20 years, 1735–55, Linnaeus named and classified all of known botany; Buffon systematized Natural History in 36 volumes; the American, John Bartram, scoured the wilderness for plants to send to correspondents in Europe; Voltaire, Montesquieu and Hume investigated the nature of man and the moral foundations of law and society; Benjamin Franklin demonstrated electricity from lightning; Dr. Johnson by himself compiled the first dictionary of the English language; Diderot and the Encyclopedists of France undertook to present all knowledge in enlightened terms; the secret of making porcelain having just previously been discovered in Europe through intensive experiments, its manufacture in a thousand forms flourished at Meissen and Dresden; clearing for the Place de la Concorde, to be the most majestic in Europe, was begun in Paris, and the fantastic cascades of Caserta constructed for the Bourbons of Naples; 150 newspapers and journals circulated in England; Henry Fielding wrote *Tom Jones*; Thomas Jefferson was born; Tiepolo painted his gorgeous masterpiece, the Four Continents, on the archducal ceilings at Wurzburg; Chardin, no less supreme, painted his gentle and affectionate domestic scenes; Hogarth, seeing a different creature in the species, exposed the underside in all its ribaldry and squalor. It was an age of enthusiasm: At the first London performance of Handel's Messiah in 1743, George II was so carried away by the Hallelujah Chorus that he rose to his feet, causing the whole audience to stand with him. A custom was thereby established, still sometimes followed by Messiah audiences.

If the twenty-year period is stretched by another ten, it includes the reverberatory voice of Rousseau's "Social Contract," Beccaria's groundbreaking study on "Crime and Punishment," Gibbon's beginning of the "Decline and Fall," and despite the Lisbon earthquake and Voltaire's "Candide," the admission of "optimism" into the Dictioinnaire de l'Académie Francaise.

Although the Enlightenment may have overestimated the power of reason to guide human conduct, it nevertheless opened to men and women a more humane view of their fellow passengers. Slowly the harshest habits gave way to reform—in treatment of the insane, reduction of death penalties, mitigation of the fierce laws against debtors and poachers, and in the passionately fought cause for abolition of slave trade. The humanitarian movement was not charity, which always carries an overtone of being done in the donor's interest, but a more disinterested benevolence—altruism, that is to say, motivated by conscience. Through recent unpleasant experiences, we have learned to expect ambition, greed or corruption to reveal itself behind every public act, but it is not invariably so. Human beings do possess better impulses, and occasionally act upon them, even in the 20th Century. Occupied Denmark, during World War II, outraged by Nazi orders for deportation of its Jewish fellow citizens, summoned the courage of defiance and transformed itself into a united underground railway to smuggle virtually all 8,000 Danish Jews out to Sweden. Far away and unconnected, a village in southern France, Le Chamben-sur-Lignon, devoted itself to rescuing Jews and other victims of the Nazis at the risk of the inhabitants' own lives and freedom. "Saving lives became a hobby of the people of Le Chamben," said one of them. The larger record of the time was admittedly collaboration, passive or active. We cannot reckon on the better impulses predominating in the world; only that they will always appear.

The strongest of these in history, summoner of the best in men, has been zeal for liberty. Time after time, in some spot somewhere on the globe, people have risen in what Swinburne called the "divine right of insurrection"—to overthrow despots, repel alien conquerors, achieve independence—and so it will be until the day power ceases to corrupt, which, I think, is not a near expectation.

The phenomenon continues today in various forms, by Algerians, Irish, Vietnamese, peoples of Africa and the Middle East. Seen at close quarters and more often than not manipulated by outsiders, contemporary movements seem less pure and heroic than those polished by history's gloss, for instance the Scots of the Middle Ages against the English, the Swiss against the Hapsburgs, Joan of Arc arousing a dispirited people against the occupier, the Albanian Scanderbeg against the Turks, the American colonies against the mother country.

So far I have considered qualities of the group rather than of the individual, except for art which is always a product of the single spirit. Happiness too is a matter of individual capacity. It springs up here or there, haphazard, random, without origin or explanation. It resists study, laughs at sociology, flourishes, vanishes, reappears somewhere else. Take Izaak Walton, author of *The Compleat Angler*, that guide to commitment as well as fishing of which Charles Lamb said, "It would sweeten any man's temper at any time to read it." Although Walton lived in distracted times of revolution and regicide, though he adhered to the losing side in the Civil War, though he lost in their infancy all seven children by his first wife and the eldest son of his second marriage, though he was twice a widower, his misfortunes could not sour an essentially buoyant nature. "He passes through turmoil," in the words of a biographer, "ever accompanied by content."

Walton's secret was friendship. Born to a yeoman family and apprenticed in youth as an ironmonger, he managed to gain an education and through sweetness of disposition and a cheerful religious faith, became a friend on equal terms of various learned clergymen and poets whose lives he wrote and works he prefaced. John Donne, vicar of the parish in Chancery Lane where Walton worked, was his mentor and his friend. Others were Archbishop Sheldon of Canterbury, George Morley, Bishop of Winchester, Richard Hooker, Sir Henry Wotton, George Herbert, Michael Drayton and the Royalist, Charles Cotton.

The Compleat Angler, published when the author was 60, glows in the sunshine of his character. In it are humor and piety, grave advice on the idiosyncracies of fish and the niceties of landing them, delight in nature and in music. Walton saw five editions reprinted in his lifetime while innumerable later editions secured him immortality. The surviving son by his second wife became a clergyman; the surviving daughter married one and gave her father a home among grandchildren. He wrote his last work, a life of his friend Robert Sanderson, at eighty-five and died at ninety after being celebrated in verse by one of his circle as a "happy old man" whose life "showed how to compass true felicity." Let us think of him when we grumble.

Is anything to be learned from my survey? I raise the question only because most people want history to teach them lessons, which I believe it can do, although I am less sure we can use them when needed. I gathered these examples not to teach but merely to remind people in a despondent era that the good in mankind operates even if the bad secures more attention. I am aware that selecting out the better moments does not result in a realistic picture. Turn them over and there is likely to be darker side, as when Project Apollo, our journey to the moon, was authorized because its glamor could obtain subsidies for rocket and missile development that otherwise might not have been forthcoming. That is the way things are.

It is a paradox of our time that never have so many people been so relatively well off and never has society been more troubled. Yet I suspect that humanity's virtues have not vanished, although the experiences of our century seem to suggest they are in abeyance. A century that took shape in the disillusion that followed the enormous effort and hopes of World War I, that saw revolution in Russia congeal into the same tyranny it overthrew, saw a supposedly civilized nation revert under the Nazis into organized and unparalleled savagery, saw the craven appeasement by the democracies, is understandably suspicious of human nature. A literary historian, Van Wyck Brooks, discussing the 1920s and '30s, spoke of "an eschatological despair of the world." Whereas Whitman and Emerson, he wrote, "had been impressed by the worth and good sense of the people, writers of the new time" were struck by their lusts, cupidity and violence, and had come to dislike their fellow men. The same theme reappeared a few months ago when a drama critic, Walter Kerr, described a mother in a play who had a problem with two "pitilessly contemptuous" children. The problem was that "she wants them to be happy and they don't want to be." They prefer to freak out or watch horrors on television. In essence, this is our epoch. It keeps turning to look on Sodom and Gomorrah; it has no view of the Delectable Mountains.

Barbara Tuchman, from *Reading, Writing*.
Reprinted by permission of Russell & Volkening Inc.
as agents for author.
Copyright 1980 by Barbara W. Tuchman

ESSAY ASSIGNMENT

The author, Barbara Tuchman, has a great deal of praise for the people of past centuries and past generations, but seems to feel that, in our era, misery seems to have taken over our creative spirits. Do you agree with this pessimistic assessment? If you do, explain to what you ascribe our lack of creative drive. If you disagree, explain the creative spirit *you* have noticed in this century, and detail the accomplishments of 20th Century man.   (90 minutes)

8 Special Notes and Tips for ESL Students

PRELIMINARY ADVICE AND STRATEGIES FOR INTERNATIONAL AND ESL STUDENTS

If you are an International Student or a student for whom English is a second language, you can get a head start on ensuring a good performance on the GWAR. Around professorial circles it is well known that international students watch TV stations that broadcast in their native language and that carry programs from their home countries. It is also well known that many such students live with family members or associate with members of their international community or study together with fellow students from their home countries, often speaking entirely in their native tongues. While these habits serve to keep the spirit of home and language alive, they end up being counterproductive to a good performance on both the essay and objective portions of the GWAR. Follow the procedures below, and begin applying them as soon as possible in order to achieve a high score.

1. Saturate yourself with English. Saturation in a foreign language provides the fastest way to acquire mastery of that language. What this means is speaking and listening to only English, forcing yourself to watch TV programs in English only, asking your friends and family to speak only English as a favor to you until you pass the test, listening to English-speaking radio shows.
2. Read magazines and newspapers at least two or three hours a day preceding the test. Studying your required course work in English does not help you acquire English, because your course work involves terms, definitions, and formulas with which you are familiar. Therefore you skip clauses connecting facts and details. Also, you are studying these materials for tests in important classes, and it doesn't help your concentration to pay attention to the English. So you need to take the time to read entertainment or news magazines and newspapers.
3. Consult your local sample test materials for the GWAR early, so that you know the kinds of items to expect on the objective portion, learn about the patterns of questions, and review sample student responses approved for passing at your university.
4. Find a role model student who speaks your native language who has passed the GWAR already, and ask for that student's advice.
5. Consult your local ESL teacher who is familiar with your university's GWAR as well as familiar with your error areas. This teacher can help you design a program of preparation.

HOLISTIC SCORING AND ESL STUDENTS

ESL students worry unnecessarily about competing against native speakers of English. It's true that unless you are well trained, you don't have a confident familiarity with idioms, particle words like prepositions and articles, and the verb tenses. Yet you have a strength working for you that you take for granted. You are a mature student with world experience. You have passed rigorous tests and screening processes to study in this country. This added maturity and experience and ability compensates for your possible lack of confidence in certain areas of English.

Special Notes and Tips for ESL Students

In other words, holistic scorers look forward to your essays, hoping you will perform well, and expecting you to use unique and mature examples. Since the holistic scorers, on average, are saturated with matters of local and regional culture, examples drawn from other cultures become quite fascinating, offering as they do a welcome contrast.

Some international students wrongly wish to disguise the fact that they are foreigners, by trying to simulate American idiom and experience. It is a better strategy to rely confidently on your background, providing exotic examples the readers can enjoy. Freely refer to examples from your experiences growing up, from your culture, from your background, and from your travels.

A QUICK OVERVIEW OF SUBORDINATION AND COORDINATION

Two ways exist for building simple sentences (independent subject-verb combinations) into more sophisticated ones.

First, you can link sentences together (called coordination), using the simple conjunctions (for, and, nor, but, or, yet, so). It is important to remember that 90 percent of the time using the simple conjunctions, the subject of the first independent clause will be the same as the subject of the second linked independent clause: *The fire department officers participated in the parade, and they brought their 1930 GM fire truck.* (The comma goes where the period would have gone if there had been no second clause!) You can also link sentences with causal relationships using the causal conjunctions (because, even though, although, since, though). In this case you can keep the same subject or switch subjects: *She lost her license, because she drove drunk.* Compare: *She lost control of the car, because the brakes failed.*

Second, you can compress information into a sentence by a process called subordination. Many ideas about one subject can be listed in the building blocks of English called simple sentences:

Farmer Ralph Brown lives in Arkansas. Farmer Brown grows wheat. Farmer Brown owns a classic 1963 blue Corvette. The Corvette has a stick shift. The Corvette has dual exhaust. Farmer Brown lives in a conservative voting district. Farmer Brown is fifty years old. Farmer Brown is a Democrat.

It would sound immature to link these ideas with coordination. But you can use subordination to bring all of the ideas smoothly together:

> *The fifty-year-old Arkansas wheat farmer, Ralph Brown, who owns a classic blue 1963 Corvette with dual exhaust, is a Democrat living in the heart of the conservative voting district.*

You can also use many subordinating connective words available in English to manage the spacing of ideas, and the discussion below expands on the use of those words.

Section A examines the meaning and usage of linking words. Section B reviews the usage of the article in English. Section C gives you a quick review of the verb tenses. Last of all, in section D a series of exercises will teach you to correct (or edit) your paper while reviewing those aspects of English that tend to give students problems. Let's begin!

A. LINKING WORDS

If ESL writers understand the meanings and usage of linking words, the tone of their papers will greatly improve. You probably have a fairly good command of such common linking words as *and, but,* and *or*, but in this section you will improve your knowledge of a wide range of linking words and learn to use them correctly. Thus, you will have a greater selection to choose from when you are writing. Also, your writing will be more cohesive. That is to say that your essay will be more unified and fluent.

First, we will examine the function and meaning of coordinating conjunctions and then analyze subordinating conjunctions. Last of all, we will discuss the meaning and usage of a special group of linking words called conjunctive adverbs.

A.1 Coordinating Conjunctions: *and, but, yet, or, nor, (neither...nor) for, so*

EXAMPLE 1:   <u>She graduated</u>, and <u>her parents are happy</u>.
     (Clause A)   (Clause B)

Can Clause A, *She graduated*, stand alone as a complete sentence?
Can Clause B, *Her parents are happy*, stand alone?

The answer to both questions is of course, yes. In fact, both clauses are independent and the word *and*, which unites these two clauses, is a *coordinating conjunction*. For a complete review of this subject refer to pp. 171–174.

Our task is to examine the meanings of the seven coordinating conjunctions by defining the relationships that may exist between clauses. Thus, you will be able to use these linking words properly.

→ **And:** This is by far the most commonly used coordinating conjunction probably because it has the possibility of representing a number of relationships. Consider the uses that follow.

EXAMPLE 2:   <u>He decided to buy the cake</u>, and <u>he included some ice cream</u>.
                 (Clause A)   (Clause B)

In the preceding sentence *and* is adding the information of Clause A to the information of Clause B. This linkage is known as an *additive* relationship.

EXAMPLE 3:   He removed the cake from its box, and he served it to his guests.

In Example 3 *and* represents that the actions happened at the same time. This is a relationship of time which is called a *temporal* relationship (temp = time).

EXAMPLE 4:   He ate the cake, and no more remains.

Last of all, the word *and* in Example 4 represents the cause and effect relationship that exists between the two clauses. This kind of pairing is known as a *causal* relationship. Notice the root word *cause* in *causal*.

Keep in mind the three basic relationships: *additive* (add), *temporal* (time), and *causal* (cause). These definitions will serve later on to define the sometimes obscure meanings of other linking words.

→ **But:** This conjunction also has the possibility of representing several meanings. Consider the following sentences.

EXAMPLE 5:   His book was interesting, *but* it was too long.

In Example 5, a simple contrast is being noted about his book.

EXAMPLE 6:   She played the piano beautifully, *but* she could not read sheet music.

Normally, we expect that if someone is able to play the piano well, he or she will be able to read sheet music. Given the information in the first clause, the information in the second clause is not expected.

EXAMPLE 7:   The clouds grew thick overhead, *but* they did not yield rain.

EXAMPLE 8:   He suffers from heart problems, *but* he jogs as if he were twenty years old.

Examples 5, 6, 7, and 8 show us how *but* can represent either a contrast or a contradiction (an *adversative* relationship).

→ **Yet:** You are probably familiar with this word as an adverb as found in the following sentences:

    He has not arrived yet. (—until now)
    Do not turn off the radio yet. (—at the present time)

However, this word can also function as a conjunction, and it has the same meaning as *but* has in Example 6. In fact, these two conjunctions are interchangeable when used to introduce information that is not expected.

EXAMPLE 9:   She studied all week, $\begin{cases} \text{but} \\ \text{yet} \end{cases}$ she did not pass the exam.

EXAMPLE 10: He did well in law school, {yet / , but} he has failed his state bar exams.

EXAMPLE 11: She worked overtime every day, {yet / , but} she still did not have enough money.

Or: This conjunction establishes a choice between two possibilities.

EXAMPLE 12: She can pursue her degree, or she can attempt to get some experience in her field.

→ **Nor:** This conjunction is not a negative form of *or*. In fact its meaning is the same as *and + not*. Many ESL writers have trouble with this conjunction because the word order in the second clause is irregular.

EXAMPLE 13: He is not a doctor. (and) He *is* (not) a lawyer.

He is not a doctor, nor *is he* a lawyer.

EXAMPLE 14: She does not understand democracy. *She does* not value freedom.

She does not understand democracy, nor *does she* value freedom.

Once you use *nor*, you no longer need the word *not*. Also, after the word *nor* there is the word order of a question.

nor <u>does</u>   <u>she</u>   <u>value</u> her freedom.
    (auxiliary)   (subject)   (verb)

→ **Neither...nor:** If *neither* (which means not one, and not the other) is used with *nor*, the verb in the first clause is not negative.

EXAMPLE 15: She does *not* understand democracy. She does *not* value her freedom. →

EXAMPLE 16: *Neither* does she understand democracy, nor *does she* value her freedom.

Note: Most writers would prefer the form: She *neither* understands democracy, *nor* values her freedom.

MINI PRACTICE EXERCISE

Combine the following sentences by using the word *nor*. Make sure to make all other necessary changes.

1. She didn't eat her meat. She didn't touch her vegetables.
2. He did not settle the trade problem. He did not impress the American people.
3. Use neither...nor to combine the next two sentences. She did not give him moral support. She did not give him financial support.

ANSWERS

1. She didn't eat her meat, nor did she touch her vegetables.
2. He did not settle the trade problem, nor did he impress the American people.
3. Neither did she give him moral support, nor did she give him financial support.
   or:
   She gave him neither moral nor financial support.

→ **For:** You are familiar with *for* used as a preposition. However, since this conjunction is not commonly used in spoken English, you may not be aware that this word may be used as a coordinating conjunction. In fact, it follows a statement and gives a reason much in the same way that the word *because* does. ***Because*** subordinates some clauses, whereas *for* **coordinates them.**

EXAMPLE 17: The production of grain was low in 1997, *for* there was a drought.

82 CSU — Writing Proficiency Exam

EXAMPLE 18: The production of grain was low in 1997 *because* of a drought.

NOTE: Whether you put a comma before *because* depends on how long the accompanying clause is. If the clause is short or lacks a combined subject-verb structure, no comma is necessary. If the clause is long and contains a complete subject-verb structure, then the comma before the *because* signals the presence of the subject-verb.

→ **So:** When this word is used as a conjunction, it introduces the *result* of the first clause.

EXAMPLE 19: The anesthesia wore off, *so the doctor had to administer a second dose.* (The phrase in italics is the result.)

EXAMPLE 20: They argued all day long, *so they decided to look for new roommates.*

PRACTICE EXERCISE

Combine the following sentences by means of one of the seven coordinating conjunctions: *and, but, yet, or, nor, for,* or *so*. Do not forget that these conjunctions are preceded by a comma and followed by a word that begins with a lowercase letter. At times, two different conjunctions may be acceptable.

1. The concept of the "discovery of the New World" is absurd to Native Americans. Their ancestors had inhabited the New World many centuries before the Europeans landed on the Eastern seaboard.

2. Many refer to the discovery of the New World as an Age of Discovery. This period should be more appropriately called an Age of Destruction, given the impact that the Europeans had on Native Americans.

3. The Europeans did not value the cultures that they found in the New World. They did not respect the ancient rites of the natives.

4. The Europeans felt that the natives were heathens. They felt an obligation to convert the Indians to Christianity.

5. The Indians could be submissive to the newcomers. They could attempt to fight for the preservation of their rights.

ANSWERS AND EXPLANATIONS

1. Clause 1 is a statement. Clause 2 is the explanation that supports what is stated in clause 1. Use "*for*" to connect the two clauses.
   — The concept of the "discovery of the New World" is absurd to Native Americans, for their ancestors had inhabited the New World for many centuries before the Europeans landed on the Eastern seaboard.

2. The information in the second clause is in contradiction to the information in the first clause. This is an adversative relationship. Either *but* or *yet* could have been used to join these two clauses.
   — Many refer to the discovery of the New World as an Age of Discovery, { *but* this period... / , *yet* this period... }

3. Either *and* (if we wish to make this an additive relationship) or *nor* (if we wish to stress that both clauses are negative) may be used.
   —The Europeans did not value the cultures that they found in the New World, and they did not respect the ancient rites of the natives.
   —The Europeans did not value the cultures that they found in the New World, nor did they respect the ancient rites of the natives. NOTE: The negative drops from the second clause, and question word order is used for the second clause.

4. *And* may be used if you want to establish a simple additive relationship.
   —The Europeans felt that the natives were heathens, and they felt an obligation to convert them to Christianity.

   So may be used to state the second clause is the result of the first.
   —The Europeans felt that the natives were heathens, so they felt an obligation to convert them to Christianity.

5. *Or* should be used to emphasize the fact that the Indians had two choices.
   —The Indians could be submissive to the newcomers, or they could attempt to fight for the preservation of their rights.

ANOTHER PRACTICE EXERCISE

Use a coordinating conjunction (*and, but, yet, or, nor, for, so*) to unite the following pairs of sentences.

1. Exotic cuisine is good.
   On a cold wintry night, a dish of hot soup is always satisfying.
   _____
   _____

2. That restaurant is famous for its split pea soup.
   People drive hundreds of miles to try it.
   _____
   _____

3. I did not appreciate the red decor.
   I did not find the food particularly tasty.
   _____
   _____

4. I could not try their famous soup recipe.
   They had stopped making it the month before.
   _____
   _____

5. We could not get what we wanted.
   We decided to go home.
   _____
   _____

ANSWERS

1. [..., but...] or [..., yet...]
2. [..., and...] or [..., so...]
3. I did not appreciate the red decor, *nor did I* find the food to be particularly tasty. (*Do not forget to put auxiliary + subject.*)
   or:
   Neither did I appreciate the red decor, *nor* did I find the food to be particularly tasty.
   or:
   I neither appreciated the red decor *nor* found the food to be particularly tasty.
4. [..., for...] (*since* might work well here)
5. [..., so...]

A.2 Subordinating Conjunctions

Consider the following clause: *because the employees did not complete the census*. This clause cannot stand by itself as an independent sentence. The word *because* at the beginning of the clause tells us that it depends on other information that can either come before or after. This dependence gives the clause its name: a <u>dependent</u> clause. (To understand the word *clause*, if you omit the *because* from the clause, then your remainder reads as follows: *the employees did not complete the census*. Any such series of words within a sentence that has **both** a subject and a predicate, and that could thus conceivably be a complete sentence, is called a <u>clause</u>. Any series of words functioning as a unit without both a subject and predicate is called a <u>phrase</u>: *The governing body, of the lake, attracted three party-goers* are all examples of phrases.)

Dependent clauses, when incorporated into writing, become <u>subordinated</u> to a main clause governing a larger sentence. This word, "subordination," suggests that dependent clauses take a supposedly lower-level position relative to the main or governing clause.

Students get potentially confused about dependent and independent clauses, because it is not always easy to tell which information in the sentence is considered "lower-level"—as contrasted with the upper-level or main clause. Truly, some information in a dependent clause may be of higher importance than that in the main clause of a sentence: *The employees had to work extra hours because they did not complete the census*. The main clause, *the employees had to work extra hours*, is the basic sentence. But it is arguably less important than the dependent or subordinated clause that follows it: *because they did not complete the census*. From a writer's point of view, it is certainly sad that the employees had to work extra hours, but failing to complete the census sounds more important in the long run.

Not surprisingly, you can also reverse the order of the sentence and start with the dependent clause: *Because they did not complete the census, the employees had to work extra hours*. But the subordinating conjunction, *because*, called by some experts a causal <u>linking</u> conjunction, determines which of the clauses gets labeled "dependent," despite the question of importance. This discussion aims at improving your writing efforts by clarifying the terms and by emphasizing the value of subordination, both for showing causal relationships and for indicating levels of importance of information within a sentence. The holistic scorers evaluating your essays are expecting you to have familiarity with mastering the skill of selecting main clauses and subject words carefully, and then subordinating less important—though essential—information along with those clauses.

Now, it might help to take a last look at the sentence example above in both of its forms and ask, "Why does no comma appear before *because* in the first version of the sentence, while one appears after *the census* in the second version?" According to the expert rule, when the dependent clause comes first, ("Because . . ."), you follow the clause with a comma; and when the independent main clause comes first, ("The employees . . .") no comma is necessary. For the GWAR you will be taking, few holistic scorers will "mark you down" for putting the comma in the sentence under both conditions, as many of them know it frequently makes good sense to do so. Even experts would include a comma in the following example:

> *A formally trained architect's progress through the hierarchies of the design industry occurs much faster than that of an apprentice, because an architect with a university education has a much more focused background of authoritative experience to consult.*

The length of the sentence suggests the courtesy of a comma before *because* to signal a clause following the connective. Frankly, it's logical to use a comma before the causal conjunctions *because, even though, although, since,* and *though* when they are both preceded and followed by complete subject-verb clauses, unless the resulting full sentence fits on one line or less.

You may notice at times that *because* and *since* can lead to <u>phrases</u> instead of clauses: *He was ejected from the party because of his bad manners*. You would never use a comma here. Writers and readers (and holistic scorers) are well aware of the possibility of such constructions, which leads us to note a second value for using the comma in cases where you have a subject-verb structure on each side of the connective word. In other words, the comma signals the oncoming clause; lack of a comma suggests an oncoming phrase.

Some ESL writers make the mistake of leaving out the subject word following the connective, since perhaps in their languages they do not need to continue to state the subject once it has been introduced. In English you must keep subjects evident.

EXAMPLE 1:   INCORRECT: She left, because was tired.
             CORRECT: She left because she was tired.

Adding the full subject after *because* is necessary so as not to set the reader up unintentionally to expect an idiomatic construction like this:

             CORRECT: She left because of exhaustion.

Sometimes in English writers and speakers use a prepositional phrase with "of" following "because" as a brief way of explaining cause and effect. You will notice that in English we don't allow predicates to "float" or exist without subjects. In other words, a predicate would never exist as a phrase by itself; it will always be part of a clause, that is, a complete subject-verb structure.

In short, subordinating conjunctions represent specific relationships of time (*temporal*), cause and effect (*causal*), or contrast/contradiction (*adversative*). Let's begin our discussion with an examination of subordinating conjunctions that represent time relationships.

Time (Temporal) Subordinating Conjunctions (Connectives). The most common temporal conjunctions are the following: *after, since, before, by the time, when, whenever, while, as, as long as, now that, until, once,* and *as soon as*. These are also called conjunctive adverbs.

All of these linking words establish *when* the action of the two clauses took place in relationship to one another. The meaning of many of these linking words should be very clear to advanced ESL writers. Let's concentrate on those linking words that might not be known to you. Also, we will look at some of the verb tenses normally used with these words. (For a review of tenses and their usage, see Section C, pages 101–107.)

Since:

EXAMPLE 2:   *Since* he left, he *has telephoned* three times.

→ Do not forget to use the present perfect (or the present perfect progressive) for the verb in the independent clause. Refer to Section C for a review of the tenses. Remember *since* may also be used to give a cause (see Example 15).

MINI PRACTICE EXERCISE

The following sentences consist of two clauses joined by *since*. Fill in the blanks with the present perfect form of the verbs given in parentheses.

1. Since the last great war finished, there _____ (*to be*) several small wars.
2. The temperature _____ (*to increase*) since the winds stopped blowing.
3. Since she _____ (*to move*) to Los Angeles, she cannot find decent employment.

ANSWERS

1. *have been*
2. *has increased*
3. *has moved*

By the time:

EXAMPLE 3:   *By the time* they returned home, the fire *had already destroyed* the building.

This expression implies that the action in the first clause took a long time. Also, when referring to the past, the simple past is used with the first clause (*returned*) and the past perfect is used in the second clause (*had destroyed*). Both actions took place in the past, but emphasis is given to the fact that one action was completed before the other action took place. (See the time line on page 106.)

> **MINI PRACTICE EXERCISE**
>
> The following sentences consist of two clauses joined by *by the time*. Fill in the blanks with either the simple past or past perfect forms of the verbs given in parentheses.
>
> 1. By the time he _____ (*to arrive*), the meeting _____ (*to finish*).
> 2. By the time Columbus _____ (*to leave*), he _____ (*to collect*) a vast number of plant species.
> 3. She _____ (*to develop*) stomach problems by the time she _____ (*to reach*) high school.
>
> **ANSWERS**
>
> 1. arrived, had finished
> 2. left, had collected
> 3. had developed, reached

This expression may also be used to speak about the future and the present habitual.

EXAMPLE 4:   By the time he <u>gets</u> here, we <u>will have finished</u> the project.
             (simple present   (future perfect)
             for
             the near future)

When/Whenever: These two linking adverbs differ slightly in meaning.

EXAMPLE 5:   *When* he finished his work, he left. (At that precise moment in the past)

EXAMPLE 6:   *Whenever* you finish your work, you may leave. (At any time)
             Whenever I see that painting, I think of my grandmother. (It stresses *every* time.)

> **MINI PRACTICE EXERCISE**
>
> Choose either *when* or *whenever* to fill the blanks in the following sentences.
>
> 1. _____ he comes home from work, he reads the newspaper.
> 2. _____ they go to New York, they visit Central Park.
> 3. She gets a horrid skin rash _____ she eats berries.
>
> **ANSWERS AND EXPLANATIONS**
>
> 1. when (at that moment. If you use *whenever*, it sounds as if he does not come home from work very often.)
> 2. when or whenever (*Whenever* stresses *every* time.)
> 3. when or whenever (*Whenever*, however, stresses the fact that it happens every time.)

While/As/As long as/So long as:
All of these conjunctions/connectives denote that the action of the two clauses happened at the same time.

EXAMPLE 7:   *While* he went to law school, he worked at the docks.
             While implies an action that lasted a long period of time (durative).

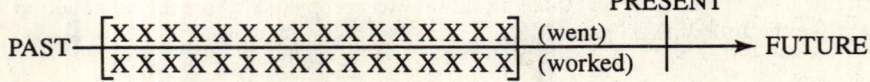

EXAMPLE 8:   *As* the graduates stood up, the crowd cheered.
             As implies at the same time.

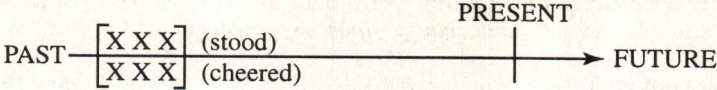

EXAMPLE 9: *As/so long as* he was attending college, he worked an extra twenty hours a week.
    This conjunction is a lot like *while*. It emphasizes that he worked an extra twenty hours *only* while he attended college.

EXAMPLE 10: *So long as* we were coworkers, she never invited me to her home. (This statement implies that we are no longer coworkers.)

For all four of these conjunctions/connectives, the two actions may also take place in the present or future.

   Present: While I *clean* the house, she *shops*.
   Future: While I *am* in France, she *will be* in Italy. (The simple present *am* may refer to the future.)

Until:
As a conjunctive adverb, this word means the period of time before something happened.

EXAMPLE 11: *Until* laws were established, countries did not hesitate to throw chemical waste into the Mediterranean Sea.
    Until laws are established, countries will not hesitate to throw chemical waste into the Mediterranean Sea.

Once:
This linking word refers to the period of time after which something happens.

EXAMPLE 12: *Once* laws were established, countries could no longer legally throw chemical waste into the Mediterranean Sea.
    Once laws are established, countries will no longer legally throw chemical waste into the Mediterranean Sea.

As soon as:
This conjunctive adverb or connective provides a way to say that two actions began at the very same time.

EXAMPLE 13: *As soon as* the new pollution laws came into effect, five countries were fined for polluting the Mediterranean Sea.
    As soon as the new pollution laws come into effect, five countries will be fined for polluting the Mediterranean Sea.

MINI PRACTICE EXERCISE

Choose among *since, by the time, when, whenever, while, as, as/so long as, until, once, as soon as* to fill the blanks in the following sentences.

1. _____ I heard the news, I ran to her house.
2. _____ she finished her degree, she applied for medical school.
3. _____ they got to Los Angeles, the sun had already risen.
4. _____ he hears her name, he begins to cry.
5. Her accomplice waited at the door _____ she robbed the bank.
6. _____ they learn to save money, they will never be able to afford a house.
7. _____ her parents are willing to support her financially, she will never make a serious effort to find employment.

ANSWERS

1. *when* or *as soon as*
2. *when, once, as soon as*
3. *by the time*
4. *when* or (even better) *whenever* (stresses every time)
5. *while, as*
6. *until*
7. *as/so long as*

Cause/Effect (Causal) Subordinating Conjunctions: Some of the most frequently used conjunctions in this category are *because, since, as, inasmuch as, so (that), in order that*.

Because:
This linking word introduces a direct reason.

EXAMPLE 14:   She left school *because* she no longer had money for tuition.

Since/As/Inasmuch as:
Circumstances that led to an event or action are expressed with these conjunctions.

EXAMPLE 15:   They sold their house *since* they had run out of money.

EXAMPLE 16:   They sold their house *as* they had run out of money.

EXAMPLE 17:   They sold their house *inasmuch as* they had run out of money.

NOTE: *Since* and *as* may also represent time relationships as well.

So (that)/In order that:
These words introduce the desired result. In the independent clause, what was done to obtain the desired result is stated.

EXAMPLE 18:   <u>He took out a loan</u> <u>so that he could pay his tuition</u>.
                what was done   desired result

EXAMPLE 19:   He took out a loan *in order that* he could pay his tuition.

MINI PRACTICE EXERCISE

Choose among *because, since, as, inasmuch as, so...that,* or *in order that*, to fill the blanks in the following sentences.

1. _____ she is such a fantastic instructor, all of her courses are full.
2. The grapes had to be harvested immediately _____ a storm was coming in.
3. He had to take four units of American history _____ he might graduate.

ANSWERS
1. *since, as, inasmuch as* (*Because* is not commonly found at the beginning of a sentence.)
2. *because, since, as, inasmuch as*
3. *so that, in order that*

Contrast/Contradiction (Adversative) Subordinating Conjunctions: The most common contrast/contradiction conjunctions are *although, even though, though,* and *whereas*.

Although/Even though/Though:
These three conjunctions have the same meaning and are interchangeable. They introduce a truth which is then denied or contradicted in the independent clause.

EXAMPLE 20:   <u>Although he studied diligently</u>, <u>he did not pass the exam</u>.
                (Truth)   (In contradiction with
                                     the first clause.)

→ Notice that the same relationship is represented by the coordinating conjunction *but*; however, *but* introduces the clause in which the contradiction is given.

EXAMPLE 21:   <u>He studied diligently</u>, *but* <u>he did not pass the exam</u>.
              (Truth)   (Contradiction)

EXAMPLE 22:   *Even though* she carefully took the medicine for ten days, she still had the ear infection.

EXAMPLE 23:   She carefully took the medicine for ten days, *but* she still had the ear infection.

Whereas:
This word means *while on the contrary*.

EXAMPLE 24:   One parent arrived on time *whereas* the others were tardy.

EXAMPLE 25:   Public universities are affordable *whereas* private universities are not.

MINI PRACTICE EXERCISE

Choose either *although*, *even though*, *though*, or *whereas* to fill the blanks in the following sentences.

1. My husband votes republican _____ I vote democratic.
2. _____ they had lived next door to each other for twenty years, they had never spoken to one another.
3. _____ a university degree takes about four years to complete, a community college degree takes about two years.

ANSWERS

1. *whereas*
2. *even though, though, although*
3. *whereas* (while)

PRACTICE EXERCISE

Choose among the subordinating conjunctions given in parentheses those that would be the most appropriate in the following sentences. Answers and explanations follow after each question.

1. Tarquin was an Etruscan king who ruled Rome with a strong hand. _____ Roman nobles rebelled against King Tarquin, Romans had little freedom. (*until, since, by the time*)
2. _____ Tarquin was driven out of Rome, the Romans had already suffered for many years. (*when, while, until, by the time*)
3. _____ Etruscan royalty left Rome, Rome became a republic. (*by the time, when, before, after, whenever*)
4. Roman generals brought back great wealth to Rome _____ Rome fought other powerful states. (*since, whenever, when*)

→ NOTE: the conjunction is in the middle of the sentence and there is no comma before it.

5. First Julius Caesar defeated his rivals. Then he ruled Rome. _____ Julius Caesar defeated his rivals, Caesar ruled Rome as a dictator. (*so long as, once, as soon as*)
6. Other states feared Rome _____ Rome was ruled by Caesar. (*so long as, until, whenever*)
7. Roman soldiers are called legionaires _____ the Roman army was divided into legions. (*so, although, because*)
8. The emperors treated the soldiers with extreme care _____ there was always great danger of mutiny. (*because, so, since*)
9. The legionaires had specially designed sandals _____ they would be able to march for miles. (*because, even though, so, in order that*)
10. _____ legionaires were not allowed to be married, many soldiers had unofficial wives and offspring (children). (*since, even though, although*)
11. _____ Roman women slaves had few rights, wealthy Roman women enjoyed many privileges. (*whereas, even though*)

ANSWERS AND EXPLANATIONS

1. *Until*. This is a temporal relationship—with the meaning of "for the entire time before the Romans rebelled."
2. *By the time*. This is a temporal relationship with the meaning that "the Romans had suffered over the period of time before Tarquin was driven out." (Note how the past perfect is used in the second clause.)

3. *When* or *After*. This is a temporal relationship, and either conjunction makes sense although the meaning changes with the conjunction that is chosen.
   when—at the same time
   after—first the Etruscans left, then Rome became a republic.
4. *Whenever* or *When*. This is a temporal relationship. The best answer is *whenever*, because it emphasizes that great wealth was brought back to Rome *every time* Rome fought other states.
5. *Once* or *As soon as*. This is a temporal relationship. Both give the idea that the moment Caesar defeated his rivals, he began his rule as a dictator, which lasted thereafter.
6. *So long as*. This is a temporal relationship. This conjunction signifies that the actions of the two clauses took place over the same period of time.
7. *Because*. This is a causal relationship. The conjunction introduces a direct reason.
8. *Because* or *Since*. This is a causal relationship. Both conjunctions will do just fine.
9. *So* or *In order that*. This is a causal relationship. These conjunctions introduce the why behind the action in the first clause, that is, why legionaires had specially designed sandals.
10. *Even though* or *Although*. This is a causal relationship. These two conjunctions are interchangeable.
11. *Whereas*. This is an adversative relationship. *Whereas* is the best choice because it emphasizes the contrast which existed between the two groups of women.

Conjunctive Adverbs

ESL writers must be especially careful with the group of linking words called conjunctive adverbs, which link together paragraphs, clauses, or even parts of phrases. Again, as in our previous discussion, we will deal with these linking words from the viewpoint of meaning (semantics) since the meanings of these connectors may not be evident to a non-native speaker. For punctuation tips refer to pages 145–155. The following chart shows the function of these connecting words.

Function	Conjunctive Adverbs
To list or rank The asterisk marks items that are used as a group. For example, if you start a paragraph with *on one hand*, the next paragraph must begin with *on the other hand*.	*first, second, third... *first of all, second of all... *on one hand, on the other hand... to begin with next, then to conclude, finally, lastly last of all
To introduce similar thoughts or thoughts that follow the same logic	equally, likewise, correspondingly, similarly, by the same token
EXAMPLE: The dumping of toxic waste must be curbed. Likewise, the emission of deadly fumes must be strictly regulated.	
To reinforce or develop an idea	also, furthermore, moreover, in addition
EXAMPLE: The committee did not approve the amendments; furthermore, it mandated that all future amendments be sent to a subcommittee.	
To summarize or develop a conclusion	therefore, thus, (these two are interchangeable) to sum up, to summarize, to conclude, in conclusion (this group is usually used at the end of an essay)

Function	Conjunctive Adverbs
To illustrate a point by example of rewording	for instance, for example, that is, that is to say, in other words

> EXAMPLE: He has one semester to raise his grade point average. In other words, if he does not get better grades, he will not get into graduate school.

To introduce a result	consequently, therefore, thus, hence (formal), as a consequence, in consequence, as a result

> EXAMPLE: He did not raise his grades; therefore, he did not get into graduate school.

To show a contrast	on the contrary, in contrast, by contrast, in comparison, by comparison

> EXAMPLE: She owned her own house. In comparison, her sister did not own anything.

To introduce a statement that is unexpected in light of what was just said	however, nonetheless, nevertheless, in any event, in any case, at any rate

> EXAMPLE: The country has a substantial national debt; nevertheless, government officials are increasing defense contracts.

PRACTICE EXERCISE

Use a conjunctive adverb to fill in the blank spaces.

1. In most Western countries the deceased (dead) were either buried or cremated. _____ (A), in New Guinea the deceased were smoked, mummified, covered with clay, and placed on a scaffold (a high shelflike construction) out in the open. _____ (B), the remains of villagers were placed on exhibit for all to see.
2. The sting of Africanized or "killer" bees is no more dangerous than that of a European bee. _____ (A), Africanized bees are deadly because they tend to attack in mass. _____ (B) if you are attacked by this type of bee, your best defense is to seek shelter in a car or building. You will still get stung, but the number of stings will be reduced.
3. The giant figures which are etched in the deserts of the U.S. Southwest were created about A.D. 890. _____ (A), scientists believe that the figures are a representation of prehistoric Indian myths.
4. White-throated swifts (a type of bird) are threatened by the toxic chemical DDT; _____ (A), the peregrine falcon, which is found on the coasts of California, is also endangered by DDT.
5. _____ (A), consumers are attracted to the price and quality of foreign automobiles. _____ (B), these same consumers are intent upon buying American products to boost the American economy.
6. Student loans greatly benefit university students. _____ (A), the money obtained from these loans allows students to pursue their education. _____ (B), since students do not have to work full time to support themselves, they are able to finish their studies earlier and enter the work force. _____ (C), students with loans do not have to depend on parental financial support.

ANSWERS

1. A. on the contrary, in/by contrast, in
   B. in other words, that is, that is to say
2. A. However, Nonetheless, Nevertheless
   B. Accordingly, Consequently, Hence, Therefore, Thus, As a consequence, As a result

> 3. A. Also, Furthermore, Moreover, In addition
> 4. A. equally, likewise, correspondingly, similarly, by the same token
>   or:
>   also, furthermore, moreover, in addition
> 5. A. On one hand
>   B. On the other hand
> 6. A and B. First... ...Second, or First of all... ...Second of all
>   C. Finally, Lastly, Last of all

A Summary of Linking Words

It is now clear that coordinating conjunctions, subordinating conjunctions, and conjunctive adverbs all link parts of sentences, full sentences, or even paragraphs together. The writer chooses each one of these connectors in accordance with the relationships that he or she is establishing. They serve as transitions to move ideas and ensure unity.

→ **All three types of connectors are followed by clauses that must have a subject that is explicitly stated.**

The following chart summarizes the three types of connectives according to type (coordinating conjunction, subordinating conjunction or conjunctive adverb) and function. The choice is up to you!

Connective Function	Coordinating Conjunctions ___ , conjunction ___ .	Subordinating Conjunctions Ind. Clause Dep. Clause	Conjunctive Adverbs ___ . conj adv. ___ ___ ; conj adv. ___ .
Additive/Linking Simply add two clauses Reinforce	and neither-nor (negative addition)		Add by numerical sequence: First, second, third. On the one hand, on the other hand, to begin with, next, then, finally, last, also, furthermore, moreover, in addition
Contrast/opposition of idea	but, yet, or, nor	although, even though though (relative truths)/ however, nonetheless, nevertheless, in any event, in any case, at any rate, whereas	by contrast, in contrast, by comparison, in opposition to
Similarity/equality of idea			likewise, similarly, equally (as), just as
Causal connectives to cause or reason	for (reason) so (result)	because (a reason) since, as, inasmuch as (gives circumstances)	consequently, therefore, hence thus, as a consequence, as a result, in consequence
Temporal/time relationships		after, since (that time), before, by the time, when, whenever, while, as, as long as, now, now that, until, soon, as soon as, once	(same list as box to left)
Summarizing			therefore, in brief, to put it simply, thus, to conclude, in short, in conclusion
Exemplification			for instance, for example, as an example, as an illustration
Rewording			that is, that is to say, to put it simply, in other words

B. THE USAGE OF THE ARTICLE

Among the types of errors that can harm your essay-writing score during the holistic grading procedures, we did not list usage of the articles. Scorers know that article usage in English is extremely complicated, in part due to the kinds of classes of nouns that require articles, and in part due to the idiomatic nature of many article applications. In other words, while you can develop the ability to determine which article goes where by following the listed rules below, in many other cases, you can only learn which articles accompany certain words by rote memorization of individual cases. As a result, holistic scorers do not penalize you too much for making occasional errors with article usage. However, they do expect you to understand the basic principles. The review below will help you strengthen your understanding of this type of article.

First of all, however, let us take a good look at how the article may be used with singular and plural, countable and noncountable nouns. You will want to refer to the following charts throughout our discussion.

Singular Countable Nouns

A or An **If emphasis is on "one"**
He bought *a car*. (meaning one nonspecific car)
They are planning *a vacation*. (one nonspecific vacation)

The **If the noun is specific**
The car he bought is expensive. (one specific car he bought)
The vacation lasted six weeks. (Here it is understood from an implicit previous discussion which specific vacation is being referred to.)

Plural Countable Nouns
Noncountable Nouns (mass, abstract, etc.)

No article **If the reference is general/nonspecific (implies "all")**
Books are very expensive. (books in general)
Honesty is the best policy. (implies all kinds of honesty)
Students should consider all options. (students in general)

The **If the noun is specific**
The books required for this course have not arrived yet. (implies some specific books)
The people of this country should all vote.
The generosity that she demonstrated will never be forgotten.

B.1 The Function of the Article *the*

NOTE: In this section we will speak about *the*. This article is used when you want to point out a specific person or thing. In many of the examples given in this section, it is possible to use *a*, but we will talk only about the article *the* and keep the discussion of *a* for the next section (B.2).

This article is used when the speaker (or writer) has in mind (and wants to point out) a very specific person (the man), group of people (the teachers), object (the table), group of objects (the tables), a feeling (the pain), and so on. In fact, this article is closely related to the adjectives *this, that, these,* and *those*. By contrast, if a subject is being spoken about in general, no definite article is used. Consider the sentences that follow:

EXAMPLE 1: Beer is produced in the state of Washington. (No article is used because we are talking about beer in general. *A* beer would make no sense, since no reason exists to discuss one nonspecific brand or type of beer.)

EXAMPLE 2: *The beer* produced in the state of Washington is known for its purity. (Here we use the article with *beer* because we are speaking specifically of the beer in Washington as opposed to beer produced in other states.)

In Example 2, *the beer in Washington* is being singled out and set apart from all other types of beer. In this case the word *beer* is specified by a prepositional phrase *in Washington*. There are many ways in which a noun may become specific. The next six sections will clarify this subject.

B.1.1 Specification that is directly given in a sentence.

A noun may be made specific by information contained in a sentence.

EXAMPLE 3:	The book *on the table* is mine.	*prepositional phrase*
EXAMPLE 4:	The book *that I told you about* is written by Bill Stanley.	*relative clause*
EXAMPLE 5:	The *red and green* book is mine.	*adjective(s)*

→ *NOTE:* Modification does *not* necessarily make a noun specific. Always keep in mind whether the noun is being spoken of in general, or if a specific object or person is being referred to. Compare the phrases that follow.

Spanish literature	(Without an article the writer is talking about Spanish literature in general.)
The literature of Spain	(The writer with this construction is specifying the literature of Spain as opposed to that of other countries.)
Women who smoke	(all women who smoke in general)
The women who smoke a pack a day	(a specific group as opposed to women in the same group who do not smoke a pack a day)

B.1.2 Specification that comes from an immediate situation.

It is possible that a noun is specific even though there is no modification of the noun in the sentence.

EXAMPLE 6:   *The dishes* are dirty.

In this example, the listener knows which exact dishes the speaker is referring to because they have just spoken about the dishes or possibly the speaker is pointing to the dishes. Removing the article *the* would imply all dishes are dirty all the time.

B.1.3 Specification that comes from shared knowledge.

Sometimes the person or object being referred to is specific to the writer or speaker, because all the members of the audience are familiar with that person or object.

EXAMPLE 7:   *The president* appeared at Camp David last week.

If both the speaker and the listener are inhabitants of the United States, both will understand that the president of the United States is being referred to. If the speaker were speaking of the president of another country, either the country or the name of the president would need mention.

EXAMPLE 8:   *The president* of Mexico was in Washington, D.C. last week.

B.1.4 Specification that is the result of the fact that only one such object or person exists in the world.

At times an object, person, or group is specific because it is unique and the only such object or person in the world, for example:

the sun	the earth	the moon
the Equator	the universe	the north
the south	the east	the west
the White House	the Vatican	the Acropolis
the Renaissance	the Roman gods	the Prince of Wales

NOTE: The word *earth* is often used without an article especially when we use expressions like *falling down, return to,* and the preposition *down:*

The meteorite *fell to earth.*
The proposal is very *down to earth.* (meaning logical)
What *on earth* are you doing? (informal expression)

Keeping this principle in mind, it is logical that the definite article be used with such expressions as the following:

- the first, the second
- the last, the first
- the same, the only
- the most, the least, the best, the most beautiful. (In English the superlative adjective must be preceded by the article *the*!)

B.1.5 Specification given by a preceding text (what you just wrote)

Very often the first time a general noun is mentioned in a text it carries a nonspecific or an indefinite article (a, an). The second time the noun is mentioned, it is given a definite article because the writer wishes to focus specifically on it and add detail for the reader.

EXAMPLE 9:   A young *man* and an elderly *woman* got on the tram at Fourth Street. *The man* was wearing a green coat, and *the lady* was wearing an old pink sweater, which looked as if it had served her for many years.

EXAMPLE 10:   Agostina bought *a* new *car* last summer. When she brought the car home, she found that *the brakes* were not working properly.

In the latter example, the word *brakes* takes the definite article *the* because from the previous text we know that these are the brakes of the specific car that Agostina bought.

→ *NOTE:* Once a topic is introduced, everything that refers to that topic becomes specific.

EXAMPLE 11:   At *an* American university *graduation, the students* and *the professors* usually wear caps on their heads and long black hooded gowns. *The colors* on *the hoods* represent academic rank, and the college attended by *the wearer.*

In Example 11, the subject is the description of a graduation. Once the subject is announced, all of the elements relating to that subject require a definite article: the student, the professors, the colors, the hoods, the wearer.

B.1.6 Specification of institutions and mass communication. Cultural institutions and aspects of mass communication and transportation are usually considered to be specific and require the article *the*, for example:

the cinema	the theater	the movies
the novel	the ballad	the drama
the opera	*the radio	the television (Here, *the* may be deleted.)
the paper(s)	the press	the news (Here, *the* may be deleted.)
*the bus	*the train	the mail

NOTE: The asterisks denote items for which the article is omitted if the word is preceded by the preposition *by.*

EXAMPLE 12:   They travel to school by *bus* every day.

EXAMPLE 13:   The news of the disaster was first communicated by *radio.* (or on the radio)

For cultural institutions such as the cinema, at times the article may refer to the building in which a movie is being shown. In any case the article *the* is still used.

EXAMPLE 14:   She went to *the cinema* on Broadway. (i.e., the specific building)

EXAMPLE 15:   She loves to go to *the cinema.* (In other words, she likes to see films in general.)

For other kinds of nouns the same principle holds true.

EXAMPLE 16:   The mail came in at six o'clock. (The actual letters)

EXAMPLE 17:   The mail should be privately owned. (The institution)

B.1.7 Specification of class nouns. These nouns are generally considered to be specific: *the poor, the lonely, the rich, the wealthy, the dead, the middle class, the abused, the sick,* and so forth.

EXAMPLE 18:   *The homeless* of this city need immediate assistance.

EXAMPLE 19:   *The hungry* need to be fed.

EXAMPLE 20:   *The illiterate* should be taught.

PRACTICE EXERCISE

Now that we have thoroughly examined what makes a noun specific, it is time to do a practice exercise.

In the following sentences, insert the article *the* where necessary. The answers will directly follow the exercise, so you will be able to correct yourself immediately.
NOTE: Ø means that no article is needed.

1. _____ potatoes that come from Idaho sell very well.
2. _____ Italian art is fascinating.
3. _____ people of America should vote.
4. _____ students who study at this university should keep careful _____ financial records.
5. _____ plants in this garden are all drought resistant.
6. _____ plants should be chosen according to their resistance to drought.
7. _____ Constitution provides for _____ liberty and _____ justice.
8. _____ constitutions establish the principles through which laws are made.
9. _____ An American wedding is full of _____ tradition. _____ bride usually wears a white gown, and _____ groom wears a tuxedo. _____ best man brings _____ wedding ring to _____ church, and _____ maid of honor helps _____ bride dress for _____ ceremony.
10. Last night they all went to _____ theater. They greatly enjoy _____ play. They also frequent both _____ opera and _____ cinema.
11. Some believe that _____ poor, _____ meek, and _____ humble shall be the first to enter _____ kingdom of God.
12. Without _____ air we cannot live.
13. Is _____ art an imitation of _____ life?
14. _____ literature of _____ nineteenth century tends toward _____ realism.
15. _____ agriculture is important to our society.
16. Many of _____ small farms of California have disappeared.
17. _____ humanity has always struggled for _____ survival.
18. _____ Japanese cars are very popular in the United States.
19. _____ practice makes perfect.
20. _____ modern art is very difficult to understand.

ANSWERS AND EXPLANATIONS

1. Two answers are possible:
    <u>The</u> potatoes = as compared to those grown in other states
    <u>Ø</u> potatoes = potatoes from Idaho in general
   The choice you make actually changes the meaning.
2. <u>Ø</u> Italian art = this type in general.
3. <u>The</u> people of America (Remember, if there is *of* after the noun you will most likely need *the*.)
4. <u>The</u> students or <u>Ø</u> students (see answer 1)
    <u>Ø</u> financial records (in general)
5. <u>The</u> plants (*in this garden* makes it specific)

> 6. Ø plants (in general)
>   Ø drought resistant (in general)
> 7. The Constitution (It is specific because we are speaking about the U.S. Constitution.)
>   Ø liberty, Ø justice (concepts in general)
> 8. Ø constitutions (in general)
> 9. Ø tradition (in general)
>   Every noun after *tradition* has the article *the*. Once the topic of *an American wedding* has been specified, every noun referring to that wedding is specific.
> 10. the theater, the play, the opera, the cinema (All are cultural institutions.)
> 11. the poor, the meek, the humble (class nouns)
>   the kingdom of God (Remember, *of* usually makes a noun specific.)
> 12. Ø air (in general)
> 13. Ø art, Ø life (in general)
> 14. The literature *of* the nineteenth century, Ø realism (in general)
> 15. Ø agriculture (in general)
> 16. the small farms (*of* makes it specific)
> 17. Ø humanity, Ø survival (in general)
> 18. Ø Japanese cars (in general)
> 19. Ø practice (in general)
> 20. Ø modern art (in general)

B.2 The Function of the Article *a/an*

***B.2.1* General reference to a countable singular noun that is *not* specific. Thus, the usage of this article is exactly the opposite of that of the definite article. Compare the two articles in the following sentences:**

EXAMPLE 21:   *A* child should be taught manners.

In Example 21 we are speaking about children in general. We are making a generalization.

EXAMPLE 22:   *The* child should be taught manners.

In the preceding sentence the speaker has a specific child in mind. Either he or she has just spoken about the child, or both the speaker and the listener have just seen the child.

***B.2.2* Reference of the indefinite article to the concept *one*. Very often this article is used with the meaning of *one*.**

EXAMPLE 23:   She walked *a mile* to school. (meaning one mile)

EXAMPLE 24:   He found *a dollar* in his pocket. (one dollar)

EXAMPLE 25:   The Wilsons have *a house* in Los Angeles and *a villa* in France.

***B.2.3* Reference of the indefinite article to refer to a general profession of a person with the verb *to be* uses an indefinite article before the profession. In many other languages this is not the case.**

EXAMPLE 26:   He is *an engineer.*

EXAMPLE 27:   She is *a medical doctor.*

> **PRACTICE EXERCISE**
>
> Fill in the blank spaces in the following sentences with *a, an,* or *the*.
>
> 1. Some people do not even drink _____ single glass of water a day.
> 2. _____ car that I have never seen before drove away.
> 3. _____ car that I bought last week is at the mechanic's for repairs.
> 4. John is _____ artist of great renown.
> 5. Peter is _____ man that changed my life.
> 6. She fixed _____ car last week that was worth as much as my house.
> 7. _____ gentleman approached him and asked him the way to London.
> 8. _____ gentleman was wearing a funny green plaid jacket.
> 9. I left _____ newspaper on the table. Have you seen it?
> 10. I would like _____ glass of water.
>
> **ANSWERS**
>
> 1. a single glass (*one*)
> 2. A car (*generic, one*)
> 3. The car (*specific*)
> 4. an artist (*profession*)
> 5. the man (*specific*)
> 6. a car (generic, *one*)
> 7. A gentleman (*generic, one*)
> 8. The gentleman (here, *he is specific*)
> 9. a newspaper (*one*), the newspaper
> 10. a glass (*one*)

B.3 General and Specific Reference *Without* Articles (Zero Article)

Of course we have seen how any noun that is neither specific nor carries the meaning of *one* will not have an article. Here are some other cases that do not require an article:

B.3.1 Reference to generalized locations, if preceded by *at, in, on, to*.

He went to town.   He went to jail.
    to church.   to bed.
    to college.   to hospital. (British)
    to school.   to class.
    to sea.   (Also: He went downtown.)

B.3.2 Reference to specific nouns of time after *at, by, after*, and *before*.

He came at *midnight*.
It happened *before dawn*.
Come home *by noon*.
Do not return *after dark*.

B.3.3 Reference to generalized meals, unless you are speaking of one particular meal.

Come to my house for *dinner*.   vs.   *The dinner* we ate was horrid.
Breakfast is served at 8:00.   vs.   *The breakfast*, which was served at 8:00, consisted of coffee and toast.

B.4 The Function of the Article Used When Referring to a Group. Consider the following:

A rose is a delicate flower. (Here, one rose represents the group of roses.)
Roses are delicate flowers. (Roses as an entire group.)
The rose is a delicate flower. (The rose as compared to other flowers.)

In all three preceding examples the noun represents the whole group. We are speaking about roses in general. Very often in essays, we speak about a subject in general. Is it possible to use any one of these three forms, whenever we want? The answer is no. Let us look carefully at each type.

B.4.1 Reference to a group with an article preceding a noun that is the subject of a sentence. In the following example and a subsequent one (both marked with an asterisk), *a rose* is NOT in the subject position, and it cannot represent the group.

*People are learning to appreciate *a rose*. (As an object, *a rose* will not represent the group, so this sentence is not grammatically correct.)

Notice the differences between the following sentences:
                  the novel.   (As a group.)
    John has studied novels.   (As a group.)
                  a novel.   (*One* novel not the group.)

Study the construction below in which you can use a noun—in this case, *a rose*—to represent the group:

    A rose *is a* symbol of love. (The article also *follows* the verb.)
        or:
    A... is a...

We cannot use "a rose" to represent the group of roses if we do not have the preceding construction as the following sentence shows:

    *A rose is popular. (There is no *a* after the verb.)

B.4.2 Reference to a class *without* an article using a plural or non-count noun.

Teachers have many duties. (Teachers as a group.)
Parents must monitor their children. (Parents as a group.)
Students should study hard. (Students as a group.)
People are learning to appreciate *roses*. (Roses in general.)
Honesty is the best policy. (Honesty in general is a non-count noun.)
Hunger is a prime mover. (Hunger in general.)
Research has proved that cigarettes are deadly. (All cigarettes.)

B.4.3 Reference to specific nouns that are subsets of larger sets using the article *the*. This form is used in particular for the following categories:

musical instruments:	Peter plays *the piano* very well. (Subset of musical instruments)
dances:	Elizabeth loves to dance *the waltz*. (Subset of dances)
nationalities:	*The British* love to drink tea. (Subset of nationalities)
adjective/noun:	*The poor* need shelter. (Subset of social classes)

PRACTICE EXERCISE

Fill the blanks in the following sentences with *the* or Ø where no article at all is needed.

1. In the past _____ young men went to _____ sea for _____ adventure.
2. _____ sea is _____ food source of _____ future.
3. He came to _____ school late. _____ students laughed as he opened _____ door. _____ teacher had little _____ patience for his antics.
4. _____ dinner served at _____ White House was very special indeed.
5. _____ breakfast should be eaten by all if _____ energy levels are to be kept high.
6. _____ parents have long recognized _____ importance of treating _____ children with _____ love and _____ respect.
7. _____ banana I ate yesterday was from Panama.
8. _____ words are _____ symbols that represent _____ actions or _____ things.
9. _____ Chinese have great respect for _____ elderly.
10. _____ samba is a fun dance to learn.

> **ANSWERS**
>
> 1. Ø young men, Ø sea, Ø adventure
> 2. the sea, the food source, the future
> 3. Ø school
>   the students, the door, the teacher (all become specific), Ø patience (in general)
> 4. the dinner, the White House
> 5. Ø breakfast, Ø energy levels
> 6. Ø parents, the importance, Ø children, Ø love, Ø respect
> 7. The banana
> 8. Ø words, Ø symbols, Ø actions, Ø things
> 9. The Chinese, the elderly
> 10. The samba

B.5 Function of the Article with Proper Nouns

Proper nouns include the names of specific people (Peter Smith), places (New York), days (Monday), and so on.

→ **B.5.1 Countering an unclear reference with the article *the*.** One rule of thumb is that a proper noun is specific in itself, and it does not generally need an article. If for some reason the reference is *not clear* you need to use an article.

- Are you speaking of the Susan Stowski that I know?

→ Also, if the proper noun has a common noun as a base, you will normally need the article *the*, for example:

- the *Queen* of England   vs.   Queen Elizabeth
- the Italian *Republic*   vs.   Italy
- the *President*   vs.   President Clinton
- the Metropolitan *Museum* of Art
- the United *States* of America   vs.   America
- the Suez *Canal*
- the *University* of California (If the modification precedes the name of the university the article is usually not needed: Stanford University, Yale University, but there are exceptions.)
- the Atlantic (*Ocean*)
- the Mediterranean (*Sea*)
- the former Soviet *Union*
- the North *Pole*
- the City of Los Angeles   vs.   Los Angeles
- the Nile (*River*)

B.5.2 Referring to specific groups of proper nouns that may require the article *the*.

- Plural islands, lakes, and mountains: *the* Bahamas, *the* Great Lakes, *the* Alps
- Buildings, businesses, and holidays, which can either have or not have an article, for example:

NO ARTICLE	ARTICLE
Los Angeles City Hall	the Empire State Building
Independence Hall	the Forum
Memorial Stadium	the Civic Auditorium
Sears Roebuck	The Hilton
Christmas	the Fourth of July

- Newspapers: *The Times, The Observer, The Daily News* (magazines do not carry the article *the*.)
- Family names in the plural:
   the Fultons
   the Murphys

This is a general guideline that will help you to make a reasonable decision. Of course, there are exceptions that *must be memorized* as you encounter them.

> **PRACTICE EXERCISE**
>
> Fill in the blanks in the following sentences with *the* or Ø where no article at all is needed.
>
> 1. _____ Colemans will be here for _____ Christmas.
> 2. _____ *Los Angeles Times* has a separate edition for _____ San Fernando Valley.
> 3. _____ Lake Erie is _____ southernmost lake of _____ Great Lakes.
> 4. _____ Department of Building and Safety of _____ City of Los Angeles has many offices all over _____ metropolitan area.
> 5. _____ Memorial Day is not as celebrated as _____ Fourth of July.
> 6. _____ Pacific Ocean has long been a favorite spot for _____ summer tourists.
> 7. _____ Madonna Inn is located on _____ Pacific Coast.
> 8. _____ Queen Elizabeth is well loved by _____ British.
> 9. _____ John Thompson who came to _____ interview was not a polite young man!
> 10. _____ College of Fine Arts at _____ University of New Mexico has a fine reputation.
> 11. _____ European Union is undergoing great social reform.
> 12. _____ Notre Dame is a famous gothic cathedral in _____ Paris.
>
> **ANSWERS**
>
> 1. The Colemans, Ø Christmas
> 2. The *Los Angeles Times*, the San Fernando Valley
> 3. Ø Lake Erie, the southernmost lake, the Great Lakes
> 4. The Department of Building and Safety, the City of Los Angeles, the metropolitan area
> 5. Ø Memorial Day, the Fourth of July
> 6. The Pacific Ocean, Ø summer tourists (in general) *or* the summer tourists (as opposed to the winter ones)
> 7. The Madonna Inn, the Pacific Ocean
> 8. Ø Elizabeth, the British
> 9. The John Thompson, the interview
> 10. The College of Fine Arts, the University of New Mexico
> 11. The European Union
> 12. Ø Notre Dame, Ø Paris

C. A QUICK REVIEW OF THE MAJOR VERB TENSES

C.1 The Present—Simple Present

(A) General Truths

You will find that the simple present is often used in essays because it serves to speak about *general truths*.

So if you are writing a description, a classification, a definition, a comparison and contrast, a cause and effect or a persuasion, you will most likely be using the simple present (unless you are referring to the past or future). You can use it when writing analysis or application. Look at the following example of comparison and contrast:

Phonics and whole language *are* two methods teachers *use* to teach young children how to read. Phonics *involves* the teaching of the relationships that *exist* between sounds and symbols. By contrast, whole language *is* a philosophy of education that focuses on language as a means of communication.

(B) Perceptions and States of Being

The simple present is also used to write about sensations and states we wish to present as occurring at the moment of speaking, which probably won't occur on a GWAR.

- The wind feels cold against my face. The rain *chills* my very soul.

(C) Habitual Actions

Also, the simple present is used to speak about actions that are repeated all the time, that is, habitual actions. (You may need this tense on a GWAR.)

- The news *is* broadcasted every hour on the hour.

C.2 The Present—Present Progressive

The present progressive tense is used to emphasize the fact that an action is ongoing.

- The condition *is getting* progressively worse. (or to rewrite, The condition worsens.)
- The two countries *are arguing* over the boundary.

→ *NOTE:* Both the simple present and the present progressive may be used idiomatically to speak about the future. (For ESL students the future tense is safer.)

- The train *leaves* at three o'clock. (near future)
- Next summer I *am going* to Brazil.

In these cases, there is usually an adverb indicating time (today, tomorrow, next year, and so on) which accompanies the verb.

MINI PRACTICE EXERCISE

Fill the blanks in the following sentences with the appropriate tense—either *simple present* or *present progressive*—of the verbs given in parentheses.

1. The numerous roads in Europe _____ (*to be*) a tribute to the Roman soldiers that built them.
2. Many countries _____ (*rebuild*) these roads which _____ (*to be*) in desperate need of repair.
3. The family _____ (*wait*) for the doctor to arrive.
4. He _____ (*hope*) that the doctor will have a cure.
5. The swallows _____ (*return*) to Capistrano every year.
6. The bus _____ (*depart*) at two o'clock this afternoon.

ANSWERS

1. *are* (fact or truth)
2. *are rebuilding* (in the process); *are* (fact or truth)
3. *is waiting* (in the process)
4. *hopes* (state of mind) or *is hoping* (to emphasize the duration of the act)
5. *return* (habitual action)
6. *departs* or *is departing* (for the future)

C.3 The Past—Simple Past

This tense is used for actions or states of being that occurred in the past and have finished. The action may have lasted over a period of time, and it may have even been a repeated action. Most important of all, the action must no longer be taking place. However, this tense has the strongest impact, since it suggests an unchangeable frozen event.

- They *received* an eviction notice.
- They *received* seven eviction notices.
- It *took* three years to evict them.

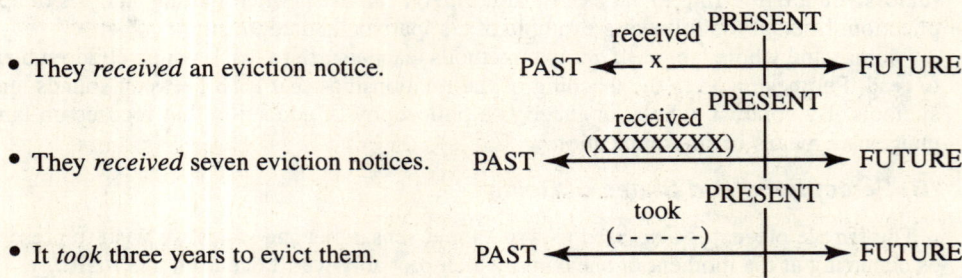

NOTE: **used to + the infinitive of a verb** may be used to speak about states of conditions and habitual actions that happened in the past. (The *s* in used sounds soft in this case.)

- I *used to eat* in restaurants every day.
- She *used to be* very short.

C.4 The Past—Past Progressive

NOTE: This tense is often misused by ESL writers. With this tense one action must be in progress when the other action takes place, and may or may not continue past the point of time a second action interrupts.

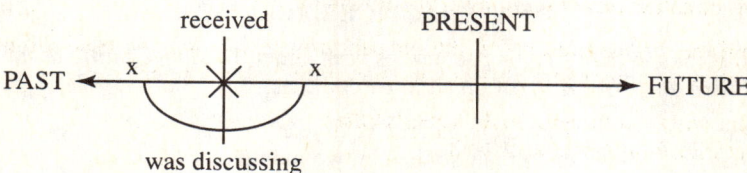

- The council *was discussing* security, when they *received* an anonymous call, which indicated that there was a bomb in the building.
- *At five o'clock*, the witness *was leaving* for work. (Then something happened.)

MINI PRACTICE EXERCISE

Fill the blanks in the following sentences with either the *simple past* or *the past progressive* tense of the verbs given in parentheses.

1. The crows _____ (*to approach*) as the sun _____ (*to begin*) to set. They _____ (*to swoop*) out of the sky and _____ (*to settle*) in the branches of the old oak trees. Their cries _____ (*deafen*) all who _____ (*observe*) them.
2. During the course of his last year at the university, he _____ (*to receive*) three job offers.
3. Last summer, they _____ (*to spend*) their vacation looking for a house to buy.
4. Emily _____ (*to live*) in New York City.
5. The merchant _____ (*to count*) the day's earnings when a thief _____ (*to enter*) the shop.
6. At ten o'clock, I _____ (*to leave*) the office.
7. Last year she _____ (*to study*) at the university when she _____ (*to decide*) to move to Europe.

ANSWERS

1. *approached, began, swooped, settled, deafened, observed* (All these actions happened and finished at one specific period of time in the past.)
2. *received*
3. *spent* (happened and finished over a period of time)
4. *lived* or *used to live* (state of condition) or (was living, if interrupted)
5. *was counting, entered* (The counting was in progress when it was interrupted by the thief.)
6. *left* (was leaving, if the writer is reporting an ongoing schedule)
7. *was studying, decided* (The studying was interrupted by her decision.)

C.5 The Future—Simple Future

There are several ways to indicate the future in English. Consider these examples:

- I will go. (Definite intention)
- I am going to go shopping. (Intention to do something)
- I go at noon. (Simple present with an adverb of time, usually in answer to a spoken question)

C.6 The Future—Future Progressive

Just like the past progressive, the future progressive may be used to indicate something that will be in progress when another action takes place or at a specific time. Also, we use this tense to stress that an action will be lasting a long time in the future (duration). With this tense writers and speakers know that the hoped-for future condition may be unattainable.

- He *will be traveling* in Spain when I arrive in Europe.
- Next summer, she *will be studying* for her university exit exams.
- By this time next week, I *will be leaving* for the Orient.

MINI PRACTICE EXERCISE

Fill the blanks in the following sentences with either the *simple future* or the *future progressive* tense of the verbs given in parentheses.

1. She _____ (*to earn*) a large income next year.
2. They _____ (*to finish*) their studies in two months.
3. The President _____ (*to visit*) Japan at the end of the month.

ANSWERS

1. *will earn* or *is going to earn* or *will be earning*
2. *will finish* or *are going to finish* or *will be finishing*
3. *will visit* or *is going to visit* or *will be visiting*

C.7 The Perfect Forms—Present Perfect

→ *NOTE:* Some other languages have a tense that may resemble the present perfect in form, but the usage is probably very different. The best way to understand this tense is to not make comparisons with other languages.

There are three main times when we use the present perfect.

EXAMPLE 1: We use this tense for actions that began in the past and are still continuing now.

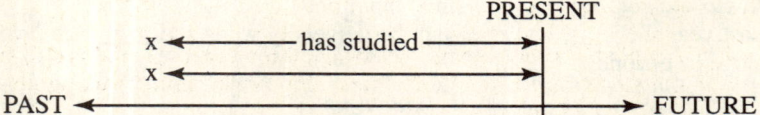

- He *has studied* ballet for three years.
- They *have known* Pat for three years.
- She *has played* soccer since he was a child.

EXAMPLE 2: We also use the present perfect for an action that happened in the past, but when this action occurred is either unknown or not indicated.

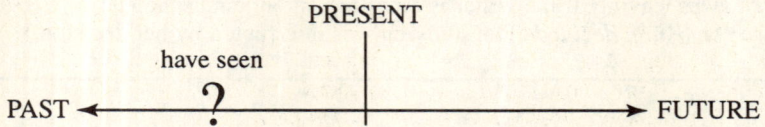

- I *have seen* this movie. (I do not remember when.)
- I *have been* to the former Soviet Union several times. (The exact times are irrelevant to the discourse.)

→ *NOTE:* This form is also used for actions that never occurred, and for actions that we do not know whether or not they occurred.

- *Have* you *been* to Tokyo?
- I *have* never *been* to Tokyo.

EXAMPLE 3: Last of all, the present perfect is used for actions that have *just* finished, or finished a short time ago.

- They *have just finished* their dinner.
- Mary *has just finished* her law degree.

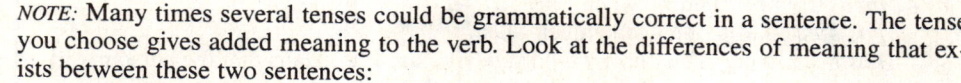NOTE: Many times several tenses could be grammatically correct in a sentence. The tense you choose gives added meaning to the verb. Look at the differences of meaning that exists between these two sentences:

I *went* to New York.   The speaker knows in his mind exactly when he went even though he doesn't say exactly when.

I *have been* to New York.   In this case, the speaker does not know when he went to New York, or perhaps thinks that when the action occurred is *not* important to the discourse.

Now, try to identify the difference in meaning between the following two sentences:

(1) *Has* Pete *gone* to Los Angeles? vs. (2) *Did* Pete *go* to Los Angeles?
    (present perfect)   (simple past)

Again, both sentences are grammatically correct. In the first, the speaker has no specific time in mind. Perhaps the action never even took place. In the second sentence, the speaker has a specific time in mind and is sure that there is a good chance that Pete actually went to Los Angeles. Maybe the speaker knows that Pete spent his vaction in California, and there is a good chance that he went to Los Angeles. Or it is possible that Pete told the speaker that he intended to go to Los Angeles. As you can see, the choice of verb tense brings different meaning to the sentence. You must choose which tense creates the strongest impact.

NOTE: The SIMPLE PAST is used for a *definite* time in the past (at least in the mind of the speaker).

The PRESENT PERFECT is used for an *indefinite* time in the past (maybe the action never even occurred).

C.8 The Present Forms—Present Perfect Progressive

The present perfect progressive is used in just about the same ways as the present perfect. The difference between the two is that the progressive form is used to emphasize the continuous nature of the action.

- He *has studied* English for three years. (He began three years ago and is still studying.)
- He *has been studying* English for three years. (He began three years ago and is still studying day, after day, after day.)

MINI PRACTICE EXERCISE

Fill the blanks in the following sentences with either the *present perfect*, the *present perfect progressive*, or the simple past of the verbs given in parentheses. In some cases, all three may be grammatically correct.

1. They _____ (*to visit*) Scotland.
2. In 1987, Nancy _____ (*to finish*) her degree.
3. They _____ (*to study*) at NYU for two years.
4. That famous actor from the 1930s _____ (*to die*).

ANSWERS AND EXPLANATIONS

1. *visited*. If the time is definite in your mind.
   have visited. If the time is indefinite in your mind.
   have been visiting. If they started visiting a while ago, and they are still visiting. Here you want to emphasize the duration of the act.
2. *finished*. The time is definite.

3. *studied*. If the action was in the past and finished.
   have studied. Either the time is indefinite, or they are still studying.
   have been studying. They started a while ago and are still studying. Emphasis is given to the duration of the action.
4. *died*. If you remember when.
   has died. If you don't remember when.
   has been dying. This form would rarely be used. It means that the person is ill and has been in the process of dying for a long time. It sounds sarcastic. Some verbs that involve actions that happen and finish quickly (to finish, to start, to die) do not usually work well in the present progressive form.

 NOTE: The tense we choose gives different meanings to the sentences.

C.9 The Perfect Forms—Past Perfect

This form is used to show how one past action happened before a later past action. Often, direct past action has been influenced or preceded by prior actions.

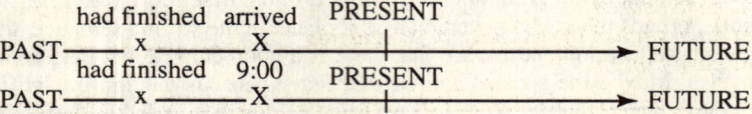

- They *had finished* their homework before we *arrived*.
- They *had finished* their homework before *nine o'clock*.

C.10 The Perfect Forms—Past Perfect Progressive

When we want to stress the fact that the past perfect action continued for a period of time, then we use the past perfect progressive form.

- He *had been watching* television before you arrived.
- They *had been studying* English before the phone rang.

MINI PRACTICE EXERCISE

Fill the blanks in the following sentences with either the *past perfect* or the *past perfect progressive* form of the verbs given in parentheses.

1. They _____ (*to meet*) before they graduated from the university.
   ANSWER: *had met*. With a verb like *to meet*, you probably would not use a progressive form unless you want to emphasize the fact that they continually meet each other.
2. By the time you arrived home, she _____ (*to finish*) all of the dessert.
   ANSWER: *had finished*
3. Before 1985, they _____ (*to live*) in California for ten years.
   ANSWER: *had lived* or *had been living*
4. Before their mother returned, they _____ (*to complete*) all of their chores.
   ANSWER: *had completed* (finished) or *had been completing* (in the act of completing)

C.11 The Perfect Forms—Future Perfect

Much like the form that we have just discussed, this form is used to speak about an action that will occur before another action or time in the future. This tense is rare on GWAR essays.

- They *will have finished* dinner before you return.
- They *will have finished* dinner before nine o'clock.

C.12 The Perfect Forms—The Future Perfect Progressive

This form is used just like the preceding one; however, since it is a progressive form, it emphasizes the continuous nature of the action.

- They *will have been studying* for one year in China, before they will return home.
- She *will have been waiting* seven hours by midnight.

MINI PRACTICE EXERCISE

Fill the blanks in the following sentences with either the *future perfect* or the *future perfect progressive* form of the verbs given in parentheses.

1. Barbara _____ (*to arrive*) in Korea by this time tomorrow.
2. Before you get home this evening, I _____ (*to cook*) dinner.
3. By the year 2000, I _____ (*to study*) for twelve years.
4. By his action, he _____ (*to prove*) his intentions.

ANSWERS

1. *will have arrived*
2. *will have cooked*
3. *will have studied* or *will have been studying*
4. *will have proven*

D. LEARNING TO CORRECT YOUR COMPOSITION BY YOURSELF/TRACKING YOUR ERROR AREAS

To greatly improve your writing, you must reserve a part of the time given to you for the correction of your paper. All of us have our weak spots. That is to say, we all tend to have a few mistakes that we repeat constantly. You should get out your old essays from your various classes and study the errors that you made. Try to categorize your mistakes. Answer the following questions to try to pinpoint where your weaknesses lie.

1. Do you have trouble with verb tenses? (See Section C.1.) ☐ yes ☐ no
2. Do your subject and verbs normally agree? ☐ yes ☐ no
3. Do you have trouble with prepositions? ☐ yes ☐ no
4. Do you often choose an incorrect article? (See Section B.) ☐ yes ☐ no
5. Do you have trouble with linking words? (See Section A.) ☐ yes ☐ no
6. Do you use relative clauses correctly? (E.g., He is the man *to whom I spoke*. [*to whom* is a relative clause]) ☐ yes ☐ no
7. Do you have trouble with reported speech? (Putting someone else's words into your words.) ☐ yes ☐ no
8. Do you make mistakes when the sentence you are writing contains the word *if*? ☐ yes ☐ no
9. Do you have trouble with choosing the correct forms of words? (Parts of speech) ☐ yes ☐ no
10. Do you find that you tend to repeat the same words over and over again? ☐ yes ☐ no
11. Do you use a lot of words that fill space but say very little? ☐ yes ☐ no
12. Is it always clear to whom or what you are referring? ☐ yes ☐ no

Once you know what types of mistakes you make, you will be able to proofread your essay specifically for these mistakes.

In this section, we will review some of the topics just mentioned. Also, we will practice correcting (or editing) papers that contain some commonly made mistakes.

Sample 1

Read the following introduction to an essay and determine its main structural defects. Later we will examine its grammatical errors.

Raising Children in the United States

The family is always been the basic unit of society in any country. It is the most important factor in any community. Any professional can tell that in a family, it is important to observe the relationship of parents to their children. There are so many duties and responsibilities that parents are facing especially here in the United States when raising their children.

Since in the United States, the culture, values and traditions are very different as compared to any other countries, parents have a different way of raising their children too. They got a different way to give their children the material things that they need, a different interpretation of what is freedom and the way to discipline their children.

First, write your comments below about this introduction from the point of view of structure and content. Then read the following evaluation.

_____
_____
_____

The person who wrote this piece knows the language fairly well and has some good thoughts on the subject. However, it seems that the writer is so tied up in words, that he is giving little thought to what he is actually saying. In fact, much of the first paragraph can be eliminated. We really don't know the thesis statement until the second paragraph. This is a common problem with ESL writers. When you write in a foreign language it is easy to over concentrate on grammar, word choice and word order to the point of losing sight of what you are actually trying to say. If you *think* and *plan* carefully before you begin to write, you will avoid this type of common error. Consider delaying the writing of your thesis or first paragraph until after you plan your examples and evaluations.

 Pointer 1. Plan exactly what you are going to say *before* you begin to write. Use your words wisely. Be concise. (See Chapter 3.)

Now let's take a look at some of the grammatical mistakes in the two sample paragraphs. What are the problems that this writer must pay particular attention to?

Your comments: _____
_____
_____

If you mentioned tenses, repetition, and unclear reference, then you have done a fine job analyzing this sample. Now, make your corrections directly onto the following text.

Raising Children in the United States

The family <u>is always been</u> the basic unit of society in any country. <u>It is the most</u>
                  1

<u>important factor in any community</u>. <u>Any professional can tell that</u> in a family, it is
        2   3

important to observe the relationship of parents <u>to</u> their children. There are so
                                            4

many duties and responsibilities that parents <u>are facing</u> especially here in the
                                          5

United States when raising <u>their</u> children.
                          6

Since in the United States, the culture, values and traditions are very different <u>as compared to any other countries</u>, <u>parents</u> have a different way of raising their
        7   8

children too. <u>They got a different way to give their children the material things that they need, a different interpretation of what is freedom and the way to discipline their children.</u>
                                 9

Special Notes and Tips for ESL Students

ANSWERS AND EXPLANATIONS

(The corrections on previous page are underlined.)

1. *is the*. Usually, when writing about a topic in general, we use the simple present tense. However, if you want to use the word *always*, you must use *has always been*.
2. This sentence repeats the thought of the first sentence. Eliminate it.
3. This phrase is wordy. Get straight to the point. The transition to *professional* is unclear.
4. *with*. You have a relationship *with* someone.
5. *face*. Use the simple present for general truths.
6. Misplaced: "...<u>face when raising children in the United States</u>."
7. In this sentence, it seems that the writer is comparing *culture, values,* and *traditions* to *countries*. Probably the writer intended the comparison to be between *culture, values, and traditions in the United States* and *culture, values, and traditions in other countries*. Thus, the sentence should read "...<u>from those in other countries</u>."
8. Which parents are being spoken of? <u>American parents</u>.
9. Repetition. When you find that you are repeating the same exact words, something is wrong. Get straight to the point! Moreover, in the rest of the essay, which does not appear here, the writer goes on to speak about the value of hard work and not the value of material things. Freedom and discipline are overlapping topics in this essay.

Here is an example of how the writer could have written the introduction in Sample 1:

> Since every culture has different values and traditions, the way parents raise their children greatly varies in each country. Visitors to the United States are quick to notice that American parents have a unique way of raising, disciplining, and teaching their children. The American method has risks and benefits; American children have more freedom, but they mismanage responsibility.

As you can see, the content of the original introductory paragraphs was very limited.

Sample 2

Study the next composition. See if you can correct all of the underlined sections of the text.

Why People Come to the United States

In many countries <u>in all over the world</u> there are a lot or problems, <u>such as</u>
                     1   2

<u>politicals, socials, and economics</u>. <u>These problems</u> <u>make people to leave</u> their
                       3   4

countries. For example, <u>Nicaragua and El Salvador for the inability to vote</u>.
                                   5

Chile, Argentina, Paraguay, Uruguay, and Peru, among others, are countries

that <u>lost</u> a lot of people. <u>They had to leave their own countries</u> <u>for</u> the political
     6   7   8

hardships. In Africa and <u>oriental countries</u> <u>is happening the same situation</u>. Al-
                     9   10

though in Europe there are many countries where people <u>could</u> get a good ed-
                                                   11

ucation and <u>they could get</u> <u>good jobs</u>, the people still <u>came</u> to the United States
          12   13

for many reasons. <u>For example, the United States is a country whose govern-</u>
                          14

110 CSU — Writing Proficiency Exam

<u>ment is chosen democratically by the people, the United States is a country</u>
                                                    14
<u>which respects everyone and anybody can manifest his/her ideas. And in the</u>
                                                    14
<u>United States there are a lot of possibilities to work and study.</u>
                                                    14

ANSWERS AND EXPLANATIONS

1. <u>All over the world</u> or <u>In many countries there...</u>
2. <u>...there are a lot of political, social, and economic problems</u>. It is much better form to use the three words as adjectives. (See the parallel rule pages 185–186.)

→ *Pointer 2.* Be careful how you use the expression *such as*. It always follows a general noun, and it gives subtypes of that noun. For example, *companies, machines,* and *professions* are all general nouns in the following sentences. Notice how *such as* introduces specific subtypes. Note the punctuation that is used.

- COMPANIES, *such as IBM and NCR*, have large research departments.
- A secretary must know how to operate many MACHINES, *such as photocopiers and word processors*.
- There are many dangerous PROFESSIONS, *such as that of the soldier and the law enforcement agent*. Notice how in the essay that we are working on *such as* was incorrectly used to introduce three adjectives, not three noun subtypes.

ANSWERS

3 and 4. <u>...and economic problems that make people leave their countries</u>.

→ *Pointer 3.* Pay special attention to preposition usage after "two-verb verbs."
  Certain verbs, such as *to make, to let,* and *to help,* are usually followed by another verb to complete their meaning. Sometimes, the second verb is preceded by *to,* and sometimes it is not. The rule is very simple. The verbs *to make, to let,* and *to have (someone do something)* are not followed by *to*. With *to help, to* is optional. Observe the following examples.

- *to is excluded*
  They *made* him *go* to the university.   no *to* is used
  They *let* him *finish* his dinner.   no *to* is used
  They *had* him *do* the work.   no *to* is used
- *to is optional*
  They *helped* him *finish* his degree.
        OR   *to* can be omitted or used
  They *helped* him (*to*) *finish* his degree.
- *All other verbs require* (*to*)
  He *permitted* him (*to*) *go*.
  We *asked* him (*to*) *stay*.
  He *was obliged* (*to*) *tell* the truth.
  They *were told* (*to*) *stop* fighting.
  Lucretia *got* the company (*to*) *donate* money.
  Bill *wants* you (*to*) *fix* the sink.
  John *expects* his children (*to*) *do* well.

ANSWER AND EXPLANATION

5. This is not a full sentence. It lacks a verb. One correction could read
   <u>People leave Nicaragua and El Salvador because of the inability to vote</u>.
   Note that "<u>for</u> the inability to vote" becomes "<u>because of</u> the inability to vote"

→ *Pointer 4.* Notice that in English, *for* does not introduce a reason as it often does in other languages.

INCORRECT: He came to the United States *for to get a better job*.
CORRECT: He came to the United States *to get a better job*. (two-verb verb: see Pointer 3)

INCORRECT:	He came to the United States *for the war*.
CORRECT:	He came to the United States *because of the war*. (because of + noun)

ANSWERS AND EXPLANATIONS

6. <u>have lost</u>. Use the present perfect because the time is very indefinite. Also, this tense emphasizes the fact that the action has occurred over many years until the present.
7. Again, if a concept must be repeated, you must stop and try to make your writing more concise. Sentences 6 and 7 should be combined to read <u>...have lost a lot of people who disagreed with the governing political regimes</u>. (Otherwise, the "They" is an unclear transition.)

→ *Pointer 5*. Prepositional phrases, relative clauses, and compound verbs all serve to make your writing concise.

CHOPPY:	He left for school. It was five o'clock.
IMPROVED:	<u>At five o'clock</u>, he left for school.
	(Prepositional phrase)
CHOPPY:	The children passed the exam. The exam was given yesterday.
IMPROVED:	The children passed <u>the exam that was given yesterday</u>.
	(Relative clause)
REPETITIOUS:	Louis ran. *Louis* tripped. *Louis* fell.
IMPROVED:	Louis <u>ran, tripped, and fell</u>.
	(Compound verb)

Learn to use these three structures effectively!

ANSWERS AND EXPLANATIONS

8. *For* cannot be used with the meaning of *because of*.
→ 9. <u>In Africa and Asia</u>. When you make a list, each element must be similar to the other ones. If the first two items are nouns, then the third item must be a noun. If the first item is a continent, then the next one must also be a continent.
10. <u>the same situation is happening</u>. Unless you are using a special construction, such as a yes/no question, in English statements usually the subject will come before the verb. Be careful because in your language a verb/subject sequence may be perfectly normal. If we change the verb, it sounds even better. ...<u>the same situation prevails</u>.
11. <u>can</u>. Use the simple present when speaking of generalities.
12. <u>a good education and jobs</u>. Be concise!
13. <u>come</u>. Again, use the simple present.
14. Notice how <u>the United States</u> is repeated three times. Besides the fact that the punctuation of this section of text is extremely poor, something must be done to put all of this information into one concise sentence. Here is one solution:

> Democracy, freedom of speech, and the possibility of self-advancement are three reasons why so many people from all over the world choose to make the United States their home.

Notice how the three concepts were neatly summarized by three nouns: democracy, freedom of speech, and self-advancement. This sentence also serves as a thesis sentence in that it tells the reader, in a clear, concise manner, that the following essay will deal with democracy, freedom of speech and self-advancement in the United States.

Now let's take a look at a revised version of the original paragraph from Sample 2:

> All over the world, there are a lot of political, social and economic problems that make people leave their countries. For example, people leave Nicaragua and El Salvador because of the inability to vote. Chile, Argentina, Paraguay, Uruguay and Peru, among others, are countries that have lost a lot of people who disagreed with the governing regimes. In Africa and Asia, the same situation prevails. Although in Europe there are many countries where people can get a good education and jobs, many Europeans still come to the United States. In reality, democracy, freedom of speech, and the possibility of self-advancement are three reasons why so many people from all over the world choose to make the United States their home.

The preceding paragraph could be further improved, but this revision is grammatically correct and directly reflects the original version.

In short, after you have written your essay within your time budget and according to the suggested procedure on page 39, re-read your paper carefully. If you have been allowed to use a pencil, you should be able to neatly repair any of your habitual problems as we have just discussed. With a serious effort you will greatly improve the quality of your writing. Remember that it is also important that you make your paper as well supported, logical, coherent, and grammatically correct as possible. Although the scorers will not expect perfect grammatical correctness, and though they will judge your essay on your overall ability to organize your thoughts and make yourself understood, it will help you to institute gradual improvement to your error areas.

9 Multiple-Choice Tests

Five universities in the California State University (CSU) system include a multiple-choice component in their Graduation Writing Assessment Requirement (GWAR) as summarized in the following chart.

Campus	Number of Questions	Length in Minutes	Question Types
Fresno	166	65	Fresno Model (CEPT plus Spelling/Punctuation Test)
Fullerton	50	35	TSWE
Hayward	72	40	CAAP Writing Skills Test
Long Beach	60	80	Long Beach Model
San Jose	72	40	CAAP Writing Skills Test

Test patterns and options are subject to change.

In this chapter, we discuss and give examples of the various multiple-choice questions required at the five campuses listed in the table. Note that the material tested in such questions comprises the rules of grammar, usage, diction, and style that are covered thoroughly in Chapter 10 of this manual, with a series of lessons which include brief summary tests and reviews.

Chapter 11 provides comprehensive review in the form of five practice examinations, complete with answers and explanations. All of these tests in Chapter 11 follow a single test format that permits a consistent testing criterion and measure of progress. Be sure to complete all the practice questions in this manual regardless of their format to achieve a maximum amount of drill. Even more important, be sure to study and review thoroughly the basics covered in Chapter 10 so your drills are grounded in substance—that is, hard and fast knowledge of the rules.

Interestingly enough, GWAR exams are limited in what they can test on the objective portions of exams. You can use the check sheet below to track how many times certain test items appear on the sample tests in this manual, to track which areas give you no trouble, and to track which ones give you difficulty.

ITEM	TYPES	FREQUENCY ON EXAM
PUNctuation	commas, splices (missing conjunctions), fused sentences (missing semicolon or period), commas in series	(Tabulate accuracy here too)
Punctuation	colons, dashes	
Subject-verb recognition	number (case) agreement between subjects and verbs, fragment recognition	

Item	Types	Frequency on Exam
Pronouns	number agreement (between pronoun and noun or pronoun it refers to), pronoun spelling	
Parallel Rule (keeping sentence units exactly the same in shape and form to fit the rest of the sentence)	subjects and nouns in series, verb forms (infinitives, participles (verb +ing or +ed), tenses, gerunds (+ing verbs used as nouns), prepositional phrases in series	
Parallel Rule	keeping units the same shape and form in <u>comparison</u> phrases and clauses. (X is as Y, X as much as Y: however long and what shape X is, Y must be the same)	
Verb Tenses	keeping time periods accurate	
Commas	enclosing inserted nonessential information	
Word Forms: (i.e., recognizing noun functions, verb functions, +ing functions, adjective functions)	so as to correct errors in parallel and find correct versions of flawed parallels by keeping functions similar	
Misplaced Modifiers	match correct noun or subject with its modifier	
Logic and Coherence	rephrasing sentences with alternate word choices and clauses and transitions	
Apostrophes	knowing contracted words and possessive pronouns from possessive nouns	
Subject/Object Pronouns (Also called Nominative and Object Pronouns)	knowing the difference between pronouns that can be subjects, and those that can't	
Paragraph and Sentence Sequence	ordering sentences within paragraphs, and paragraphs within essays	

FRESNO MODEL

As part of the writing examination, CSU Fresno gives a multiple-choice test that has two components:

- **CEPT** (College English Placement Test), a 106-question test given over 45 minutes. CEPT measures how well a student understands the basic structure of the English language and how effectively the student can manipulate that language.

- **SPELLING AND PUNCTUATION**, two 30-item tests given together in a 20-minute period with no break or separate timing between the two. The spelling test measures the student's ability to use the structures of English words in order to spell correctly. On this test, students are also asked to divide words into syllables and follow the rules of spelling in joining roots, prefixes, and suffixes. The punctuation test gauges how well a student understands the rules governing the use of punctuation marks.

CEPT Practice Test

Question Type A (Proofreading and Editing)

Read the sentences below and decide in each case whether a correction needs to be made.
1. The horse that came in first is related to the great Citation.
    Circle A. if a comma should be inserted after *horse*.
    B. if *that* should be changed to *which*.
    C. if a comma should be inserted after *first*.
    D. if *came* should be changed to comes.
    E. if NO CHANGE needs to be made.
2. If the engine was tuned properly, Jim and I would not have been stranded in the desert.
    Circle A. if the comma after *properly* should be removed.
    B. if *I* should be replaced with *me*.
    C. if *was* should be replaced with *were*.
    D. if *desert* should be capitalized.
    E. if NO CHANGE needs to be made.
3. After having lunch at Solley's, it started to rain so heavily that all traffic stopped in the main square.
    Circle A. if *main square* should be capitalized.
    B. if the comma after *Solley's* should be changed to a semicolon.
    C. if *After having lunch at Solley's* should be changed to *Because we had lunch at Solley's*.
    D. if *it started to rain* should be changed to *we watched it raining*.
    E. if NO CHANGE needs to be made.
4. The bride really ought to have been accompanied by her father.
    Circle A. if *bride* should be capitalized.
    B. if *ought to have been accompanied* should be changed to *ought to have accompanied*.
    C. if *father* should be capitalized.
    D. if *ought* should be replaced with *oughten*.
    E. if NO CHANGE needs to be made.

Question Type B (Diction)

Which word best fills the blanks in the sentences below?
5. The Honduran mahogany desk was _____ to a fine finish.
    A. filed
    B. ground
    C. polished
    D. burnished
    E. rasped
6. & 7. The tax measures were _____ in April, too late to _____ current tax returns.
    A. affected
    B. effected
    C. inflected
    D. affect
    E. effect
8. The old man retired with _____ despite his abrupt dismissal.
    A. admiration
    B. bravura
    C. dignity
    D. feistiness
    E. egoism
9. The motorist was quite _____ when he realized that his car had been towed away.
    A. irascible
    B. steamed
    C. upset
    D. grouchy
    E. testy

Question Type C (Effective Writing)

Which sentence below expresses the thought most effectively?

10. A. The garage door springs had snapped and because of this we had to park the cars outside all night.
    B. Being that the garage door springs had snapped, we had to park our cars outside all night.
    C. Because the garage door springs had snapped, we had to park our cars outside all night.
    D. Because we had to park our cars outside all night, the garage door springs had snapped.
    E. The garage door springs had snapped; we had to park our cars outdoors all night.
11. A. My son is a soldier with the 3rd Armored Division and he drove an M1A1 tank in the Persian Gulf War.
    B. Having driven an M1A1 tank in the Persian Gulf War, my son is a soldier with the 3rd Armored Division.
    C. My son is a soldier with the 3rd Armored Division. He drove an M1A1 tank in the Persian Gulf War.
    D. My son, a soldier with the 3rd Armored Division, drove an M1A1 tank in the Persian Gulf War.
    E. In the Persian Gulf War, my son was a soldier with the 3rd Armored Division and he drove an M1A1 tank.
12. A. Mrs. Wilson was embarrassed and she had gone outside to pick up the paper in her pajamas.
    B. In her pajamas, the paper was picked up by Mrs. Wilson who was embarrassed.
    C. Mrs. Wilson, in her pajamas and embarrassed, had picked up the paper when she had gone outside.
    D. Mrs. Wilson was embarrassed that she had gone outside in her pajamas to pick up the paper.
    E. Having gone outside in her pajamas, the paper was picked up by Mrs. Wilson.
13. A. It was too late to take the final examination; Egbert failed.
    B. Egbert failed to take the final examination and it was too late.
    C. Having been too late to take the final examination, Egbert failed.
    D. Egbert failed because it was too late to take the final examination.
    E. Because Egbert failed, it was too late to take the final examination.

Spelling and Punctuation Practice Test

Question Type D (Spelling)

Choose the correct spelling for the word parts combined below:

1. argue + ment
   A. argument
   B. arguement
   C. argumant
2. nine + th
   A. nineth
   B. ninthe
   C. ninth
3. explore + ation
   A. exploreation
   B. exploration
   C. exploretion
4. dis + service
   A. diservice
   B. disservice
   C. discervice
5. refer + ing
   A. refering
   B. reffering
   C. referring

Question Type E (Spelling)

Choose the correct spelling.
6. A. roommates
   B. roomates
   C. roomaits
7. A. perfessor
   B. proffesor
   C. professor
8. A. developes
   B. devellopes
   C. develops
9. A. ocurrence
   B. occurrence
   C. occurance
10. A. bussineses
    B. bussinesses
    C. businesses

Question Type F (Syllabication)

Choose the word division that best shows the meaningful parts of the word.
11. barkeeper
    A. bar/keep/er
    B. bar/kee/per
    C. bark/ee/per
12. barbarian
    A. barb/ar/i/an
    B. bar/ba/ri/an
    C. bar/bar/i/an
13. marshmallow
    A. mar/sh/mal/low
    B. marsh/mal/low
    C. mar/sh/mall/ow
14. exhibition
    A. ex/hi/bi/tion
    B. ex/hib/i/tion
    C. ex/hibit/ion
15. slovenly
    A. slo/ven/ly
    B. slov/en/l/y
    C. slov/en/ly

Question Type G (Punctuation)

Choose the correct word and put it in the blank.
16. Show the possession:
    The _____ bicycles were all covered with snow.
    A. childrens'   B. children's
17. The poker was _____ .
    A. red-hot   B. red hot
18. The _____ poker burned a hole in the leather belt.
    A. red-hot   B. red hot
19. Show possession:
    The _____ accounting books were always kept in the safe.
    A. business's   B. business'
20. My _____ birthday was a gala affair at the Waldorf Astoria.
    A. mother's-in-law   B. mother-in-law's

Question Type H (Punctuation)

Decide what mark of punctuation would be placed in the underlined spaces.
  Every spring _____ (21) the girls in the town celebrated three events _____ (22) the Spring Prom, May Day, and the Tulip Festival.

21. A. no punctuation
    B. (,)
22. C. (.)
    D. (;)
    E. (:)

John spent a great deal of time preparing his tackle ___ (23) and he was well ___ (24) prepared on the day of the casting contest.

23. A. (;)
    B. (,)
24. C. no punctuation
    D. (-)
    E. (,)

Until the morning of the reunion ___ (25) not one of us had ever seen Mark, Bill ___ (26) or Steven.

25. A. (:)
    B. (,)
26. C. no punctuation
    D. (,)
    E. (;)

"Will you meet me after school ___ (27) she asked ___ (28)

27. A. ("?)
    B. (?")
28. C. (?)
    D. (!)
    E. (.)

The house ___ (29) that they really wanted to buy ___ (30) was on the crest of the hill.

29. A. no punctuation
    B. (,)
30. C. no punctuation
    D. (,)
    E. (—)

Answers and Explanations: Fresno Model

CEPT Practice Test

1. **E** The sentence is correct as it stands.
2. **C** The *if* clause is contrary to fact and therefore requires the use of the subjunctive verb *were*.
3. **D** Unless the subject of the main clause is changed to *we*, the participial phrase at the beginning of the sentence, *After having lunch at Solley's*, becomes a dangling modifier because it does not modify a logical noun or pronoun.
4. **E** The sentence is correct as it stands.
5. **C** Only the word *polished* is appropriate here, because *polishing* results in a fine finish; the actions suggested by the other verbs do not.
6. **B** *Effected* is a verb meaning "brought about."
7. **D** *Affect* is a different verb and means "to have influence over."
8. **C** Only the word *dignify* carries the intent of the sentence. All of the other choices convey other meanings which are either nonsensical or logically meaningless.
9. **C** *Upset* is standard American English; *steamed* is slang. The other choices are not meaningful.
10. **C**
11. **D**
12. **D**
13. **D**

SPELLING AND PUNCTUATION Practice Test

1. **A.** argument
2. **C.** ninth
3. **B.** exploration
4. **B.** disservice
5. **C.** referring
6. **A.** roommates
7. **C.** professor
8. **C.** develops
9. **B.** occurrence
10. **C.** businesses
11. **A.** bar/keep/er
12. **C.** bar/bar/i/an
13. **B.** marsh/mal/low

14. **A.** ex/hi/bi/tion
15. **E.** slov/en/ly
16. **B.** children's (The word *children* is a plural noun.)
17. **B.** red hot (Hyphenate compound adjectives only when they occur *before* the noun they modify.)
18. **A.** red-hot (See previous answer.)
19. **A.** business's (Although less formal usage permits the use of the apostrophe alone to indicate possession in nouns ending in *s*, most authoritative sources favor the apostrophe -*s* combination.)
20. **B.** mother-in-law's (For compound words, make the last word in the group possessive.)
21. **B.** (,) (Set off introductory phrases and clauses with a comma.)
22. **E.** (Use the colon to introduce anticipated supporting material such as these apositives.)
23. **B.** (,) (Use a comma to separate coordinate clauses joined by means of a coordinating conjunction.)
24. **C.** (Compound words and adjectives do not take the hyphen when they occur *after* the noun they modify.)
25. **B.** (,) (Set off introductory phrases and clauses with a comma.)
26. **D.** (Set off items in a series with commas.)
27. **B.** (The quote is a question, and so requires that the question mark be included before the quotation marks.)
28. **E.** (The fact that the subject asked the question is itself a statement, not a question.)
29. **A.** (The adjective clause *that they wanted to buy* is a restrictive modifier and so cannot be separated from the noun it is modifying.)
30. **C.** (The clause *that they wanted to buy* is not set off. See previous answer.)

TEST OF STANDARD WRITTEN ENGLISH (TSWE)

The TSWE, used at CSU Fullerton as part of its Examination in Writing Proficiency (EWP), tests some basic principles of grammar and usage such as agreement of subject and verb and of pronoun and antecedent; in addition, it presents more complicated writing problems such as whether or not the comparisons made in a sentence are logical. The test begins with 25 usage questions, then has 15 sentence correction questions, and ends with 10 more usage questions. You are given 35 minutes to complete this sequence of 50 questions.

Question Type A (Usage)

DIRECTIONS: Some parts of each sentence below are underlined and lettered. Decide which underlined part is in error and mark its letter on your answer sheet. If you spot no errors, do not hesitate to mark the (E) No error choice. No sentence contains more than one error.

1. The U.S. <u>Coast Guard</u> is <u>capable</u> of <u>effecting</u> rescues even during <u>sea gales</u> and hurricanes. <u>No error</u>.
         A   B   C   D   E

2. She <u>knew</u> that <u>her</u> mother <u>would enjoy</u> receiving flowers that smelled so <u>sweetly</u>. <u>No error.</u>
       A   B   C   D   E

3. Willets seems <u>introverted</u>, but you will find few salesmen more engaging <u>than</u> <u>him</u> when it comes to <u>closing</u> a sale. <u>No error</u>.
                 A   B C
       D   E

4. "<u>The War of the Worlds,</u>" one of the most memorable <u>hoax</u> of all time, <u>was</u> a radio program <u>produced</u> by Orson Welles. <u>No error</u>.
        A   B   C
      D   E

5. By the time <u>they were able</u> to rescue the little girl and bring her <u>off the ice</u>, her hands had <u>nearly</u> <u>froze</u>. <u>No error</u>.
                A   B
       C   D   E

6. The plant manager expressed concern about the large amount of chairs that had dis-
       A   B   C
   appeared since the new facility opened in June. No error.
       D   D   E

7. To stay home and read a good book, to do a little gardening in the afternoon, and
      A   B
   watching a good baseball game on television is my idea of a peaceful, relaxing day.
   C   D
   No error.
   E

8. Very tired. Mike lay his gun on the counter and lay down on the same bed he had lain
        A   B   C   D
   in all his life. No error.
                    E

9. The senator's son had spoken against him at the student rally; yet no one was more
       A   B   C
   fond of his father than him. No error.
                            D   E

10. President Norquist, whom the faculty respected, had given the student protesters
                        A   B
    neither open or implied support. No error.
    C   D   E

11. Because of the fog, they mistakenly supposed the driver to be I. No error.
    A   B   C   D   E

12. After reviewing your final paper for a second time, I am convinced that neither of your
    A   B   C
    hypotheses are correct. No error.
               D   E

13. One of my new Michelin tires are almost flat. No error.
        A   B C   D   E

14. Herman Melville, who is now believed to be one of the greatest American novelists,
                                A   B   C
    was virtually unknown when he died. No error.
                  D   E

15. Considering how long it's been since Jurgen saw her last, I can't hardly believe that
                A   B   C   D
    he would remember her. No error.
                           E

16. After the production schedule meeting, the same impulse sent the three of us in two
                  A   B
    directions—they back to the San Francisco plant and me back to San Diego. No error.
                 C   D   E

17. Many a box of rosy peaches have been sent to New York by proud Washingtonians.
    A   B   C   D
    No error.
    E

18. In spite of our frequent disagreements, I feel there is no real animosity between you
                A   B   C
    and I. No error.
        D   E

19. Florence Chadwick had swum the English Channel several times before she set the
                            A   B   C   D
    record. No error.
            E

20. The following petition, together with the minutes of the town meeting, present our
                           A   B   C
    main objections to the new airport. No error.
         D   E

21. The class felt very badly when their teacher burst into tears because of all the talking.
                 A   B   C   D
    No error.
    E

22. Each of the horses were meticulously combed before the auction. No error.
                     A   B   C   D   E

23. The new department was located in the bungalow furthest from the administrative wing. No error.
                             A   B   C   D   E

24. My children have always been more ambitious than their mother or me. No error.
                        A   B   C   D E

25. Every employee who applied for a paid leave hoped that their request would be granted by June. No error.
                  A B   C   D
    D   E

Question Type B (Grammar, Sentence Structure, Punctuation, Diction)

DIRECTIONS: Part or all of each sentence below is underlined. Select the lettered answer that contains the best version of the underlined section. Answer A always repeats the original underlined section exactly. If the sentence is correct as it stands, select A.

26. He walked closer and closer to the rare Siberian butterfly, quietly, cautiously, and with slow movements.
    A. and with slow movements.
    B. and by acting in a slow manner.
    C. and he used slow motion.
    D. and slowly.
    E. and with slowness.

27. When the time to speak had arrived, Dean Scott picked up his papers and walked to the podium.
    A. When the time to speak had arrived
    B. When it was time to speak
    C. When the time to speak had finally come
    D. When the time to speak had came
    E. When it was going to be time to speak

28. When reminiscing about the war, a tone of deep sadness creeps into his voice.
    A. When reminiscing
    B. When there is a reminiscence
    C. When describing about
    D. When he reminisces
    E. In reminiscing

29. How much has food costs raised during the past three decades?
    A. has food costs raised
    B. have food costs raised
    C. will food costs have raised
    D. has food costs rose
    E. have food costs risen

30. If you drink when you drive, you will loose your driver's license.
    A. you will loose your driver's license.
    B. you'll loose your driver's license.
    C. you will lose your driver's license.
    D. you will lose you're drivers license.
    E. you'll lose you're driver's license.

31. There should be no protest against him winning the MVP Cup since all the newspaper reporters voted for him.
    A. against him winning
    B. against he winning
    C. against the winning of
    D. against his winning
    E. against him having won

32. Neither Camerinda or Aimee knows how to speak French.
    A. or Aimee knows
    B. or Aimee knew
    C. nor Aimee knows
    D. nor Aimee know
    E. or Aimee know
33. If I were a Persian Prince, I would not want any other wife than you.
    A. were a
    B. was a
    C. had been a
    D. has been a
    E. would have been a
34. Because he was a popular lawyer, because he was widely respected throughout Illinois, and that he spoke so well at meetings, Lincoln was considered a very strong candidate.
    A. that he spoke
    B. in that he spoke
    C. although he spoke
    D. because he speaks
    E. because he spoke
35. All aspects of UNICEF strive to improve the lives of children.
    A. strive to improve
    B. strives to improve
    C. are intended to improve
    D. have striven to improve
    E. should have striven to improve
36. Appearing in Los Angeles for the first time, the Swedish star's popularity rose to celebrity elevations.
    A. Appearing
    B. As she appeared
    C. When she appeared
    D. Though she appeared
    E. As if appearing
37. The entire Los Angeles Community College District, including such large schools as L.A. Trade Tech, L.A. City College, L.A. Valley College, and L.A. Pierce College, derives from one school, L.A. City College.
    A. College, derives from
    B. College—derives from
    C. College; derives from
    D. College, derive from
    E. College, has gotten its derivation from
38. To quell the rising fears of American isolationism, it required that we establish new trade agreements with all of our trading partners.
    A. isolationism, it required that we
    B. ostracism, it required that we
    C. isolationism, we needed to
    D. isolationism, it was required that we
    E. isolationism, it needed us to
39. Sprawled lazily around the huge fireplace in the den, accounts of our most recent trips were described by each of us.
    A. accounts of our most recent trips were described by each of us.
    B. accounts narrating our most recent trips were told.
    C. we each described our most recent trips.
    D. we each told accounts that described our most recent trips.
    E. we each described and told accounts about our most recent trips.
40. Regardless of the possibility that the branch could break, the fireman began inching out toward the kitten.
    A. Regardless of
    B. Irregardless of
    C. Regarding
    D. Irregardless to
    E. Disregardless of

Question Type A (Usage)

DIRECTIONS: Some parts of each sentence below are underlined and lettered. Decide which underlined part is in error and mark its letter on your answer sheet. If you spot no errors, do not hesitate to mark the (E) No error choice. No sentence contains more than one error.

41. Myra and <u>myself</u> <u>were planning</u> to <u>get married</u> in August of the same year <u>we met</u>.
              A   B   C   D
    <u>No error.</u>
    E

42. The plans for the campus dedication <u>included a Dixieland band</u>, a chorus of <u>beautiful</u>
                                                     A   B
    <u>women dressed</u> as Vikings, a full orchestra, three keynote <u>speakers and</u> a <u>seven-course</u>
        B   C   D
    dinner. <u>No error.</u>
              E

43. My <u>immediate</u> family <u>includes</u> two <u>brother-in-laws</u>, a sister, two <u>children</u>, and my
           A   B   C   D
    wife. <u>No error.</u>
          E

44. <u>Neither</u> of the two <u>bystanders</u>, Rachel <u>or</u> Edith, had the composure to call the fire
       A   B   C
    department until long after the fire <u>had gone</u> out of control. <u>No error.</u>
                                                  D   E

45. After <u>tolerating</u> the distraction <u>for most</u> <u>of the seminar</u>, Professor Romero lost his
            A   B   C
    patience with <u>Maria filing</u> her nails. <u>No error.</u>
                    D   E

46. Either dried onion or cabbage <u>do</u> well <u>in this kind</u> of soup, but my <u>preference</u> is onion
                                        A   B   C
    because of the wonderful taste <u>it</u> contributes to the flavor. <u>No error.</u>
                                     D   E

47. In many of the <u>towns and small cities</u> of the United States, <u>they</u> still <u>have</u> <u>old-fashioned</u>
                          A   B   C   D
    town meetings where the people of the town make public policy. <u>No error.</u>
                                                                                  E

48. <u>Taking into account the rise in the cost of jet fuel</u>, the airline was <u>anything</u> but <u>profitable</u>;
                                    A   B   C
    in fact, <u>it was</u> almost insolvent. <u>No error.</u>
              D   E

49. <u>Etching</u> <u>is when</u> you pour acid <u>over an item</u> and <u>produce</u> a frosty texture on its surface.
       A   B   C   D
    <u>No error.</u>
    E

50. <u>Stop!</u> <u>that</u> ratchet <u>assembly</u> <u>is going</u> to fly apart. <u>No error.</u>
     A   B   C   D   E

Answers and Explanations: Test of Standard Written English

Question Type A

1. **E** The sentence is correct as it stands.
2. **D** Flowers smell *sweet*; the use of the adverb *sweetly* suggests that the flowers are performing the actions.
3. **C** The full phrase is *than he is*.
4. **B** *Hoaxes* needs to be plural because the radio program is cited as one of a memorable group of hoaxes.
5. **D** The past participle of the verb *freeze* is *frozen*.
6. **B** Items that are distinguishable as individual, and able to be counted separately, like chairs, take the pronoun *number* rather than *amount*.
7. **C** The word *watching* disturbs the parallel series of infinitives that structures the sentence, *to stay, to do,* and *to watch.*

8. **B** The verbs *lay*, "to place or put somewhere," and *lie*, "to rest in a horizontal position," are two different verbs. The past tense of *lay* is *laid*.
9. **D** Literally, "than *he was*."
10. **D** The correlatives *neither* and *nor* are used together, as are *either-or*.
11. **E** The sentence is correct as it stands. (*Driver* is a subject word as is *I*.)
12. **D** Literally, the last clause in the sentence reads, "...that neither *one* of your hypotheses *is* correct.."
13. **C** *One* of the tires *is* flat.
14. **E** The sentence is correct as it stands.
15. **D** The words *can't hardly* create a double negative.
16. **C** Literally, the impulse sent *them* back to San Francisco.
17. **B** Literally, a *box has been sent*.
18. **D** The object of the preposition takes the objective case, as in the prepositional phrase *between you and me*.
19. **E** The sentence is correct as it stands.
20. **C** The subject of the sentence is the noun *petition*, which is singular and therefore takes the singular verb *presents*.
21. **B** The class felt *bad*. In this case, *bad* is a predicate adjective modifying the subject *class*. If the adverb *badly* is used in this context, it modifies the verb *felt* and confuses the statement.
22. **A** The subject of the sentence is the singular pronoun *each*, which requires the singular verb *was combed*.
23. **C** The adverb *farthest* refers to physical distance, *further* to time or degree.
24. **D** Literally, *than I have been*.
25. **C** The subject *employee* is singular and so takes a singular pronoun such as *his* or *her*.

Question Type B

26. **D** In order to maintain a parallel sentence, the series it contains must be three adverbs, *quietly, cautiously,* and *slowly*.
27. **B** The more economical phrase is the simple *When it was time to speak*.
28. **D** Unless the subject *he* is included with the verb *reminisces*, the clause at the beginning dangles and suggests that the noun *tone* is engaged in reminiscence.
29. **E** The basic sentence from which this question is derived is *Food costs have risen during the past three decades*.
30. **C** *Lose* and *loose* are two different verbs.
31. **D** The word *winning* is a gerund, and therefore a noun which takes a possessive pronoun.
32. **C** The correlatives *neither* and *nor* are used together.
33. **A** The sentence is correct as it stands, containing a subjunctive verb in a contrary-to-fact statement.
34. **E** The past tense and the *because* clause are necessary to maintain the parallel series that structures this sentence.
35. **C** All other options illogically give the noun *aspects* the ability *to strive*.
36. **C** The other versions either have a dangling modifier which gives the noun *popularity* the ability to appear, or inappropriate transitional phrases.
37. **A** The sentence is correct as it stands. Other versions are either wordy or employ punctuation incorrectly.
38. **C** Only the version that uses the pronoun *we* as the subject of the main clause makes sense. The other versions contain dangling modifiers.
39. **C** The subject of the main clause must be the pronoun *we* if the sentence is going to make sense. Versions *D* and *E* are wordy.
40. **A** The sentence is correct as it stands. The other versions either make no sense or employ a non-existent word, *irregardless*.

Question Type A

41. **A** Reflexive pronouns must refer to words within the same sentence and so cannot be used as subjects or direct objects in sentences.
42. **C** Use commas to set off items in a series. (...three keynote speakers, and a seven-course dinner.)
43. **C** The plural of *brother-in-law* is *brothers-in-law*.
44. **C** The correlatives *neither* and *nor* are used together, as are *either-or*.

45. **D** The gerund phrase *filing her nails* is a noun and therefore requires a possessive pronoun, as in the phrase *Maria's filing her nails*.
46. **A** Literally, *either one does well*.
47. **B** The use of the pronoun *they* is incorrect without a previously stated antecedent.
48. **A** The participial phrase *Taking into account the rise in the cost of jet fuel* is incorrect because it is modifying the noun *airline*, a construction that is nonsensical. Airlines are inanimate corporate organizations which are incapable of taking anything into account.
49. **B** The conjunction *when* usually introduces a clause intended to modify a verb. It cannot modify a noun or a gerund like *etching*.
50. **B** The word *Stop!* Is an expletive and technically a sentence. The word *that* begins a new sentence.

CAAP MODEL

The CAAP (California Assessment of Academic Proficiency) Writing Skills Test at Hayward and San Jose is comprised of 72 questions given in a 40-minute span.

> **DIRECTIONS:** Most of the underlined sections in the following passages contain errors or inappropriate expressions. You are asked to compare each with the four alternatives in the answer column. If you consider the original version best, choose **A** or **F: NO CHANGE**. For each question, blacken the alternative on the answer sheet that you think best. Read each passage through before answering the questions based on it.

Consider this example:

Humdrum as life may seem, we all <u>had</u> dramatic
                                      1
moments, some comic, some tragic, as do people

we read about in novels.

1. **A.** NO CHANGE
   B. have had
   C. has
   D. have

Response D, *have*, is the correct choice, because the sentence is set in the present tense (note the tense of the verb *do* in the last clause). Choice C is also in the correct tense but does not agree in number with the subject "we."

Passage I

(1)

Typical diseases associated with overweight are

hypertension, or high blood pressure, atherosclerosis, or

fatty deposits in blood vessels, <u>which consequently for</u>
                                          1
<u>those reasons</u> restrict the flow of blood, and coronary
    1
heart disease. Other diseases occur far more often among

the overweight than <u>for those who have ordinary weight</u>,
                            2
including diabetes, respiratory ailments, gallbladder and

kidney diseases, and some kinds of cancer.

1. **A.** NO CHANGE
   B. which therefore in that manner
   C. which
   D. OMIT the underlined portion.

2. **F.** NO CHANGE
   G. among normal-weighted people
   H. others
   J. among persons with normal weight

(2)

Most all people who are trying to lose weight are
         3
doing so mainly for social reasons. In today's informed
society, being fat is no longer a symbol of good health
and prosperity, as they used to think; and it also keeps a
                        4
person from looking their best, as do, incidentally, being
                        5   6
underweight. For one thing, to be overweight is
     6   7
embarrassing, and even being only slightly overweight
can damage self-esteem, because having a good self-
image has been important to emotional well-being.
     8

Doctors now consider being able to keep one's weight
                       9
at a proper level one of the most important aspects of
preventive medicine, which attempts to keep people
healthy by preventing illness.

(3)

About 25 percent of the population is overweight, a
figure that makes obesity "one of the curses of
affluence" and, according to the American Medical
              10
Association, the nation's most crucial health problem.

(4)

Some slightly overweight people never seem to notice
their obesity, and they even look attractive to others.
     11

3. A. NO CHANGE
   B. Among those people
   C. Most people
   D. Most of those people

4. F. NO CHANGE
   G. as it once has been
   H. as was once thought to be
   J. as it once was

5. A. NO CHANGE
   B. his
   C. his or her
   D. her

6. F. NO CHANGE
   G. as is, incidentally, being underweight
   H. as does incidentally, being underweight
   J. as does, incidentally, being underweight

7. A. NO CHANGE
   B. being overweight
   C. being burdened with overweight
   D. being several pounds overweight

8. F. NO CHANGE
   G. could be important
   H. is important
   J. will be important

9. A. NO CHANGE
   B. knowing how to keep their weight
   C. knowing that one has kept his weight
   D. keeping one's weight

10. F. NO CHANGE
    G. and according
    H. and according,
    J. and; according

11. A. NO CHANGE
    B. obesity. And they
    C. obesity and they
    D. obesity; and they

Therefore, mortality rates among even the slightly obese are significantly higher than among persons in the same age group with normal weights. Insurance companies are well aware of the seriousness of obesity, and rank being overweight as a high-risk category. [13]

An overweight person is likely to be constantly tired and unable to do much. Eventually, obese people are simply unable to be active in any endeavor. Unfortunately, this lack of activity is not the only problem that comes with being overweight. Health problems begin to manifest themselves, especially as a person gets older and eventually approaches middle age. [15]

Passage II

A convincing way to prove the need for nurses is the long lines in hospital waiting rooms. An additional problem in most hospitals is the terrible food, which is usually prepared by contract service firms. One only has to pick up a newspaper or turn on the radio to be informed about the very critical shortage of skilled nurses. The argument then begins about responsibility for the shortage. [18] Without nurses, a hospital might as

12. **F.** NO CHANGE
    G. However,
    H. For this reason,
    J. Consequently,

13. Choose the sequence of paragraph numbers up to this point (paragraphs 1–4) that makes the structure of the passage most logical.
    A. NO CHANGE
    B. 1, 4, 3, 2
    C. 2, 3, 4, 1
    D. 4, 3, 1, 2

14. **F.** NO CHANGE
    G. approaching middle age.
    H. as a person gets older, approaching middle age.
    J. as a person approaches middle age.

15. The writer could most effectively strengthen the passage at this point by adding which of the following?
    A. Reports by life insurance firms linking weight and morbidity
    B. A list of euphemisms for *overweight* like "full-figured" or "pleasingly plump"
    C. A bibliography of diet books
    D. More specific details about what constitutes overweight, including height and weight comparisons

16. **F.** NO CHANGE
    G. is to point to the long lines in hospital waiting rooms.
    H. are the long lines in hospital waiting rooms.
    J. always has been the long lines in hospital waiting rooms.

17. **A.** NO CHANGE
    B. Place this sentence at the end of the paragraph.
    C. Place this sentence at the beginning of the paragraph.
    D. OMIT this sentence.

18. A quick scan of this passage shows it to be a summary argument in favor of more training facilities for nurses. In view of this fact, what kinds of further arguments would be appropriate in the rest of this paragraph?
    F. Detailed, exhaustive explanations
    G. No arguments at all
    H. Short, one-line summary arguments
    J. Long, emotional appeals

well pack away its sheets. <u>Yes, there are many nurses</u>[19] <u>licensed who are not in practice, but this tendency of nurses to "drop out" has always existed, and, yes, health care agencies which employ nurses, particularly hospitals, could improve, and are improving, working conditions but the fact remains that there are more vacant positions for nurses than there are available applicants.</u>[20]

[21] Hospitals have had to close wards and <u>they have had</u>[22] <u>to tell patients that they are unable to treat them</u> because of a lack of nursing staff. [23]

19. A. NO CHANGE
    B. OMIT this sentence.
    C. Move this sentence to end of paragraph.
    D. Move this sentence to beginning of paragraph.

20. F. NO CHANGE
    G. Although there are many nurses licensed who are not in practice, and although this tendency of nurses to "drop out" has always existed, and, yes, health care agencies which employ nurses, particularly hospitals could, and are improving working conditions but the fact remains that there are more vacant positions for nurses than there are available applicants.
    H. Yes, there are many nurses licensed who are not in practice, but this tendency of nurses to "drop out" has always existed. Yes, health care agencies which employ nurses, particularly hospitals, could improve, and are improving, working conditions. The fact remains that there are more vacant positions for nurses than there are available applicants.
    J. Because there are many nurses licensed who are not in practice, and because health care agencies, particularly hospitals are improving conditions, there are more vacant positions for nurses than there are available applicants.

21. The writer could most effectively strengthen his arguments at this point by adding:
    A. a daily log from a critical care nursing station in a large, municipal hospital.
    B. a summary of the vacant nurse positions in all of the city's hospitals.
    C. testimony from two or three patients in a large hospital.
    D. a list of inactive nurses which explains why each nurse is not working.

22. F. NO CHANGE
    G. turn them out
    H. turn away patients
    J. tell patients "no go"

23. The first paragraph suggests that it is representing both sides of an "argument." How could the argument be made more fair or evenhanded?
    A. Bolster the position that there is a critical shortage of nurses by giving statistics, pay scales, etc.
    B. Bolster the position that nurses are really in good supply by presenting numbers of nurses now available and of nursing students soon to be graduated.
    C. Bolster both positions with testimony of patients that have received adequate hospital care and patients that have received poor care.
    D. Bolster the position that nurses are really in good supply by compiling lists of registry applicants who have earned Master's Degrees in nursing.

According to the Los Angeles Hospital Council, there is a 20 percent vacancy for budgeted, registered nurse positions. Therefore, there is a ready-made job market for graduates with Associate Degrees in nursing. The employment and career opportunities are greater than other community college programs. Students all have jobs before graduation (contingent upon licensure) if they so desire. This is further demonstrated by the waiting lists of applicants for programs. [26]

The Associate Degree nursing programs are appealing to the disadvantaged individual who could not afford the expenses and other requirements of university programs. Associate Degree programs attract ethnic minorities, men, and older students who could not otherwise be served in the educational system. The Associate Degree nursing program provides disadvantaged people with a salable skill, thereby enabling them to enjoy a better way of life while meeting the nursing shortage which helps all members of the community. The health care profession has historically been represented by ethnic minorities, and a program at Los Angeles Mission College would help to correct this problem. [30]

Passage III

On the morning of June 8, 1988, Joyce McBride left her home to attend a garage sale. As she left, McBride locked her front door with a double dead-bolt lock which required a key either to open it from inside or outside.

24. F. NO CHANGE
    G. than still more
    H. than several more
    J. than those in other

25. A. NO CHANGE
    B. This need for a larger program
    C. This job glut
    D. This excess of jobs

26. Readers are likely to regard the passage as best described by which of the following terms?
    F. Inspirational
    G. Informative
    H. Persuasive
    J. Confessional

27. A. NO CHANGE
    B. has not been able to afford
    C. cannot afford
    D. up to now, could not afford

28. F. NO CHANGE
    G. men and older students
    H. men; older students
    J. men: older students

29. A. NO CHANGE
    B. shortage, a public service which
    C. shortage that
    D. shortage, a philosophy which

30. This passage is probably written for readers who:
    F. are patients in hospitals.
    G. are other community college instructors.
    H. are members of a hospital governing board.
    J. are members of a state licensure panel or other group likely to rule on whether a nursing school should be opened at L.A. Mission College.

31. A. NO CHANGE
    B. to open it from inside or outside either.
    C. to either open it from inside or outside.
    D. to open it from either inside or outside.

While McBride was away, her next-door neighbor, Peggy Frobush, looked out her bathroom window and saw William Goode standing by McBride's front door. Peggy had known Goode for years; he was a good friend of her son, Chuck, and had been living in his car parked outside the Frobushes' home. It had appeared to her that Goode had just closed McBride's front door behind him. Thinking a burglary had just taken place,

Peggy screamed, "Police!" She noticed at that moment that McBride's back door was open. Peggy, by the way, is an extremely attractive woman. [36] The police told McBride about the burglary upon her return home. Several items were missing, including a guitar, power tools, and jewelry. Police investigators discovered the front-door dead bolt shut and assigned as a cause the back door was the point of entry behind the house.

Later that morning, Chuck approached a neighbor of McBride and offered to sell a gold bracelet and necklace. Chuck left the jewelry with the neighbor, who returned the articles to McBride. These items were taken in the burglary. [39]

On July 15, 1988, Detective Bruno Pilsner interviewed Goode about the burglary. Goode told the detective he had been living in his broken-down car for

32. F. NO CHANGE
    G. Frobushe's home.
    H. Frobushes's home.
    J. Frobushes home.

33. A. NO CHANGE
    B. has appeared
    C. appeared
    D. appears

34. F. NO CHANGE
    G. screamed "Police"!
    H. screamed, "Police"!
    J. screamed "Police!"

35. A. NO CHANGE
    B. By the way, Peggy is an extremely attractive woman.
    C. Peggy is an extremely attractive women, by the way.
    D. OMIT this sentence

36. F. NO CHANGE
    G. Begin a new paragraph with the following sentence.
    H. Delete the rest of this paragraph.
    J. Place the rest of this paragraph at the beginning of the passage.

37. A. NO CHANGE
    B. theorized that
    C. laid that fact on
    D. put the saddle on the right horse that

38. F. NO CHANGE
    G. on the nether side of the house.
    H. OMIT the underlined portion.
    J. toward the rear of the house.

39. Is the use of the gold bracelet and necklace effective in this paragraph?
    A. No, because it does not give enough evidence to convincingly accuse Chuck.
    B. Yes, because Chuck had to sell the stolen goods right away in order to buy drugs.
    C. Yes, because this whole passage is about an actual case and attempts to report facts.
    D. No, because a person in Chuck's situation would not sell stolen goods to a neighbor.

several weeks, parking it outside the Frobushes' residence. <u>In working</u> on his car, Goode heard Chuck call to him from McBride's house. After walking to the front door, he saw his friend inside the residence. Chuck opened the front door and asked him to help take McBride's property, but Goode refused. He decided to leave when Peggy yelled for the police. [41]

After further investigation, Goode was interviewed again. <u>It was with no minor irritation that Detective Pilsner belabored</u> Goode's earlier version because the front door could not have been opened without <u>a key, he accused</u> Goode of planning the burglary with Chuck. Replying, "You are right," Goode told Pilsner the following story: Chuck, needing money to buy drugs, asked for Goode's help in burglarizing the McBride house. Goode agreed. Chuck planned to enter the house from the back and let Goode in through the front, <u>thus</u> he could not open the door. Goode turned to leave when he heard Peggy scream, and fled the area on foot.

At trial, Goode denied participating in the crime. He testified that Chuck approached him that morning, told him he needed money for drugs, and asked for Goode's help in carrying tools from the McBride house. Goode's final version of the story was that he refused to participate. [45]

40. F. NO CHANGE
    G. While working
    H. For working
    J. When working

41. Suppose that at this point the writer decided to add more information about the police department in this town. Would this addition be an appropriate one, and, if so, which of the following would be most relevant to the passage as a whole?
    A. A brief biography of Detective Pilsner and his family.
    B. A discussion of the structure of the local police department, including the duties of each branch.
    C. No addition would be appropriate. This is a very lean summary of a case; additional detail is not required.
    D. A summary of exceptional cases Detective Pilsner has helped to solve.

42. F. NO CHANGE
    G. Detective Pilsner was angry about
    H. Detective Pilsner pooh-poohed
    J. This time, Pilsner told Goode he did not believe

43. A. NO CHANGE
    B. a key, he accused
    C. a key. He accused
    D. a key; he accused

44. F. NO CHANGE
    G. but
    H. however
    J. nevertheless

45. This passage was probably written for readers who:
    A. are detective and mystery fiction buffs.
    B. are law enforcement students learning about criminal behavior.
    C. need summary details about this case for a subsequent discussion or determination.
    D. are avid readers and would especially appreciate the technique and style of this author.

Passage IV

(1)

The person or persons suing someone are called the PLAINTIFFS; the person or persons being sued are called the DEFENDANTS. Neither plaintiffs <u>nor</u> defendants may bring a lawyer to represent them in Small Claims Court.

46.
F. NO CHANGE
G. or
H. however or
J. and nor

(2)

<u>Having appeared on the Court Calendar</u>, the plaintiffs simply explain why they feel the defendant owes them the money they have asked for, and present any evidence or witnesses they can to help them prove their case. After <u>having heard</u> from both sides, the judge will decide who is right.

47.
A. NO CHANGE
B. When their suit comes before the judge,
C. When the court calendar determines the time of the hearing,
D. When the suit is brought before the court calendar,

48.
F. NO CHANGE
G. they spoke
H. he heard
J. hearing

(3)

Any person who is eighteen or older may file suit in Small Claims Court. A minor may do so only if he or she has a parent or guardian <u>and who is to come</u> with him when the suit is filed. The judges of Small Claims Courts are members of the Justice and Municipal Courts. They set aside certain days and times to hold Small Claims <u>Court which</u> may be different for each county.
[51]

49.
A. NO CHANGE
B. to have come
C. come
D. whom to come

50.
F. NO CHANGE
G. court, which
H. court that
J. court, whom

51. The writer could most effectively strengthen the passage at this point by adding which of the following?
A. A visual description of a typical small claims court
B. A description of some of the more unusual small claims suits in recent years
C. A few examples to illustrate the general points being made
D. Testimony from both defendants and plaintiffs of what they think of the Small Claims Court

(4)

The Small Claims is a special court in which an individual can sue another who owes him money. By the same token, the maximum amount of money litigants can collect is $2500. If the suing party's claim is larger, he may either speak to an attorney about taking the case to a higher court, or may accept the $2500 and give up any claim to the rest.

(5)

In some cases, plaintiffs must file their suit at the court located in the district where the defendant lives or works at. If, for example, the complaining party lives in Boston, but the store where a defective vacuum cleaner was bought is in Worcester, the plaintiff must file suit in Worcester. [58]

(6)

Unfortunately, there are usually no translators in Small Claims Court, so if either the plaintiff or the defendant does not speak English, it is advisable to bring along someone who can act as an interpreter. Also, due to the fact that there are very few night courts, litigants will almost always have to attend court during working hours. [60]

52. F. NO CHANGE
    G. are
    H. claims to be
    J. was

53. A. NO CHANGE
    B. her
    C. him or her
    D. them

54. F. NO CHANGE
    G. However,
    H. Furthermore,
    J. Granted that,

55. A. NO CHANGE
    B. partys'
    C. partys
    D. parties

56. F. NO CHANGE
    G. the defendant
    H. the plaintiff
    J. the judge

57. A. NO CHANGE
    B. has worked
    C. is working
    D. works

58. Suppose this passage were written for an audience that was familiar with the small claims court and other legal systems. Which of the following additions would be most relevant to the passage as a whole?
    F. A clear, *simple* enactment of a *typical* small claims case
    G. A recounting of several typical small claims actions, together with decisions rendered
    H. Discussions of fine points of law that have made some decisions very difficult to determine
    J. A detailed, step-by-step day in the life of a small claims judge

59. A. NO CHANGE
    B. owing to the fact that
    C. since
    D. in the light of the fact that

60. Choose the sequence of paragraph numbers that makes the structure of the passage most logical.
    F. NO CHANGE
    G. 6, 1, 4, 2, 3, 5
    H. 1, 4, 3, 5, 6, 2
    J. 4, 1, 2, 3, 5, 6

Passage V

(1)

Environmental issues appear frequently, especially in states where liberal groups are at odds with the establishment, in Nevada, for example, voters will be asked to withdraw from a five-state nuclear waste compact. Massachusetts will offer a measure that would ban the generation of electricity by nuclear plants that produce radioactive waste. Washington State voters will decide on the issue of whether to impose a tax on hazardous substances to help finance toxic waste cleanup. In general, throughout the nation, environmental initiatives are to be found everywhere, from bottle bills in Montana to surface-mine reclamation in South Dakota. Many other issues will be brought up by initiatives in this year's general elections. Several states are voting on new minimum wage levels, and at least three are considering measures mandating AIDS testing. Others are deciding such mixed-up issues as personal property taxes, cigarette and beer taxes, mandatory health insurance, tuition tax credits, state park expansion, farm animal abuse, safety inspections, funding of abortions, homeless shelters, gambling, seat belt laws, official language laws, and school financing. [67]

(2)

Initiatives are citizen-sponsored ballot measures that circumvent the normal legislative process of placing referendums before the public. Considered by most advocates to be an important and useful safety valve for popular action when citizens are frustrated by state and

61. **A.** NO CHANGE
    B. establishment. In
    C. establishment in
    D. establishment; In

62. **F.** NO CHANGE
    G. on a tax
    H. whether a tax
    J. whether to impose a tax

63. **A.** NO CHANGE
    B. surface mine reclamation
    C. surface, mine reclamation
    D. surface and mine reclamation

64. **F.** NO CHANGE
    G. Begin new paragraph with this sentence.
    H. OMIT the underlined portion.
    J. Place this sentence at beginning of paragraph as it now exists.

65. **A.** NO CHANGE
    B. diverse
    C. wildly arrayed
    D. confusing

66. **F.** NO CHANGE
    G. laws and schools
    H. laws, and school,
    J. laws and, school

67. Suppose at this point in the passage the writer wanted to add more information about the diversity of initiative subjects. Which of the following would be most relevant to the passage as a whole?
    A. Several detailed paragraphs about *one* really interesting initiative
    B. A history of the initiative process in England
    C. Two more paragraphs detailing more initiatives to be on ballots this year
    D. A summary of the election results

local legislatures, and which the initiative process has
                        ―――――――――
                              68
been a significant factor in elections throughout this nation's history. In the 1970s, for example, the subject of most initiative propositions was state endorsement of a national nuclear freeze. During the late '70s and early '80s, the popular subject initiatives involved the taxpayers' revolt. In contrast, however this year the
                    ―――――――――――――――
                           69
initiative targets are very diverse, ranging from

automobile insurance and tort liability and they also
                                       ―――――――――――
                                            70
address mandatory AIDS testing of prisoners. [71]
――――――――――――――
       70

(3)

Some initiative watchers are alarmed by recent "judicial activism" that has seen judges nix dozens of
                                              ―――
                                               72
voter-sponsored referendums because petitions used to place measures on the ballot were not printed in Spanish or other languages that reflect the demographic makeup of the state, as well as in English. Other reasons that initiatives have been declared invalid is that they address
                                       ――
                                       73

more than one subject, they intrude upon the domain of
              ―――――――――――
                   74

the legislature, or they bear too colorful a title. [75]

68. F. NO CHANGE
    G. and the
    H. the
    J. which the

69. A. NO CHANGE
    B. In contrast,
    C. Moreover,
    D. In addition,

70. F. NO CHANGE
    G. to mandatory
    H. they address mandatory
    J. addressing

71. Readers are likely to regard the passage so far as best described by which of the following terms?
    A. Romantic
    B. Journalistic
    C. Fantastic
    D. Persuasive

72. F. NO CHANGE
    G. deep-six
    H. pull the plug on
    J. strike down

73. A. NO CHANGE
    B. have been
    C. are
    D. has been

74. F. NO CHANGE
    G. subject; They
    H. subject. They
    J. subject they

75. Choose the sequence of paragraph numbers that makes the structure of the passage most logical.
    A. NO CHANGE
    B. 3, 2, 1
    C. 2, 1, 3
    D. 1, 3, 2

Answers and Explanations: CAAP Model

1. **C** The original version (A) and choice B are wordy. The underlined portion cannot be omitted (D) because the pronoun *which* is needed.
2. **J** Repetition of the preposition *among* creates a phrase that is parallel with *among the overweight*. In choice G *normal-weighted* is awkward.
3. **C** The other options are awkward or wordy.
4. **J** The only choice that employs the proper pronoun and tense is J. The others either use a pronoun without an antecedent (F), omit a necessary pronoun (H), or use a tense incompatible with the tense of the sentence (G).
5. **C** The use of *his* or *her* or any such reflection that there are two sexes is now expected in popular English. The antecedent, *person*, is singular; therefore the pronoun which refers to it must be singular.
6. **J** The verb (*does*) must agree with its singular subject (*underweight*). In addition, the parenthetical adverb *incidentally* must be set off by two commas.
7. **B** Actually, choices A and B would be equal options if it were not for the phrase *being...overweight* in the following clause, with which the subject must be parallel. Choices C and D are unnecessarily wordy.
8. **H** This paragraph is written in the present tense.
9. **D** The simple gerund phrase *keeping one's weight* is clear and direct; the other choices are wordy or awkward.
10. **F** The phrase *according to the American Medical Association* is parenthetical and must be set off by commas.
11. **A** Coordinate clauses need to be separated by a comma. The two clauses are short and closely related and so do not require a stronger mark of separation like a semicolon or a period.
12. **G** *However* is the only transitional phrase listed that signals the contrasting statement that follows.
13. **C** Paragraph 2 is clearly an introductory statement. Paragraphs 3, 4 and 1 each become more specific and concrete.
14. **J** This choice is the most economical; the others are either redundant (F and H) or use an incorrect verb form (G).
15. **D** More specific details that define overweight would support the general statements made in the passage; the other suggestions are not relevant to the subject.
16. **G** A *way* to prove the need for nurses is not the long lines, but rather *to point out* the long lines. As this sentence appears (F), the predicate is not compatible with the subject.
17. **D** While somewhat related, this sentence has no bearing on the main arguments of the passage.
18. **H** Longer, more detailed, or emotional explanations and arguments would depart abruptly from the concise, one-line strategy of the passage. Obviously, arguments are necessary (G).
19. **B** This sentence is more remote in relevance than first appears. There is no reference to a hospital without nurses.
20. **H** Too many data in one sentence can obscure its main point. This is the only choice that presents the facts concisely and logically in keeping with the pattern of the passage.
21. **B** A summary of unfilled positions is the only information listed here that is appropriate in this paragraph. The other information is at least vaguely off the topic.
22. **H** The infinitive phrase *(to) turn away patients* is economical; the other choices are wordy (F), contain a pronoun without an antecedent (G), or are inappropriate in style (J).
23. **B** This paragraph really does not represent the opposing opinion very well, and should support it with more detail.
24. **J** The opportunities are not greater than *programs*, but rather greater than opportunities *in* other programs.
25. **B** The pronoun *this* is almost never adequate alone; an explanatory noun is needed (*this need*). The other options supply nouns that are incompatible with the meaning of the sentence.
26. **H** From beginning to end, this passage is an attempt to persuade the reader that more nurses must be trained.
27. **C** The passage is written in the present tense.
28. **F** Separate three or more items in a series with commas.

29. **B** The pronoun *which* dangles without a clear antecedent like *service*. Meeting a shortage is not a philosophy (D).
30. **J** The target of this persuasive attempt to support the opening of another nursing school must be a body that can make such a decision.
31. **D** The conjunction *either* applies only to the prepositions *inside* and *outside*, and so must be placed just before them.
32. **F** The plural of the proper name *Frobush* is *Frobushes*; the possessive is formed by adding the apostrophe after the pluralizing *s*.
33. **C** The tense of this passage is the simple past.
34. **F** A quotation must be separated from the preceding text by a comma; the exclamation point should be placed *inside* the quotation marks because the quoted utterance is the exclamation.
35. **D** This sentence has no bearing on the meaning of the passage and should be removed.
36. **G** A new paragraph begins at this point because a new subject (the police investigation) and line of action begins.
37. **B** Only the verb *theorized* results in an economical and meaningful sentence; the other options are either wordy or slang.
38. **H** The prepositional phrase *behind the house* is redundant; the words *back door* already convey that meaning.
39. **C** The point is that the passage is about a real burglary; among the items taken (jewelry) were a gold bracelet and necklace. We have not been told that Chuck is on drugs (B), and people do not always act sensibly (D).
40. **G** The phrase *While working* works best; the other options suggest the wrong meaning.
41. **C** From the outset, this narrative appears to be a very lean summary of a case; embellishment would be inappropriate.
42. **J** The correct answer maintains the strict, economical style of the passage; the other options are either incompatible in style or misleading in what they say.
43. **C** Without a period or semicolon, the sentence becomes a comma splice or run-on sentence. The period and new sentence option is most appropriate because of the significant statement made in the second clause, that is, being charged formally with a crime.
44. **G** The conjunction at the beginning of the second clause must logically signal contrast. The words *but* and *however* do just that, but *however*, being a conjunctive adverb, requires a semicolon. *But* is the only possible choice.
45. **C** Because of its sparse, businesslike style, this passage is clearly one that provides background for a subsequent discussion on a point of law or trial procedure.
46. **F** The correlative conjunction *neither* means "not one of two," and is followed by *nor*; *either* means "one of two" and is followed by *or*.
47. **B** The correct choice presents a concise adverb clause properly modifying the following verb *explain*. There is no need for reference to the court calendar.
48. **J** Only the gerund *hearing* maintains the sequence of tenses; all other choices confuse the time of the sentence.
49. **C** Only the infinitive *come*, with the *to* elliptically omitted, sounds natural in this position; the other options are awkward.
50. **G** The adjective clause *which may be different for each county* is nonrestrictive, modifying *days and times*, and therefore must be set off by a comma.
51. **C** Some specific details illustrating the plea of a plaintiff, for example, would support the general points made in this passage. The inappropriate alternative answers stray far from the thesis of the passage.
52. **F** Other options either disagree with the subject in number (G), employ a verb that makes little sense (H), or use the wrong tense (J).
53. **C** The use of *him and her* or other such recognition that there are two sexes is not expected.
54. **G** A transitional word signaling contrast is needed here.
55. **A** A singular noun takes an apostrophe and *s* to indicate possession.
56. **H** Always use the principal noun enough to establish its presence in the sentence or paragraph.
57. **D** The correct answer (*works*) is parallel with the preceding verb (*lives*).
58. **H** Discussion of legal subtleties is compatible with the presence of a trained legal audience; the other options are either trivial or irrelevant.
59. **C** The correct choice is concise and clear; the others are awkward, wordy, or ungrammatical.
60. **J** Paragraph 4 begins with a clear, simple sentence explaining the point of the selection.

138   CSU — Writing Proficiency Exam

61. **B** The two clauses that join at this point contain enough substance to require a full-fledged sentence for each. Options A and C are wrong because they create run-on sentences. In D the word after the semicolon is incorrectly capitalized.
62. **J** The correct choice is clear and economical; the others are either wordy or result in an incomplete statement.
63. **A** Hyphenate a compound adjective that precedes the noun it modifies.
64. **G** The topic abruptly and completely moves from environmental initiatives to other initiatives, mandating a new paragraph.
65. **B** The adjective *diverse* is in keeping with the style of the passage and the sense of what follows.
66. **F** The conjunction *and* that marks the end of this long series of nouns needs itself to be preceded by a comma.
67. **C** Only the correct answer addresses the issue posed in the question. The other options deal with irrelevant material.
68. **H** The participial phrase preceding the underlined matter of this question is subordinate; *initiative process* is the subject of the sentence, and cannot be introduced by a relative pronoun.
69. **B** *In contrast* and *however* are both transitions indicating contrast; only one is required. The other options signal addition.
70. **G** The idiom *ranging from...to...* is completed by choice G. The other choices disrupt the structure of the sentence.
71. **B** The facts presented are simple and sparse; that is, the passage is journalistic.
72. **J** The phrase *strike down* is the only one compatible with the rest of the passage; the other options represent colloquial usage or slang and are therefore unsuitable.
73. **C** The subject (*reasons*) is plural, and so the verb must be; options B and D change the tense inappropriately.
74. **F** The three clauses at the end of this sentence are members of a series and require separation by commas.
75. **C** Paragraph 2 clearly introduces the subject, and must be the first paragraph in the passage.

LONG BEACH MODEL

The CSU Long Beach multiple-choice test consists of 60 questions to be answered in 80 minutes. There are four sections in the test, each featuring a different question design. Each question relates to a single type of error.

Section I

Question Type A (Proofreading and Editing)

DIRECTIONS: In each of the following, select the best answer from the four suggested.

1. What the structural engineer discovered is what I had dreaded for ___ house was sinking on the west side.
   A. years: the
   B. years, the
   C. years-the
   D. years; the
2. Malcolm refuses to eat ___
   A. meat however he will eat cheese and eggs.
   B. meat but he will eat cheese and eggs.
   C. meat; however, he will eat cheese and eggs.
   D. meat, however, he will eat cheese and eggs.
3. Once emptied by the garbage collectors ___
   A. , Mrs. Fillmore put the cans tidily behind the garage.
   B. the cans were put tidily behind the garage by Mrs. Fillmore.
   C. , the cans were put tidily behind the garage by Mrs. Fillmore.
   D. Mrs. Fillmore put the cans tidily behind the garage.

4. Do you know whether ___ going to keep the library or any of ___ collections of rare books and prints?
   A. their...her
   B. they're...it's
   C. there...its
   D. they're...its
5. Dad gave both ___ new cars for Christmas.
   A. he and I
   B. him and I
   C. him and me
   D. he and me

Question Type B (Proofreading and Editing)

DIRECTIONS: In each of the following items, three of the four sentences illustrate a similar type of error. Choose the correct sentence.

6. A. Scientists are working on DNA typing and to give all people a genetic "fingerprint."
   B. They have begun a systematic collection methodology and to collect genetic samples.
   C. They are working with military and federal agencies as so that they can build files.
   D. They hope to build a military file by 1995 and genetically identify every person in the armed forces.
7. A. Some of the brothers were embarrassed on hazing night.
   B. Each of the pledges were reluctant to go on stage with the propeller cap.
   C. Not one of them were willing to make a fool of themselves at a serious civic meeting.
   D. Finally a recruit from Fresno and his pledge brother was persuaded to make the dash.
8. A. Everyone must develop his own level of productivity and accomplishment, the drive to create and grow has to come from within.
   B. That inner spark has to be there, there is no use in planning and setting up priorities without it.
   C. The need to accomplish has complex roots; it is related to a person's self-concept and self-confidence.
   D. Even the creative drive can go awry, though it can become obsessive.
9. A. In the face of insurmountable odds, he worked like a Trojan and is able to finish his projects on time.
   B. He routinely starts early in the day and to finish late.
   C. In this manner, he met his objectives and earned the respect of his peers.
   D. Eventually, he will display what he has accomplished and gets high grades from his instructors.
10. A. Mabel loved sewing, cooking, and especially to ice skate on the local pond.
    B. George was willing to prove that he had collected the receipts from all the merchants, that he had then gone directly to the Central Bank, and that he has deposited the money directly.
    C. Mildred resented her neighbor's letting his dog have the run of her entire yard, playing loud music after 10:00 P.M., and tuning his cars' engines at 6:00 in the morning.
    D. Fred brought Lydia to the faculty party, to the new campus dedication, and they also went to the senior talent show.

Section II

Question Type C

DIRECTIONS: In this section, you are to rewrite sentences in your head after first viewing the original version. You will be told how to begin your new sentence. Keep in mind that your new sentence should have the same meaning and contain essentially the same information as the sentence given to you.

Consider this example:

> Never having been in the big city, Lettie cautiously walked the streets of New York in undisguised astonishment.
> Rewrite, beginning with Although...; the next words will be:
> A. she had never been
> B. she was cautious
> C. astonished
> D. she walked the streets
>
> The correct answer is **A**. Your rephrased sentence should read: "Although she had never been in a big city, Lettie cautiously walked the streets of New York in undisguised astonishment." A sentence that used one of the alternate phrases would either change the meaning of the original sentence, be poorly written, or be less effective.

11. For a non-profit form of business, it is necessary that the CEO's executive salary derive from the approved tax laws published by the Internal Revenue Service.
    Rewrite, beginning with The approved tax laws . . . the next words will be:
    A. for a non-profit form
    B. of the Internal Revenue Service
    C. are necessary
    D. derive a CEO's salary

12. Sometimes students are given much credit for personal, unsolicited scholarship; sometimes they are vilified by their instructors for delving into a scholarly enclave reserved for the esoteric.
    Rewrite, beginning with When students do research...; the next word(s) will be:
    A. in a subject
    B. they
    C. and are vilified
    D. they are given credit

13. Because much of the architectural work had already been completed, the Bakers were reluctant to tell the architect that they had decided to dispense with the west wing.
    Rewrite, beginning with Reluctant...; the next words will be:
    A. to do the architectural work
    B. to dispense
    C. to tell
    D. to complete

14. Aware of the additional dangers paratroopers routinely endure, John, nevertheless, enlisted in the 82nd Airborne Division.
    Rewrite, beginning with Although...; the next words will be:
    A. aware of the dangers
    B. enlisting in the 82nd Airborne
    C. enduring the additional dangers
    D. nevertheless aware of the

15. Each of the cadets was very nervous, because he was expected to pass the physical endurance test, as well as survive a formidable battery of psychological assessments.
    Rewrite, beginning with Expected...; the next word(s) will be:
    A. to test
    B. to survive both
    C. to assess
    D. cadets

Section III

Question Type D

DIRECTIONS: Choose the numbered sequence that rearranges sentences in logical paragraph order.

Consider this example:

> Choose the most logical order:
> 1. The arrow is also attracted by any mass of metal—a truck, your rifle, your helmet, and even electrical power lines.
> 2. The arrow on the compass points to magnetic north.
> 3. Thus, be sure to use your compass away from metal objects so it will not give a wrong reading.
> 4. Use your compass to determine or follow an azimuth.
>   **A.** 3, 1, 2, 4
>   **B.** 4, 2, 1, 3
>   **C.** 1, 2, 4, 3
>   **D.** 2, 4, 1, 3
>
> The correct answer is **B**. That sentence order would form the most logical paragraph, that is, the ideas follow a cause-effect sequence. Even though you might prefer a sequence not listed, you must select one of these four answers.

16. Choose the most logical order:
    1. The mouth-to-nose method is similar to mouth-to-mouth except that a rescuer blows into the nose while holding the lips closed with the hand at the chin.
    2. In some cases, it may be necessary to separate the casualty's lips to allow the air to escape.
    3. When mouth-to-mouth rescue breathing cannot be performed because the casualty has jaw injuries or spasms, the mouth-to-nose method may be more effective.
    4. The rescuer then removes his or her mouth to allow air to escape.
       A. 1, 2, 3, 4
       B. 4, 3, 1, 2
       C. 3, 1, 4, 2
       D. 2, 4, 1, 3

17. Choose the most logical order:
    1. Finally, there was a fireworks display that was simply spectacular.
    2. Then there was a spirited concert featuring patriotic marches and folk songs.
    3. First, the huge crowd came into the Bowl early, most of them gathering for a picnic lunch or a little wine and cheese before the concert.
    4. The Hollywood Bowl Fourth of July Concert was one of the real highlights of my visit to Los Angeles.
       A. 4, 3, 2, 1
       B. 1, 2, 3, 4
       C. 3, 4, 1, 2
       D. 3, 2, 4, 1

18. Choose the most logical order:
    1. He had recently separated from his wife of many years, who had given him ten children.
    2. In addition, he was engaged in a romantic liaison with a young woman only eighteen years old, Ellen Ternan.
    3. When Charles Dickens wrote *A Tale of Two Cities*, he had more on his mind than a split between two grand cities.
    4. He and Ellen frequently went to Paris for a weekend sojourn.
       A. 3, 4, 2, 1
       B. 3, 1, 2, 4
       C. 3, 2, 1, 4
       D. 1, 4, 2, 3

19. Choose the most logical order:
    1. First, they are not raising revenues enough to pay their teachers—by far their most important employee group—a living wage.
    2. Second, they are so inundated with non-English-speaking students that they are losing their ability even to teach basic skills.
    3. For that simple reason, they are losing their teaching force.

4. Most large school districts in America today are on the verge of collapse.
   A. 4, 1, 2, 3
   B. 4, 2, 1, 3
   C. 1, 2, 3, 4
   D. 3, 2, 1, 4

20. Choose the most logical order:
    1. Add to that the cost of school, food, transportation alone, and you begin to wonder how *any* single person in *any* circumstances makes it anyway.
    2. The mortgage payment alone frequently takes most of the husband's paycheck.
    3. It is becoming more and more difficult for a family to make it economically without both husband and wife working full time.
    4. The real answer is that many do not; they become street people.
       A. 1, 2, 3, 4
       B. 1, 4, 3, 2
       C. 3, 2, 1, 4
       D. 4, 1, 3, 2

Section IV

Question Type E

DIRECTIONS: Each of the following items presents a paragraph in which a sentence is missing. Read each paragraph and then choose from the four sentences that follow it, the one that is most suitable as the missing sentence.

Consider this example:

> "Good words are worth much and cost little." _____ It is a widely accepted fact that articulate, direct speakers, the people with just the right word for their statement, are the people who succeed in all endeavors today, in business, in science, in the humanities. We all owe ourselves no less than a good start in the lifelong habit of vocabulary development.
> **A.** The practice of speech reaps benefits in many ways, not the least of which is the ability to persuade your fellow man.
> **B.** A good dictionary helps sharpen your sense of nuance and precision.
> **C.** The poet George Herbert made this observation in the seventeenth century, but his meaning is probably truer now than ever before.
> **D.** Good words are valuable and cheap.
>
> The correct answer is **C** because it places the quotation that begins the paragraph properly in the context of the discussion and gives it purpose. The other sentences ignore the quotation.

21. *Frankenstein* is an example of the Gothic novel popular in Mary Shelley's day. It is characterized by a somber Gothic setting, remote and distant time and locale, and usually some psychological aberration on the part of the protagonist. _____ He seemed excessively concerned with his own feelings and emotions, his reasons for undertaking the creation of another being, and the personal intensity that defied his own control.
    A. Usually there is an ancient castle with forbidden vaults and chambers.
    B. It is clear that Frankenstein's *mind* is one of the main focal points of the story.
    C. The gothic background also highlights the peril of the townspeople.
    D. Notre Dame was an example of an ancient Gothic cathedral.

22. Many special activities or groups have their own special language out of necessity. At times, however, such esoteric language begins to feed upon itself; _____. Unfortunately, the language of government, business, science, and even the arts is often designed to impress the general public rather than to communicate clearly.
    A. its perpetrators form complex-sounding phrases where plain English would be more appropriate.
    B. its perpetrators will have formed complex-sounding phrases where plain English would be more appropriate.
    C. it perpetrators do much special research that results in exciting innovations that improve the quality of life.
    D. its perpetrators, by relying on a special vocabulary, strengthen the universal language for all people in all groups.

23. Not all writers are pessimistic about man's future. Recurrently, throughout literary history, authors have written of a better future for us all. In a time of war and social upheaval (1516), Sir Thomas More wrote his *Utopia* (the word means "no place" in Greek), an essay romance describing an imaginary commonwealth in which political organization, education, religion, and industry approach perfection. _____ Hope and optimism about the future of man typify Francis Bacon's *New Atlantis* (1626), Thomas Hobbe's *Leviathan* (1651), and H.G. Wells's *A Modern Utopia* (1905).
    A. Similarly, Edward Bellamy's *Looking Backward* is about a man who slept for about 113 years, awakening to a bright, modern world.
    B. Similarly, Edward Bellamy wrote *Looking Backward* in 1888, another era of spiritual and social disruption.
    C. Similarly, *Looking Backward* is about an urban Rip Van Winkle.
    D. Similarly, Edward Bellamy predicted in his *Looking Backward* in 1888 that there would be another era of spiritual and social disruption.
24. If he is inside a foxhole during a nuclear attack, a soldier should take protective actions. A blast wave can enter the foxhole with great force, and the debris it carries can cause injury. Lying face down on the ground offers worthwhile protection. The best position, however, is on the back with knees drawn up to the chest. _____. Bulky equipment such as packs or radios can be stored in an adjacent pit.
    A. This belly-up position might seem less dignified, but the more radiation-resistant arms and bent legs will not be evident outside the foxhole at any rate.
    B. This belly-up position might seem less vulnerable, and the less radiation-resistant arms and bent legs will probably not protect the head and trunk.
    C. This belly-up position might seem vulnerable, but the more radiation-resistant arms and bent legs will protect the head and trunk.
    D. This belly-up position might seem less useful; nevertheless, the head and trunk need some cover.
25. New findings concerning the health risks to nonsmokers posed by public smoking are strong evidence that we need laws to protect nonsmokers. Nonsmokers should not be subjected to cigarette smoke at all, anywhere. They should not be put in the position of constantly battling the excesses of thoughtless smokers if they are outspoken about their rights. _____. Smokers have to face the fact that they are free to put themselves at risk, but they are not free to subject anyone else to their deadly smoke.
    A. And they should not breathe fumes because they are meek.
    B. Nor should they be put in a position of arguing with people who are also breathing deadly fumes because they want to.
    C. Nor should he protest too much about what has been considered a civil right for years.
    D. Nor should they be put in the position of breathing fumes that have been proven deadly to them just to avoid making a scene.

Answers and Explanations: Long Beach Model

Question Type A

1. **A** Use a colon as a signal to call attention to what follows.
2. **C** Always set off conjunctive adverbs such as *however* with semicolons.
3. **C** Set off introductory phrases and clauses with a comma. Versions A and D contain dangling modifiers.
4. **D** *They're* is the contraction for *They are*; *its* is a possessive pronoun and does not need an apostrophe.
5. **C** The objective pronouns *him* and *me* are indirect objects in this sentence.

Question Type B

6. **D** All the other sentences contain errors in predication; the sentences begin one way, and continue with a different, incompatible structure.
7. **A** All of the other sentences have a subject that disagrees in number with the main verb of the sentence.
8. **C** All of the other sentences contain comma splices, or two clauses improperly joined together with a comma.
9. **C** All of the other sentences contain awkward and ungrammatical shifts in tense.
10. **C** All of the other sentences contain an unparallel series.

Question Type C

11. **A** Your new sentence would read: *The approved tax lax laws for a non-profit form of business published by the Internal Revenue Service are necessary for deriving the CEO's executive salary.*
12. **A** The final sentence is, *When students do research in a subject their instructors consider a scholarly enclave, they are sometimes vilified, and sometimes given much credit.*
13. **C** The final sentence is, *Reluctant to tell the architect, who had already completed much of the architectural work, the Bakers decided to dispense with the west wing.*
14. **A** The final sentence is, *Although aware of the dangers paratroopers routinely endure, John enlisted in the 82nd Airborne Division.*
15. **B** The final sentence is, *Expected to survive both a physical endurance test as well as a formidable battery of psychological assessments, each of the cadets was very nervous.*

Question Type D

16. **C** The order of this paragraph is sequential, each phase of the resuscitation process logically occurring before the next.
17. **A** The order here is chronological, beginning with a general statement, and then continuing with the three events that occurred in straightforward order.
18. **B** The order in this paragraph is chronological, beginning with an introductory statement, and following with three sentences clearly cued by transitional words and plain logic.
19. **A** The order of this paragraph is causal; after the introductory statement of the problem, two of the three sentences are naturally cued by transitional phrases (*First, Second,*). Sentence 3 is easily recognized as the concluding statement.
20. **C** The order of this paragraph is causal; after the introductory statement of the problem (sentence 3), the order of the three is logically determined (*mortgage payment*, then *school, food, transportation*). The statement about the consequence (*street people*) follows logically.

Question Type E

21. **B** The tip-off is the pronoun *he* in the sentence following the blank space. Only choice B provides an antecedent.
22. **A** Only choice A fits. Choice B employs an incompatible tense; choices C and D are illogical, running contrary to the train of thought introduced early in the paragraph.
23. **A** Only this choice continues and moves forward the prevailing theme in the paragraph, that not all writers are pessimistic about the future of humanity.
24. **C** The alternate choices are considerably less logical.
25. **D** Choice D is the most natural choice; it expresses a counterpoint to the sense of the previous sentence.

10 English Review and Practice

English usage and mechanics are governed by a set of consistent, logical rules called Standard American English. English has evolved its punctuation, usage, and mechanics to represent these logical rules, to reveal the locations of subjects and verb structures in sentences, to indicate subordination and coordination, to show insertion of required or helpful information, to keep track of parallel units, to mark introductory and transitional elements, and to indicate where sentences end so new ones can begin. Understanding the logic of punctuation and usage is equal to creating logical and clear ideas when you write, for the first serves as a tool to carry out the second. (See the index for locations of definitions of these terms in this manual.) This chapter is dedicated to a comprehensive review of those rules, along with their exceptions, and includes some review exercises to help you determine whether it's all "sinking in." Break this chapter up into bites, and concentrate on your error areas first.

In addition, those of you who will be taking a multiple-choice test along with your writing assessment have a double reason to read and study this chapter carefully. These tests are quite straightforward, not tricky or devious. They seek to measure your ability to recognize clear and meaningful prose, and to identify word combinations that are either incorrect or less effective than others.

If you feel unsure of your prose "ear" (the language sense you've developed over the years), your best strategy is to review this chapter several times. As you examine each section, think of the materials presented to you as a general review of problem areas, rather than as specific data to memorize. The English language has too many options to commit to memory. In each lesson, try to see the general rule and its purpose.

USAGE/MECHANICS

Punctuation

The Comma

Among its many functions, the comma is used to set off independent clauses, items in a series, coordinate adjectives, parenthetical expressions, and nonrestrictive (helpful, but not essential) phrases or clauses.

Use a comma to separate independent clauses joined by a coordinating conjunction (*and, but, for, or, nor,* or *yet*).

EXAMPLES: He wanted to be a salesman, but he found no jobs were available.
The people refused to send their children to school, and the school building stood empty the entire year.

Be sure you understand that this rule applies to the joining of *independent clauses*, that is, complete sentences. The use of the coordinating conjunction to join compound subjects (*Clinton* and *Dole* participated in a town meeting), pairs of phrases (The food at that restaurant is prepared *without care* and *without taste*), compound verbs (Phil *ran* the office and *acted* as athletic director), or the like, requires omitting the comma.

Use commas to separate all items in a series.

EXAMPLES: Friendly, small, and innovative are adjectives that accurately characterize this college.
He went to the basement, set the trap, and returned to the kitchen to wait.

Use a comma to separate coordinate adjectives modifying the same noun.

EXAMPLES: He washed his new, black, shiny pickup.
Himalayan cats have long, silky, heavy fur.

To test whether adjectives are coordinate, reverse their order or insert *and* between them. If the phrase still makes sense, they are coordinate adjectives and require a comma. The first example makes sense using either method: *shiny, black, new pickup,* or *new and shiny and black pickup.*

Non-coordinate adjectives have a special relationship with the nouns they modify. To some degree, they create a word group that itself is modified. They should not be preceded by commas.

EXAMPLE: They all admired the tall, powerful *football player*.

In this sentence, *football* is a non-coordinate adjective, different from the coordinate adjectives *tall* and *powerful*. You cannot put *and* between *powerful* and *football* nor can you move the word *football*. Other examples of non-coordinate adjectives are *doll* house, *art* museum, *computer* science, and *wheat* bread.

Use a comma to set off an introductory phrase or clause from the main clause.

PARTICIPIAL CLAUSE: Having spent his last penny, Luster tried to borrow a quarter from his boss.
PREPOSITIONAL PHRASE: At the beginning of each game, a noted singer gives his rendition of "The Star-Spangled Banner."
ADVERBIAL CLAUSE: When the composer was finished with the prelude, she began work on the first movement.

Use a pair of commas to indicate inserted nonrestrictive (amplifying or explanatory) phrases and clauses within a sentence.

EXAMPLES: Mary Jennings, who was my best friend, dropped the class.
The first offer on the Blake house, which had been on the market for almost a month, was very disappointing.

Be sure to distinguish between these *nonrestrictive* interrupters and the *restrictive modifiers*, which are *not* set off by commas. Nonrestrictive modifiers add information but do not limit or change the meaning of the sentence. Note how the meaning changes when the clause is restrictive.

RESTRICTIVE: The young woman who was my best student dropped the class.

The young woman is now identified as the best student. Here is another example of a restrictive clause:

EXAMPLE: Cardiac patients who have artificial valve implants are required to take anticoagulants for the rest of their lives. (only those with implants)

Use a comma to set off nonrestrictive phrases and clauses that follow the main clause.

EXAMPLES: Jessica wanted to see the ice show, not the circus.
The captain maneuvered the tugboat, taking care to maintain a safe distance from the tanker.

Use commas to insert an appositive. (An appositive is a noun or noun phrase that renames or explains the noun it follows.)

EXAMPLE: The novel, a mystery about a secret island off the Washington coast, was an instant bestseller.

Use commas to respect names in direct address. (Names in direct address identify the ones being spoken to.)

EXAMPLE: Excuse me, Beth, but aren't you late for your tennis lesson?

A comma can indicate an omitted word or phrase.

EXAMPLE: The Capitol Bank is located in a shopping mall; the Investors Bank, in the heart of town. (The verb phrase "is located" is implied by the last comma.)

A comma is sometimes needed for clarity.

EXAMPLES: Ever since, we have taken the plane rather than the train.
In May, Marcia went to Washington, D.C.

PRACTICE EXERCISE

Decide whether the punctuation is correct or incorrect at each numbered point in the following paragraph. Then place a check in the proper column.

CORRECT   INCORRECT

_____   _____   1. When a writer begins a story﹐he must start
_____   _____   2. the pages smoking right away﹐not bore the
_____   _____   3. reader with verbiage about setting﹐
_____   _____   4. characterization, and theme. The
_____   _____   5. author must present a protagonist, and
_____   _____   6. an antagonist﹐and he must also give
_____   _____   7. them a cause worth arguing over. The
_____   _____   8. complication, a series of battles the
_____   _____   9. protagonist always loses, comes next
_____   _____   10. just before the crisis, to end all crises. The climax is
_____   _____   11. the long-awaited, conclusive, high point of the tale.
_____   _____   12. There cannot be art without form, and there cannot be
          form without businesslike
_____   _____   13. craft. Any writer, who believes art flows
_____   _____   14. from emotion alone, is not likely to write
_____   _____   15. the kind of disciplined, organized short
_____   _____   16. story, that reflects the real world.

ANSWERS AND EXPLANATIONS

1. INCORRECT. An introductory clause is set off by a comma.
2. INCORRECT. Set off a nonrestrictive phrase that follows the main clause.
3. INCORRECT. Use commas to separate items in a series.
4. CORRECT. See explanation, item 3.
5. INCORRECT. Pairs of words (here, the compound objects *protagonist* and *antagonist*).
6. INCORRECT. Independent clauses linked by a coordinating conjunction are separated from each other by a comma.
7. CORRECT. The phrase *worth arguing over* is restrictive (defines *cause*) and should not be separated from the main clause by a comma.
8. CORRECT. Interrupters, in this case a nonrestrictive appositive, are set off by commas.
9. INCORRECT. Nonrestrictive concluding phrases are set off by commas.
10. INCORRECT. The infinitive phrase *to end all crises* is restrictive (defines *crisis*) and should not be set off by a comma.
11. INCORRECT. The adjective *high* in the phrase *high point* is not a coordinate adjective and should not be preceded by a comma.
12. CORRECT. Use a comma to separate independent clauses joined by a coordinating conjunction.
13. INCORRECT. The adjective clause *who believes art flows from emotion alone* restricts the meaning of the word *writer* to those writers who hold the same belief. It should not be set off by commas.
14. INCORRECT. See explanation, item 13. This is the second comma of the pair used mistakenly to set off the adjective clause.
15. CORRECT. The adjective *short* in the phrase *short story* is not a coordinate adjective. It should not be preceded by a comma.
16. INCORRECT. The adjective clause *that reflects the real world* is restrictive (directly defines *short story*) and should not be set off by a comma.

The Semicolon

The semicolon is generally used to link independent clauses in a sentence, without the use of coordinating conjunctions. Most often, it is used between related ideas that require punctuation weaker than a period, but stronger than a comma. As a second function, the semicolon can divide three or more items in a series when the items themselves contain commas.

Use a semicolon between related independent clauses not joined by a coordinating conjunction. (The independent clauses must relate directly to a single subject.)

EXAMPLES: A mature male gorilla may be six feet tall and weigh 400 pounds or more; his enormous arms can span eight feet.
New York has twelve major stadiums; Los Angeles has fifteen.

Use a semicolon between independent clauses joined by a conjunctive adverb.

Frequently, two independent clauses are joined, not by a coordinating conjunction, but by a transitional word (conjunctive adverb) introducing the second clause. A semicolon must be used between the clauses, because these transitional words (*accordingly, also, consequently, finally, furthermore, however, indeed, meanwhile, nevertheless, similarly, still, therefore, thus,* and the like) are *not* coordinating conjunctions.

EXAMPLE: A female coyote will not bear pups if her diet consists of fewer than fifty rodents a week; thus, Mother Nature achieves a population balance.

Use a semicolon to separate coordinate clauses if the clauses themselves have commas.

EXAMPLE: The warranty on the car covered extensive repairs to the electrical system, front end, transmission, fuel injection system, and valves; but the amount of time and inconvenience involved in returning each time to the dealer cannot be ignored.

Use a semicolon to separate items in a series when the listed items themselves contain internal punctuation.

Normally, three or more items in a series are set off by commas; however, when they are made more complex by commas and other punctuation, they are separated by semicolons.

EXAMPLE: The trio was composed of a cellist named Grosz, who had been a European virtuoso for many years; a pianist named Rosen who had won a major music festival in 1954, 1955, and 1958; and a violinist named Struik who had studied in Budapest, Vienna, and Munich.

PRACTICE EXERCISE

Each of the following sentences contains a numbered punctuation mark. Decide whether the mark is correct or should be changed to a semicolon. Then check the appropriate space to the left.

CORRECT   INCORRECT

_____   _____   1. He hit the ball well, however, he was not much of a
                              1
                       fielder.

              2. He had played his entire repertoire: a short piece by
                 Mozart that, in spite of its difficulty, was his favorite
                 sonata; a prelude by Liszt that once had caused an
                 audience to erupt in cheers, in spite of the fact that he
                 was not finished, and finally a mazurka by Brahms that
                                           2
_____   _____   was popular with musicians, composers and the
                 general audience alike.

              3. The movie had segments unsuitable for children,
                 including violent scenes, nudity, and inappropriate
                 language, but the general theme was inspirational.
                              3
_____   _____   4. Life is hard work; life can be a pleasure.
                                   4

ANSWERS AND EXPLANATIONS

1. **INCORRECT.** When a transitional word (conjunctive adverb) is used between clauses, the clauses must be separated by a semicolon.
2. **INCORRECT.** This sentence contains a series of items, each a noun modified by an adjective clause, and each containing commas. They should be separated from each other by semicolons.
3. **INCORRECT.** The general rule is to use a comma to separate independent clauses joined by a coordinating conjunction. However, when the clauses themselves contain a number of commas, a semicolon is used for clarity.
4. **CORRECT.** A semicolon is used to separate related independent clauses not linked by a coordinating conjunction.

The Colon, Hyphen, and Apostrophe

THE COLON

The colon is a signal that something is to follow: a rephrased statement, a list or series, or a formal quotation. Use a colon in a sentence if you can logically insert *namely* after it.

Use a colon only at the end of a complete sentence to show anticipation—that is, to show that amplifying details follow, such as a list, a series of items, a formal quotation, or an explanation.

EXAMPLES: Of all the gauges in an airplane cockpit, three are crucial: the altimeter, the gas gauge, and the crash-warning indicator.
After five minutes of silence, the actor uttered those famous words: "To be or not to be; that is the question."
A popover has four common ingredients: flour, milk, salt, and butter.

Problems that occur in the use of the colon usually result from the following lapses:

1. A colon incorrectly follows an incomplete sentence.

    INCORRECT: Tasks that I must complete today: mow the lawn, read two chapters of history, and tidy my room.
    CORRECT: I must complete several tasks today: mow the lawn, read two chapters of history, and tidy my room.

2. A colon incorrectly separates a second part of a sentence that *must* flow directly from the first part.

    INCORRECT: In updating my computer, I added: a hard disk, a laser printer, and a fine-resolution monitor. (The colon separates the verb from its direct objects.)
    CORRECT: In updating my computer, I added some new components: a hard disk, a laser printer, and a fine-resolution monitor.
    ALSO CORRECT: In updating my computer, I added a hard disk, a laser printer, and a fine-resolution printer.

3. More than one colon appears in a sentence.

    INCORRECT: The success of the action depended upon three variables: that the weather would hold out, that the supplies would arrive on time, and that the enemy would be short on three things: planes, ammunition, and food.
    CORRECT: The success of the action depended on three variables: that the weather would hold out, that the supplies would arrive on time, and that the enemy would be short on planes, ammunition, and food.

HYPHEN

The hyphen has two main uses: to divide syllables at the end of a line and to link words in certain combinations. It is also used in compound numbers from twenty-one to ninety-nine.

Hyphenate a compound adjective (an adjective made up of two or more words) when it precedes the noun it modifies. The hyphen is ordinarily not used when the words follow the noun.

EXAMPLES: She wore a well-used raincoat.
            BUT
Her raincoat was well used.
The past-due bill lay unnoticed behind the couch.
The bill, past due, lay unnoticed behind the couch.

NOTE: A compound adjective with an adverbial *-ly* modifier is never hyphenated: the *poorly designed* interchange. When the *-ly* modifier is an adjective, a hyphen is properly used: a *friendly-looking* dog.

APOSTROPHE

In addition to indicating possession, the apostrophe is used to take the place of omitted numbers (class of '87) and omitted letters or words in contractions (wasn't [was not], o'clock [of the clock], and sometimes to indicate plurals (A's, I.D.'s).

Use an apostrophe to show the possessive case of nouns and indefinite pronouns.

1. The possessive case of singular nouns (either common or proper) is indicated by adding an apostrophe and an *s*.

EXAMPLES: George's speech, the senator's campaign, anyone's opinion, the boss's office, Charles's book.

2. The possessive case of plural nouns ending in *s* is formed by adding only the apostrophe.

EXAMPLES: the girls' softball team, the waitresses' union, the Harrisons' antique cars.

NOTE: Irregular plurals, such as *men* or *children*, form the possessive by adding an apostrophe and an *s*: men's, children's.

A common error is to confuse possessive pronouns and contractions, particularly *its* and *it's* (meaning *it is*), *their* and *they're (they are)*, and *whose* and *who's (who is)*. Possessive pronouns have no apostrophe.

Subject Pronoun + To Be	vs.	Possessive Pronoun
I am = I'm		My/mine
We are = we're		Our
You are = you're		Your/yours
He is = he's		His
She is = she's		Her/hers
They are = they're		Their/theirs
It is = it's		Its (belonging to it—possessive built-in)
Who is = who's		Whose

PRACTICE EXERCISE

Decide whether the punctuation at each numbered point is correct or incorrect. Then place a check in the proper column.

CORRECT   INCORRECT

Into the circus arena paraded all the

_____   _____   1. performers and animals; first the
                       1
_____   _____   2. high stepping horses and bareback riders, then the
                       2
                    lumbering elephants with their trainers, followed by

                    the cartwheeling clowns and the

_____   _____   3. brightly costumed trapeze artists.
                       3
_____   _____   4. Louis's expertise at skateboarding amazed his friends.
                       4

		5. The long awaited furniture finally
		5
		6. arrived at the Jameses house.
		6
		In saving a threatened species, a basic
		7. step is: the study of it's diet, mating and
		7 8
		8. reproductive processes, range patterns, and
		social behavior.

ANSWERS AND EXPLANATIONS

1. INCORRECT. Use a colon, not a semicolon, to introduce a list after a complete statement.
2. INCORRECT. Hyphenate a compound adjective that occurs *before* the noun.
3. CORRECT. Do not hyphenate a compound adjective if its first member is an adverb ending in *-ly*.
4. CORRECT. To form the possessive, add an apostrophe and an *s* to a singular noun.
5. INCORRECT. See explanation, item 2.
6. INCORRECT. To form the plural possessive of a proper name, add an apostrophe to the plural (Jameses').
7. INCORRECT. A colon should not be used if it separates essential parts of a sentence (the verb *is* should not be separated from its object, *the study of...*).
8. INCORRECT. The possessive personal pronoun *its* does not take an apostrophe.

The Dash, Question Mark, and Exclamation Point

DASH

The main function of the dash, like parentheses, is to enclose emphasized information within a sentence. Dashes are more forceful and should be used sparingly, since they highlight the ideas and items they enclose.

Use dashes to indicate hesitation, or a sudden break in thought or sentence structure, or to set off appositives and other explanatory or parenthetical elements. The dash adds emphasis to any part of a sentence that can be separated from the rest of the sentence.

EXAMPLE: The skydiver—in spite of his broken leg—set a new record for endurance.

Some specific uses of the dash follow:

1. To interrupt continuity of prose

EXAMPLE: "I really can't tolerate—Well, never mind."

2. To emphasize appositives

EXAMPLE: The items she had asked for in the new car—tape deck, mileage computer, stick shift—were all included.

3. To set off phrases or clauses containing commas.
When a modifier itself contains commas, dashes can make its boundaries clear.

EXAMPLE: General Motors—which has manufactured tanks, cannons, and mobile cranes—has always been far more than an automobile assembler.

4. To set off parenthetical elements

EXAMPLE: The child was sitting—actually sprawling—at his desk.

QUESTION MARK

A question mark indicates the end of a direct question. A question mark in parentheses signals doubt or uncertainty about a fact such as a date or a number.

Use a question mark after a direct question.

EXAMPLES: When are we going to eat?
Ask yourself, what are the odds of winning?
(It is also correct to capitalize the word *what*.)

A question mark in parentheses may be used to express doubt.

EXAMPLE: The Dean's notes, published in 1774 (?), are considered the novel's origin.

NOTE: The use of the question mark as a mark of irony or sarcasm is not usually considered proper: The superintendent's important (?) announcements took all morning.

The question mark is unlikely to cause you trouble on the English test. Problems mainly occur (a) because of failure to distinguish between *direct* and *indirect* questions (an *indirect* question is always followed by a period: My friend asked why I didn't have my car.) or (b) because of mistaken combinations of question marks with other punctuation marks. A question mark should never be combined with a comma, period, exclamation point, or other question mark. When quoting someone's question, keep the question mark inside the quote marks.

EXCLAMATION POINT

An exclamation point is an indicator of strong *emotional* feelings, such as anger, joy, shock, surprise, or fear. It may also be used to express irony or emphasis. Like the dash, it should be used sparingly.

Use an exclamation point after a command, an interjection, an exclamation, or some other expression of strong emotion, which appears only rarely in GWAR essays.

COMMAND: Stop!
INTERJECTION: Wow! Fire! Help!
EMOTIONAL EXPRESSION: Don't tell me you did it again! How wonderful!

An exclamation point should not be used with commas, periods, other exclamation points, or question marks.

PRACTICE EXERCISE

Decide whether the punctuation at each numbered point is correct or incorrect. Then place a check in the proper column.

CORRECT   INCORRECT

_____   _____   1. The tornado headed—no, *hurtled*—our way.

_____   _____   2. The doctor—an imposter, actually—cleared his throat.

_____   _____   3. The book—which was expensive—had been his favorite for many years.

_____   _____   4. Don't tell me you're leaving already.

_____   _____   5. Is this the building you want to study!

_____   _____   6. Mr. Williams asked when I could rake his lawn?

7. Last Tuesday, I'll never forget it, was the first time we
   saw Michael Jordan play.

8. The famous diva—who had performed in such eminent
   opera houses as the Met, LaScala, and Covent Garden—
   was not willing to sing at our school.

ANSWERS AND EXPLANATIONS

1. CORRECT. Dashes can be used to signal a dramatic or emphatic shift in tone.
2. CORRECT. Dashes can be used to emphasize an appositive.
3. INCORRECT. Commas, not dashes, should be used to set off simple adjective clauses such as this one. Remember, though, that dashes *can* be used to set off adjective and other clauses that contain commas or other marks of punctuation.
4. INCORRECT. An exclamation point is called for here, to show dismay.
5. INCORRECT. This sentence is a direct question and requires a question mark.
6. INCORRECT. An indirect question takes a period, not a question mark.
7. INCORRECT. Use dashes to signal an abrupt change of thought.
8. CORRECT. Nonrestrictive clauses that are long and contain internal commas can properly be set off by dashes.

Quotation Marks and Parentheses

QUOTATION MARKS

Quotation marks function to signal the exact words of a writer or speaker. Quotation marks are also used to enclose the titles of short literary or musical works (articles, short stories or poems, songs), as well as words used in a special way. Commas and periods go inside the quote marks; semicolons and colons go outside.

Enclose direct quotations in quotation marks.

EXAMPLE: "We will wage war wherever it takes us," Winston Churchill pledged.

Quotation marks should enclose only the exact words of the person quoted.

EXAMPLE: Winston Churchill pledged that "we will wage war wherever it takes us." (NOT...pledged "that we will...")

NOTE: When a quoted sentence is interrupted by a phrase such as *he said* or *she replied*, two pairs of quotation marks must be used, one for each part of the quotation. The first word of the second part of the quoted material should not be capitalized unless it is a proper noun or the pronoun *I*.

EXAMPLE: "There are two sorts of contests between men," John Locke argued, "one managed by law, the other by force."

Commas and periods *always* belong *inside* quotation marks; semicolons and colons, outside. Question marks and exclamation points are placed inside the quotation marks when they are part of the quotation; otherwise, they are placed outside.

EXAMPLE: What did he mean when he said, "I know the answer already"?
"The case is closed!" the attorney exclaimed.

PARENTHESES

Parentheses, like dashes, enclose words of explanation and other secondary supporting details—figures, data, examples—that help the main sentence or paragraph. Parentheses are less emphatic than dashes and should be reserved for ideas that are less pivotal to the meaning of the sentence.

Use parentheses to enclose an explanatory or parenthetical element that is not closely connected with the rest of the sentence.

EXAMPLE: The speech that she gave on Sunday (in the room adjacent to the exposition hall) was her best.

If the parenthetical item is an independent sentence that stands alone, capitalize the first word and place a period inside the end parenthesis. If it is a complete sentence within another complete sentence, do not begin it with a capital letter or end it with a period. A question mark or exclamation point that is part of the parenthetical element should be placed inside the end parenthesis.

EXAMPLES: On Easter, I always think of the hot cross buns I used to buy for two cents apiece. (At that time, the year was 1939, and I was three years old.)
A speech decrying the lack of basic skills on campuses today was given by Congressman Jones (he was the man who once proposed having no entrance standards for community college students).
The absurd placement of the child-care center (fifteen feet from a classroom building!) revealed amateur architecture at its worst.

PRACTICE EXERCISE

Decide whether the punctuation or capitalization at each numbered point is correct or incorrect. Then place a check in the proper column.

CORRECT   INCORRECT

_____ _____ 1. He had said "that he is nobody to fool with."
                     1

_____ _____ 2. Fred wrote a poem for Barbara, which he entitled "Barbaric Barbara."
                        2   2

_____ _____ 3. Joseph Pummell (he was the senator who authored the antifraud bill.) offered to speak at our first meeting.
                                                                        3

_____ _____ 4. "I knew for sure," she said, "when he didn't ask me to the prom".
                                                                                    4

_____ _____ 5. The measure designed to lower inflationary pressures on the economy resulted in a cost-of-living increase of 12 percent (some measure, some reduction!).
                                                                                                                                               5

_____ _____ 6. "There is no doubt," he asserted, "That the enormous
                                                        6
national debt will be a major problem in the next century."

ANSWERS AND EXPLANATIONS

1. INCORRECT. Only the actual words spoken can be in quotation marks. He said, "I am nobody to fool with."
2. CORRECT. Quotation marks are used in titles of shorter literary works.
3. INCORRECT. A complete sentence enclosed in parentheses within another sentence does not take a period.
4. INCORRECT. A period always belongs inside the quotation mark.
5. CORRECT. An exclamation point that is part of the parenthetical phrase is placed within the parentheses.
6. INCORRECT. The second part of a direct quotation that is interrupted by a phrase like *he asserted* does not begin with a capital unless the first word is a proper noun or *I*.

FOCUS ON THE TEST

The following sample questions represent ways in which the above skills might be tested on your writing test.

What lies behind the creative genius of our greatest <u>authors</u> has been the subject of speculation over the past
₁
two centuries. There is little doubt that many of the <u>worlds</u> creative geniuses experienced miserable <u>lives</u>
₂ ₃
most often, they suffered a personal and extreme brand of deprivation that profoundly affected the quality of their daily lives. Almost <u>always,</u> the depth of their
₄
misery is related to the greatness of their genius. One who reads both Emily Bronte's <u>*Wuthering Heights*</u> and
₅
the <u>best known</u> critical discussion about her work
₆
cannot escape the <u>conclusion,</u> that Emily was the
₇
product of a punitive and abusive <u>environment,</u> it is
₈
difficult to avoid the further conclusion that the strength and authenticity of her <u>novel</u> especially regarding the
₉
vulnerabilities and palpable yearnings of its main characters—are <u>related however, faintly</u> to her personal
₁₀
affliction.

1. A. NO CHANGE
   B. authors'
   C. authors,
   D. author's

2. F. NO CHANGE
   G. world's
   H. worlds'
   J. world's,

3. A. NO CHANGE
   B. lives:
   C. lives;
   D. lives,

4. F. NO CHANGE
   G. always;
   H. always—
   J. always:

5. A. NO CHANGE
   B. "Wuthering Heights"
   C. Wuthering Heights
   D. Wuthering-Heights

6. F. NO CHANGE
   G. best, known
   H. best-known
   J. "best known"

7. A. NO CHANGE
   B. conclusion;
   C. conclusion—
   D. conclusion

8. F. NO CHANGE
   G. environment;
   H. environment—
   J. environment?

9. A. NO CHANGE
   B. novel;
   C. novel—
   D. novel:

10. F. NO CHANGE
    G. related; however faintly,
    H. related, however faintly,
    J. related (however faintly)

ANSWERS AND EXPLANATIONS

1. **A** The noun *authors* is a simple object in this sentence and requires no punctuation.

2. **G** The plural *geniuses* are a possession of the world and require that it signal that possession with an apostrophe.

3. **B** The words occurring after *lives* form an independent clause and so must be set off with a stronger mark of punctuation. The colon is the best choice in this context because the following statement gives specific focus to the general statement made in the sentence's introductory clause.

4. **F** Set off introductory phrases with a comma.

5. **A** Underline (set in italics) novels and other larger works of literature.

6. **H** Hyphenate compound adjectives preceding the noun they modify.

7. **D** The adjective clause following the noun *conclusion* is a restrictive modifier and so does not take separating punctuation.

8. **G** The clause that follows necessitates a strong mark of punctuation. Since it is closely related in meaning to the previous independent clause, the most appropriate choice is the semicolon.

9. **C** The dash at the end of this phrase requires a matching dash at the beginning. Dashes are appropriately used to give special emphasis to parenthetical phrases such as this one.

10. **H** The phrase *however faintly* is parenthetical and must be set off by commas.

Basic Grammar and Usage

Subject-Verb Agreement

Nouns, verbs, and pronouns often have special forms or endings that indicate *number*—that is, whether the word is singular or plural. A verb must agree in number with the noun or pronoun that is its subject.

A verb agrees in number with its subject. A singular subject requires a singular verb; a plural subject, a plural verb.

SINGULAR	PLURAL
The *house has* three bathrooms.	Many *houses have* more than one bathroom.
UCLA is my choice.	*UCLA, Berkeley, and Stanford are* my favorites.
My *cat*, a Persian named Gus, *is* awake all night.	*Cats*, according to this article, *are* almost always nocturnal.
Mandy, together with the other girls, *wants* a pizza for lunch.	*Mandy and the other girls want* a pizza for lunch.

Do not let **intervening words obscure the relationship between subject and verb.** Find the subject and make the verb agree with it.

> EXAMPLES: A column of wounded prisoners, townspeople, and exhausted soldiers *was spotted* struggling over the horizon. (*Was spotted* agrees with its subject, *column*, not with the intervening plural nouns.)
> She, her brother, and her friends from upstate *have always bought* tickets to the rock concert. (The verb agrees with the plural subject.)

Singular subjects followed by such words and phrases as *along with, as well as, in addition to, together with,* **or** *with* **require singular verbs.**

> EXAMPLE: The *carrier*, together with three destroyers and two frigates, *was dispatched* to the Mediterranean Sea.

Indefinite pronouns like *anybody, each, either, everyone, neither,* **and** *one* **are always singular, and take a singular verb, regardless of intervening words. Other indefinite pronouns, like** *all, any, none,* **or** *some* **may be either singular or plural.** *Both, few, many,* **and** *several* **are always plural.**

EXAMPLES: *Neither* of my children *has* an interest in music.
All *is* not lost BUT *all* of us *are going*.
Few of the golfers *were* professionals.

Compound subjects joined by *and* usually take a plural verb. (An exception is a compound subject that names one person, thing, or idea: *Ham and eggs* is a favorite breakfast.)

EXAMPLES: The *Toyota* and the *Ford are* low on gas.
The *Pendletons*, the *Riveras*, and the *Kleins are coming* to dinner.

In sentences that begin with *there is* or *there are*, the subject follows the verb, and the verb must agree with it.

EXAMPLE: There *are* (verb) many *reasons* (subject) for the war in the Middle East.

Singular subjects joined by *or* or *nor* take a singular verb. If one subject is singular and the other plural, the verb should agree with the nearer subject.

EXAMPLES: Either the *vegetable* or the *pan is creating* this awful taste. (Singular subjects)
Either the *pan* or the *vegetables are creating* this awful taste. (The verb agrees with the nearer subject.)

Collective nouns (*bunch, committee, family, group, herd, jury, number, team*) may be either singular or plural, depending upon whether the group is regarded as a unit or as individuals.

SINGULAR: The number of homeless families *increases* every year.
The *committee has* the serious responsibility of selecting a new dean.

<u>Notice that the same nouns are considered plural when the reference is to individual members of the group.</u>

PLURAL: A *number* of homeless people *were* ill enough to require hospitalization.
The *committee have* not *agreed* on a date for the picnic.

NOTE: A good rule to follow with *number, total*, and similar nouns is that, preceded by *the, number* is singular; preceded by *a*, it is plural. Another test, A *number of* should be treated as plural if it signifies several or many.

Words like *aeronautics, cybernetics, mathematics*, and *physics* or like *news* and *dollars*, are plural in form but usually singular in usage.

EXAMPLES: *Mathematics is* a subject essential to the sciences.
Eighty-five *dollars* for that coat *is* a bargain.

PRACTICE EXERCISE

Decide whether the verb in the following sentences should be singular or plural. Then indicate your answer by placing a check in the appropriate space.

1. Some of us is ( ) are ( ) studying for the test.
2. The Board of Trustees is ( ) are ( ) making a decision about tuition increases this Wednesday.
3. The committee is ( ) are ( ) arriving in Chicago at different times.
4. There is ( ) are ( ) several options available to the opera buff in Chicago.
5. A large shipment of automotive parts has ( ) have ( ) been delayed.
6. Peanuts is ( ) are ( ) high in cholesterol.
7. Neither the mechanics nor the shop manager was ( ) were ( ) able to solve the problem.
8. Hospital expense, as well as doctor's fees, is ( ) are ( ) skyrocketing.
9. The cat and the dog is ( ) are ( ) getting a flea bath today.
10. Few of us realize ( ) realizes ( ) how much work went into the senior prom.

ANSWERS AND EXPLANATIONS

1. ARE studying. The indefinite pronoun *some* here signifies more than one and consequently requires a plural verb.
2. IS making. The Board of Trustees is a single body acting officially as a legal entity.
3. ARE arriving. The reference is clearly to individual members of the committee; therefor, the verb is plural.
4. ARE. The subject of the sentence is *options*, and the plural verb *are* agrees in number.
5. HAS been delayed. The subject of the sentence, *shipment* requires a singular verb.
6. ARE. The plural subject *peanuts* requires a plural verb.
7. WAS. If a singular subject and a plural subject are joined by *nor*, the verb agrees with the nearer subject ("manager *was*").
8. IS skyrocketing. The singular subject *expense* requires a singular verb.
9. ARE getting. Use a plural verb with two singular subjects joined by *and*.
10. REALIZE. The subject of this sentence is the indefinite pronoun *few*, which requires the plural verb *realize*.

Principal Parts of Verbs

All verbs have four principal parts: the *present* (NOW), the *past* (YESTERDAY), the *present participle* (the -ING form of the verb), and the *past participle* (the form of the verb with HAVE). To find the principal parts of a verb, just remember the clues NOW, YESTERDAY, -ING, and HAVE.

```
            PRESENT:  (you) work (NOW)
               PAST:  (you) worked (YESTERDAY)
PRESENT PARTICIPLE:  (you are) work (ING)
   PAST PARTICIPLE:  (you HAVE) worked
            PRESENT:  (he) buys (NOW)
               PAST:  (he) bought (YESTERDAY)
PRESENT PARTICIPLE:  (he is) buy (ING)
   PAST PARTICIPLE:  (he HAS) bought
```

Participles are used:

1. as part of the main verb of the sentence

EXAMPLES: Sylvia *was buying* a dress.
Ed *had swum* a mile last Sunday.

2. as an adjective

EXAMPLE: *Protesting* loudly at the podium, Mr. McCracken insisted that an environmental study be held. (The present participle *protesting* modifies the noun *Mr. McCracken*.)

3. as a noun (sometimes functioning as a subject)

A gerund is the present participle, or *-ing* form of the verb, used as a noun.

EXAMPLE: *Smoking* is indisputably a danger to one's health. (The gerund *smoking* is the subject of this sentence.)

When the main verb is separated from its helping verbs (like *has, have, be, does*) by intervening parts of a sentence, sometimes, through omission, an error in verb formation results. The verb formation *did not swum*, for example, is obviously wrong when seen out of context, but notice how difficult it is to spot in a sentence. Since the verbs refer to different time periods, they must be included in their entirety.

INCORRECT: Florence Chadwick *had swum* the English Channel twice before in treacherously cold weather, but last winter she *did not*.
CORRECT: Florence Chadwick *had swum* the English Channel twice before in treacherously cold weather, but last winter she *did not swim*.
INCORRECT: The rebel groups never *have* and never *will surrender* to any government forces.
CORRECT: The rebel groups never *have surrendered* and never *will surrender* to any government forces.

Another error involving principal parts of verbs results from a confusion of the simple past and the past participle. As in the preceding examples, such errors are more likely to occur in sentences where subject and verb are separated by modifiers. Note the following examples:

EXAMPLES:	PRESENT	PAST	PAST PARTICIPLE
We *saw* (not *seen*) the dog just last week.	see	saw	seen
The Dodgers finally *did* (not *done*) it.	do	did	done
My family had *gone* (not *went*) there for several summers.	go	went	gone
The music *began* (not *begun*) as the ship slid into the sea.	begin	began	begun
Jose Canseco had *broken* (not *broke*) his favorite bat.	break	broke	broken
The guests had *eaten* (not *ate*) before the wedding party arrived.	eat	ate	eaten
The Liberty Bell had *rung* (not *rang*) every Fourth of July for a century.	ring	rang	rung

Verbs like *sit, set, rise, raise, lie,* and *lay* cause trouble because of similarity of form.

EXAMPLES:	PRESENT	PAST	PAST PARTICIPLE
My cats usually *lie* (not *lay*) in the sun.	lie (to recline)	lay	lain
The president *lay* (not *laid*) down for his afternoon rest.			
The wounded soldier had *lain* (not *laid*) on the battlefield for three days.			
If you *lay* (not *lie*) your jacket on the counter, it may become soiled.	lay (to place)	laid	laid
Phillip *laid* (not *lay*) the new sod on the prepared soil.			
The contractors have recently *laid* (not *lain*) the fresh cement for our new driveway.			
At the sound of "Hail to the Chief," everyone usually *rises* (not *raises*).	rise (to get up or move up)	rose	risen
The flag *rose* (not *raised*) to the strains of "The Marine Hymn."			
We feel that the faculty and staff have *risen* (not *raised*) to the challenge.			
The college trustees intend to *raise* (not *rise*) student fees.	raise (to cause to rise)	raised	raised
The students *raised* (not *rose*) the dress-code issue again.			
The neighbors had *raised* (not *risen*) the third side of the barn by noon.			

Some errors arise from the confusion of the present tense with another principal part. Look at the following examples:

EXAMPLES: The students protested that the test was *supposed* (not *suppose*) to be on Chapter Three.
They *used* (not *use*) to have dinner together every Friday.
Shirley *came* (not *come*) to see how you are.

The following list of principal parts features verbs that sometimes cause trouble in speaking and writing. (See also pages 48 and 49.)

PRESENT	PAST	PAST PARTICIPLE
become	became	become
begin	began	begun
bid (offer)	bid	bid
bid (command)	bade	bidden
bite	bit	bit, bitten
blow	blew	blown
break	broke	broken
bring	brought	brought
burst	burst	burst
catch	caught	caught
choose	chose	chosen
come	came	come
dive	dived, dove	dived
do	did	done
drag	dragged	dragged
draw	drew	drawn
drink	drank	drunk
drive	drove	driven
eat	ate	eaten
fall	fell	fallen
fly	flew	flown
forget	forgot	forgot, forgotten
freeze	froze	frozen
get	got	got, gotten
give	gave	given
go	went	gone
grow	grew	grown
hang (suspend)	hung	hung
hang (execute)	hanged	hanged
know	knew	known
lay	laid	laid
lead	led	led
lend	lent	lent
lie (recline)	lay	lain
lie (speak falsely)	lied	lied
lose	lost	lost
pay	paid	paid
prove	proved	proved, proven
raise	raised	raised
ride	rode	ridden
ring	rang, rung	rung
rise	rose	risen
run	ran	run
see	saw	seen
shake	shook	shaken
shrink	shrank	shrunk
sing	sang, sung	sung
sink	sank, sunk	sunk
speak	spoke	spoken
spring	sprang	sprung
steal	stole	stolen
swim	swam	swum
swing	swung	swung
take	took	taken
tear	tore	torn
throw	threw	thrown
wear	wore	worn
weave	wove	woven
wring	wrung	wrung
write	wrote	written

PRACTICE EXERCISE

Find the verb errors in the following sentences. Not every sentence has an error. Place a check in the appropriate column.

CORRECT   INCORRECT

_____   _____   1. Within five minutes, the fireman had climbed the ladder, plowed his way through mountains of debris, and did the impossible by putting out the fire.

_____   _____   2. The play was completely staged by July and began in early August.

_____   _____   3. She was very weary and simply wanted to lay down until dinner.

_____   _____   4. The price of football tickets had rose dramatically since 1974.

_____   _____   5. The New Zealand crew had lost a man overboard and tore the spinnaker.

_____   _____   6. He had driven his bike to the trail head, run to the lake, and swum to the base camp.

_____   _____   7. When we were down at the lake on weekends, we use to sit on the sand and watch the girls.

_____   _____   8. After my mother removed the sheets from the washer, my sister hanged them on the line.

ANSWERS AND EXPLANATIONS

1. INCORRECT. *Had climbed*, [had] *plowed*, and [had] *done*.
2. INCORRECT. *Was staged* and [was] *begun*.
3. INCORRECT. The infinitive form of the verb *lie* (meaning *to recline*) is *to lie*.
4. INCORRECT. *Rose* is the past tense of the verb *rise*; the past participle required here is *risen*.
5. INCORRECT. *Had lost* and [had] *torn*.
6. CORRECT. *Had* combines with each verb: driven, run, swum.
7. INCORRECT. The past tense *used* is needed here.
8. INCORRECT. The past tense of *hang* (to suspend) is *hung*.

Verb Forms and Verbals

A high percentage of verb-related errors occurs because the reader confuses *verb forms*—that is, the different forms that an action word can assume—with entirely different structures known as *verbals*—words formed from verbs but not used as verbs in a sentence. Known as *participles*, *gerunds*, and *infinitives*, verbals form important phrases within the sentence.

INFINITIVES

An infinitive is ordinarily preceded by *to* and is used as a noun, an adjective, or an adverb.

NOUN: *To err* is human. (Subject)
ADJECTIVE: The survivors had little *to celebrate*. (To celebrate modifies the noun little.)
ADVERB: *To please* his children, Jerry bought a new pool. (*To please* modifies the verb *bought*.)

Sometimes, infinitives omit the word *to*.

EXAMPLES: Who dares [to] *challenge* a champion?
Please [to] *go*.
Make him [to] *turn* on the radio.
We saw him [to] *leave*.

Because both gerunds and participles have an *-ing* ending, they can be harder to distinguish between. However, a sentence that equates the two presents an error in parallel structure. If you understand the function of each in the sentence, you will be sure to spot this error if it occurs on the English test.

GERUNDS

A gerund always ends in *-ing* and functions as a noun.

SUBJECT: *Writing* is very rewarding.
SUBJECTIVE COMPLEMENT: My favorite occupation is *binding* books.
DIRECT OBJECT: He now regrets *resigning*.
OBJECT OF PREPOSITION: After *sealing* the letter, he went for a walk.

PARTICIPLE

A participle acts as an adjective in the sentence.

EXAMPLES: *Growling* threateningly, the gorilla intimidated the crowd. (*Growling* modifies *gorilla*.)
The floor *invaded* by termites was made of oak. (*Invaded* modifies *floor*.)

There are two forms of participles, present and past. Present participles end in *-ing*; past participles assume many different forms (e.g., *bought, granted, shown, heard, hung, hidden, shot, torn*).

Other verb forms that may give trouble are the progressive and the passive. Progressive verb forms are regular action words that emphasize continuing action: "I *am running*" rather than "I *run*." Passive verbs transform the sentence in such a way that the subject is receiving action instead of performing it: "I *was given*" instead of "I *gave*."

Note the similarities of form in the following groups:

VERBS: *Simple*—I *hit* the clay target fifty times.
Progressive—I *am hitting* the ball better than ever.
Passive—I *was hit* by a snowball.
VERBALS: *Infinitive*—*To hit* a child is considered criminal.
Gerund—*Hitting* golf balls at a driving range is essential preparation for a match.
Participle—The man *hitting the ball* is also the coach.

See the definition of the parallel rule on page 51.

PRACTICE EXERCISE

The following items may have errors in the use of verbals and verb forms. Indicate with a check in the proper column whether the sentence is correct or incorrect.

CORRECT   INCORRECT

_____   _____   1. By providing day care will help the working mother, as well as the economy.

_____   _____   2. He made me to see this was a mistake.

_____   _____   3. Sue is playing golf this morning, having lunch at the clubhouse, and expected home at three.

_____   _____   4. Sylvia has traveled often, taking her little sister with her.

_____   _____   5. To give underprivileged children gifts at Christmas and serving poor people a meal at this holiday made him happy.

_____   _____   6. He wanted to start a cooperative family grocery outlet and selling a variety of household products.

ANSWERS AND EXPLANATIONS

1. INCORRECT. Although the gerund *providing* seems to be the subject of the verb *will help*, it is not. It is the object of the preposition *by*. To correct the sentence, omit *by*.
2. INCORRECT. Drop the *to* of the infinitive after the verb *make* ("He made me see ...").
3. INCORRECT. The progressive forms *is playing* and *[is] having* are incorrectly made parallel with the passive form *[is] expected*. The correction is to use the progressive form: "*[is] expecting* to arrive home at three."
4. CORRECT. The participle *taking* modifies *Sylvia*.
5. INCORRECT. The infinitive *to give* is not parallel with the gerund *helping* in the compound subject of this sentence. The verbals must both be infinitives or must both be gerunds.
6. INCORRECT. The compound direct object of this sentence combines an infinitive (*to start*) and a gerund (*selling*). The elements must be parallel (*to start* and *to sell*).

Pronouns

Pronouns are most often employed as substitutes for nouns, but some can also be used as adjectives or conjunctions. To master pronouns and be able to spot errors in their use, you need to understand pronoun *case* (nominative or subject case, possessive, objective), pronoun *number* (singular or plural), and pronoun *class* (personal, demonstrative, interrogative, relative, indefinite).

PERSONAL PRONOUNS

A personal pronoun indicates by its form the person or thing it takes the place of: the person speaking (first person), the person spoken to (second person), or the person or thing spoken about (third person). See also the pronoun charts on pages 151 and 165.

First-Person Pronouns

	SINGULAR	PLURAL
Nominative or subject case	I	we
Possessive case	my, mine	our, ours
Objective case	me	us

Second-Person Pronouns

	SINGULAR	PLURAL
Nominative or subject case	you	you
Possessive case	your, yours	your, yours
Objective case	you	you

Third-Person Pronouns

	SINGULAR	PLURAL
Nominative or subject case	he, she, it, who	they, who
Possessive case	his, hers, its, whose	their, theirs
Objective case	him, her, it, who, whoever	them, whom, whomever

Some common errors in pronoun case occur frequently in everyday speech and may well appear on the writing test. Study the following applications to see if you have been using the correct forms.

Use the nominative case of a pronoun in a compound subject.

EXAMPLE: Betty and *I* watched the Olympics on television.

Use the nominative case of a pronoun following any form of the verb *to be*. This use may not sound right to you, but it is standard written English, the language of the writing test.

EXAMPLES: It is *she*. The winner was *I*. (She is it, or I was the winner.)

Use the objective case when the pronoun is the object of a preposition.

EXAMPLES: This is just between you and *me*.
Doug looks like *me*. (Like, as well as *but*, can be used as a preposition.)
Nadine made coffee for Allan, Ken, and *me*.

When there are intervening words, eliminate them to find the correct pronoun to use. "Nadine made coffee for *I*" sounds ridiculous, yet some people might say, "Nadine made coffee for *Allan, Ken, and I*." Similarly, in the sentence "*We (Us) homeowners want better roads*," eliminate the word *homeowners* to choose the correct word: "*We want better roads*."

Use the objective case when the pronoun is the object of a verb.

EXAMPLE: The noise frightened Karen and *me*. (The noise frightened me.)

Use the nominative case for pronouns that are subjects of elliptical clauses (clauses that are incomplete or unexpressed).

EXAMPLES: My children are as excited as *I* [am].
She raked more than *he* [raked].

As and *than* are subordinating conjunctions that introduce elliptical clauses. Mentally complete the clause to determine the pronoun case or jot it down on scratch paper.

Use a possessive pronoun before a gerund. Just as you would say *My car*, you would also say *My smoking* bothers her.

EXAMPLE: We have always regretted *her* leaving for California.

DEMONSTRATIVE PRONOUNS

Demonstrative pronouns (*this, that, these, those*) take the place of things being pointed out.

EXAMPLES: *These* are Mary's.
            I don't like *this*.

They are called demonstrative adjectives when used before nouns:
These seats are comfortable.

INCORRECT: *Them* are the new watches I ordered.
CORRECT: *Those* are the new watches I ordered.
            (Demonstrative pronoun)

Do not substitute a personal pronoun for a demonstrative pronoun or a demonstrative adjective.

INCORRECT: Look at *them* diamonds!
CORRECT: Look at *those* diamonds! (Demonstrative adjective)

INTERROGATIVE PRONOUNS

Interrogative pronouns (*who, whom, whose, which,* and *what*) are used in questions. *Who, which,* and *what* are used as subjects and are in the nominative case. *Whose* is in the possessive case. *Whom* is in the objective case, and, like all objects, it is the receiver of action in the sentence.

The most common error involving interrogative pronouns is the tendency to use *who* instead of *whom*.

When the pronoun is receiving action, the objective form *whom* must be used.

INCORRECT: *Who* did you contact?
CORRECT: *Whom* did you contact? (You did contact whom?)

When the pronoun is performing the action, the nominative (or subject case) *who* must be used.

INCORRECT: *Whom* did you say is running the dance?
CORRECT: *Who* did you say is running the dance?
            (*Who* is the subject of *is running*.)

RELATIVE PRONOUNS

Relative pronouns (*who, whom, whose, which, what,* and *that*) refer to people and things. When a relative pronoun is the subject of a subordinate clause, the clause becomes an adjective modifying a noun in the sentence.

EXAMPLE: The rumor *that plagued him all his life* was a lie. (*That* [subject] *plagued him all his life* modifies *rumor*.)

Which and *that* can also act as subordinating conjunctions to introduce subordinate clauses.

EXAMPLE: Bob knew *that* Boston would win.

INDEFINITE PRONOUNS

Indefinite pronouns (*all, another, any, both, each, either, everyone, many, neither, one, several, some,* and similar words) represent an indefinite number of persons or things. Many of these words also function as adjectives ("*several* men").

Indefinite pronouns present few problems. One thing to remember:

Use a singular pronoun with an indefinite antecedent like *one, everyone,* and *anybody*.

INCORRECT: Everyone needs to prepare *themselves* for retirement.
CORRECT: Everyone needs to prepare *himself* (or *herself*) for retirement.

And a final caution:

The antecedent of a pronoun should be clear, specific, and close to the pronoun. Reword the sentence if necessary.

CONFUSING: The coach told Eric that *he* could practice after school.
CLEAR: The coach said that Eric could practice after school.

Possessive Pronoun–Gerund Combination Drill

If you have the habit of using objective-case pronouns with gerunds and gerund phrases, a very common error, try to remember this: *Gerunds are always nouns; therefore any pronoun placed before them must always be a possessive pronoun.* Here is an easy way to develop an ear for the use of the correct pronoun case. The following sentences are all correct. Just read the list several times, preferably aloud.

1. She resented *my* going out and having business lunches.
2. *Your* wanting to get up and leave was obvious to everyone.
3. *Her* having to cook dinner as well as take care of the children was the last straw.
4. The girls were irritated at *our* referring to the old fraternity all evening.
5. *Your* wanting to rebuild the city is very moving to me.
6. George resented *their* imposing a filing fee for new candidates.
7. The commission ruled against *my* giving away free balloons at the fair.
8. *Your* car-pooling can help rid the city of gridlock.
9. Edna began to feel embarrassed at *his* jumping into every conversation and immediately monopolizing it.
10. *Our* letting Brock eat table scraps from the table produced a spoiled animal.
11. *Your* sponsoring our son will not be forgotten.
12. *Their* having turned their backs on Kuwait and Saudi Arabia could possibly signify the end of the PLO.
13. *My* getting married should have no impact on you.
14. He felt strongly that he did not have to explain *his* enlisting in the Navy to anyone.
15. The world in general deeply resents *Saddam Hussein's* setting those oil fires and causing the world's largest oil spill.
16. The *industrial world's* treating oil as the only economical source of energy has brought us to a critical state of dependence.
17. *Janet's* brushing her hair every night has certainly made a difference in her appearance.
18. The house mistress felt that *Yvonne's* obvious flaunting of her intelligence would lead to some animosity among the women.
19. *Her* knowing that he did not have much money, yet ordering prime rib and lobster tails, was an example of raw greed.
20. *Bertha's* consuming four entire chickens in front of the Jungle Chicken stand was not the kind of endorsement the management hoped for.
21. Mary thinks *Phil's* chewing gum is the reason they did not get the part.
22. *Jill's* losing her wallet started off a very bad day.
23. The whole city was shocked by *his* refusing to take the oath.
24. *Their* running and jumping on our grass is going to ruin our front lawn.
25. *My* taking lunch to work every day has saved hundreds of dollars so far.
    (Compare: By taking lunch to work every day I have saved hundreds of dollars.)

PRACTICE EXERCISE

Find the pronoun errors in the following sentences. Not every sentence has an error. Place a check in the appropriate column to indicate whether the sentence is correct or incorrect.

CORRECT   INCORRECT

_____   _____   1. Who do you think is coming?

_____   _____   2. I can tell the culprit. It was he.

_____   _____   3. I play more tennis than her, but she has a natural talent.

_____   _____   4. They nominated everybody but Rosa and he.

_____   _____   5. Frank and him have been using the word processor.

_____   _____   6. Everyone must pat themselves on the back once in a while.

_____   _____   7. The broker was surprised at him wanting to buy 5,000 shares of that penny stock.

_____   _____   8. Who did you see in the play.

_____   _____   9. The IRS required Lee, Carlotta, and I to produce more detailed records.

_____   _____   10. Us Chicagoans don't appreciate our city nearly enough.

ANSWERS AND EXPLANATIONS

1. CORRECT. *Who*, the subject of *is coming*, is performing the action.
2. CORRECT. The nominative case is used with all forms of the verb *to be*. *He* is correct.
3. INCORRECT. To correct this sentence, supply the missing verb: "I play more tennis than *she* [does]..."
4. INCORRECT. *But* in this sentence is used as a preposition; its object must be in the objective case (*him*), not the nominative.
5. INCORRECT. Use the nominative case for a pronoun in a compound subject (Frank and *he*).
6. INCORRECT. The pronoun should be *himself* (or *herself*) to agree with the singular form *everyone*.
7. INCORRECT. *Wanting to buy stock* is a gerund phrase; it takes the possessive pronoun *his*.
8. INCORRECT. *Whom* is needed, because it is the object of *did see*. (I saw him/whom)
9. INCORRECT. The pronoun *I* should be in the objective case (*me*) because it is a direct object of *required*.
10. INCORRECT. The pronoun *us* should be in the nominative case (*we*) because it modifies *Chicagoans*, the subject of the sentence. (*We don't*...)

FOCUS ON THE TEST

The following sample questions represent ways in which the above skills might be tested on your writing test.

Operators and manufacturers of nuclear reactor power facilities are making increased use of robots to improve operations and maintenance, lower operating costs, <u>increasing</u> plant availability and equipment
₁

1. **A.** NO CHANGE
   B. increases
   C. increase
   D. increased

reliability, <u>enhanced</u> worker safety, and reduce worker
₂
exposure to radiation. There is no doubt in the field that

2. **F.** NO CHANGE
   G. enhancing
   H. enhances
   J. enhance

advanced telerobotic systems <u>can have made</u> more
₃
effective use of human operators, expert systems, and

3. **A.** NO CHANGE
   B. can make
   C. can be made
   D. can be making

intelligent machines; in fact, <u>few</u> of the world's leading
₄
nuclear plant designers believe that a facility without

4. **F.** NO CHANGE
   G. some
   H. one
   J. none

modern robotic and telerobotic systems <u>will have
₅
become</u> obsolete in a very few years. The design of
₅
future nuclear plants and supporting facilities—

5. **A.** NO CHANGE
   B. would have become
   C. becomes
   D. will become

particularly <u>these</u> involving fuel recycling—should
₆
incorporate considerations for use of robotic systems.
A committee of scientists critical of the move toward

6. **F.** NO CHANGE
   G. they
   H. those
   J. that

robotics <u>believe</u> that existing methods for controlling
₇

7. **A.** NO CHANGE
   B. believes
   C. believed
   D. have believed

and preprogramming the typical robot <u>is</u> appropriate for
₈
only a limited number of jobs in nuclear facilities,

8. **F.** NO CHANGE
   G. were
   H. are
   J. will be

mainly because it <u>simply require</u> too much supervision.
₉
In addition, existing robots are limited in their ability to

9. **A.** NO CHANGE
   B. it simply required
   C. they simply require
   D. it simply requires

sense their surroundings and <u>interpreting</u> sensor data, a
                                          10
prerequisite for handling unexpected problems during
the routine executions of tasks.

10. F. NO CHANGE
    G. interpret
    H. interpreted
    J. has interpreted

ANSWERS AND EXPLANATIONS

1. **C** The verb *increase* needs to be an infinitive to be parallel with the series of infinitive phrases that comprise the end of the sentence.

2. **J** The verb *enhance* needs to be an infinitive to be parallel with the series of infinitive phrases that comprise the end of the sentence.

3. **B** The passage is written in the present tense, and employs the present tense in generally true statements.

4. **G** *Some* is the more logical choice of indefinite pronoun here; the use of *few* in the text renders the sentence meaningless.

5. **D** The future tense is made necessary by the trailing phrase "in a very few years."

6. **H** Demonstrative pronouns take the place of things *being pointed out*. In this case, the word *those* is more appropriate for the antecedent *facilities* because those facilities will be built in the future.

7. **B** The subject of the verb is the singular noun *committee*.

8. **H** The subject of the verb *are* is the plural noun *methods*.

9. **D** The subject of the verb is the singular personal pronoun *it*, the antecedent of which is the noun *robot*.

10. **G** *Interpret* is one of a pair of parallel infinitives (*to sense* and *to interpret*) modifying the noun *ability*.

SENTENCE STRUCTURE

In addition to a NO CHANGE response, the questions on the writing test that deal with sentence structure will offer three alternatives, each one a restructuring of the underlined part. Errors in sentence structure include such items as sentence fragments, run-on sentences, misplaced modifiers, and lack of parallelism. These topics are reviewed in this section.

Sentence Fragments

A sentence fragment is a part of a sentence that has been punctuated as if it were a complete sentence. It does not express a complete thought but depends upon a nearby independent clause for its full meaning. It should be made a part of that complete sentence.

INCORRECT: I was not able to pick up my child at her school. *Having been caught in heavy traffic.* (Participial phrase)
REVISED: Having been caught in heavy traffic, I was not able to pick up my child at her school.
OR
I was not able to pick up my child at her school. I had been caught in heavy traffic.

INCORRECT: The cat sat on the water heater. *Unable to get warm.* (Adjective phrase)
REVISED: Unable to get warm, the cat sat on the water heater.

INCORRECT: The salesman tightened the wire around the burlap feed bag with a spinner. *Which twisted the wire loops until they were secure.* (Adjective clause)
REVISED: The salesman tightened the wire around the burlap feed bag with a spinner, which twisted the wire loops until they were secure.

INCORRECT: We will probably try to find another insurance company. *When our policy expires.* (Adverb clause)
REVISED: When our policy expires, we will probably try to find another insurance company.

Run-on Sentences

Probably the most common error in writing occurs when two sentences are run together as one. There are two types of run-on sentences: the *fused* sentence, which has no punctuation mark between its two independent clauses, and the *comma splice*, which substitutes a comma where either a period or a semicolon is needed, or where a comma and conjunction are needed.

FUSED: Jean had no luck at the store they were out of raincoats.
COMMA SPLICE: She surprised us all with her visit, she was on her way to New York.

To correct a run-on sentence, use a period, a semicolon, or a coordinating conjunction (*and, but, or, nor, for, yet*) to separate independent clauses.

Note the following examples of run-on sentences and the suggested revisions.

FUSED: Eric is a bodybuilder he eats only large amounts of meat.
REVISED: Eric is a bodybuilder; he eats only large amounts of meat.

COMMA SPLICE: He had never been so prepared, he even had backup copies of his study sheets!
REVISED: He had never been so prepared. He even had backup copies of his study sheets!

COMMA SPLICE: His father was an artist, his mother was an accountant.
REVISED: His father was an artist, and his mother was an accountant.

PRACTICE EXERCISE

Most of the following items contain sentence fragments or run-on sentences. Place a check in the proper column to indicate whether the item is correct or incorrect.

CORRECT   INCORRECT

_____   _____   1. Bert used his manuscript for scratch paper. Having received rejection notices from twelve publishers.

_____   _____   2. The bank changed its hours and hired more security officers. After a wave of bank robberies hit the neighborhood.

_____   _____   3. We have to leave now it will be dark soon.

_____   _____   4. Having been declared fit by his doctor, Cleveland planned a weekend hike to the top of Mount Washington.

_____   _____   5. It was an embarrassment to hear Colonel Wilkinson talk about the medals he won with his marching corps. In front of all those wounded veterans!

_____   _____   6. Erica played softball for Taft High School, she hit a home run every week.

_____   _____   7. Our Himalayan cat Mathilda gave birth to seven beautiful kittens. All little white bundles of purring fluff.

_____   _____   8. Boris accidentally stepped on the little girl's foot he felt terrible.

_____   _____   9. It is necessary to vacuum around and under your refrigerator at least once a month. To prevent it from overheating.

_____   _____   10. Several of us want to give Dr. Kellogg a birthday party. Because he is so kind and generous.

_____   _____   11. Human cloning will soon become a reality; people will be able to produce improved versions of themselves.

_____   _____   12. Jared was warned, he was offending too many of his superiors.

ANSWERS AND EXPLANATIONS

1. INCORRECT. *Having received rejection notices from twelve publishers* is a participial phrase modifying the proper noun *Bert* and must be attached to the main clause.
2. INCORRECT. The adverb clause *After a wave of bank robberies hit the neighborhood* modifies the verbs *changed* and *hired*, and should be joined to the rest of the sentence.
3. INCORRECT. This is a fused sentence, which needs a period, semicolon, or coordinating conjunction between the words *now* and *it*. If a period is used, the word *it* should begin with a capital letter.
4. CORRECT. The dependent phrases, *Having been declared fit by his doctor* and *to the top of Mount Washington*, have been included in one complete sentence.
5. INCORRECT. *In front of all those wounded veterans* is a prepositional phrase that should be made part of the sentence containing the word it modifies, *talk*.
6. INCORRECT. This sentence is a comma splice; that is, a comma is used where a stronger mark of separation belongs, such as a period, semicolon, or coordinating conjunction.
7. INCORRECT. *All little white bundles of purring fluff* is an appositive phrase modifying *kittens*. It cannot stand alone.
8. INCORRECT. See explanation, item 3.
9. INCORRECT. The infinitive phrase *To prevent it from overheating* should be part of the previous sentence.
10. INCORRECT. *Because he is so kind and generous* is a dependent adverb clause that should be attached to the independent clause containing the verb it modifies.
11. CORRECT. The independent clauses are properly separated by a semicolon.
12. INCORRECT. See explanation, item 6.

Connectives

Connectives that join two independent clauses are called coordinating conjunctions (*and, so, but, or, nor, for, yet*). Connectives that introduce a dependent clause are called subordinating conjunctions (*after, although, since, when*).

Coordinating conjunctions link words, phrases, and clauses that are equal grammatically.

EXAMPLES: The pilot *and* the crew boarded the plane.
The road ran through the valley *and* along the river.

Compound sentences are formed when coordinating conjunctions link two independent clauses.

EXAMPLE: You can sign the loan papers on Friday, *or* you can sign them on Monday.

Subordinating conjunctions are used in sentences to subordinate (connect) a dependent clause to an independent one. As a result one idea is made subordinate (dependent on) to another. Some of the important conjunctions allowing subordination include *after, as, because, before, if, in order that, once, since, unless, until, whenever, wherever, though, even though, although*.

EXAMPLES: We covered up the newly planted citrus trees *when* the temperature began to drop.
Until I saw her in person, I thought Cher was a tall woman.

Another form of connective is the *conjunctive adverb*, an adverb that functions as a coordinating conjunction. The principal conjunctive adverbs are *accordingly, also, besides, certainly, consequently, finally, furthermore, however, incidentally, instead, likewise, nevertheless, otherwise, similarly*, and *undoubtedly*. When they join clauses, conjunctive adverbs are usually preceded by a semicolon and followed by a comma.

EXAMPLE: The Hansons wish to see a Broadway musical; *undoubtedly,* they'll have to get tickets far in advance for one of the hit shows.

Subordinating ideas is a necessary skill for writers because coordinating them can be overdone. Unfortunately, if every significant idea in every sentence receives equal weight by coordination, then the main ideas compete illogically.

FAULTY
COORDINATION: The real power in the company lies with Mr. Stark, and he currently owns 55 percent of the stock; in addition to that, his mother is semiretired as president of the firm.
REVISED: The real power in the company lies with Mr. Stark, who currently owns 55 percent of the stock and whose mother is semiretired as president of the firm.

Notice that subordinating two of the independent clauses tightens the sentence and adds focus.

Subordinating too many parts of a sentence, however, can also cause confusion. Consider the following example:

EXCESSIVE
SUBORDINATION: Standing on the corner were many aliens who had entered the country illegally, and most of whom had applied for amnesty, and even more important to them though, who had families back in Mexico or El Salvador who needed food and shelter.
REVISED: Standing on the corner were many illegal aliens, most of whom had applied for amnesty. Even more important to them, though, was the fact that they had families needing food and shelter back in Mexico or El Salvador.

Notice how a judicious balance of coordination and subordination helps clarify a confusing stream of excessively entwined modifiers.

You must also keep in mind the *logic* of subordination. What you choose to subordinate in a sentence has to make sense to the reader. For example, the sentence "Sue happened to glance at the sky, amazed to see an enormous flying saucer hovering over the barn" gives greater importance to the fact that Sue glanced at the sky. A more logical version of that sentence is, "Happening to glance at the sky, Sue was amazed to see an enormous flying saucer hovering over the barn."

BACKWARD
SUBORDINATION: She studied medicine with great intensity for fifteen years, becoming a doctor.
LOGICAL REVISION: She became a doctor, having studied medicine with great intensity for fifteen years.

BACKWARD
SUBORDINATION: The pitcher momentarily let the runner on first base take a wide lead, when he stole second.
LOGICAL REVISION: The runner stole second when the pitcher momentarily let him take a wide lead.

BACKWARD
SUBORDINATION: He ran over with a fire extinguisher, saving the driver's life.
LOGICAL REVISION: Running over with a fire extinguisher, he saved the driver's life.

PRACTICE EXERCISE

Most of the following sentences contain either faulty coordination or subordination, or backward subordination. Place a check in the appropriate column to indicate whether the sentence is correct or faulty.

CORRECT   FAULTY

_____   _____   1. I had prepared myself by practicing, and I was able to beat Phil at racquetball.

_____   _____   2. Realizing that the Mafia does not forgive breaches of security, Lefty went into hiding.

_____   _____   3. As a terrible storm began, we were eating.

_____   _____   4. George found out about the burglary, and he was so shocked at first, and he could not remember his telephone number.

_____   _____   5. Between Big Sur and Carmel, the roads were in very bad condition, because the State Highway Agency is repairing them.

_____   _____   6. He bought a secondhand car, which had a sun roof, and it began to leak, so he took the car back to the dealer, who replaced the roof.

_____   _____   7. The V-2 Project was manned by prisoners who had no contact with the outside world, because it was completed in total secrecy.

_____   _____   8. Janine is a ballet dancer, and her sister is a gymnast.

ANSWERS AND EXPLANATIONS

1. FAULTY. This sentence is an example of faulty coordination. The sentence would be improved by subordinating the less important idea: Having prepared myself by practicing, I was able to beat Phil at racquetball.
2. CORRECT. In this sentence, the less important idea is properly subordinated.
3. FAULTY. This sentence is an example of illogical or backward subordination. The important idea is the storm, not the eating: A terrible storm began as we were eating.
4. FAULTY. This sentence is an example of faulty coordination. Improve it by subordinating two of the independent clauses: When George found out about the burglary, he was so shocked at first that he could not remember his telephone number.
5. FAULTY. This is an example of illogical or backward subordination. The fact that the roads were being repaired is the main idea of the sentence. We know that because the other clause gives the reason that the roads are being repaired. *Revised:* Because the roads between Big Sur and Carmel were in very bad condition, the State Highway Agency is repairing them.
6. FAULTY. This is an example of both faulty coordination and excessive subordination. *Revised*: He bought a secondhand car with a sun roof. When the sun roof began to leak, he took the car back to the dealer, who replaced the roof.
7. FAULTY. This sentence is an example of illogical subordination. Of the two ideas, *The V-2 Project was manned by prisoners* and *it was completed in total secrecy*, the second is the more important one. *Revised*: Because the V-2 Project...world, it....
8. CORRECT. This is an acceptable compound sentence, pairing two equal ideas logically.

Modifiers

ADJECTIVES AND ADVERBS

The purpose of adjectives and adverbs is to describe, limit, color—in other words, to *modify*—other words. Adjectives modify nouns or pronouns, and generally precede the words they modify. Adverbs describe verbs, adjectives, or other adverbs. Some words can be used as either adjectives (He has an *early* appointment) or adverbs (He arrived *early*).

ADJECTIVES: *fuzzy* peach
impressive view
sour milk

ADVERBS: He grumbled *loudly*.
She smiled *broadly*.
It poured *unmercifully*.

Although most adverbs end in *-ly*, some do not (*fast, hard, long, straight*). A few adjectives also have an *-ly* ending (*lovely* day, *lively* discussion).

ADJECTIVES

Problems that students face with adjectives frequently relate to the use of degrees of comparison. There are three degrees: the *positive*—the original form of the word (*straight*); the *comparative*—used to compare two persons or things (*straighter*); and the *superlative*—used to compare more than two persons or things (*straightest*). If not understood, the spelling and form changes involved can sometimes confuse the unwary student.

1. Most adjectives form the comparative and superlative degrees by adding *-er* and *-est*:

    POSITIVE: nice
    COMPARATIVE: nicer
    SUPERLATIVE: nicest

2. Other adjectives form the comparative and superlative by using *more* and *most*:

    POSITIVE: challenging
    COMPARATIVE: more challenging
    SUPERLATIVE: most challenging

3. Some adjectives change completely as they form the comparative and superlative degrees:

    POSITIVE: little   good   poor
    COMPARATIVE: less   better   worse
    SUPERLATIVE: least   best   worst

Be alert for double comparisons, which incorrectly use *more* or *most* with adjectives that already express a degree: *more softer* or *most strongest*.

Also, watch for the illogical use of the comparative or the superlative with adjectives that cannot be compared, such as *square, round, perfect, unique*. It is meaningless to write *rounder* or *most perfect*.

When comparing only two nouns, use the comparative degree: Mars is the *larger* of the two planets. When comparing more than two, use the superlative: Gibson is the *most dangerous* hitter on their team.

ADVERBS

Adverbs (either as words, phrases, or clauses) describe the words they modify by indicating *when, how, where, why, in what order,* or *how often*.

WHEN: He studied *until 10:00 every night*.
HOW: She testified *with quiet dignity*.
WHERE: Bring the paper *here*.
WHY: They rejected the offer *because it was too little*.
IN WHAT ORDER: *One after another*, the townspeople told the judge their story.

NOTE: *Anywheres, nowheres,* and *somewheres* are not words or correct adverb forms. Use *anywhere, nowhere, somewhere*.

The adjectives *good* and *bad* should never be used as adverbs in academic or professional writing.

NOT
She doesn't sing so *good*.
He wants that job *bad*.
BUT
She doesn't sing so *well*.
He wants that job *badly*.

Standard English requires the use of a formal adverb form rather than a colloquial version.

NOT
This was a *real* good clambake.
He *sure* doesn't look happy.
BUT
This was a *really* good clambake.
He *surely* doesn't look happy.

NOTE: Usually it's best to avoid such intensifiers.

PRACTICE EXERCISE

Some of the following sentences combine errors in the use of adjectives or adverbs. Determine whether *a* or *b* is the correct word to use. Then place a check in the appropriate column.

a   *b*

_____ _____ 1. The new Turbo-B ran *real/really* well during the first race.
                                  a   b

_____ _____ 2. Mike is the *more/most* active of the twins.
                            a   b

_____ _____ 3. I *sure/surely* would like that leather jacket.
                  a   b

_____ _____ 4. Portia was even more *fussier/fussy* than Elena.
                                     a   b

_____ _____ 5. These earrings are *unique/most unique*!
                                   a   b

_____ _____ 6. He had many friends in Chicago, where he lived *previous/previously*.
                                                               a   b

ANSWERS AND EXPLANATIONS

1. *b* The adverb *really* is needed to modify the adverb *well*. (Only adverbs can modify other adverbs.)
2. *a* The comparative degree is used when two are compared.
3. *b* In colloquial speech, the word *sure* is accepted. In the writing test, as in all secondary school and college writing, the norm is standard English, which requires the adverb *surely* in a construction like this.
4. *b* With the comparative degree *more*, only the positive degree *fussy* is correct. *More fussier* is a double comparison.
5. *a* It is illogical to add degrees to absolutes like *unique*. Something is either unique or not unique.
6. *b* The adverb *previously* is the correct choice to modify the verb *lived*. *Previous*, an adjective, cannot modify a verb.

Probably the most persistent and frustrating errors in the English language involve either *incorrect modification* or else *inexact modification* that is difficult to pin down.

In most cases, if you can keep your eye on the *word or phrase being modified*, it is easier to avoid the following pitfalls.

MISPLACED MODIFIERS

To avoid confusion or ambiguity, place the modifying words, phrases, or clauses near the words they modify.

Misplaced Adverb Modifiers

Adverbs like *scarcely, merely, just, even,* and *almost* must be placed near the words they modify.

CONFUSED: Last week during the cold spell, I *nearly* lost all of my flowers.
  CLEAR: Last week during the cold spell, I lost *nearly* all of my flowers. (The adverb *nearly* modifies the pronoun *all*.)

CONFUSED: Acme *just* cleaned my rugs last month.
  CLEAR: Acme cleaned my rugs *just* last month. (The adverb *just* modifies the adverbial phrase *last month*.)

Misplaced Phrase Modifiers

CONFUSED: *To plant tomatoes*, it was a good growing year.
  CLEAR: It was a good growing year *to plant tomatoes*.

CONFUSED: *Like a sleek projectile*, the passengers saw the new train approach the station.
  CLEAR: The passengers saw the new train approach the station *like a sleek projectile*.

Misplaced Clause Modifiers

CONFUSED: He packed all of his books and documents into his van, *which he was donating to the library*.
  CLEAR: He packed all of his books and documents, *which he was donating to the library*, into his van.

CONFUSED: The new series of seminars will focus on how to prevent inflation, *which will benefit us all*.
  CLEAR: The new series of seminars, *which will benefit us all*, will focus on how to prevent inflation.

DANGLING CONSTRUCTIONS

A dangling modifier literally hangs in the air; there is no logical word in the sentence for it to modify. Frequently it is placed close to the wrong noun or verb, causing the sentence to sound ridiculous. *Driving through the park, several chipmunks could be seen.*

Dangling Participles

A participle is a form of the verb that is used as an adjective. Unless there is a logical word for it to modify, the participial phrase will dangle, modifying either the wrong noun or none at all.

INCORRECT: Having run out of gas, John was late for dinner.
  REVISED: Because the car ran out of gas, John was late for dinner.

INCORRECT: Driving along the parkway, several deer were spotted.
  REVISED: Driving along the parkway, we spotted several deer.

Dangling Gerunds

A gerund is the *-ing* form of a verb serving as a noun (*Smoking is bad for your health*). When a gerund is used as the object of a preposition ("by *hiding*," "after *escaping*," "upon *realizing*"), the phrase can dangle if the actor that it modifies is missing.

INCORRECT: After putting a bloodworm on my hook, the flounders began to bite.
REVISED: After putting a bloodworm on my hook, I found that the flounders began to bite.

INCORRECT: In designing our house addition, a bathroom was forgotten.
REVISED: In designing our house addition, we forgot to add a bathroom.

Dangling Infinitives

Unlike the participle and the gerund, the infinitive performs more than one job in a sentence. While the participle acts like an adjective, and the gerund like a noun, the infinitive phrase can take the part of a noun, adjective, or adverb. Note the following examples of dangling infinitive phrases:

INCORRECT: To skate like a champion, practice is essential.
REVISED: To skate like a champion, one must practice.

INCORRECT: To make a good impression, a shirt and tie should be worn to the interview.
REVISED: To make a good impression, Jeff should wear a shirt and tie to the interview.

ILLOGICAL COMPARISONS

Occasionally, a writer will mistakenly compare items that are not comparable.

INCORRECT: Her *salary* was lower than a clerk. (The *salary* is incorrectly compared with a *clerk*.)
CORRECT: Her *salary* was lower than a *clerk's* (salary).

INCORRECT: The cultural *events* in Orlando are as diversified as *any other large city*. *Events* are being compared with a large city.
CORRECT: The cultural events in Orlando are as diversified as *those in any other large city*.

Another form of illogical comparison results when a writer fails to exclude from the rest of the group the item being compared.

INCORRECT: She is taller than *any girl* in her class.
CORRECT: She is taller than *any other girl* in her class.

PRACTICE EXERCISE

In the following sentences, find the errors that involve modifiers. Not every sentence has an error. Place a check in the appropriate column to indicate whether the sentence is correct or incorrect.

CORRECT   INCORRECT

_____   _____   1. The corn was roasted by the boys skewered on the ends of long, pointed sticks.

_____   _____   2. It was still pouring, so Uncle Maurice went out to the sty to feed the hogs with an umbrella.

_____   _____   3. Coming nearer to it, the building certainly seemed dilapidated.

_____   _____   4. Henry's sales record will be as good as any of the top salespeople.

_____ _____ 5. Coiled in a corner of the garage and ready to spring, Mrs. Lampert was surprised by a rattlesnake.

_____ _____ 6. Having been asked to speak at the senior dinner, Fred spent many evenings preparing his speech.

_____ _____ 7. To be well baked, you have to leave the pork roast in the oven for three hours.

_____ _____ 8. We saw the impressive Concorde on the porch this morning.

ANSWERS AND EXPLANATIONS

1. INCORRECT. The participial phrase *skewered on the ends of long, pointed sticks* should be placed closer to corn, the noun it is intended to modify: *Skewered...sticks, the corn...*
2. INCORRECT. The prepositional phrase *with an umbrella* is misplaced. It seems to modify the *hogs* or *to feed* but should modify the verb *went*.
3. INCORRECT. This sentence is missing the noun that the participial phrase *Coming nearer to it* is meant to modify. A corrected version might be *Coming nearer to the building, we noticed that it certainly seemed dilapidated.*
4. INCORRECT. This sentence contains an illogical comparison. The correct sentence should include the pronoun *that: Henry's sales record will be as good as that of any of the top salespeople.*
5. INCORRECT. The participial phrase beginning this sentence seems to modify *Mrs. Lampert*. It should modify *rattlesnake*. The correction, of course, is to place the word *rattlesnake* close to the participial phrase.
6. CORRECT. The participial phrase is placed close to *Fred*, the noun it logically modifies.
7. INCORRECT. The infinitive phrase *To be well baked* here incorrectly modifies *you* instead of *roast*, the noun it is intended for.
8. INCORRECT. The Concorde was not on the porch, as this sentence seems to imply. *Revised: As we sat on the porch this morning, we saw the impressive Concorde.*

FOCUS ON THE TEST

The following sample questions represent ways in which the above skills might be tested on your writing test.

The life of famed watchmaker Abraham-Louis Breguet was, from beginning to end (1747–1823). A
₁
steady progression toward fame and fortune. Breguet soon revealed a lively interest that developed into a veritable passion for things mechanical in his
₂
stepfather's shop. He studied with the famed jeweler
₂

1. **A.** NO CHANGE
   B. (1747–1823), a
   C. (1747–1823) a
   D. (1747–1823); a

2. **F.** NO CHANGE
   G. (Place at the beginning of the sentence.)
   H. (Place after the verb *revealed*.)
   J. (Delete altogether; the phrase is not related.)

Abbot Marie for twelve <u>years, his vocation</u> was
                                    3

henceforth decided. <u>Living in the Swiss cantons</u> on the
                         4

French border, watchmaking had already been

developed on a large scale by refugee French families,

<u>because</u> it was limited almost exclusively to inexpensive
5

products. <u>Young Breguet, on the contrary,</u>
              6
<u>demonstrating very early a decided disgust for shoddy</u>
              6
<u>workmanship, as well as a genius for precision work,</u>
              6
<u>had an attitude he never lost.</u>
              6

<u>In 1802, Breguet, receiving the gold medal at an</u>
              7
<u>exhibition of industrial products, sat at the table of the</u>
              7
<u>first consul.</u> Throughout his reign, Napoleon's interest
     7

in the works of the watch master, principally those of

high precision, never slackened. <u>The face studded with</u>
                                        8
<u>brilliant diamonds and rubies, Napoleon acquired</u>
              8
<u>Breguet's most ambitious creation the day after it was</u>
              8
<u>completed.</u>
     8

<u>The fall of the empire did not affect either his</u>
                      9
<u>fortunes adversely or his renown, which had spread</u>
              9
<u>throughout Europe.</u> The exhibition of 1819 in which
         9
Breguet presented a collection of his most important

3. **A.** NO CHANGE
   B. years his vocation
   C. years, then his vocation
   D. years, and his vocation

4. **F.** NO CHANGE
   G. (Place this phrase after *border*.)
   H. (Place this phrase after *families*.)
   J. (Delete altogether; the phrase is not related.)

5. **A.** NO CHANGE
   B. but
   C. even though
   D. however

6. **F.** NO CHANGE
   G. Young Breguet, on the contrary, demonstrating very early a decided disgust for shoddy workmanship, as well as a genius for precision work, an attitude he never lost.
   H. Young Breguet, on the contrary, demonstrated very early a decided disgust for shoddy workmanship, as well as a genius for precision work, an attitude he never lost.
   J. Young Breguet, on the contrary, demonstrated very early a decided disgust for shoddy workmanship, as well as a genius for precision work, and had an attitude he never lost.

7. **A.** NO CHANGE
   B. In 1802, Breguet, receiving the gold medal at an exhibition of industrial products, sitting at the table of the first consul.
   C. In 1802, Breguet received the gold medal at an exhibition of industrial products, and he sat at the table of the first consul.
   D. In 1802, Breguet sat at the table of the first consul, receiving the gold medal at an exhibition of industrial products.

8. **F.** NO CHANGE
   G. The face studded with brilliant diamonds and rubies, Breguet's most ambitious creation, the day after it was completed, was acquired by Napoleon.
   H. The face studded with brilliant diamonds and rubies the day after it was completed, Napoleon acquired Breguet's most ambitious creation.
   J. Napoleon acquired Breguet's most ambitious creation, the face studded with brilliant diamonds and rubies, the day after it was completed.

9. **A.** NO CHANGE
   B. The fall of the empire did not adversely affect either his fortunes or his renown, which had spread throughout Europe.
   C. Adversely, the fall of the empire did not affect either his fortunes or his renown, which had spread throughout Europe.
   D. The fall of the empire did not affect either his fortunes or his renown adversely, which had spread throughout Europe.

works was a triumphant compendium of his life,

by then more than seventy years old.
           10

10. **F.** NO CHANGE
    G. (Place this phrase at the beginning of the sentence.)
    H. (Place this phrase, bracketed with commas, after the word *Breguet*.)
    J. (Delete this phrase; it is not relevant.)

ANSWERS AND EXPLANATIONS

1. **B** This sentence contains the parenthetical interruption *from beginning to end (1747–1823),* which must be set off by commas. Any stronger mark of punctuation after the parentheses results in two fragmented sentences.

2. **G** The only logical position in this sentence for the prepositional phrase *in his stepfather's shop* is at the beginning of the sentence where it will correctly modify the noun *Breguet*.

3. **D** A compound sentence is the most appropriate vehicle for these two ideas of equal importance. A comma is used before the coordinating conjunction that joins coordinate clauses.

4. **H** The only logical position in this sentence for the participial phrase *Living in the Swiss cantons* is next to the noun it logically modifies, *families*.

5. **B** Only a connective signaling contrast like *but* makes sense in this context, especially in light of the next sentence.

6. **H** This choice allows the main clause to emphasize the major characteristic of the subject, and correctly subordinates the parenthetical phrase, *an attitude he never lost*.

7. **C** The act of receiving the gold medal is logically as important as sitting with the first consul, and should not be subordinated in a participial phrase.

8. **J** The phrase *The face studded with brilliant diamonds and rubies* modifies the noun *creation* and so must be placed next to it.

9. **B** The adverb *adversely* logically modifies only the verb *affect* and should be placed near it.

10. **H** The phrase *By then more than seventy years old* appropriately modifies the noun *Breguet* and should be placed next to it, set off by commas since it is a parenthetical addition.

Consistency and Tense

VERBS IN SUBORDINATE CLAUSES

    Because *tense* indicates the time of the action and *voice* indicates whether the subject is the agent of the action (*active:* Tom *saw*) or the recipient of the action (*passive:* Tom *was seen*), both of these verb forms are central to the consistency of a sentence or passage.

Tense

A verb in a subordinate clause should relate logically in tense to the verb in the principal clause. Avoid any unnecessary shift.

    INCORRECT: As the wedding *began* [past], the bride's mother *starts* [present] to cry.
    CORRECT: As the wedding *began* [past], the bride's mother *started* [past] to cry.

    INCORRECT: He *had intended* [past perfect] to finish his third novel by the end of the year, but he *has been very sick* [present perfect] until Thanksgiving.
    CORRECT: He *had intended* [past perfect] to finish his third novel by the end of the year, but he *had been very sick* [past perfect] until Thanksgiving.

    INCORRECT: By the time the fire *had been extinguished* [past perfect], the priceless paintings *had been destroyed* [past perfect].
    CORRECT: By the time the fire *was extinguished* [past], the priceless paintings *had been destroyed* [past perfect]. (The past perfect expresses action that took place before the simple past.)

    NOTE: For clarification refer to the timelines on pages 86, 87, 102–104, and 106.

Voice

A verb in a subordinate clause should relate logically in voice to the verb in the main clause. It is generally better to avoid voice shifts within a sentence.

INCORRECT: Sighs of appreciation *could be heard* [passive] as the waiters *brought* [active] huge trays of roast beef and Yorkshire pudding.

REVISED: The guests *sighed* [active] with appreciation as the waiters *brought* [active] huge trays of roast beef and Yorkshire pudding.

INCORRECT: If the fishing boat *had been reached* [passive] in time, the Coast Guard *might have saved* [active] it with floats. (Note that the subject shifts as well as the voice.)

CORRECT: If it *had reached* [active] the fishing boat in time, the Coast Guard *might have saved* [active] it with floats.

THE PRESENT INFINITIVE

Always use the present infinitive (*to run, to see*), after a perfect tense (a tense that uses some form of the helping verb *have* or *had*).

EXAMPLES: He *has decided to order* the Jaguar Model S-1. (Present Perfect + Present Infinitive)
They *had hoped to hold* a spring picnic. (Past Perfect + Present Infinitive)

Keep in mind that the objective portions of the GWAR tests usually offer three substitute choices for each underlined part. Frequently, even though you may not remember the grammatical terms involved, your prose sense will lead you to the right answer.

Look at the following set of responses. Which is correct?

A. Fran would of wanted to see the show.
B. Fran would have wanted to had seen the show.
C. Fran would have wanted to have seen the show.
D. Fran would have wanted to see the show.

Choice **D** is correct. If you selected this answer, did you apply the grammatical principle involved (use the present infinitive after a perfect tense), or were you guided by your prose "ear"? Chances are that it may have been your own language sense that suggested this answer. The point is that you already possess language sense that should help you on the test. With more preparation, you should do even better.

THE SUBJUNCTIVE MOOD

Verbs may be expressed in one of three moods: the *indicative*, used to declare a fact or ask a question; the *imperative*, used to express a command; and the *subjunctive*, generally used to indicate doubt or to express a wish or request or a condition contrary to fact. The first two moods are fairly clear-cut.

INDICATIVE: This cake is tasty. Who baked it?
IMPERATIVE: Please leave now. Go home.

NOTE: The imperative mood has only one subject (*you*) and one tense (the present).

The subjunctive mood presents more of a problem. It suggests *possibilities, maybes, could have beens*, or *wishes that it had been*, and its uses are sometimes more difficult to understand. The subjunctive mood appears more frequently in formal English than in standard written English.

Notice the following uses, including some traditional ones:

EXAMPLES: I insist that the new road *be started* this spring.
The company requires that the check *be certified*.
Had she *been* certain of her facts, she would have challenged the teacher.
If need *be*, we can use our pension money.

> *Should* the swarm *reappear*, I will call a beekeeper.
> If he *were* honest, he would return all the money.
> I move that the budget *be accepted*.
> Far *be* it from me to suggest that he is lying.
> *Would* that I *were* sixteen again!
> I wish I *were* on a plane to Tahiti.

NOTE: Today, the subjunctive is most often used to express doubt, wishes, or conditions contrary to fact. However, the indicative can also be used for some of these same feelings.

SUBJUNCTIVE MOOD: If it *be* true, I will be delighted.
INDICATIVE MOOD: If it *is* true, I will be delighted.

SPECIAL USE OF THE PRESENT TENSE

Use the present tense to express universally true statements or timeless facts.

EXAMPLES:
Ice *forms* at 32° F.
The rainy season seldom *arrives* in California.
She told the campers that mosquitos *are* part of nature.

THE HISTORICAL PRESENT

In writing about a poem or describing events in fiction or plays, use the present tense. This convention is called the *historical* present.

EXAMPLE: In *A Tale of Two Cities*, Dr. Manette *is restored* to his daughter after twenty years in jail.

PRACTICE EXERCISE

In the following sentences, find any errors in mood or tense. Not every sentence has an error. Place a check in the appropriate column to indicate whether the sentence is correct or incorrect.

CORRECT   INCORRECT

_____   _____   1. If I knew about winning the lottery, I would not have sold my boat.

_____   _____   2. In his poem *In Memoriam*, Tennyson wrote a eulogy for his friend Arthur Henry Hallam.

_____   _____   3. The children have gone fishing for trout.

_____   _____   4. By the time the tide had covered the sand castles, we had already put the children to bed.

_____   _____   5. Groans and catcalls could be heard as the opposing team took the field.

_____   _____   6. When the earthquake struck, we all run out of our houses.

_____   _____   7. If I was you, I would take the job.

_____   _____   8. If we reach an accord by Monday, we will offer it to the membership by Monday night.

ANSWERS AND EXPLANATIONS

1. INCORRECT. The past tense *knew* does not go back in time far enough to permit the use of the present perfect tense later in the sentence. The correction is to change *knew* to *had known* (the past perfect).
2. INCORRECT. Use the historical present for statements about literary works (*poet...writes*).

> 3. INCORRECT. Use the present infinitive after a perfect tense. The children have gone *to fish* for trout.
> 4. INCORRECT. Watch the sequence of tenses: The children had been put to bed *before* the tide covered the sand castles. *Covered* is the correct tense.
> 5. INCORRECT. Both the subject and the voice shift in this sentence. *Revised*: The opposing team heard groans and catcalls as they took the field.
> 6. INCORRECT. Maintain a consistent verb tense: When the earthquake struck [past], we all *ran* [past] out of our houses.
> 7. INCORRECT. Use the subjunctive mood for a condition contrary to fact: If I *were* you...
> 8. CORRECT. There are no awkward shifts of subject or voice in this sentence. The sequence of tenses is also correct.

Predication

Predication refers to the process of joining the *naming* part of the sentence (the *subject*) to the *doing* or *describing* part of the sentence (the *predicate*).

SUBJECT	PREDICATE
People	are buying more fish.
Cecelia	is a counselor.

It is not likely that a writer or reader will have trouble linking the subjects and predicates of sentences as short as these. It is in the use of longer, more detailed sentences that predication errors come about. Illogical predication equates unlike constructions and ideas. Look at the following incorrect examples.

INCORRECT: By working at such technical plants as Lockheed and Bendix gives the engineering students insight into what will be expected of them. (*By working* does not give them insight; *working* does.)

According to one authority, the ages of thirty to forty are subject to the most pressures concerning self-identity. (The *ages* are not subject to the pressures, but rather the *people* of those ages.)

The sheer simplicity of frozen food may soon replace home-cooked meals. (*Simplicity* will not replace the meals; *frozen food* will, *because* of its simplicity of preparation.)

Paying bills on time causes many worries for young families. (*Paying* bills does not cause worries, but *not paying* them does.)

IS WHEN, IS WHERE, IS BECAUSE

The use of *is when, is where, is because* is always incorrect. The reason is simple: *when, where,* and *because* introduce adverbial clauses; and a noun subject followed by a form of the verb *to be* must be equated with a noun structure, not with an adverb clause.

INCORRECT: Lepidopterology *is where you study butterflies and moths.*
CORRECT: Lepidopterology *is the study of butterflies and moths.* (Here, the adverb clause *where you study...* has been changed to a subject complement: *lepidopterology = study.*) Or *lepidopterology requires the study...*
INCORRECT: The reason they won *is because they had better coaching.*
CORRECT: The reason they won *is that they had better coaching.* (The noun clause *that they had better coaching* equates with the noun *reason.*)
  OR
They *won because* they had better coaching. (The adverb clause modifies the verb *won.*)

NOTE: To eliminate the possibility of making such errors, always focus on stronger, more active verb use.

> **PRACTICE EXERCISE**
>
> In the following sentences, find any errors in predication. Not every sentence has an error. Place a check in the appropriate column to indicate whether the sentence is correct or incorrect.
>
> CORRECT   INCORRECT
>
> _____   _____   1. By building a more efficient engine will save fuel.
>
> _____   _____   2. Maintaining a healthy weight causes problems for many millions of Americans.
>
> _____   _____   3. Vertigo is when a person becomes dizzy and is unable to maintain his balance.
>
> _____   _____   4. Heart failure results from the inability of the heart to pump enough blood to maintain normal bodily functions.
>
> _____   _____   5. My first sight of Niagara Falls was inspiring, joyful, emotional.
>
> _____   _____   6. The reason that our team did not win was because our key players had injuries.
>
> **ANSWERS AND EXPLANATIONS**
>
> 1. INCORRECT. *Building* a more efficient engine may save fuel, but not *by building*.
> 2. INCORRECT. The problem does not lie in *maintaining* a healthy weight. It lies in *not maintaining* a healthy weight.
> 3. INCORRECT. *Is when* is always incorrect. *Revised*: Vertigo is a condition in which ...
> 4. CORRECT. This sentence has no errors in predications.
> 5. INCORRECT. *The sight* was not inspiring, joyful, or emotional; the speaker's *feelings* were.
> 6. INCORRECT. Equate a noun (*reason*) with a noun structure (the clause *that our key players had injuries*).

Parallelism

Parallel ideas in a sentence should be expressed in the same grammatical form. If they are not, the sentence will be unbalanced.

A series of coordinated elements should be parallel in form.

INCORRECT: He enjoys *plays, exhibitions,* and *to walk* every morning. (An infinitive is paired with two nouns.)

CORRECT: He enjoys *going* to plays, *visiting* exhibitions, and *walking* every morning.
OR
He enjoys *plays, exhibitions,* and morning *walks*.

INCORRECT: The union wanted *pay increases for every employee* and *that there would be shorter working hours*. (A noun is paired with a noun clause.)

CORRECT: The union wanted *pay increases* for every employee and shorter *working hours*.

The constructions that follow correlative conjunctions (*both-and, either-or, neither-nor, not only-but also, whether-or*) should be parallel in form.

INCORRECT: He was *neither qualified* to lead this country *nor was he willing*.
CORRECT: He was *neither qualified nor willing* to lead this country.

Do not use *and* before *which* or *who* unless the sentence has a previously expressed *which* or *who* clause with which to be parallel.

INCORRECT: She is a well-known surgeon from New York, and who has written many books on brain surgery.

CORRECT: She is a well-known surgeon from New York, who has lectured at many medical schools and who has written many books on brain surgery.

NOTE: A sentence may lack logical parallelism even though its parts are *grammatically* parallel. If the ideas are not logically equal, then the flow of ideas is not parallel.

INCORRECT: The dean introduced new faculty members, explained some curriculum strategies, began an exploratory discussion of the accreditation process, *spilled coffee on his tie*, reviewed the budget for the fiscal year, and *went to lunch with Don Love*. (Although the italicized phrases are grammatically parallel, they are not parallel with the other ideas expressed.)

PRACTICE EXERCISE

In the following sentences, find any errors in parallelism. Not every sentence has an error. Place a check in the appropriate column to indicate whether the sentence is correct or incorrect.

CORRECT   INCORRECT

1. William Faulkner wrote *As I Lay Dying, The Sound and the Fury, Sartoris*, and he was also the author of *The Reivers*.

2. Cluster secretaries answer calls about special programs, file important papers, sort mail, and they do typing and stuffing envelopes.

3. He bought a new scooter with an electric starter, and which has dual pipes and a digital clock.

4. My sister's tamale pie is made with ground meat, chili seasoning, olives, and it has onions and beans as well.

5. Playing racquetball is more taxing than to jog or play basketball.

6. The union stood firm on its demands for a realistic wage, a better health plan, and a more generous pension package.

7. The pool is eighteen feet in length and twelve feet wide.

8. Most citizens felt gas rationing to be a necessity and fair.

ANSWERS AND EXPLANATIONS

1. INCORRECT. *Made parallel:* William Faulkner wrote *As I Lay Dying, The Sound and the Fury, Sartoris*, and *The Reivers*. (*He was also the author of* is unnecessary.)
2. INCORRECT. *Made parallel:* Cluster secretaries answer calls about special programs, file important papers, sort mail, type, and stuff envelopes.
3. INCORRECT. *Made parallel:* He bought a new scooter with an electric starter, dual pipes, and a digital clock. (A sentence that contains *and which* is not parallel unless it has a previously expressed *which* clause.)
4. INCORRECT. *Made parallel:* My sister's tamale pie is made with ground meat, chili seasoning, olives, onions, and beans.
5. INCORRECT. *Made parallel:* Playing racquetball is more taxing than jogging or playing basketball. (In the original, the infinitives *to jog* and [*to*] *play* are not parallel with the gerund phrase *playing racquetball*.
6. CORRECT. The structures in this sentence—*wage, plan,* and *package*—are parallel.
7. INCORRECT. *Made parallel:* The pool is eighteen feet long and twelve feet wide. (Or match the phrase *in length* with the phrase *in width*.)
8. INCORRECT. *Made parallel:* Most citizens felt gas rationing to be necessary and fair. (In the original sentence, an adjective, *fair*, is paired with a noun, *necessity*.)

English Review and Practice 187

> **TRANSITION RULE**: Each sentence on a GWAR essay should be connected to the sentence before it by a transitional word, phrase, or expression. Writers can best use these words within the first four or five words of a sentence. Similarly, the first sentence of a paragraph, excepting the introductory paragraph, should contain a transitional idea referring to the paragraph(s) before it. Transitional words and phrases allow writers to (1) keep the subject going, (2) change to a new subject, or (3) imply a connection to a related idea.

Transitional Words and Phrases

Words of transition help the reader to follow the writer's flow of ideas. Confusion can result, however, when a transition is omitted or an illogical or incorrect connective is used. The following list includes more commonly used transitional words and phrases, and the concepts they suggest.

CONCEPT

Addition	also, furthermore, moreover, similarly, too
Cause and effect	accordingly, as a result, consequently, hence, so, therefore, thus
Concession	granted that, it is true that, no doubt, to be sure
Conclusion	in short, that is, in brief
Contrast	although, but, however, nevertheless, on the contrary, on the other hand
Example	for example, for instance

Watch for errors in logic during use of transitional words. For example:

INCORRECT: At many gas stations, drivers have to pump their own gasoline; *therefore,* at Ken's Union Station, full service is still the rule.

CORRECT: At many gas stations, drivers have to pump their own gasoline; *however*, at Ken's Union Station, full service is still the rule.

PRACTICE EXERCISE

In the following sentences, find any transition errors. Not every sentence has an error. Place a check in the appropriate column to indicate whether the sentence is correct or incorrect.

CORRECT   INCORRECT

1. Her apple pie won a blue ribbon at the county fair; nevertheless, we all wanted the recipe.

2. Bud and Jake climbed to the top of the falls, and Jake had a fear of heights.

3. I have been meaning to learn more about electronics, so I just bought a book on the subject.

4. I have just finished preparing my tax return after four weeks of figuring and frustration; furthermore, I refuse to fill out any other forms for at least a month!

5. Maria has spent almost twelve years of her academic life studying medicine; however, she feels well qualified to treat sick people.

ANSWERS AND EXPLANATIONS

1. INCORRECT. The connective *nevertheless* is obviously illogical here, with its implication of contrast. A better transitional word might be *consequently*.
2. INCORRECT. A contrast like *although* is needed in this sentence.

> 3. CORRECt. This is a typical cause-and-effect sentence, correctly using the word *so*.
> 4. INCORRECT. The speaker refused to fill out another form *because of* his work on the tax return. Needed here is a causal transition like *as a result*.
> 5. INCORRECT. The connective *however* does not make sense here because it implies contrast. A causal word like *accordingly* is required.

FOCUS ON THE TEST
The following sample questions represent ways in which the above skills might be tested on your writing test.

Crime and Punishment by Fyodor Dostoevsky is a topical novel dealing with philosophical doctrines, political₁ and social issues widely discussed in Russia just after the 1861 reforms. By most critical essays,₂ treating Dostoevsky's work has employed₃ psychological or biological points of view. Because *Crime and Punishment* is a passionate, masterly portrayal of internal psychological conflict, a general assumption has evolved in the general critical world that the author wrote, at least in part, from personal experience. Nevertheless,₄ Dostoevsky's biography has been endlessly probed, explored, and it was thoroughly analyzed.₅ In 1849, Dostoevsky was convicted of consorting with known radical factions; however, he was sentenced₆ to a four-year prison term. Many critical commentaries on *Crime and Punishment* consider this experience

1. A. NO CHANGE
    B. politically
    C. politics
    D. that are political

2. F. NO CHANGE
    G. Because of most critical essays
    H. Most critical essays,
    J. Most critical essays

3. A. NO CHANGE
    B. have employed
    C. should employ
    D. employ

4. F. NO CHANGE
    G. Hence,
    H. On the contrary,
    J. Furthermore

5. A. NO CHANGE
    B. and being analyzed.
    C. and analyzed.
    D. subject to analysis.

6. F. NO CHANGE
    G. factions, yet, he was sentenced
    H. factions and was sentenced
    J. factions; moreover, he was sentenced

formative and essential—certainly a major source of the creative impulses that eventually resulted in Dostoevsky's execution of the novel. The epilogue of the novel had been set in Siberia, where he was
                                      7

imprisoned. If, indeed, he were talking to his fellow
                       8
prisoners, then he found an opportunity to focus on crime and guilt, and thus thought about the psychology of the criminal mind granted that he lived among
                                9
hardened convicts. One must ask, though, why he waited until 1865 to write *Crime and Punishment*. One possible answer is because he wrote the novel in part to
                      10
speak against foreign ideas adopted by the Russian radicals of the 1860s.

7. **A.** NO CHANGE
   B. is set
   C. was set
   D. has been set

8. **F.** NO CHANGE
   G. he was talking
   H. he had talked
   J. he had been talking

9. **A.** NO CHANGE
   B. as he
   C. knowing that he
   D. considering that he

10. **F.** NO CHANGE
    G. is when
    H. is where
    J. is that

ANSWERS AND EXPLANATIONS

1. **C** A noun is necessary in this position to be parallel with the other noun objects in this series, *doctrines* and *issues*.

2. **J** As it stands, this sentence contains an error in predication, beginning with one construction, *By most critical essays*, and continuing with a different one, *treating Dostoevsky's work has employed...points of view*. It is incorrect to separate a subject from its verb by a comma, as in choice H.

3. **D** The verb must agree with its plural subject *essays* and maintain the established present tense.

4. **G** The logic of the sentence requires a cause/effect transitional marker like *Hence*, not the contrast or addition markers suggested by the alternative choices.

5. **C** The parallel series of past participles in this sentence requires this option: *has been probed, explored, and analyzed*.

6. **H** The logic of this sentence requires a transitional word suggesting either *cause* or *addition*. Since the acts of *conviction* and *sentencing* seem to be of equal weight, the conjunction *and* is a sound choice.

7. **B** Use the historical present tense when relating events that occur in fiction.

8. **F** The subjunctive is the logical choice of mood in this *if* clause because it expresses a supposition.

9. **B** The use of the subordinating conjunction *as* is a sound choice in this position because it creates an adverb clause that modifies the verbs *focused* and *thought*. The other choices create modifiers of the subject to little effect.

10. **J** Only the use of the words *is that* in this spot forms a noun structure that equates with the noun *answer*. The other choices form adverb clauses that cannot equate with the noun.

RHETORICAL SKILLS

Strategy

Some questions on the writing test might ask you to choose the most effective introductions and conclusions, both of paragraphs and essays. Others will ask you to select the most logical transitions between sentences or between paragraphs. You will most likely be asked if a passage is appropriate for a particular audience or what kinds of supporting details should be added to strengthen a paragraph. You may be asked whether a particular sentence or paragraph is relevant to the selection. A good way to prepare for such questions is to look over writing strategies and some of the principles that apply to each.

Description

Descriptive writing usually relies on sense impressions—records of what the eye sees, the ear hears, the nose smells, the tongue tastes, and the skin feels. If you are asked how a descriptive selection can be strengthened, be sure to consider the addition of more specific sense impressions, if that is an option you are given. (Mood also results from sense impressions.)

In addition to sense impressions, descriptive writing often employs a *dominant impression* at the outset of the selection, a controlling idea or value judgment that helps unify the passage and encompass the specific details employed.

Narration

Narration is usually a series of events presented in chronological sequence, all of which have one purpose: *to tell what happened*. Narration, primarily used in storytelling, biographical histories, diaries, and journals, is a fundamental strategy in all writing. To be effective, narration requires coherent order and also a good deal of rich, descriptive detail.

It is probable that any test choices dealing with the structure of the narrative passage will focus on the *order* of events that make up the narrative. The exact chronological relationships among the events are signaled by tenses, transitions, and time markers. Notice how the author of the following selection uses each of these cues to establish coherent order.

> In the past, this type of literature—whether in books or magazines—was published under such titles as *Travel Adventures, Wonder Stories, Fantastic Tales,* or *Mysteries of the Universe*. It took garish "headlines" like these to draw attention to the special nature of this material.
>
> In 1929, Hugh Gernsback, a New York magazine publisher and one of the great pioneers in the field we are exploring here, provided the much-needed common denominator by coining the inspired term *science fiction*.
>
> Instantly and universally, science fiction was defined and accepted as a form of literature distinct and apart from all others, a form that imposed on the writer none of the shackles that confine traditional writing to the limits of so many rules and precedents.
>
> Comfortably settled under the aegis of its brand-new generic name, science fiction prospered in spite of a worldwide depression and World War II. Other entertainment media contributed their share. The movies gave us Boris Karloff as Frankenstein's monster and Fredric March as Dr. Jekyll. In 1938, a science fiction radio program about Martian invaders threw the East Coast of the United States into a panic.

Note that the events in the development of science fiction are carefully presented in a clear, coherent sequence and include clues that leave no doubt about the order in which these events took place. For instance, the use of *in the past, this type of literature ... was published* in the first paragraph establishes the fact that science fiction existed in some form *before* the events described in the subsequent paragraphs. In the next three paragraphs, such transitions and time markers as *in 1929, instantly and universally, comfortably settled under ... brand-new ... name, worldwide depression, World War II,* and *in 1938* firmly establish the relative order of events.

Explanation of a Process

Explaining a process is, in some ways, similar to narration; however, you have to be even more careful with the sequence of events. Narration adheres *in general* to a sequence; a process depends *exactly* on a sequence, one that can be repeated time after time with the same results. In explaining a process, the use of transitional signals such as *after, before, next, immediately, while the [glue] is still [wet],* and *when [this] is done,* to indicate the sequence of steps, is an essential writing strategy. To evaluate the sequence of steps in a process passage, pay careful attention to transitional words and phrases.

Classification and Division

Classification helps organize detailed material into different groups so that it can be dealt with in steps or stages, can be seen more clearly, or can be explained or illustrated in all its diversity.

Suppose that you are a newspaper writer who specializes in restaurants and that you want to do an article on international food available in a certain town. You might divide the restaurants in the following way:

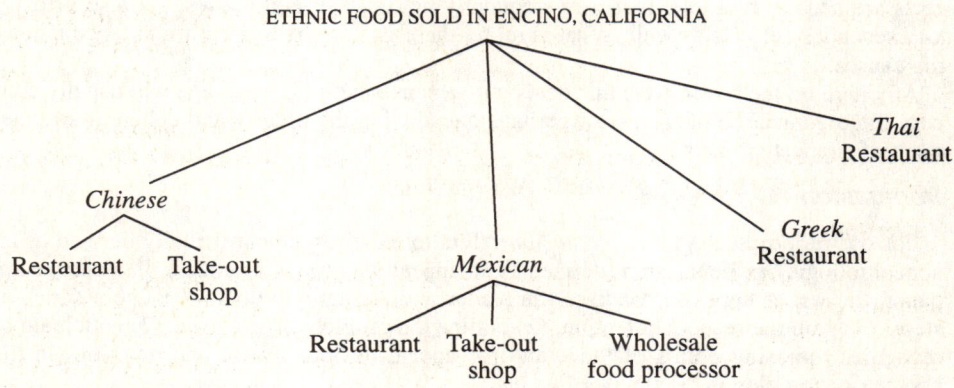

Each division and subdivision of a subject must make sense, that is, it must be necessary for the writer's purpose and also understandable to the reader. The division must be based upon some clear principle: in the diagram of ethnic food sales in Encino, for instance, each ethnic group heads a category. Restaurants, take-out shops, and a wholesale food processor are placed in a subdivision. (When you plan your essay use a quick diagram to organize your categories.)

Definition

A definition usually takes the form of one or more paragraphs within a larger piece of writing. The writer has decided at that point in the essay that an explanation is needed of the nature or essential qualities of something.

A definition begins by placing the term being defined into a *class*; then it lists the details by which the term can be *distinguished* from other members of that class. For example, a blender is in the class of small kitchen appliances; it can be distinguished from other members of that class—like toasters, can openers, and waffle irons—by the fact that it blends liquids. Here are some other examples:

TERM BEING DEFINED	CLASS TO WHICH IT BELONGS	DISTINGUISHING CHARACTERISTICS
A stove is	a kitchen appliance	designed to heat and cook food.
Freedom is	a political condition	without restraints or limitations.
A lion is	a feline animal	that inhabits wide plains areas.
Psychiatry is	the medical field	dealing with physical and behavioral disorders of the mind.

An extended definition begins with this simple form and builds upon it, using any of the techniques common to other strategies.

Comparison and Contrast

A common way to explain something is to show how it is *similar to* or *different from* something else—in other words, to *compare* or *contrast*. You have two main options in comparing and contrasting: (a) you can present the similarities or differences point by point, turning first to one subject and then to the other each time, or (b) you can treat each subject as a whole, finishing with one during the first half of the essay, and then with the other.

In either case, strict organization of the specific differences and similarities between one item and the other is essential. In addition, some balance and sense of equal treatment of each subject will establish coherence.

Cause and Effect

Cause-and-effect essays can be immensely complicated and, as a result, require more careful organization than any other strategic approach. The cause-and-effect essay or paragraph usually begins with a clear, detailed examination of the *effect* that is the essay subject (such as the slow death of Monterey pine trees around Lake Arrowhead in Southern California) and then proceeds to discuss each of the causes in detail, usually in order of importance or chronological sequence.

What can be more troublesome about cause-and-effect essays is that both causes and effects are usually multiple; there are frequently not only several causes, but also primary *and* secondary effects as well. What is more, there is a progression of importance among the causes.

Any item on the writing test that deals with a cause-and-effect passage will usually concern the organization of the essay, perhaps questioning the orderly and coherent arrangement of supporting facts.

Persuasion

For our purposes, the term *persuasion* refers to either argument (usually defined as an appeal to logic), or persuasion (defined as an appeal to emotion or ethics). In a persuasion paper, the writer hopes to *convince* the reader and attempts to do so through a series of steps: (1) gain the reader's attention, (2) outline the problem or situation, (3) anticipate or recognize opposing points of view, and (4) appeal to both reason and emotion (in the choice of examples and details).

PRACTICE EXERCISE

Identify the appropriate writing strategy for developing a paragraph on each of the following topics. Choose your answer from the following list and write the letter of your choice in the space to the left.

A. Description
B. Narration
C. Explanation of a Process
D. Classification and Division
E. Definition
F. Comparison and Contrast
G. Cause and Effect
H. Persuasion

WRITING
STRATEGY   TOPIC

_____   1. Types of diets

_____   2. An inspiring moment

_____   3. American students and Japanese students

_____   4. Why so many high school students drop out

_____   5. My grandmother's kitchen _____

_____   6. How to install a three-way switch

_____   7. The meaning of commitment

_____   8. Don't let them cut the homeowner's tax deduction.

> **ANSWERS AND EXPLANATIONS**
>
> 1. **D** *Classification and Division.* Whenever a plural topic (diets) is to be broken down into subtypes, the written material will be detailed and will require classification, division, and subdivision.
> 2. **B** *Narration.* The word *moment* is an important clue. Obviously something happened to make that moment memorable. Narration presents a series of events.
> 3. **F** *Comparison and Contrast.* A topic with such clear polarity has to fall into this strategy. When two items are being discussed, it is almost impossible to avoid a discussion of similarities and differences.
> 4. **G** *Cause and Effect.* The effect is the dropout rate; the cause is the main substance of a paper on this topic (*why* such a phenomenon occurs). It is clearly a complicated topic, with multiple causes and effects.
> 5. **A** *Description.* Grandmother's kitchen is full of smells and visual impressions that can only be approached *through a descriptive essay*.
> 6. **C** *Explanation of a Process.* The words *How to* signal a process paper, a paper that explains the exact and repeatable steps to take to achieve the same result each time—in this case, an operating three-way switch.
> 7. **E** *Definition.* Definition writing is required when a word must be placed in a class—in this case, a class of philosophical stances—and then distinguished from other members of that class, to achieve a clear and understandable definition.
> 8. **H** *Persuasion.* The very form of this topic ("...Don't let them...") indicates that it is a form of argument in which the writing is meant to convince the reader.

Organization

The Main Idea

If a passage of prose can be viewed as a liquid and boiled in a pan until just one drop is left, that one drop can be considered the *essence* or *main idea* of that passage. It is essential to realize that every piece of writing that can stand on its own has one *main idea* from which the entire work, no matter how large or small, is derived.

It should not be too difficult to discover the central idea in each of the short selections that are often a part of the writing tests. If you get in the habit of formulating the main idea as you read each passage, you will find that the rhetorical questions, especially those concerning organization, can be answered more easily. Remember that the main idea must always be a complete sentence, not a word or topic. Only a full sentence expresses the full *idea* of the passage.

For example, a passage might be about exercise (the *topic*). But what does it state about exercise? If the selection points out that exercise makes a person more alert, more fit, more productive, and more likely to live longer, the central idea is probably something similar to "Exercise is essential to a healthy, productive life." On the other hand, if statements are made concerning bruised heel bones, pulled hamstrings, shinsplints, and muscle pain, then the main idea might be something similar to "Exercise can do more harm than good."

Whatever sentence you decide expresses the main idea of the passage, you must test it to make sure it really does represent the thrust of the entire selection. For example, you can ask, "In what way can exercise do more harm than good?" Or, "In what way is exercise essential to a healthy, productive life?" If every sentence and paragraph in the passage pertains to the main idea you have chosen, then you know your choice is sound. However, if you find that the passage contains sentences and paragraphs that support other ideas, then you need to start over and formulate another main idea.

Questions that test your ability to determine the central idea can be expressed in a number of ways:

The main point the author makes is ...
The author seems chiefly concerned with ...
The main idea of this passage is ...
Which of the following titles could best be used for this selection?
Which of these statements best expresses the idea of the passage?

Supporting Material

The supporting material that makes up the larger portion of most selections (often called the *body of the writing*) contains the essential material of the work—specific details, anecdotes, allusions, references, or reasons—by which a writer substantiates the main thought.

Keep in mind that supporting material may vary considerably from one context to another. The specific details in a report on a scientific discovery, for example, may be very different from the kind of detail needed in a biographical selection.

Try to be continually mindful of the logical order of paragraphs within a selection, and of the logical order of sentences within each paragraph. Transitional words and phrases usually highlight paragraph or essay coherence, and should provide great clues when you are asked whether or not a sentence or paragraph seems out of place.

At times, the writing test will include a question about the *readers* or *audience* for whom the selection is intended. The relative quality and sophistication of the supporting details will supply the basis for the answer to such questions. For example, a selection intended for children would probably include simple explanations and supporting details that would be unnecessary or inappropriate for adult readers.

Transition

Transitional words and phrases make clear the relationships between phrases, clauses, and sentences, and lend coherence to the sequence of paragraphs.

A transitional paragraph is used to link larger parts of an essay. Such a paragraph may be just a single sentence that eases the progression from one idea to the next:

EXAMPLE: Sometimes a solution is based upon a study of the past. Let us review what has taken place in new architecture so far this century.

Most of the time, however, transitions are individual words or phrases that provide transition while signaling a concept like addition, contrast, example, or time. The following list reinforces the functions of some transitions.

CONCEPTS	TRANSITIONS
Addition and continuation	also, and, another, besides, finally, likewise, furthermore, in addition, indeed, moreover, similarly, then, too
Cause and effect	accordingly, as, as a result, because, consequently, for this reason, since, then, therefore, thus
Concession	certainly, granted that, it is true that, no doubt, of course, still, to be sure
Conclusion or repetition	in other words, in particular, in short, in summary, once again, that is, to repeat
Contrast or limitation	although, but, however, if, in contrast, instead, nevertheless, on the contrary, on the other hand, otherwise, provided that, still, yet
Example	for example, for instance, in particular, likewise, specifically, that is, to illustrate
Place	above, behind, below, elsewhere, here, in back of, north of, on this side, there, to the right of, underneath
Time	afterward, before, earlier, eventually, immediately, later, meanwhile, next, now, since, soon, until

Openings and Closings

Being able to spot beginning and ending paragraphs is important when you are asked on the ACT to rearrange paragraphs that are obviously scrambled. The beginning paragraph will often include signals that will help you determine the proper order of subsequent paragraphs.

The *opening paragraph* is crucial. In a few words, the author must make clear the central purpose of the work and also convince the reader that he should continue. Sometimes, an author will use the opening paragraph to establish his authority for the task or to create a question in the reader's mind that he or she needs or hopes to have answered—by continuing to read.

> The land that became the United States was in colonial times an extension of the Old World into the New. Through the centuries, the descendants of the

original colonists blended their European heritage into the new Nation that evolved. But for the courage and resourcefulness of the Europeans who first explored and settled the unknown wilderness, that evolution would not have been possible.

The simplest *closing paragraphs* summarize the gist of the entire passage in a sentence or two. Others invite or challenge the reader to engage in further research on the topic. A good concluding paragraph will complete the passage logically and clearly, leaving the reader with the certainty that the main idea has been adequately developed. Also, good concluding paragraphs identify a truth or principle.

> The amalgamation of such rich and diverse national, cultural, and racial elements into a free and democratic society has created the United States of America—a blending of cultures, languages, and traditions that mirrors the hopes and aspirations of all mankind.

PRACTICE EXERCISE

The sentences in the following paragraphs have been deliberately rearranged so that the thoughts are not coherent. You will find, however, that they contain enough key words and ideas for you to identify the central idea and then rearrange the sentences to form a well-crafted, coherent paragraph. In the space at the left, indicate the correct sequence of sentence numbers.

Paragraph I

_____

(1) More flowed at Concord, and much more along the route of the British as they retreated to Boston, harassed most of the way by an aroused citizenry. (2) About 77 militiamen confronted the redcoats when they plodded into Lexington at dawn. (3) What once had been merely protest had evolved into open warfare; the American War of Independence had begun. (4) After some tense moments, as the sorely outnumbered colonials were dispersing, some blood was shed.

Paragraph II

_____

(1) It was not just the Iranian hostage crisis or the Soviet invasion of Afghanistan, but the fear, felt by many of our friends, that America could not, or would not, keep her commitments. (2) We need to remember where America was in the late 1970s. (3) Other nations were saying that it was dangerous—deadly dangerous—to be a friend of the United States. (4) We need to recall the atmosphere of that time—the anxiety that events were out of control, that the West was in decline, that our enemies were on the march. (5) Pakistan, the country most threatened by the Afghan invasion, ridiculed the first offer of American aid as "peanuts."

Paragraph III

_____

(1) Finally, and probably most important, inflation must be brought under control so that the country can enjoy a period of disciplined growth. (2) Another would be to increase investment in human capital, particularly skilled workers and technical personnel, through training in the workplace and in institutions of higher education. (3) The U.S. government can do much to create an environment in which the innovative capacity of American business and labor can be maximized. (4) It is clear that it would be impossible for the United States to emulate the much-vaunted Japanese form of industrial policy. (5) To do so would require a very different system for allocating capital investments, a different government-business-labor relationship, and perhaps a different set of cultural institutions. (6) Yet there are some lessons to be learned

from the successes of Japan, as well as from those of industrial countries. (7) Increasing the level of investments and savings would be a desirable goal.

ANSWERS AND EXPLANATIONS

The answers have been rearranged in the logical order.

PARAGRAPH I: 2, 4, 1, 3. About 77 militiamen confronted the redcoats when they plodded into Lexington at dawn. After some tense moments, as the sorely outnumbered colonials were dispersing, some blood was shed. More flowed at Concord, and much more along the route of the British as they retreated to Boston, harassed most of the way by an aroused citizenry. What once had been merely protest had evolved into open warfare; the American War of Independence had begun.

Commentary: Note that the second, third, and fourth sentences of the rearranged paragraph begin with the transition clues that place them after a key statement in the previous sentence. For example, in the second sentence, the phrase *After some tense moments* clearly belongs after the event described in the initial sentence. Similarly, the word *More* in the next sentence has as its antecedent the word *blood* in the sentence before, and the summation of the last sentence applies to the paragraph as a whole.

PARAGRAPH II: 2, 4, 1, 5, 3. We need to remember where America was in the late 1970s. We need to recall the atmosphere of that time—the anxiety that events were out of control, that the West was in decline, that our enemies were on the march. It was not just the Iranian hostage crisis or the Soviet invasion of Afghanistan, but the fear, felt by many of our friends, that America could not, or would not, keep her commitments. Pakistan, the country most threatened by the Afghan invasion, ridiculed the first offer of American aid as "peanuts." Other nations were saying that it was dangerous—deadly dangerous—to be a friend of the United States.

Commentary: Again, each sentence has a clue to help you determine where it belongs. The first sentence has the phrase *We need*, echoed by the second sentence, which then goes on to speak of events out of control. The next sentence actually lists events out of control and also mentions the fear, on the part of our friends, that we would not meet our commitments. These "friends," Pakistan and other nations, are identified in the next two sentences.

PARAGRAPH III: 4, 5, 6, 7, 2, 3, 1. It is clear that it would be impossible for the United States to emulate the much-vaunted Japanese form of industrial policy. To do so would require a very different system for allocating capital investments, a different government-business-labor relationship, and perhaps a different set of cultural institutions. Yet there are some lessons to be learned from the successes of Japan, as well as from those of other industrial countries. Increasing the level of investments and savings would be a desirable goal. Another would be to increase investment in human capital, particularly skilled workers and technical personnel, through training in the workplace and in institutions of higher education. The U.S. government can do much to create an environment in which the innovative capacity of American business and labor can be maximized. Finally, and probably most important, inflation must be brought under control so that the country can enjoy a period of disciplined growth.

Commentary: The key to unraveling this set of sentences is the phrase *To do so* in the second sentence. A cursory look at all of the sentences in the paragraph reveals that only one (the sentence beginning *It is clear that* ...) makes sense in an earlier position. The other sentences occur naturally in order from that point on. The contrast indicator *yet* signals a departure from the "it is impossible to emulate" position of the first two sentences, with the sentence it begins stating that "there are some lessons to be learned." The next two sentences list two of those lessons, and the last two sentences add two more steps that could be taken by the U.S. government.

NOTE: Understanding transitional movement will help you identify the original sentence sequence of a paragraph for which sentences have been scrambled.

Style

As you read each passage on the test, it serves you to analyze/figure out the author's style of writing. You may be asked a question about style, and its characteristics, or about a portion of the test that departs from that style. A fundamental principle of writing is that style should remain consistent throughout any writing selection. If there is an obvious shift in style in one of the selections, you will probably be questioned about it.

There are several levels of formality in the prose that most secondary and postsecondary students encounter: formal, informal, popular, elevated, and esoteric.

Formal Writing Style

Formal style is characterized by long and complex sentences, a scholarly vocabulary, and a consistently serious tone. Grammatical rules are observed, and the subject matter is substantial. The selection may include references to literary works or allusions to historical and classical figures. Absent are contractions, colloquial expressions, and an identified speaker, with the impersonal *one* or *the reader* frequently used as the subject.

> The California coast, endowed with a wonderful climate and peopled by docile Indians, was ideally suited for the pastoral mission system by which New Spain had been slowly extending her northern frontiers. Elsewhere in the present United States the system had either failed or met with only moderate success; in California it thrived and reached perfection. Nevertheless, California was the last area in the United States to be penetrated by Spain—and not until the frontier lay virtually dormant elsewhere. Located as it was so far out on the lifelines of the Spanish Empire in the New World, California was sparsely populated and neglected.
>
> *Explorers and Settlers,* Government Printing Office

A formal writing style is used in serious essays, research papers, and legal documentation. Although this type of writing is not likely to appear on the test, you should be prepared to identify it.

Informal Writing Style

Informal style uses the language of everyday speech, characterized by contractions, colloquialisms, and occasional slang. The topics are often light, and the approach, or tone, is conversational. Sentences are usually uncomplicated, and the writer makes no attempt to distance himself from the reader, frequently using *I* or *we* as the subject.

> Animals talk to each other, of course. There can be no question about that; but I suppose there are very few people who can understand them. I never knew but one man who could...This was Jim Baker. According to Jim Baker, some animals have only a limited education, and use only very simple words, and scarcely ever a comparison or a flowery figure; whereas, certain other animals have a large vocabulary, a fine command of language and a ready and fluent delivery; consequently these latter talk a great deal; they like it; they are conscious of their talent, and they enjoy "showing off."
>
> Mark Twain, *A Tramp Abroad*

Popular Writing Style

The popular style is the writing style most students use in school work. Less colloquial and relaxed than the informal, the popular style consists of longer sentences, with no contractions but some colloquialisms when necessary for clarity and immediacy. Usually the tone of the work is serious, and the content is substantial and informative. The popular style is characteristic of the language used in newspapers, magazines, and contemporary literature. Look at the following student essay, written in popular style.

> Fishing has always been an art form to the practitioner of the sport. The techniques involved in outsmarting fish are passed down from generation to generation. Sometimes this information is related in the form of direct instruction or through the use of illustrated books, but most neophytes learn by watching others fish or by being asked to "mind my pole." That is usually the time when

the best fish of the day is caught. Such an occurrence can and does drive expert anglers to distraction, causing them to mutter under their breath and cast sidelong glances at a youngster who is doing everything wrong but still manages to bring in a whopper.

Elevated Writing Style

The elevated style is poetic in tone and is intended for certain solemn occasions that exist infrequently today – for example, addressing a king or memorializing a national hero. Heightened funeral orations or eulogies now seem inappropriate, most expressions of grief or commemoration being couched in more popular styles. Literary allusions, biblical phrases, figures of speech, ornate language, graveness of tone—all are characteristic of the elevated style. Although this type of writing is not likely to appear on all of the writing tests, it is a good idea to be familiar with it, in case you are asked to differentiate it from another style of writing. The following excerpt is from a eulogy that appeared in a July 1852 newspaper.

> Alas! who can realize that Henry Clay is dead! Who can realize that never again that majestic form shall rise in the council-chambers of his country to beat back the storms of anarchy which may threaten, or pour the oil of peace upon the troubled billows as they rage and menace around?

Esoteric Writing Style

The word *esoteric* refers to knowledge that is limited to a small group. This writing style uses technical or specialized phraseology (sometimes referred to as jargon) characteristic of a particular profession, trade, or branch of learning. Groups employing such language include medical personnel, astronauts, air traffic controllers, jazz musicians, and a variety of others. The following excerpt is from a medical journal.

> Morphologic changes in the myocardium are caused by coronary obstruction leading to infarction and hemorrhaging within the wall of the sclerotic coronary vessel.

PRACTICE EXERCISE

Identify the following items according to the writing style used: formal (F), elevated (EL), informal (I), popular (P), or esoteric (ES). Put the correct letter in the space to the left of each item.

_____ 1. If gold were the first valuable product to be found in America, wood of the *Caesalpina* species, known in English as brazilwood, or simply logwood, had become the second by 1510.

_____ 2. Before the sale started, I spotted an old beat-up table, drop-leaf style, that was pure cherry, as far as I could see.

_____ 3. Parry made the crucial connection between this "formulaic" diction and the possibility, long speculated on, that Homer was an oral bard rather than a literate writer.

_____ 4. The essential difference between capitalizing with discount rates, GRMs, and overall capitalization rates is that specific forecasting of periodic cash flows is required when using discount rates.

_____ 5. Of course, this man was an eccentric. In fact, an eccentric among eccentrics. Most furniture forgers use old wood. And where do these crooks get two-hundred-year-old wood? The answer's simple. From two-hundred-year-old houses.

_____ 6. Alas, in those dark hours, which, as they come in the history of all nations, must come in ours—those hours of peril and dread which our land has experienced, and which she may be called to experience again—to whom now may her people look up for that counsel and advice, which only wisdom and experience can give?

_____ 7. Second-rate matadors lived at that pension because the address on the Calle San Jeronimo was good, the food was excellent, and the room and board was cheap.

> **ANSWERS AND EXPLANATIONS**
>
> 1. F   Note the factual approach, the scholarly tone and vocabulary.
> 2. I   This sentence is colloquial and conversational, and uses the subject *I*.
> 3. F   Phrases like *"fomulaic" diction* and *oral bard*, as well as the scholarly tone and subject matter, indicate the writing style.
> 4. ES It is easy to identify this style by the specialized vocabulary and technical approach.
> 5. I   Informal style uses colloquialisms, slang, contractions, and short, uncomplicated sentences.
> 6. EL Extravagant sentiment and ornate phrases mark the elevated style.
> 7. P   The popular style has no contractions or slang and is less colloquial than the informal style.

Word Choice

Diction

Some of the questions on the writing test will require you to decide the appropriateness of a word in its context. In a technical passage about the development of the transistor, for example, the use of a flowery or ornate word or phrase would stand out as inappropriate. Similarly, words that are illiterate or colloquial, or used in spoken English, for the most part, are not appropriate in a formal literary passage.

A word is *appropriate* if it fits the reader, occasion, and purpose for which the writing is intended. In general, most language can be categorized as either formal, informal (colloquial), or popular.

FORMAL DICTION

Formal diction is seldom used in everyday conversation and writing. It is found in writing that serves a serious purpose (for example, a research paper) and concerns weighty or substantial topics, such as death, crime, philosophy, scholarship, science, and literature.

Formal language employs a more scholarly vocabulary than popular English (*eccentric* for *strange*, *extenuation* for *excuse*, *immaculate* for *clean*, *tantamount* for *equivalent*, and so on). Another characteristic is grammatical exactness.

INFORMAL DICTION

Informal diction is *colloquial* language, that is, the language of everyday conversation. It includes contractions (always improper in formal writing), slang, colloquialisms, dialect and turns of phrase peculiar to local areas (*provincialisms*) and shortened word forms (*TV* for *television*, *phone* for *telephone*, *stereo* for *stereophonic set*, and so on).

POPULAR DICTION

Popular diction lies somewhere between formal and informal (colloquial) diction. It is not as free as colloquial, nor does it include slang or provincialisms, but it relaxes many of the rules and restrictions of formal written English. Generally, popular diction is the language of mass-media publications. Its aim is to appeal to and communicate clearly with the average reader.

The following expressions have no place in formal prose.

Cool it.	yeah
guys	turn-on
high (intoxicated)	guts
spaced-out (on drugs)	I've had it!
for sure	stuck-up
creep (obnoxious person)	an awful lot
macho	screwball

This list contains some common misspellings, provincialisms, illiterate expressions, and incorrect forms to be avoided.

NOT	BUT
aggravate	annoy; exasperate
a half an hour	a half hour *or* half an hour
a lot	a lot
alright	all right
and etc.	etc. or et cetera
anywheres	anywhere
being that, being as how	as, because, since
can't seem to	seem unable to
considerable sick	quite sick
dark-complected	dark-complexioned
different than	different from
hadn't ought	ought not
heighth	height
irregardless	regardless, irrespective
no-account; no-good	worthless
off of	off, from
out loud	aloud
outside of	except; beside
should of, would of	should have, would have
the reason is because	the reason is that
tote	carry
try and give	try to give
use to	used to
visit with	visit
won him	beat him

Some colloquialisms and short forms are appropriate in everyday conversation and informal writing, but should not be used in formal written English.

NOT	BUT
ad	advertisement
at about; at around	about; around
can't help but	cannot help but
center around	center on
get going	go
guess so, reckon so	think, suppose
has got to go	has to go
he is liable to be there	he is likely to be there
hold on	wait
kids	children
kind of a, sort of a	kind of, sort of
mighty hard	very hard
okay	all right
out loud	aloud
packs quite a punch	delivers a strong blow
phone	telephone
show up	appear to be superior
TV	television
wait a bit	wait

Here is a list of frequently misused or confused words. Be sure you can distinguish their meanings.

accept: to receive; to agree to
except: to exclude
except: a preposition meaning *but, other than*

affect: to influence
effect: to bring about
effect: a noun meaning *result*

allusion: indirect reference
illusion: false perception or image

all ready: everything is ready
already: by this time

alumna: a female graduate
alumnae: two or more female graduates
alumnus: a male graduate
alumni: two or more male graduates; also, a universal term for college graduate

amount: used for noncountable bulk or weight (an amount of milk)
number: used for things that can be counted as individual units (a number of gallons of milk)

compare: to deal with similarities
contrast: to deal with differences

complement: to complete or strengthen (or "match")
compliment: to praise

continual: frequently repeated
continuous: without interruption; never ending

emigrate: to move out of a country or region
immigrate: to move into a country or region

fiancé: engaged man (plural: fiancés)
fiancée: engaged woman (plural: fiancées)

former: first
latter: last

healthful: giving health
healthy: having good health

imply: to suggest or hint by word or manner (He *implied*, by the way he ignored me, that he did not want to talk to me.)
infer: to gain an opinion or understanding from what one reads or hears (I *inferred* from the mayor's announcement that he was going to run.)

incredible: unbelievable (A story is *incredible*.)
incredulous: unwilling or unable to believe (A person is *incredulous*.)

less: used with noncountable items (We had *less* information about the earthquake than they did.)
fewer: used with countable items (There were *fewer* students every year.)

principal: main, most important; a sum of money; a school official
principle: a rule of conduct; a general truth

than: a conjunction used to express a comparison
then: at that time; therefore

BASIC SPELLING LIST

Group I
absence
accidentally
accommodate
accompanying
accomplish
accustom
achievement
acknowledge
across
address
a lot
all right
always
almost
although
altogether
amateur
among
amount
analyze

Group II
annual
answer
apartment
apology
apparent
appearance
approaching
arctic
argument
ascend
association
athlete
attendance
audience
bachelor
balance
before
beginning
believe
benefited

Group III
breathe
brilliant
bureau
buried
business
calendar
candidate
career
carrying
certain
changeable
changing
characteristic
clothes
coming
committee
comparison
competition
conceive
conferred

Group IV
conscience
conscientious
consciousness
convenient
course
courteous
criticism
criticize
curiosity
dealt
definite
desirable
despair
desperate
dictionary
different
dining
disagree
disappear
disappoint

Group V
disastrous
discipline
dissatisfied
dormitory
eighth
eligible
embarrass
enthusiastic
environment
equipped
especially
exaggerated
excellent
existence
experience
explanation
extraordinary
extremely
familiar
fascinating

Group VI
February
foreign
formerly
forty
fourth
friend
generally
genius
government
grammar
guidance
handle
height
humorous
imagination
immediately
indefinitely
independent
inevitable
infinite

Group VII
intelligent
interesting
itself
knowledge
laboratory
led
lightning
literature
loneliness
loose
lose
mathematics
meant
minute
mischievous
necessary
ninth
noticeable
nowadays
occasionally

Group VIII
occurred
occurrence
original
paid
parallel
particularly
pastime
perform
perhaps
piece
pleasant
possible
preferred
prejudice
principal
principle
privilege
probably
proceed
professor

Group IX
psychology
quantity
quiet
quite
really
receive
recommend
referred
relieve
religious
restaurant
rhythm
schedule
separate
sergeant
severely
sophomore
speech
stopped
strength

Group X
stretch
studying
succeed
surprise
temperature
thorough
till
together
tragedy
truly
Tuesday
unnecessarily
until
usually
weather
whether
wholly
woman
writing
written

Imagery and Figurative Language

Writers in search of clear, vivid, and forceful prose often use devices called figures of speech to gain a desired effect. Note the image conveyed by Phillip Wylie's description of a very thin woman as "a trellis for varicose veins." Among the important figures of speech are *simile, metaphor, synecdoche, metonymy,* and *personification*. Inappropriate expressions that you may need to *rule out* on the writing test could involve misuse of these figures of speech.

SIMILE

A simile is a figure of speech that uses **like** or **as** **to compare two dissimilar things.**

EXAMPLES: "... mountains like thirsty giants"—*National Geographic*
"a complexion like the belly of a fish"—*Charles Dickens*

Some similes have been used so much that they are no longer effective and are considered clichés.

INEFFECTIVE SIMILES: old as the hills
dull as dishwater
American as apple pie
teeth like pearls

METAPHOR

A metaphor is a figure of speech that suggests a likeness between two ideas or objects. *As* or *like* is not used.

EXAMPLES: This monstrous human error, the megalopolis...
"She is the rose, the glory of the day."—*Edmund Spenser*

As with similes, some metaphors have become trite through overuse.

INEFFECTIVE METAPHORS: the black sheep of the family
a wolf in sheep's clothing
a sea of troubles

A mixed metaphor results when metaphors occurring in the same sentence or paragraph create ludicrous images. If a woman is said to be a rose, and her arms petals, then she cannot be a jewel in the next sentence.

EXAMPLES: The floodgates of atheism and permissiveness are stalking arm in arm throughout the land. (Floodgates cannot stalk.)
The harvest sown by the crooked politicians came home to roost. (Two mixed metaphors here: *seeds,* not a *harvest,* are sown, and *chickens,* not a *harvest,* come home to roost.)

SYNECDOCHE

Synecdoche uses the part to represent the whole: *ranch hands,* for example, for a group of men performing labor with their hands, or *daily bread* for food. Here are a few more synecdoches:

EXAMPLES: The pen [writing] is mightier than the sword [fighting].
Five hundred souls [people] were lost.

METONYMY

Metonymy substitutes something closely related for the thing actually meant. The *White House* stands for the president, for example; *the Blue and the Gray,* for the Union and Confederate forces.

EXAMPLES: "Scepter and crown [the king] must tumble down."
The Dodgers need to add more bats [good hitters] to their team.
I'm going to complain directly to City Hall [the mayor].

PERSONIFICATION

Personification is a form of metaphor in which an inanimate object or abstract idea—for example, a car, or a quality like love—is treated as if it has human characteristics, feelings, or actions.

EXAMPLES: "I have seen the ambitious ocean swell and rage and foam."
William Shakespeare
Justice hung her head.

We use personification often in daily conversation when we speak of the "bitter wind," "nasty weather," "gentle breeze," "cruel sea," "unforgiving clock," or "bountiful Mother Nature."

Errors involving these figures of speech on one of the writing tests will most probably consist of mixed or confused examples, so be alert for any absurd, illogical, or meaningless expressions or comparisons.

PRACTICE EXERCISE

Most of the following sentences contain errors in diction, imagery, or logical expression. Place a check in the appropriate space to indicate whether the sentence contains appropriate diction and sound expressions, or uses faulty language, or uses flawed expressions. Note that all sentences should be phrased in standard written English.

CORRECT	FAULTY OR FLAWED	
_____	_____	1. It was a near perfect day to have a picnic.
_____	_____	2. Quick as a flash, the horse and rider jumped the gun and sailed around the track at full steam.
_____	_____	3. Paul excepted the invitation to compete in the biathlon.
_____	_____	4. The college has finally untangled itself from the briar bush of debt and is now in smooth water.
_____	_____	5. I was tickled pink to discover that the Senate had passed the revised income tax legislation.
_____	_____	6. He use to be a catcher for the Mets.
_____	_____	7. You hadn't ought to aggravate the Doberman!
_____	_____	8. Though the other political party keeps dragging the national debt red herring across our path, it misfires every time.
_____	_____	9. The issue of increased subway fares has become a political football.
_____	_____	10. They discovered a large amount of gold coins.

> **ANSWERS AND EXPLANATIONS**
>
> 1. FAULTY. This is a colloquial use of *near* (an adjective), instead of *nearly* (an adverb), to modify *perfect*.
> 2. FLAWED. This sentence contains two overused expressions (the simile *Quick as a flash* and the metaphor *jumped the gun* and a mixed metaphor (*sailed...at full steam*).
> 3. FAULTY. The correct word to use here is *accepted* (agreed), not *excepted* (excluded from).
> 4. FLAWED. The college is likened first to an animal or person becoming tangled in a bush, then to a ship at sea.
> 5. FAULTY. *Tickled pink* is a colloquial expression.
> 6. FAULTY. *Use to* should be changed to *used to*.
> 7. FAULTY. Use *ought not*, not *hadn't ought*. *Annoy* is a better word choice than *aggravate*.
> 8. FLAWED. A red herring cannot fire (or misfire) like a gun.
> 9. CORRECT. The metaphor presents a clear, vivid picture of an unpopular issue that is being tossed back and forth by politicians.
> 10. FAULTY. *Number* is used for a countable noun like *coins*. (But it would be correct to use *a large amount of gold*.)

Wordiness

To avoid wordiness, eliminate language that either duplicates what has already been expressed or adds nothing to the sense of the statement.

WORDY: At the present time, you can call up the library on the telephone if you want to receive that particular information.
REVISED: Now you can call the library for that information.

WORDY: A factor in the cause of the decline in stock prices was unwarranted growth.
REVISED: One cause of the decline in stock prices was unwarranted growth.
OR
A factor in the decline in stock prices ...

WORDY: As a pet, the llama is easygoing in its habits and has a friendly personality.
REVISED: As a pet, the llama is easygoing and friendly.

Expressions like *there are* and *it is* usually add unnecessary words to your sentences.

EXAMPLES: [There are] several people at school [who] have promised to help with the gardening at the new campus.
[It is] the way you swing the club [that] amazes me.

A *redundant* expression is characterized by unnecessary repetition. To say *adequate enough* is to be redundant, because *adequate* and *enough* have nearly the same meaning.

EXAMPLES: The two clubs joined [together] to feed the poor at Christmas.
They circled [around] the field.
For a list of ski areas in the state, refer [back] to page 25.

Avoid redundancies and roundabout phrases (*circumlocutions*) like the following:

WORDY	CONCISE
advance planning	planning
contributing factor	factor
due to the fact that	because
during the course of	during
exact same symptoms	same symptoms; exact symptoms
for the purpose of	for
in the event that	if

in the near future	soon
large in size	large
past experience	experience
past history	history
revert back	revert
sufficient enough	sufficient; enough

Omissions

A common error in written English is the careless omission, especially the omission acceptable in speech but not in writing. Some of the errors on the writing test are likely to be such omissions.

THE CARELESS OMISSION

Do not omit a needed verb, preposition, or conjunction.

FAULTY:	The Coast Guard always has and always will assist boaters in distress.
CORRECT:	The Coast Guard always has *assisted* and always will assist boaters in distress.
FAULTY:	Carol will graduate high school in June.
CORRECT:	Carol will graduate *from* high school in June.
FAULTY:	Liza was both allergic and fond of cats.
CORRECT:	Liza was both allergic *to* and fond of cats.
FAULTY:	He eats as much or more than anyone else in the family.
CORRECT:	He eats as much *as* or more than anyone else in the family.

THE INCOMPLETE COMPARISON

Include every word needed to make a complete comparison.

It may seem obvious to state that a comparison expresses a relationship between *two* things: for example, *Johnny is older than Sue*. A surprisingly common error, however, is the incomplete comparison.

INCOMPLETE:	Our new lawn requires less water.
REVISED:	Our new lawn requires less water *than our old one did*.
INCOMPLETE:	A subcompact's mileage is better than a large sedan.
REVISED:	A subcompact's mileage is better *than that of* a large sedan.
INCOMPLETE:	He wanted that medal more than his competitors. (Did he want the medal or the competitors?)
REVISED:	He wanted that medal more than his competitors *did* [want].

THE MISSING TRANSITION

Without logical transitions, the flow of ideas can lack natural progression and unity. Note the following.

WITHOUT TRANSITION:	He wanted so much to do well on the test; he had not studied enough.
REVISED:	He wanted so much to do well on the test, *but* he had not studied enough.
WITHOUT TRANSITION:	The multimillionaire Getty lived in London; most of his holdings were in the United States.
REVISED:	The multimillionaire Getty lived in London, *although* most of his holdings were in the United States.

Sexist Language

Throughout most of the history of the English language, masculine pronouns have been used to represent either sex. In addition, women have been routinely excluded from many nouns intended to represent humanity. Still worse, traditional use of sexist language tends to place men and women in stereotyped roles.

It is not necessary to begin using awkward terms to avoid sexist language. Terms like *mail carrier, firefighter,* or *police officer* are reasonable alternatives to *mailman, fireman,* and *policeman.*

The use of the sexist pronoun is more difficult to avoid. One alternative is to use the plural: instead of *A voter must do his duty,* say, *Voters must do their duty.* An occasional use of *he or she* is acceptable, though the phrase tends to be cumbersome.

EXAMPLE: When a person is called by the IRS for an audit, *he or she* should go over last year's return.

You can avoid the construction by rewording the sentence.

EXAMPLE: A person called by the IRS for an audit should go over the past year's return.

PRACTICE EXERCISE

Most of these sentences are either wordy or incomplete in some way. Place a check in the appropriate column to indicate whether the sentence is correct or faulty.

CORRECT   FAULTY

1. His appeal was his good looks as well as his natural charm.

2. Mexican food is as well liked by Europeans as Americans.

3. Because of the unlikely possibility that rain will occur this weekend, we will not venture to have the canoe race.

4. The teacher impatiently repeated the answer again.

5. Is it true that snow tires are safer?

6. She always let her cat out at 5 A.M. in the morning.

7. The comma, semicolon, and colon are punctuation marks used to separate components of a sentence.

8. New materials to construct long-lasting batteries have and continue to be developed by Bell scientists.

9. In my opinion, I think the autobiography of her life would make a good movie.

10. I admire Dylan more than Cherie does.

11. The baby was crying as if she were hungry; she had been fed only an hour ago.

12. The motion picture *Gone With the Wind* is a movie that still has great audience appeal.

ANSWERS AND EXPLANATIONS

1. FAULTY. Revised: His appeal was *due* to his good looks as well as his natural charm.
2. FAULTY. Revised: Mexican food is as well liked by Europeans as *it is by* Americans.
3. FAULTY. Revised: Because of the possibility of rain this weekend, we will not have the canoe race. (Excessive words omitted.)
4. FAULTY. *Repeated ... again* is redundant.
5. FAULTY. Revised: Is it true that snow tires are safer *than other types of tires?*
6. FAULTY. *In the morning* is unnecessary with A.M.
7. CORRECT. This sentence is neither wordy nor incomplete.
8. FAULTY. Revised: New materials to construct long-lasting batteries have *been* and continue to be developed by Bell scientists.
9. FAULTY. *In my opinion* and *I think* express the same idea. Also, *autobiography of her life* is a redundant phrase.
10. CORRECT. The thought in this sentence is complete.
11. FAULTY. A transitional word like *yet* is needed in this sentence.
12. FAULTY. Revised: The motion picture *Gone With the Wind* still has great audience appeal.

FOCUS ON THE TEST

The following sample questions represent ways in which the above skills might be tested on your writing test.

(1)

Modern literary criticism is a literary specialty composed of many varying and inharmonious parts. There are, however, five major trends in contemporary criticism that take into account almost every significant critical essay written in the twentieth century. It is the critics' differing opinions on the purpose of literature that create the divisions or schools of modern criticism. These schools or approaches to literature are the moral, the psychological, the sociological, the formalistic, and the archetypal. [1]

(2)

The oldest view, the moral approach, originated with Plato when he ordered Homer banished from his fictional utopian republic. Poetry, said Plato, by its very nature appeals to the emotions rather than to the

1. This entire passage was probably written for readers who are:
   A. college or college-bound literature students.
   B. poor readers who require supplemental material.
   C. interested in the scientific method.
   D. foreign students preparing for an English proficiency test.

intellect and is, therefore, potentially dangerous. Here is the first expression of concern over the effect of literature on life, and this concern becomes the primary concern of the moral critic, who gauges all literature by its ability to aid and comfort man, and convey a higher ideal of life. [2]

(3)

As you can imagine, the psychologists got into the act and started linking novels with Freud and Jung and that crowd and their theories that man is a victim of society and his own biological drives. Psychological critics argue that literature that advocates chastity, gentility, and other virtues is frustrating to the normal drives of man and is therefore unhealthy. The psychological school studies the author's life as a means of understanding his writings, the characters and their motivation in the literature itself, and the creative process as a psychological evolution.

(4)

Looking at what it is that makes folks tick when they get together in towns and the like is what the sociological critic does. A literary work is studied in order to discover the degree to which it acts as a mirror

2. Which of the following statements is best supported by the details supplied in paragraph number 2?
   F. The moral view is the most important by far.
   G. The moral approach is really a religious view.
   H. The moral approach is the oldest and most noble of the critical modes.
   J. The moral critical view requires rigid standards of behavior of its adherents.

3. Which of the suggested sentences below make the best introduction to paragraph 3 and the best transition from paragraph 2?
   A. NO CHANGE
   B. In contrast to this idea is the psychological approach to literature, a school that originated with Freud and his theory that man is a victim of both the repressive mores of society and his own biological compulsions.
   C. The psychological approach to literature is our next mode of criticism.
   D. Next, we have the psychological school of criticism, a hands-on way of looking at the nitty-gritty of an author's life.

4. Suppose at this point in the passage the author wanted to revise the third paragraph so that it is more appropriate for younger students? Which of the following revisions of this sentence would accomplish that purpose most effectively?
   F. NO CHANGE
   G. The Freudian and post-Jungian school focuses upon the subject's experiential past as a means of explicating his creative output, personality projections, and basic drives, as well as the genesis of the creative process.
   H. This way of talking about a book we have read lets us think about the author's life to see if it is related to the story, to think about the characters in the story and decide whether or not they make sense, and to ask why the author wrote the book.
   J. Psychological criticism tells us to look at the authors first, as if the author's life really always tells you that much. Anyway, you study the author's life and supposedly learn more about the book from an analytical, what-makes-us-tick point of view.

5. A. NO CHANGE
   B. As the boy's choir did in William Golding's novel *The Lord of the Flies*, man tends to organize his ruling bodies according to his inner drives.
   C. When people get together, whether they are savages or yuppies, they form social units. This process is what the sociological critic studies.
   D. The study of man's drives when he is organized into a state is the province of the sociological critic.

of society through contemporary social theory and practice. [6]

(5)

Used as an isolated method, each approach to literary commentary has serious drawbacks, leading to narrow and restrictive headings. Used collectively, however, the five approaches can deal with every facet of a work, enabling a balanced and complete interpretation of literature. [7]

(6)

The most influential method of contemporary criticism, however, is the formalistic, or "new" criticism. Assuming that literature has intrinsic meaning, the school advocates the close study of texts themselves, rather than extrinsics such as society or the author's biography. <u>The primary route by which a formalistic critic reveals and expresses his views on a classic work of literature is by means of a very ambitious and comprehensive examination and scrutiny of the text of the novel itself.</u>
8

(7)

The archetypal approach studies literature in its relation to all men, assuming a "collective unconscious" that binds all men from all time. The archetypal critic <u>eyeballs</u> a work in an attempt to disclose its reliance on
9
either a specific myth or a universal pattern of thought, both of which might reveal a man's subconscious attempt to link himself with all humanity, past and present. [10]

6. What kind of supporting details could strengthen this paragraph?
   F. A list of American states and major cities.
   G. A list of authors that have written "sociological novels."
   H. Examples of ways a novel can mirror contemporary society.
   J. A consistent way to gauge the quality of life.

7. This paragraph is organized according to which of the following schemes?
   A. A general statement followed by a number of specific examples.
   B. A narrative structure controlled by the events being described.
   C. A typical classification/division format where the topic is broken down into groups and labeled.
   D. A simple contrasting paragraph, with the point of the first sentence contrasting sharply with the next.

8. F. NO CHANGE.
   G. A close, in-depth examination of a work's structure and language is the primary characteristic of this highly analytical mode of commentary.
   H. A close, in-depth examination in which scholars scrutinize very minutely the actual text of a work of literature is the main primary characteristic of this highly analytical mode of commentary.
   J. The main way a critic reports on a book is really by looking very closely at the words and sentences.

9. A. NO CHANGE
   B. peruses
   C. ponders
   D. studies

10. Choose the sequence of paragraph numbers that makes the structure of the passage most logical.
    F. 1, 3, 5, 6, 7, 4, 2.
    G. 1, 2, 4, 3, 7, 6, 5.
    H. 1, 2, 3, 4, 6, 7, 5.
    J. 1, 2, 7, 6, 5, 4, 3.

ANSWERS AND EXPLANATIONS

1. **A** The subject and tone of the passage clearly address serious students of literature.

2. **H** The details supplied in paragraph 2 bear out solely this statement.

3. **B** This choice highlights the obvious contrast between the critical schools described in the two paragraphs, and effectively introduces the topic that is supported in the paragraph. The other choices either fall short of introducing the paragraph topic or depart markedly from the style and tone of the passage.

4. **H** This choice is written for a younger reading level, yet roughly covers the main points of the original sentence. The other choices (G and J) either do not communicate the main points of the original sentence, or are not written for young readers.

5. **D** Only this choice concludes the paragraph clearly and effectively, while maintaining the style of the passage.

6. **H** The original paragraph *does* lack specific examples of literary works that mirror their contemporary society. The information conveyed in the other choices is off the topic of the paragraph.

7. **D** The paragraph does, indeed, contain two sentences, one contrasting sharply with the other.

8. **G** This choice is the only one that expresses the primary characteristics of the formalistic critic with economy of language and in a style consistent with that of the passage. The other choices are either wordy or lacking in content or compatible style.

9. **D** The word *studies* is consistent with the tone of the passage. The other choices suggest activities that are other than scholarly.

10. **H** The paragraphs in this passage are linked to each other by means of transitional statements, and by means of the controlling order established near the end of paragraph 1.

212 CSU — Writing Proficiency Exam

PRACTICE TEST

The passages in the following tests cover a wide range of topics and are written in different styles. In responding to questions, you should be aware of these differences in writing style. Before you begin to answer the questions, quickly skim the passage. Then, answer each question in light of its context. If you are unsure of a question or your answer, read the sentences immediately before and after the sentence with the underlined part.

Think about the principles of usage involved in each question and focus on the one that applies. Many of the questions concern more than one aspect of usage, especially in the answer options. Be sure that the answer you choose does not introduce another error while correcting the first!

DIRECTIONS: The following test consists of 60 items. Some concern underlined words and phrases in context; others ask general questions about the passages. Most of the underlined sections contain errors or inappropriate expressions. You are asked to compare each with the four alternatives in the answer column. If you consider the original version best, choose letter **A** or **F**: NO CHANGE. For each question, select the alternative you think best. Read each passage through before answering the questions based on it.

NOTE: Answers and explanations can be found at the end of each passage.

Passage I

A peaceful oasis in the midst of the bustling San Fernando Valley, San Fernando Mission has been declared a historic cultural monument by the City of Los Angeles, according to a bronze plaque at the entrance to the mission. In addition to being an active religion center, many tourists come to the mission each year to stroll through the well-tended grounds and
<u>they admire</u> the unique architecture of the restored mission buildings.

The entrance to the mission quadrangle opens <u>onto</u>

1. **A.** NO CHANGE
   B. religions
   C. religious
   D. more religious

2. **F.** NO CHANGE
   G. many tourists are invited to the Mission each year
   H. it is a place where many tourists come each year
   J. people come

3. **A.** NO CHANGE
   B. they were admiring
   C. admiring
   D. admire

4. **F.** NO CHANGE
   G. out into
   H. wide into
   J. for

the east garden, a large, grass-covered courtyard in the middle of which is a flower-shaped fountain modeled after one that stands in Cordova, Spain. Wind rustles through the branches of the trees, and water tinkles in the fountain, also the sounds of traffic outside the walls only accentuate the tranquility of the setting. Strolling about the grounds, the smell of spring flowers scenting the air and the sunlight warm upon your back, one can easily imagine being back two hundred years during the time of the founding of the mission. The present-day mission compound, however, with its air of serenity and unhurried repose, is nothing like the mission in its heyday, when it was the scene of bustling activity and hundreds of Indians at diligent labor under the direction of a few Spanish Franciscan padres.

San Fernando Mission, founded in 1779 by Padre Fermin Lasuen and named for a saintly king of thirteenth-century Spain, it was the seventeenth of California's twenty-one missions stretching in a chain from San Francisco to San Diego. The purpose of the mission chain was to create centers of Christian civilization who would want to convert the California Indians and prepare them for Spanish citizenship.

Mission San Francisco was established centrally between the missions of San Buenaventura and San Gabriel, at a distance of one day's journey from each.

5. A. NO CHANGE
    B. grass-covered
    C. grass covering
    D. grass, covered

6. F. NO CHANGE
    G. while
    H. moreover,
    J. furthermore,

7. A. NO CHANGE
    B. you can easily
    C. it seems easy to
    D. one can easily

8. F. NO CHANGE
    G. diligent labor by hundreds of Indians
    H. the labor was industrious by hundreds of Indians
    J. labor that was diligent by hundreds of Indians

9. A. NO CHANGE
    B. it had been
    C. it will be
    D. was

10. F. NO CHANGE
    G. and it stretched
    H. that was stretching
    J. widely stretched out

11. A. NO CHANGE
    B. which was hoping
    C. seeking
    D. needing

12. F. NO CHANGE
    G. in a great spot
    H. well within and
    J. OMIT the underlined phrase.

The site chosen for the mission—land that had been used by Don Francisco Reyes, first mayor of the Pueblo de Los Angeles, to graze cattle—was rich in water, in fertile, arable soil, and it had an Indian population, all necessary elements for a successful mission.

The chapel—an exact replica of the original, which was built between 1804 and 1806 and destroyed by the 1971 earthquake—is long and narrow, with adobe walls decorated by frescoes of native designs. The overall effect of the frescoes, the colorful Spanish altar hangings, and the Stations of the Cross are, as one writer put it, "a glorious, if barbaric spectacle!" Although there is a number of windows on the south wall of the chapel, there is only one window on the north wall. It is not known whether this architectural detail was meant to keep out cold winds from the nearby mountains or as a defense against a potential attack by hostile Indians.

Behind the chapel is a cemetery, where many of the natives and other early settlers attached to the mission were buried. Only a few wooden crosses and there is one large gravestone mark the final resting places of approximately 2,000 persons buried there. Beyond the burial grounds is a fountain: fed by a small stream and surrounded in foliage and a flower garden.

13. A. NO CHANGE
    B. cite chosen
    C. sight chose
    D. site choosed

14. F. NO CHANGE
    G. Mission: land
    H. Mission; land
    J. Mission. Land

15. A. NO CHANGE
    B. there also were Indians,
    C. it had Indians,
    D. in an Indian population,

16. F. NO CHANGE
    G. was
    H. is
    J. will have been

17. A. NO CHANGE
    B. were a number of
    C. are a number of
    D. should be a number of

18. F. NO CHANGE
    G. hostile Indians.
    H. defending against an Indian attack.
    J. an attack against hostile Indians.

19. A. NO CHANGE
    B. one large gravestone
    C. there might have been a gravestone
    D. there most likely is a gravestone

20. F. NO CHANGE
    G. fountain. Fed
    H. fountain; fed
    J. fountain fed

21. A. NO CHANGE
    B. overhead in the
    C. about with
    D. by

English Review and Practice 215

Across the compound, stands the "convento"—the
largest original mission building in California—with its
famous corridor of twenty-one Roman arches that today
front San Fernando Mission Road. Two stories high,
with four-foot-thick adobe walls that keeps the inside
cool on even the hottest summer day. It served as living
quarters for the missionaries and visitors in the early
1800's. Tourists taking pictures inside the mission
should bring high-speed color film.

Just inside the entrance hall an atmosphere is able to
be felt of great age, perhaps due in part to the stillness
that seems to echo within the brick-floored rooms. Then
again, this feeling might be due to the odor, emanating
from the nearby wine cellar, a musty smell that grows
stronger as one moves slowly down the whitewashed
stairs—past a deep tub cut from rock where grapes were
once pressed underfoot. [30]

22. F. NO CHANGE
    G. Across the compound, stood
    H. Across the compound stands
    J. Across the compound, is standing

23. A. NO CHANGE
    B. fronts
    C. fronting
    D. fronted

24. F. NO CHANGE
    G. walls, that keep
    H. walls that keep
    J. walls, that keeps

25. A. NO CHANGE
    B. day, it
    C. day—it
    D. day: it

26. F. NO CHANGE
    G. Retain the position of this sentence in the passage but place it in its own paragraph.
    H. Move this sentence to the beginning of the paragraph.
    J. OMIT the underlined sentence.

27. A. NO CHANGE
    B. may be felt an atmosphere
    C. one feels an atmosphere
    D. an atmosphere can be felt

28. F. NO CHANGE
    G. odor; emanating
    H. odor. Emanating
    J. odor emanating

29. A. NO CHANGE
    B. stairs, passed
    C. stairs; passed
    D. stairs, past

30. Is the mention of the odor appropriate and effective at the end of this passage?
    F. No, because it introduces a new element at the end of the passage.
    G. Yes, because the musty odors of old buildings and old wine presses appropriately reflect the age of this historic mission.
    H. Yes, because the description of the odor is somewhat suspenseful, and mentioning it gives a mysterious quality to the passage.
    J. No, because an odor is generally perceived as offensive.

Answer Key

1.	C	6.	G	11.	C	16.	H	21.	D	26.	J
2.	H	7.	B	12.	J	17.	C	22.	H	27.	C
3.	D	8.	F	13.	A	18.	G	23.	B	28.	J
4.	F	9.	D	14.	F	19.	B	24.	H	29.	D
5.	B	10.	F	15.	D	20.	J	25.	B	30.	G

ANSWER EXPLANATIONS

1. **C** The underlined word is intended to modify the noun *center* and so must be an adjective.

2. **H** The introductory phrase *In addition to being an active [religious] center* clearly refers to the mission, not the tourists. Therefore, the main clause must begin with the word *mission* or with the referent pronoun *it*.

3. **D** The infinitive *to admire* is parallel in construction with *to stroll*, with which it is paired: *to stroll ... and [to] admire*.

4. **F** No other choice is idiomatically correct.

5. **B** Hyphenate a compound adjective that precedes the noun it modifies.

6. **G** Conjunctive adverbs (such as *also, moreover*, and *furthermore*) used to join clauses must be preceded by a semicolon. *While*, a subordinating conjunction used to introduce an adverb clause, is properly preceded by a comma.

7. **B** Avoid a shift in point of view, from the second person *your* to the third person *one*. Choice C incorrectly makes *it* the word modified by the introductory participial phrase.

8. **F** Answer choices G, H, and J are wrong because a scene of labor is much less clear than a scene of Indians at labor.

9. **D** The sentence has two subjects: *San Fernando/it*. *It* is unnecessary.

10. **F** The participial phrase *stretching in a chain ...* correctly modifies the noun *missions*. Choice G incorrectly uses *it* to refer to the plural word *missions*. H also incorrectly uses a singular form, *was*, which does not agree with *missions*, the antecedent of *that*. J is wordy.

11. **C** The other options either carry meanings inappropriate to the sense of the passage or contain faulty grammar.

12. **J** *Centrally* repeats the idea of *at a distance of one day's journey from each*. *In a great spot* is too colloquial for this passage. Choice H is wordy.

13. **A** The correct word to use here is *site*, meaning location. The verb forms *chose* and *choosed* in choices C and D are incorrect.

14. **F** A pair of dashes precedes and follows an interrupting parenthetical element.

15. **D** Only this option is parallel with the other prepositional phrases: *in water, in ... soil, and in ... population*.

16. **H** The singular subject *effect* requires the singular verb *is*. The predominant tense of the passage is the present.

17. **C** The phrase *a number of* is plural in meaning and takes the plural verb *are*. Choice B is wrong, since the predominant tense of the passage is the present. D changes the meaning of the clause.

18. **G** The infinitive phrase *to keep out* needs a parallel second object: *to keep out cold winds ... or hostile Indians*.

19. **B** A simple noun is needed to form the other half of the compound subject: *crosses and ... gravestone*.

20. **J** The participial phrase *fed by a small stream* is a restrictive modifier and should not be separated from the noun it modifies, *fountain*, by a punctuation mark. Choice G introduces a sentence fragment.

21. **D** The correct idiom is *surrounded by*.

22. **H** In an inverted sentence, do not use a comma to separate a short adverb construction from the verb it modifies.

23. **B** The subject of the verb *front* is the relative pronoun *that*, which refers to the singular noun *corridor*, not the plural *arches*. Thus, the correct verb form is *fronts*. Choice C is a participle, not a verb form. D shifts to the past tense.

24. **H** The subject of the verb *keep* is the relative pronoun *that*, which refers to the plural noun *walls*. Do not use a comma to separate a restrictive clause from the word it modifies (G and J).

25. **B** A comma is used to separate the introductory phrase *two stories high ... day* from the main clause of the sentence. Choice A creates a sentence fragment.

26. **J** This sentence has no bearing on the topic of the passage.

27. **C** As a rule, it is better to avoid the passive voice. The active voice is more direct and forceful.

28. **J** The participial phrase *emanating from the nearby wine cellar* is a restrictive modifier and cannot be set off by commas. Choice H introduces a sentence fragment.

29. **D** A comma is called for at this point for clarity. A dash is too great a mark of separation. Choices B and C incorrectly substitute the verb form *passed* for the preposition *past*.

30. **G** This descriptive paragraph adds a meaningful sense impression to the passage.

English Review and Practice

Passage II

Each of the paragraphs in this passage is numbered, but may not be in the most logical position. The last question asks you to select the correct number order.

(1)

Sometime around the middle of January, after reading about standard organic gardening techniques, prospective home gardeners should make a list of the vegetables most enjoyed by their families. Sitting down with a few seed catalogs, preferably those from local companies such as Santa Rosa Gardening Co. Or Burbank Farms,—whose catalogs contain detailing planting instructions for Southern California, including the proper planting dates for each of the distinct climatic regions—they should review the directions for growing vegetables, narrowing the choices to crops easy to grow. And although January is an ideal time here to plant such winter vegetables such as beets, broccoli, peas, lettuce, and swiss chard, novice gardeners might do well to plan a spring garden as a first effort. For one thing, summer vegetables like tomatoes, zucchini, and beans are easy to grow, they require little in the way of additional care once they have been planted and are growing well. And for another, spring—traditionally a time of renewal—seems the right time of year to begin a gardening project.

1. **A.** NO CHANGE
   B. Farms—whose
   C. Farms; whose
   D. Farms. Whose

2. **F.** NO CHANGE
   G. details of
   H. detailed
   J. in detailed

3. **A.** NO CHANGE
   B. like
   C. such as;
   D. as

4. **F.** NO CHANGE
   G. grow. Since these vegetables require
   H. grow. Requiring
   J. grow, requiring

(2)

These differences make it impossible that gardeners in Southern California to follow in an explicit way the advice given in nationally circulated magazines and books on organic gardening. Instead, these methods

5. **A.** NO CHANGE
   B. to be a gardener
   C. to go on being a gardener
   D. for gardeners

6. **F.** NO CHANGE
   G. explicitly
   H. in a more explicit way
   J. explicitly and definitely

must be adopted to the particular climate in this area.
7
Some suggestions follow that may be helpful to fellow gardeners in the San Fernando Valley region.

(3)

Just as organic gardening differs from gardening with the help of a chemical company. Gardening in Southern
8
California differs dramatically from gardening in almost every other part of the country. For one thing, crops will be planted here almost any time during the year,
9
whereas spring gardens are the rule in most other parts of the country. Diversity of weather systems within the relatively small area that encompassing Southern
10
California is another distinction. For instance, coastal communities experience cool, damp weather for much of the year, while the San Fernando and San Gabriel valleys are blistering hot in summer and cold in winter—some inland valleys even encounter frost and
11
freezing temperatures! Thus, although these areas separate by fewer than fifty miles, the climates are
12
disparate, necessitating the use of distinct gardening techniques for each locale.

(4)

After deciding what vegetables to grow, a rough draft
13
is made of the garden, which should be located in an
13
area of flat well-drained ground that has gotten at least
14   15
six full hours of sun daily. Taller-growing crops should be put on the north side of the garden so that they do

7. A. NO CHANGE
   B. should be adopted
   C. must be adapted
   D. must adopt

8. F. NO CHANGE
   G. company; gardening
   H. company, gardening
   J. company: gardening

9. A. NO CHANGE
   B. can be planted
   C. have been planted
   D. ought to be planted

10. F. NO CHANGE
    G. encompassed
    H. has encompassed
    J. encompasses

11. A. NO CHANGE
    B. winter;—some
    C. winter—Some
    D. winter, some

12. F. NO CHANGE
    G. are separated
    H. must be separated
    J. were separated

13. A. NO CHANGE
    B. a rough draft should be made
    C. the gardener should make a rough draft
    D. it is necessary to make a rough draft

14. F. NO CHANGE
    G. flat, well-drained
    H. flat, well drained
    J. flat and well drained

15. A. NO CHANGE
    B. will have gotten
    C. got
    D. gets

not shade any low-growing vegetables; except those that
cannot survive the intense summer sun. The latter
include lettuce and many other greens. The rows, or
beds, should be wide enough to accommodate the
particular kind of a crop to be grown. The wider the

rows, of course, the more crops the garden will have
produced. This is known as "intensive gardening" and is
ideal for small backyard gardens. One suggestion is to
make the beds three feet wide, with enough space
between them to allow easy access for cultivating,
weeding, and to harvest mature plants. However, two-

foot beds are also okay.

(5)

After the plan has been drawn up and the seeds will
be ordered, the next step is to prepare the soil properly,
one of the most important procedures in ensuring a
successful harvest. Testing the soil for deficiencies is a

must; soil-testing kits are available from most home
improvement stores and gardening centers. The organic
gardening books and magazines mentioned earlier go
into heavy detail regarding soil composition, testing,
and preparation. Following their recommendations will

contribute for the success of the gardening project.

16. F. NO CHANGE
    G. vegetables except
    H. vegetables: except
    J. vegetables. Except

17. A. NO CHANGE
    B. kind of a
    C. kinds of a
    D. OMIT the underlined words.

18. F. NO CHANGE
    G. would of produced.
    H. will produce.
    J. is producing.

19. A. NO CHANGE
    B. This kind of spacing
    C. Which
    D. This here spacing

20. F. NO CHANGE
    G. harvesting
    H. to be harvesting
    J. so we can harvest the

21. A. NO CHANGE
    B. alright.
    C. all right.
    D. allright.

22. F. NO CHANGE
    G. should be ordered,
    H. were ordered,
    J. have been ordered,

23. A. NO CHANGE
    B. properly. One
    C. properly; one
    D. properly, it is one

24. F. NO CHANGE
    G. must, as soil-testing
    H. must, soil-testing
    J. must because soil-testing

25. A. NO CHANGE
    B. much detail
    C. exquisite detail
    D. a lot of detail

26. F. NO CHANGE
    G. in the success
    H. to the success
    J. for the successfulness

(6)

Once the condition of the soil is ascertained by the person doing the gardening, deficient elements (such as phosphorus, potassium, magnesium, or sulphur) can be added. In addition to these minerals; however, enough fertilizer to get the seedlings off to a good start should be incorporated into the soil. [29] [30]

27. A. NO CHANGE
    B. Once the condition of the soil is ascertained by the gardener, elements that are lacking in sufficient quantity (such as phosphorus, potassium, magnesium, or sulphur) can be added by the gardener.
    C. Once the gardener ascertains the condition of the soil, he or she can add deficient elements (such as phosphorus, potassium, magnesium, or sulphur).
    D. Once, the gardener ascertains the condition of the soil, deficient elements (such as: phosphorus, potassium, magnesium, or sulphur) can be added.

28. F. NO CHANGE
    G. minerals however,
    H. minerals, however—
    J. minerals, however,

29. This passage is most likely directed to readers who:
    A. are experts in gardening and need little advice.
    B. are residents of Southern California and have never had a garden.
    C. are residents of Freeport, Maine, and are just curious about gardening in a warmer state.
    D. have gardened so much that they hope never to see another bud.

30. Select the correct order of the numbered paragraphs so that the passage will read in logical sequence.
    F. NO CHANGE
    G. 3, 2, 1, 4, 5, 6
    H. 1, 2, 4, 5, 3, 6
    J. 4, 2, 3, 1, 5, 6

Answer Key

1. B	6. G	11. A	16. G	21. C	26. H
2. H	7. C	12. G	17. D	22. J	27. C
3. D	8. H	13. C	18. H	23. A	28. J
4. J	9. B	14. G	19. B	24. F	29. B
5. D	10. J	15. D	20. G	25. B	30. G

ANSWER EXPLANATIONS

1. **B** A pair of dashes is used to separate a parenthetical element from the rest of the sentence; a comma is not used with the dash. Choice D introduces a sentence fragment.

2. **H** The correct choice is the past participle *detailed*, which acts as an adjective to modify the noun phrase *planting instructions*. The present participle *detailing* carries meaning that does not apply to this sentence. Choice J adds a word that does not make sense in the structure of the sentence.

3. **D** The sentence already contains the word *such* (*such winter vegetables as*). Choice B offers an ungrammatical construction, *such ... like*.

4. **J** This is the only correct option. The other choices produce sentence fragments or a comma splice.

5. **D** Idiomatic English requires the construction *impossible for gardeners ... to follow*.

6. **G** The other choices are wordy or redundant.

7.	C	The correct word here is *adapted*, meaning modified to suit. *Adopted* means taken as is.		20.	G	The gerund *harvesting* is required, to be parallel with the other gerunds, *cultivating* and *weeding*.
8.	H	Use a comma to separate an introductory adverb clause from the main clause.		21.	C	Choice A is colloquial. B and D are misspellings.
				22.	J	The verb must agree in tense with *has been drawn*.
9.	B	The verb phrase *can be planted* also means *are planted* in the context of this sentence. The other options do not carry this essential additional meaning.		23.	A	Set off a nonrestrictive appositive phrase with a comma. Choice B introduces a sentence fragment; D, a comma splice.
10.	J	Use the present tense to express generally true statements.		24.	F	A semicolon is used to separate independent clauses that are closely related. The transitional words in Choices G and J change the meaning. H creates a comma-splice sentence.
11.	A	A dash is used for emphasis to separate a parenthetical comment from the rest of the sentence. It is not used together with a semicolon. Choice C incorrectly capitalizes the word *some*. D introduces a comma splice.		25.	B	The other options are either inappropriate or incorrect.
				26.	H	The correct idiom is *contribute to*.
12.	G	The passive voice is required when the subject is acted upon. The present tense is consistent with the rest of the passage.		27.	C	The passive voice (*is ascertained* and *can be added*) is less forceful and usually results in more wordy sentences than the active voice. Choice D incorrectly places a comma after the conjunction *Once* and a colon after *such as*.
13.	C	Without a logical noun to modify (*gardener*, for example), the introductory phrase would dangle.				
14.	G	Place a comma between coordinate adjectives. The compound adjective *well-drained* takes a hyphen when it precedes the noun it modifies.		28.	J	The word *however* is used here as an adverb, not as a conjunctive adverb introducing a clause, and so should be set off by commas as a simple parenthetical word.
15.	D	The predominant tense in this passage is the present.				
16.	G	Do not use a punctuation mark to separate a restrictive phrase from the word it modifies. The phrase beginning *except those ... limits low growing vegetables*. Choice J would create a sentence fragment.		29.	B	The references to the Southwestern climate, to aids for novice gardeners, and to gardening techniques indicate that this article is addressed primarily to first-time gardeners in Southern California.
17.	D	The other choices are unnecessarily wordy and also introduce an error. (*Kind of a* is not idiomatic English.)		30.	G	Paragraph 3 is clearly the introduction to this passage; it makes general statements about the topic that are supported by data in subsequent paragraphs. The phrase *These differences* that begins paragraph 2 directly relates to the ending of paragraph 3. The step-by-step process begins with paragraph 1 and continues in order with paragraphs 4, 5, and 6.
18.	H	The simple future tense, showing expectation, is appropriate here, because the passage is set in the present tense. *Would of* is incorrect grammatically.				
19.	B	The pronoun *This* needs a specific antecedent for clear reference. Since there is none, the meaning of *this* has to be clarified. Choice C is still unclear, D is redundant, as *here* repeats the meaning of *this*.				

11 Sample Tests

TEST A

45 Minutes—75 Questions

DIRECTIONS: The following test consists of 75 underlined words and phrases in context, or general questions about the passages. Most of the underlined sections contain errors and inappropriate expressions. You are asked to compare each with the four alternatives in the answer column. If you consider the original version best, choose letter **A** or **F**: NO CHANGE. For each question, circle the letter of the alternative you think best. Read each passage through before answering the questions based on it.

Passage I

(1)

Americans are living longer. The number of citizens sixty years or older totaled more than forty million in 1988, and one out of every nine Americans <u>were</u> sixty-five or older. Because advances in medical science and a more healthful life-style have lengthened the life spans of <u>we Americans,</u> more and more of us are finding that the time comes when we either no longer want to—<u>or can</u>— live on our own.

1. **A.** NO CHANGE
   B. is
   C. have been
   D. was

2. **F.** NO CHANGE
   G. we, Americans,
   H. us Americans
   J. us, Americans,

3. **A.** NO CHANGE
   B. to or can live
   C. to, or can live
   D. to, or can, live

(2)

Unfortunately, in the past the words *retirement home* often brought to mind images of impersonal, lonely places. [4] However, conditions in retirement homes can vary, some homes earning awards for excellence in nursing care, and others earning citations for

4. This idea (of "impersonal, lonely places") could best be illustrated in this passage by employing which of the following writing strategies?
   F. Explaining a process
   G. Persuasion
   H. Defining
   J. Description

222

negligence. [5] Regulations regarding nursing homes are becoming <u>stricter than a research clinic</u>, and it is possible to find retirement conditions that are positive and comfortable. [7]

(3)

But at the same time, the sad fact remains that, although most nursing homes are now licensed by the state, <u>unclean and unhealthy conditions can still be found</u>. Even if the homes follow the licensing procedures perfectly, the law does not guarantee a <u>warm friendly</u> staff or atmosphere. [10]

(4)

When looking at nursing homes, <u>qualities should be placed</u> in priority order. Family members should remember, as they look, that attitude toward patients— the morale and personal contact—can be just as

5. Which of the following writing strategies would permit the writer to present details about both housing extremes?
   A. Classifying and dividing
   B. Narration
   C. Comparison and contrast
   D. Persuasion

6. F. NO CHANGE
   G. stricter
   H. stricter than clinics
   J. stricter than they once were

7. Suppose that at this point in the passage the writer wanted to add more information about the impact of government regulations on retirement home conditions. Which of the following additions would be most relevant to the passage as a whole?
   A. A description and brief history of the agencies regulating nursing homes.
   B. A bibliography of government reports and summaries published by regulating agencies
   C. A separate paragraph summarizing briefly the recent activity and success of regulating agencies
   D. Inclusion of a typical case report on an existing nursing institution

8. F. NO CHANGE
   G. one can still find unclean and unhealthy conditions.
   H. conditions can be found of uncleanliness and unhealthiness.
   J. many of them have unclean and unhealthy conditions.

9. A. NO CHANGE
   B. warm - friendly
   C. warm: friendly
   D. warm, friendly

10. The writer could most effectively strengthen this paragraph by adding:
    F. a list of retirement homes found to be substandard in cleanliness.
    G. an anecdote about a woman who has lived in a home for 20 years.
    H. details and examples that typify unclean and unhealthy conditions.
    J. details of the licensing procedure that homes are required to complete.

11. A. NO CHANGE
    B. interested parties should place qualities
    C. qualities are certainly to be placed
    D. the patient should place qualities

important as new buildings which, if they do not contain human warmth, can be little better than prisons.

(5)

For these reasons, it <u>behooves us</u> to take the time to
                        12
carefully check out the nursing homes the family is considering. If members of the family cannot carry out all of the necessary steps, they should have a friend or relative help with the evaluation.

(6)

Not everyone who is in a nursing home requires the 24-hour skilled care offered there. Many residents are in homes because they can no longer care for themselves at home, and have nowhere else to go. However, alternatives to nursing homes do exist for people who need less care. [13]

(7)

Home care <u>services, which</u> allow a patient to stay in a
              14
familiar environment rather than being placed in a nursing home, are an option if the elderly person needs only limited help, since home care causes far less disruption to normal life. Such services are provided by a variety of public, voluntary, and private agencies. [15]

12. **F.** NO CHANGE
    G. best suits us
    H. is very important
    J. is not a bad idea

13. Which of the following means of discussing alternatives to 24-hour skilled nursing care would be most compatible with the methods employed so far in this passage?
    A. Detailed interviews with nursing home inmates who have experienced both forms of care
    B. Insertion of medical records of patients who have been moved from occasional care to 24-hour care
    C. A short paragraph mentioning several alternatives to 24-hour care
    D. Inclusion of a personal diary written by an elderly patient who made the change to permanent care

14. **F.** NO CHANGE
    G. services which
    H. services that
    J. services

15. Choose the sequence of paragraph numbers that make the structure of the passage most logical.
    A. NO CHANGE
    B. 7, 2, 3, 1, 5, 4, 6
    C. 1, 2, 3, 5, 4, 6, 7
    D. 1, 2, 7, 3, 4, 5, 6

Passage II

Cultural activities form the loom on which the talents, skills, and dreams of individuals <u>can sprout</u> into
₁₆
something colorful and <u>distinctive—a play, pageant</u>, art
₁₇
center, music festival, museum, library, garden, park— to enrich community life. 18

Cultural activities are central to Rural Areas Development, a nationwide effort by rural people and those in public service and private endeavors who work with <u>it</u>
₁₉
to enrich the quality of life. 20

What may not be recognized by area leaders whose primary interest is in economic development <u>is when</u>
₂₁
cultural activities can be part of the steam that supplies the drive.

The first heritage festival of Lawrence County in Arkansas illustrates how a cultural activity may emerge from a ferment of economic development and, in turn, engender still newer ideas for <u>farther</u> social and
₂₂
economic gain, as well as other cultural activities. Lawrence County, a mainly rural area in northeastern Arkansas, had a population of 17,000 in <u>nineteen-sixty.</u>
₂₃
Its eastern half is fertile. The Black River runs beneath the delta—planted with rice, soybeans, and cotton—and the hills, where the farms specialize in livestock and

16. F. NO CHANGE
    G. can be woven
    H. can be sprouted
    J. can swell

17. A. NO CHANGE
    B. distinctive, a play, a pageant
    C. distinctive. A play, a pageant
    D. distinctive; a play, a pageant

18. Which of the following terms needs to be more carefully defined if the first paragraph is to carry substantial meaning?
    F. Pageant
    G. Cultural activities
    H. Loom
    J. Music festival

19. A. NO CHANGE
    B. they
    C. him
    D. rural people

20. Which of the following suggestions would improve the beginning of this passage?
    F. NO CHANGE
    G. OMIT the second paragraph.
    H. Combine the first and second paragraphs.
    J. Move the second paragraph to the end of the passage.

21. A. NO CHANGE
    B. is that
    C. is because
    D. is for

22. F. NO CHANGE
    G. even farther
    H. further
    J. furthermore

23. A. NO CHANGE
    B. nineteen-sixty A.D.
    C. 1960
    D. nineteen hundred and sixty

poultry. Family-type farms employ a third of the work force. [25]

Farmers nevertheless made up the largest occupational group in the Lawrence County Development Council when it was organized in 1962. Seventeen members of the Council were farmers—nine in general farming, six livestock and poultry producers, one a dairyman, another a rice grower. Also on the Council were an industrial worker, two bankers, and several local businessmen and homemakers.

Addressing itself to the economic advancement of the county, the Council spent its first two years of existence. It supported a one-mill tax to guarantee construction of an industrial building in Walnut Ridge, the county seat and the largest town. It was instrumental in getting a comprehensive manpower inventory and economic base study of the area it arranged for workshops in farm management. It helped leaders of Imboden to initiate a housing project for twenty elderly persons. [30]

24. F. NO CHANGE
    G. Family type farms
    H. Family type-farms
    J. Family, type farms

25. This paragraph contains a major organizational problem. Which of the following critical statements best describes this problem?
    A. The paragraph does not contain enough specific details to support the main point.
    B. The first sentence of the paragraph presents an idea that is not developed in the body of the paragraph.
    C. No beginning thesis or topic is presented.
    D. There are many ideas in the paragraph, none of them developed.

26. F. NO CHANGE
    G. on the contrary
    H. however
    J. thus

27. A. NO CHANGE
    B. —nine in general farming, six in livestock and poultry production, one in dairy production, another in rice farming.
    C. —nine are general farmers, six as livestock and poultry producers, one a dairyman, another a rice grower.
    D. —nine as general farmers, six livestock and poultry producers, one a dairyman, another a rice grower.

28. F. NO CHANGE
    G. During its first two years, the Council addressed the economic advancement of the county.
    H. Addressing itself to the economic advancement of the county, the Council spent its first two years of existence.
    J. The Council spent its first two years of existence while addressing itself to the economic advancement of the county.

29. A. NO CHANGE
    B. area, it
    C. area. It
    D. area but it

30. Which of the following is a major flaw in the structure and sense of this passage?
    F. It omits all mention of children; children are certainly an important part of rural America.
    G. It fails to mention public works projects.
    H. The whole point of the passage is that cultural activities can "supply the drive" for social and economic development, but the passage does not address that issue at all.
    J. The passage does not list enough accomplishments of the Lawrence County Development Council.

Passage III

Of all the musical instruments produced by human skill, the three <u>of which are the most distinguished</u> are
the violin, the piano, and the pipe organ. Of these, the violin still remains the instrument of the virtuoso. No method <u>to play it</u> has yet been <u>discovered</u> except by the slow and tedious process of learning it. It is the

instrument of the <u>accomplish</u> musician. [35]

On the other hand, self-playing devices have been employed successfully with both the piano and the organ—but with this difference. Piano music derives some of its <u>essentialness</u> from the personality of the player. The touch of human fingers has never been exactly reproduced by mechanical devices. In some compositions, however, the mechanical piano player <u>approaches the pianist</u>, although not by any means

in all. [38]

The pipe organ <u>consequently</u> is made for automated playing. There is virtually nothing the organist can do with his or her hands or feet that cannot be duplicated

31. A. NO CHANGE
    B. that are most distinguished
    C. of those that are distinguished
    D. most distinguished

32. F. NO CHANGE
    G. playing at
    H. in playing it
    J. of playing it

33. A. NO CHANGE
    B. invented
    C. divined
    D. developed

34. F. NO CHANGE
    G. accomplishing
    H. accomplished
    J. more accomplished

35. Which of the following writing strategies would permit the writer to present details about all three types of instruments?
    A. Classifying and dividing
    B. Narration
    C. Comparison and contrast
    D. Persuasion

36. F. NO CHANGE
    G. pith
    H. quality
    J. life-blood

37. A. NO CHANGE
    B. approaches the playing of the pianist
    C. comes close to the piano
    D. typifies the piano

38. The writer could most effectively strengthen the passage at this point by adding:
    F. documentation and detail to support opinions delivered as facts.
    G. a review of all the orchestral instruments, including their musical ranges.
    H. a discussion of the great violin makers of the past.
    J. a detailed description of organ structure and mechanism.

39. A. NO CHANGE
    B. on the contrary
    C. to be sure
    D. similarly

by mechanical devices. When an organ manual is touched, the resulting tone is the exact same, whether
₄₀

the touch be hard or soft, slow or quick. The tone
₄₁   ₄₂
continues at the same volume until the key is released. Brilliancy, variety, and other qualities are obtained by other sets of pipes, and these pipes are brought into play by pulling out stops. Such stops can be pulled by mechanical means just as effectively as by human fingers. If the organ music is correctly cut in the music roll, with all the stops, couplers, and swells operated at the proper places, the most acutest ear cannot
₄₃

distinguish between the human organist and the organist
₄₄
who is mechanical. [45]
₄₄

40. F. NO CHANGE
    G. exact identical
    H. same
    J. equal

41. A. NO CHANGE
    B. is
    C. was
    D. has been

42. F. NO CHANGE
    G. soft, slow, or quick.
    H. soft: slow or quick.
    J. soft slow or quick.

43. A. NO CHANGE
    B. the acute ear
    C. the more acute ear
    D. the most acute ear

44. F. NO CHANGE
    G. the organist, who is mechanical.
    H. the mechanical organist.
    J. the organist who is a nonhuman.

45. The main purpose of this passage
    A. leans toward a discussion of the virtues of the mechanical organ.
    B. involves a history of music.
    C. represents a comparison of the violin, piano, and organ.
    D. discusses mechanized musical instruments.

Passage IV

Until his death, Charles Darwin complained that even many of his scientific critics failed to grasp the meaning of his theory of selection; it is not unlikely that if he
₄₆
were still alive the complaint would be repeated. [47] Even where full comprehension of his theory of the causes of organic evolution has been reached, precise

46. F. NO CHANGE
    G. it is not likely
    H. it is likely
    J. it is probable

47. When a passage mentions that a famous figure *complained* about a fact or situation, how might the reader be given greater understanding of the personality and character of that subject?
    A. By inclusion of a description of the occurrence
    B. By quoted examples of what he or she actually said
    C. By references to how other persons present at the time reported the conversation
    D. By a speculative commentary on what he or she meant

determination of the degree of its adequacy—for
                                         48
adequate in great measure it surely is—has not yet been
attained. The generalization that underlies it is broad,
the facts by which it must be verified or limited are
                                                    49
always, it seems, accumulating, and the problems
        49
interrelated with it are intricate; therefore, finality with
regard to it must be indefinitely postponed. That must
                                                50
be left for the biology of the future.

   Moreover, there need be little hesitation in expressing
   51
an estimate of the great naturalist and his thought. They
are obviously among the greatest intellectual forces of
the early twentieth century, as they were of the
nineteenth. Notwithstanding certain limitations, which
Darwin himself unduly emphasizes, he was one of the
                           52
greatest of men intellectually, and, without qualification,
one of the most attractive of personalities; this must
                                                53
always remain true, whatever may be the ultimate
verdict of science in regard to details of his hypotheses.
Persons thus grandly molded have nothing to fear from
the perspective of time. He was one cool cucumber at
                         54
one of history's junctures.
        54
   Darwin insisted that the principle of natural selection
is only one of the causes of evolution of species, "the
main but not the exclusive means of modification" and he
                                        55
was also profoundly aware of the evolutionary
importance of the underlying problems of variability,
heredity, and isolating that has occupied recently the
               56   57
attention of the post-Darwinians. Naturalists, almost

48. F. NO CHANGE
    G. adequacy; for
    H. adequacy, for
    J. adequacy for

49. A. NO CHANGE
    B. are so always accumulating
    C. are accumulating
    D. are constantly accumulating

50. F. NO CHANGE
    G. This
    H. Those
    J. That judgment

51. A. NO CHANGE
    B. In addition,
    C. In other words,
    D. However,

52. F. NO CHANGE
    G. emphasize
    H. emphasized
    J. had emphasized

53. A. NO CHANGE
    B. this assessment
    C. this alone
    D. this quality

54. F. NO CHANGE
    G. He has been one cool cucumber at one of history's junctures.
    H. He is one cool cucumber at one of history's junctures.
    J. OMIT this sentence.

55. A. NO CHANGE
    B. modification," and he
    C. modification." He
    D. modification;" and he

56. F. NO CHANGE
    G. isolatability
    H. isolation
    J. isolate

57. A. NO CHANGE
    B. had occupied
    C. has been occupied
    D. have occupied

without exception, no longer doubt that natural selection, as expounded by him, is a cause of the evolution of species, and a most important one, and stood as a general law that explains the causation of
₅₈

organic evolution. This view will be supported by the
₅₉
biology of the future, if Darwin's place in the history of
₅₉

science cannot be far below that of Newton. [60]

58. F. NO CHANGE
  G. has stood
  H. stands
  J. will have stood

59. A. NO CHANGE
  B. If this view is supported by the biology of the future, Darwin's place
  C. This view will be supported by the biology of the future, although Darwin's place
  D. Nevertheless, this view is supported by the biology of the future, when Darwin's place

60. Readers are likely to regard the passage as best described by which of the following terms?
  F. Biographical
  G. Confessional
  H. Laudatory
  J. Inspirational

Passage V

Almost everywhere spread through the British Isles
₆₁
are to be found antiquities. These are carefully marked

on governmental, and many private maps and historians
₆₂ ₆₃
describe them in publicly available guides. Governmental
₆₃
agencies, the National Trusts, and private landlords are

most accommodating in permitting visits to these

unattended sites, most of which are unsupervised yet
₆₄
immaculate. [65]
₆₄

61. A. NO CHANGE
  B. widely dispersed through
  C. throughout
  D. all over, in nook and crook

62. F. NO CHANGE
  G. governmental; and many private
  H. governmental—and many private
  J. governmental and many private

63. A. NO CHANGE
  B. and described
  C. and describing
  D. and descriptively

64. F. NO CHANGE
  G. most of which are unsupervised although immaculate.
  H. most of which are immaculate.
  J. most of which are unsupervised.

65. Suppose this passage were written for an audience that was unfamiliar with antiquities and British history. The writer could most effectively strengthen the passage by:
  A. including a brief summary of the biographies of British monarchs.
  B. describing with detail and illustration just what an *antiquity* is.
  C. supplying a current map of England.
  D. defining in great detail the term *National Trust*.

With interesting exceptions, the rock graphics of the British Isles are a collection of pits, rings, and grooves, as well as <u>carefully-carved</u> symbols of Neolithic power
                                               66
(axheads, fertility symbols, etc.) and roughly sculpted monoliths. The pit, ring, and groove sites usually are found on horizontal surfaces, <u>because</u> many power
                                                                 67
symbols are found on vertical surfaces of menhirs (upright monoliths), <u>lintels and the walls</u> of constructions.
                                        68

In the more than <u>five hundred</u> megalithic stone
                       69
constructions, many have a number of menhirs whose natural shape has been abetted by human enterprise into a variety of shapes. Stonehenge is the incorporating universal structure <u>by which</u> one can discern many of
                         70
the features found elsewhere. In Scotland <u>are found</u> a
                                            71
special series of menhirs that depict symbols, both pre-Christian and Christian, as well as human figures, angels, and scenes. ⬚72

   Surely one of the earliest stones to be erected is the one near present-day Edinburgh in an area that came under Britannic control by A.D. 480. ⬚73 Christianity came to this region between the fifth and the seventh centuries: St. Ninian founded the Candida Case monastery near Whithorn on the Solway in A.D. 379–398; St. Oran established holy places in Iona, Mull, and Tiree

66. **F.** NO CHANGE
    G. carefully, carved
    H. carefully carved
    J. carefully and carved

67. **A.** NO CHANGE
    B. while
    C. although
    D. yet

68. **F.** NO CHANGE
    G. lintels, and the walls
    H. lintels; and the walls
    J. lintels, the walls

69. **A.** NO CHANGE
    B. 500
    C. 5 hundred
    D. five-hundred

70. **F.** NO CHANGE
    G. with which
    H. for which
    J. in which

71. **A.** NO CHANGE
    B. was found
    C. has always been found
    D. is found

72. Readers are likely to regard the passage as best described by which of the following terms?
    F. Fictional
    G. Scholarly
    H. Dramatic
    J. Persuasive

73. How can this paragraph be changed so that it will be more meaningful and understandable to a young reader?
    A. Include a chart of rock types, listing origins, scientific names, and descriptions.
    B. Provide a detailed description of many European prehistoric stoneworks.
    C. Describe more fully the one stone mentioned in the first sentence.
    D. Add a comparison of Easter Island monoliths with the Stonehenge monuments.

before A.D. 548. [74] The form of Christianity was the monastic and hermetic type traditionally called Celtic, which demanded poverty and obedience from its clergy, who were all monks. [75]

74. Look over the structure of this paragraph as it has unfolded so far. With which one of the following characterizations do you agree?
   F. It is surely and soundly organized, consisting of a general statement at the beginning which is supported throughout.
   G. It is not organized very well. It begins with a statement about monastic order, but does not develop that idea.
   H. It is not organized very well. It begins with a statement about a stone, but then switches to the history of Christianity in the region.
   J. It is not organized very well. It begins with a brief history of Britannic rule, and then seems to shift to a history of Pict temples.

75. This paragraph would be strengthened by:
   A. supplying more details about the Christian leaders.
   B. beginning the paragraph with a general statement that encompasses the details presented in the body.
   C. including a short lesson on rock formation.
   D. defining the hermitic form of Christianity.

TEST B

45 Minutes—75 Questions

DIRECTIONS: The following test consists of 75 underlined words and phrases in context, or general questions about the passages. Most of the underlined sections contain errors and inappropriate expressions. You are asked to compare each with the four alternatives in the answer column. If you consider the original version best, choose letter **A** or **F**: NO CHANGE. For each question, circle the letter of the alternative you think best. Read each passage through before answering the questions based on it.

Passage I

(1)

Abraham Lincoln has been quoted as advising a new lawyer, "Young man, it's more important to know what cases not to take than it is to know the law." New attorneys soon learn to recognize what cases will probably be unprofitable, or they quickly end up looking for new jobs <u>in the newspaper because of lack of funds.</u> [2]

(2)

During the initial interview with the client, the lawyer discovers whether or not a case is meritorious. Examples of cases without merit include an argument with neighbors over a pesky dog or an accident that results from the victim's own negligence, such as someone falling in a local supermarket because <u>they were drunk</u>. This <u>questionable and dubious</u> type of case can be easily seen as lacking merit, because each of the elements of a tort (a civil wrongdoing) was not present, and thus no law was broken. <u>We must all try to behave as adults as we wend our way through this troubled interval.</u>

1. **A.** NO CHANGE
   B. because of lack of funds.
   C. in the newspaper.
   D. OMIT the underlined portion.

2. Is the quotation from Abraham Lincoln an appropriate way to begin this passage?
   F. Yes, because quotations are always better than straight prose as attention-getters.
   G. No, because it misleads the reader, suggesting that Lincoln is the topic of the passage.
   H. No, because it is too short a quotation to add any meaning.
   J. Yes, because Abraham Lincoln is an authority figure, often quoted because of the truth and simplicity of his statements.

3. **A.** NO CHANGE
   B. he or she was drunk.
   C. they had been drinking.
   D. they were considerably under the influence.

4. **F.** NO CHANGE
   G. OMIT the underlined portion.
   H. questionable
   J. dubious

5. **A.** NO CHANGE
   B. We must all try to be mature.
   C. We must all do our best.
   D. OMIT the underlined portion.

(3)

Finally, there is the type of case in which the prospective client has been represented in the matter by another attorney. Accepting such a case can be risky, <u>although</u> multiple lawyers are evidence of a worthless
⁶

<u>case an</u> uncooperative client, or a client who does not
⁷

pay his or her bill. Even if the reason for the <u>client's</u>
⁸

changing attorneys is a good <u>one—let's say</u> a
⁹
personality clash between the client and the prior attorney—it makes the new lawyer's task of reaching a fair settlement with the other party strategically difficult.

(4)

There are some cases that seem to have merit but are economically unfeasible for a new attorney to handle. Such cases are easy to spot once a <u>full, adequate enough</u>
10
<u>disclosure</u> of the facts has been obtained from the client
10
during the initial interview. One type of unprofitable case is the "hurt feelings" case stemming from an incident where the defendant has <u>been guilty of caddish</u>
11
<u>behavior—but what young man in springtime has been</u>
11
<u>able to resist the pull of the heart?</u>—but where the
11
victim cannot prove he or she has been specifically damaged, or where damages are nominal. For instance, in an action for slander, not only is it difficult to prove <u>slander but also</u> the monetary damage to the victim
12
resulting from the slanderous action may be small or even nonexistent. In these kinds of cases, a prospective

6. **F.** NO CHANGE
   G. when
   H. because
   J. similarly

7. **A.** NO CHANGE
   B. case. An
   C. case, an
   D. case: an

8. **F.** NO CHANGE
   G. clients
   H. client
   J. clients'

9. **A.** NO CHANGE
   B. one, let's say
   C. one (let's say
   D. one let's say

10. **F.** NO CHANGE
    G. full, adequate disclosure
    H. full, adequate, complete disclosure
    J. full disclosure

11. **A.** NO CHANGE
    B. been guilty of caddish behavior—but sometimes that happens to young people—
    C. been guilty of wrongful behavior,
    D. OMIT the underlined portion.

12. **F.** NO CHANGE
    G. slander, but also
    H. slander. But also
    J. slander; but also

client may be so righteously angered as to say that he or she does not care about the money, that it is the principle that <u>matters, that may</u> be true for the
₁₃
prospective client, but the attorney cannot pay his secretary's salary, his office rent, or his malpractice insurance <u>premium will not be reduced</u> with a client's
₁₄

"principle." [15]

13. A. NO CHANGE
    B. matters that
    C. matters. That
    D. matters: that

14. F. NO CHANGE
    G. premium reduction
    H. premium reduced
    J. premium

15. Choose the sequence of paragraph numbers that makes the structure of the passage most logical.
    A. NO CHANGE
    B. 1, 4, 2, 3
    C. 1, 3, 2, 4
    D. 1, 2, 4, 3

Passage II

(1)

Of all the many differences between people, there is one that goes <u>more deeper</u> than any other or than all
₁₆
combined, and that is whether the person <u>are parents or</u>
₁₇
<u>not</u>. Variations in cultural background, religion, politics,
₁₇
or education do not come close to parent versus nonparent differences. [18]

(2)

Conversely, few if any knickknacks remain whole in a home with small <u>children, the only</u> plants left are those
₁₉
hanging, brown and wilted, from a very high ceiling.

Instead, <u>toys strewn</u> carelessly about the various living
₂₀
areas. The <u>somewhat disheveled rooms</u> usually look
₂₁
slightly askew, since little ones delight in moving

16. F. NO CHANGE
    G. deeper
    H. deep
    J. deepest

17. A. NO CHANGE
    B. is a parent or not.
    C. is parents or not.
    D. are a parent or not.

18. This passage was probably written for readers who:
    F. are experts in child development.
    G. are expecting a child.
    H. are general readers.
    J. are childless.

19. A. NO CHANGE
    B. children the only
    C. children: the only
    D. children. The

20. F. NO CHANGE
    G. toys strew
    H. toys were strewn
    J. toys are strewn

21. A. NO CHANGE
    B. disheveled rooms
    C. rooms
    D. somewhat, disheveled rooms

furniture around and are especially prone to do so unless
                                                    22
a guest or two are expected. Walls are usually smudged
              23
with the prints of tiny hands and feet (yes, feet—don't ask me how) and decorated with children's artwork, which also adorns the refrigerator, kitchen cabinets, message center, and any other available blank space. To a parent, there is no such thing as a sparkling clean mirror or window. A handy way to clean windows and mirrors
                  24
is by using crushed newsprint. Children simply cannot
        24
keep from touching—with their hands, noses, mouths, whatever—clean mirrors and windows. It has something to do with marking one's territory, I believe. [25]

(3)

The very way a house is decorated proclaims the owner's status. My childless friends have plants, expensive accessories, and elegant knickknacks placed strategically about their finely-furnished homes.
                                    26
Framed prints hang on their spotlessly white walls, while their mirrors and windows sparkle. [27]

(4)

Another distinguishing great difference between
        28
people without children and people with them is their attitude toward life. Before my daughter came along five years ago, I was a competent legal secretary, a faithful wife, and a person who enjoyed a quiet lifestyle interspersed with an occasional party or outing. I was

22. F. NO CHANGE
    G. after
    H. as
    J. when

23. A. NO CHANGE
    B. are expecting.
    C. is expected.
    D. will be expected.

24. F. NO CHANGE
    G. OMIT the underlined portion.
    H. Clean windows with newsprint.
    J. A handy way to clean windows is with newsprint.

25. Which of the phrases below demonstrate the intent of the writer to be whimsical and humorous?
    A. toys strewn carelessly
    B. marking one's territory
    C. sparkling clean mirror
    D. available blank space

26. F. NO CHANGE
    G. finely furnished
    H. finely, furnished
    J. furnished

27. Examination of paragraphs 2 and 3 reveals that the author of this passage wants to emphasize:
    A. fine art in American homes.
    B. styles and decor in contemporary homes.
    C. the impact of children on a home.
    D. indoor plant styles in contemporary American homes.

28. F. NO CHANGE
    G. OMIT this word
    H. discriminating
    J. differentiating

well-adjusted but ill-prepared for chaotic living, and, I
see now, quite naive. [30]

29. A. NO CHANGE
    B. well adjusted but ill-prepared
    C. well adjusted but ill prepared
    D. well-adjusted but ill prepared

30. Choose the sequence of paragraph numbers that makes the structure of the passage most logical.
    F. NO CHANGE
    G. 1, 3, 2, 4
    H. 1, 3, 4, 2
    J. 1, 4, 2, 3

Passage III

(1)

The very idea of a community among nations are unique. From the city-states of ancient Greece to the modern nations of our era, communities have to join forces to defend their individual interests. Economic, political, and military conditions have imposed their own imperatives, requiring shifting alliances and coalitions of expedience. But the contemporary community of nations—a free association based on shared principles and an increasingly shared way of life; emerged only with the evolution of the democratic idea. Just as a free people argue the issues and choose their own government, so do free nations choose their friends and allies. We are joined not just by common interests but also by ideals of freedom and justice that transcends the dictates of necessity. [36]

31. A. NO CHANGE
    B. had been
    C. is
    D. were

32. F. NO CHANGE
    G. had
    H. will have had
    J. have had

33. A. NO CHANGE
    B. life—emerged
    C. life: emerged
    D. life, emerged

34. F. NO CHANGE
    G. its
    H. his or her
    J. our

35. A. NO CHANGE
    B. transcending
    C. transcended
    D. transcend

36. Is the reference to ancient Greece in the second sentence appropriate in this passage?
    F. No, because there is no connection between two eras thousands of years apart.
    G. Yes, because ancient Greece is a model for democratic societies.
    H. No, because the United States does not have city-states.
    J. Yes, because this is one of the earliest historical instances of communities joining forces for the common good.

(2)

Our community and our heritage has enemies. Over
                            37
the past two centuries, as separate entities or in concert, free peoples have defended themselves against marauders and tyrants, against militarists and imperialists, against Nazis and the Leninist totalitarians of our time. We have seen our heritage shaking to its roots. The graves of
                              38
Normandy and the death camps of the Third Reich bears
                                                       39
permanent witness to the vulnerability of all we cherish.

(3)

Within the last twenty years we have seen other evidence of the determination of our former adversaries. The Berlin Wall once stood mute as a symbol of the fear
                                    40
our civilization and its values evoked in a totalitarian world. The Soviets, of course, had their values as well. They valued a regime that imposed an unchallenged order in their own sphere and fomented instability and
         41
division elsewhere. [42]

(4)

This community has long been a minority of humanity. In our own time, however, we have seen our
            43
numbers increase. In recent decades we have been
      43
joined by like-minded nations around the Pacific Basin; by the struggling young democracies of Latin America; and, of course, by Israel, whose very existence is a constant reminder of the sacrifices and struggles that

37. **A.** NO CHANGE
    B. have had
    C. had
    D. will have had

38. **F.** NO CHANGE
    G. shaken
    H. shook
    J. shaked

39. **A.** NO CHANGE
    B. bear
    C. bore
    D. borne

40. **F.** NO CHANGE
    G. in a mute way
    H. mute and silent
    J. mutely

41. **A.** NO CHANGE
    B. its
    C. there
    D. they're

42. Is the reference to the Berlin Wall meaningful at this place in the passage?
    F. No, because it virtually changes the subject.
    G. No, because the Berlin Wall is an inanimate object, and the passage is about people.
    H. Yes, because the Berlin Wall was created after World War II.
    J. Yes, because it is a specific example of the determination mentioned in the first sentence of the paragraph.

43. How do you regard the supporting material that follows this statement?
    A. It is ineffective; it does not support the initial statement at all.
    B. It is effective because it lists countries that have made human rights a paramount concern.
    C. It is ineffective because it does not list numbers or demonstrate with charts.
    D. It is effective because it ends with a quotation from Lincoln.

may be required if civilization is to be secured. Together, we stand for something that no other alliance in history has <u>represented; the</u> advancement of the rights of the individual, and the conviction that governments founded on these rights are, in Lincoln's words, "the last best hope of men on earth." ⟦45⟧

44. F. NO CHANGE
    G. represented, the
    H. represented: the
    J. represented. The

45. Choose the sequence of paragraph numbers that makes the structure of the passage most logical.
    A. NO CHANGE
    B. 1, 4, 2, 3
    C. 1, 3, 2, 4
    D. 1, 4, 3, 2

Passage IV

(1)

My Ántonia depicts life on the Nebraska prairie during the early 1900s, mirroring Willa Cather's own experiences as a girl living on the "Great Divide," as that part of Nebraska <u>had been called</u>. The protagonist of the novel<u>, Antonia Shimerda</u> was modeled on Annie Sadilek, an <u>actual living</u> Bohemian girl hired by one of Willa Cather's neighbors in the town of Red Cloud. ⟦49⟧

46. F. NO CHANGE
    G. was called
    H. is called
    J. called

47. A. NO CHANGE
    B. , Antonia Shimerda,
    C. Antonia Shimerda
    D. novel Antonia Shimerda,

48. F. NO CHANGE
    G. actual, living
    H. living
    J. actual

49. This paragraph serves as a summary of the novel being discussed in this passage. How might it be strengthened?
    A. NO CHANGE
    B. It should describe the Great Plains setting more fully.
    C. It should give us the entire plot of the story, not part of it.
    D. It should supply more details regarding the family background of the Shimerdas.

(2)

A close friend of Willa Cather, the author of *My Ántonia*, has written, "Willa forever preferred rural life, although she was never quite so inartistic as to announce that 'the country is preferable to the <u>city'."</u> Certainly, *My Ántonia*, Willa Cather's third prairie novel, is a joyous song of praise for "the virtues of a settled agricultural existence" as opposed to life in the

50. F. NO CHANGE.
    G. city'".
    H. city.'"
    J. city."

cities. Her belief that the ideal civilization is to be found in the country, albeit a country tempered with such desirable urban qualities as cultural refinement and order, is developed by the use of multi-level contrasts and comparisons, both obvious and symbolic. [53] [54]

51.
A. NO CHANGE
B. nevertheless
C. and
D. yet

52.
F. NO CHANGE
G. multi level
H. multilevel
J. many level

53. This paragraph begins with a quotation from a close friend of Willa Cather. Is the use of the quotation relevant to the passage?
A. No, it is irrelevant and has no bearing on the passage or paragraph.
B. No, it is misleading, dealing with Willa Cather's life, rather than the substance of the passage.
C. Yes, it is a valuable insight from a reliable source; in addition, it is relevant to the paragraph and passage.
D. Yes, it is a humorous touch that does no harm.

54. This passage was probably written for readers who:
F. are beginning readers in a youngsters' educational program.
G. are mature students of literature who are interested in critical analysis.
H. are middle-westerners who want to learn more about their heritage.
J. are authors themselves.

(3)

A richly creative novel, *My Ántonia* has been analyzed through a number of critical approaches. John H. Randall's criticism derived from broad thematic questions regarding Cather's arguments for certain values and ideas, such as the urban versus the bucolic life, using the mythic or archetypal school of criticism to explain many of the symbols employed by the author to show her beliefs. James E. Miller explains the symbolism of the three different cycles used by Cather in the novel: the seasons of the year, the phases of Antonia's life, and, most important to this essay, the people move westward in cycles to America's frontiers. Wallace Stegner, a novelist in his own right, wrote an essay about *My Ántonia.* In which he applies archetypal criticism to Antonia's identification with the land, and

55.
A. NO CHANGE
B. had derived from
C. derives from
D. has been derived from

56.
F. NO CHANGE
G. being employed
H. employing
J. employ

57.
A. NO CHANGE
B. the people moved westward in cycles
C. the cycles in the movement of people westward
D. the people were frequently moving westward in cycles

58.
F. NO CHANGE
G. *My Ántonia*, in which
H. *My Ántonia*; in which
J. *My Ántonia*—in which

the psychological approach to Cather's life and character as crucial to the novel's contrasting themes of country and city values. [59] [60]

59. This paragraph begins with the general statement: "... *My Ántonia* has been analyzed through a number of critical approaches." In what ways does the rest of the paragraph support or fail to support this statement?
   A. It supplies the names of several critical approaches and defines them in detail.
   B. It avoids the mention of critical approaches, but names three critics and discusses their ideas.
   C. It names three critics, but says little about critical approaches.
   D. It names three critics and their specific critical approaches to the novel, identifying the critical schools employed by two of them.

60. Choose the sequence of paragraph numbers that makes the structure of the passage most logical.
   F. NO CHANGE
   G. 2, 3, 1
   H. 3, 2, 1
   J. 3, 1, 2

Passage V

(1)

It is impossible to adhere rigidly to a particular global vision without accepting the fact that, in practice, a certain number of contradictions and inconsistencies will always arise in the process of translating philosophy into <u>concrete and tangible</u> action. The fact that a nation
61

possesses <u>a notion of its clear</u> international priorities,
62
however, serves to minimize the chances that its policies will merely drift in the tide of global events or become deadlocked by their mutual incompatibility. [63]

61. A. NO CHANGE
    B. concrete, tangible, and material
    C. concrete
    D. concrete and palpable

62. F. NO CHANGE
    G. a notion clear of its
    H. a notion
    J. a clear notion of its

63. The writer could most effectively strengthen the passage at this point by adding which of the following?
    A. A list of countries that comprise the international population
    B. A clearer introductory statement concerning what is meant by "translating philosophy into concrete action"
    C. A list of "global events"
    D. A list of "contradictions and inconsistencies"

(2)

By leading the more complex international decision-making structure of the 1990s, the United States will have to recognize and accept that our major international cronies will occasionally have priorities and interests that differ from our own. This is inherently a healthy sign of the pluralistic nature of modern international politics, we need not be reluctant about working for the advancement of our own interests, but we should not despair when we sometimes fail to achieve all that we desire. In practical terms, however, our prospects for success can be increased though we are sensitive to the particular constraints and policy goals that influence the actions of other nations, states, and governments. [70]

(3)

At the outset, we need to recognize that the solutions to the major foreign policy issues of the future will largely be determined on the basis of collective leadership. The United States will no longer be able simply to undertake unilateral action to resolve specific international situations. We have now grown beyond the era in which the global power of the United States was absolute and unchallenged, and it would be dangerous and futile to attempt a restoration of the postwar balance

64. F. NO CHANGE
G. Leading
H. In order to lead
J. Although leading

65. A. NO CHANGE
B. partners
C. buddies
D. pals

66. F. NO CHANGE
G. These priorities
H. This priority
J. Their independence

67. A. NO CHANGE
B. politics we
C. politics. We
D. politics yet we

68. F. NO CHANGE
G. if
H. but
J. unless

69. A. NO CHANGE
B. nations and governments.
C. nations.
D. nations, states, governments, provinces, and entities.

70. Readers are likely to regard the passage thus far as best described by which of the following terms?
F. Conciliatory
G. Hostile
H. Apologetic
J. Confessional

71. This sentence alone indicates that the intention of the author is to be:
A. descriptive.
B. persuasive.
C. poetic.
D. sentimental.

72. F. NO CHANGE
G. unchallenged and
H. unchallenged. And
J. unchallenged: and

of forces. The overwhelming truth is that human beings have created destructive weaponry they are no longer able to control. Instead we must move toward an appreciation of the central role that the United States will continue to play in reconciling competing international interests. 74 75

73. A. NO CHANGE
    B. Human beings have created destructive weaponry.
    C. OMIT the underlined portion.
    D. Human beings have created destructive weaponry they cannot control.

74. The word *instead* at the beginning of the last sentence serves as a transition between which of the following stances?
    F. From unchallenged global power to peacemaker
    G. From peacemaker to warrior
    H. From unchallenged global power to warrior
    J. From hostility to aggressiveness

75. Choose the sequence of paragraph numbers that makes the structure of the essay most logical.
    A. NO CHANGE
    B. 3, 1, 2
    C. 3, 2, 1
    D. 1, 3, 2

TEST C

45 Minutes—75 Questions

DIRECTIONS: The following test consists of 75 underlined words and phrases in context, or general questions about the passages. Most of the underlined sections contain errors and inappropriate expressions. You are asked to compare each with the four alternatives in the answer column. If you consider the original version best, choose letter **A** or **F**: NO CHANGE. For each question, circle the letter of the alternative you think best. Read each passage through before answering the questions based on it.

Passage I

(1)

The knowledge, attitudes, and skill that children acquire concerning money come from a variety of sources. The most important is the family.

(2)

What a child learns at home is reinforced, weakened, or otherwise modified by the influence of his or her <u>friends adults</u> outside the home, and pressures in the
₁

social world at large. [2]

(3)

There are several important principles involved with sound money management <u>and that</u> children need to
₃
learn. The most important is to spend wisely in such a way as to get full enjoyment and satisfaction. Another is to save for future purchases. Still another is <u>understanding</u> credit and how to use it well. Finally,
₄

1. **A.** NO CHANGE
   B. friends—adults
   C. friends: adults
   D. friends, adults

2. Suppose that at this point in the passage the writer wanted to add more information about pressures in the social world of a child. Which of the following additions would be most relevant to the passage as a whole?
   F. A brief classification of the social strata that may be part of children's lives.
   G. A scientifically accurate definition of *social pressure*.
   H. A simple anecdote about the way a child was influenced by others' spending behavior.
   J. A case history of a mentally disturbed teenager with a history of antisocial behavior.

3. **A.** NO CHANGE
   B. and which
   C. and whom
   D. that

4. **F.** NO CHANGE
   G. comprehending
   H. to understand
   J. earning

children need to have experience in earning money for their own use. [5]

(4)

In other words, he needs to learn that money is
                    —6—
valuable as a tool in reaching goals rather than as a goal in itself. The implication for parents is that they need to resist the temptation to regard money only as a restricting, rather than also as a facilitating, element in their lives. Being as how adults overemphasize the
              —7—
importance of money, they should not be surprised when children also do so.

(5)

These pressures are strong. Children themselves have become important consumers, having control over more money at earlier ages than ever before. A rise in family incomes, as well as an increase in the number of working adults, have meant that more parents can give
                        —8—
children more money for their own use. Business is fully aware of this. Modern advertising regards children
              —9—
and teenagers as awesome targets. The cost of clothes is
                       —10—   —————11—————
rising at a truly alarming rate. All of these factors
——————11——————
emphasize the need to teach children how to manage money.

(6)

On the other hand, unless adults in the company of
                        —12—
children can enjoy some of the many fine things in the

5. This paragraph is organized according to which of the following schemes?
   A. A series of comparison/contrast sentences.
   B. "Nested" classifications, with a subdivision of each topic.
   C. A general statement followed by specific examples.
   D. A narrative, with one event after another.

6. F. NO CHANGE
   G. he or she needs
   H. one needs
   J. they need

7. A. NO CHANGE
   B. If
   C. Although
   D. Thus,

8. F. NO CHANGE
   G. has meant
   H. will have meant
   J. meant

9. A. NO CHANGE
   B. that
   C. that children are more mature
   D. that more purchasing power exists

10. F. NO CHANGE
    G. massive
    H. major
    J. herculean

11. A. NO CHANGE
    B. The cost of children's clothes has remained stable.
    C. OMIT the underlined portion.
    D. The cost of clothes is just one of the factors that have contributed to inflation.

12. F. NO CHANGE
    G. until
    H. when
    J. although

246 CSU — Writing Proficiency Exam

world that require no expenditure of money and can consistently meet children's needs for affection and <u>companionship, they</u> are well on the way toward teaching
₁₃
these children the proper place that material possessions <u>and worldly goods</u> should have in their lives. ▢15
₁₄

13. A. NO CHANGE
    B. companionship they
    C. companionship: they
    D. companionship. They

14. F. NO CHANGE
    G. OMIT the underlined portion.
    H. and, thus, more worldly goods
    J. and goods

15. Choose the sequence of paragraph numbers that makes the structure of the passage most logical.
    A. NO CHANGE
    B. 1, 2, 6, 4, 3, 5
    C. 1, 2, 5, 3, 4, 6
    D. 1, 5, 6, 3, 4, 2

Passage II

(1)

Feet and shoes travel many miles. An average, healthy 7-year-old boy may take 30,000 steps every day, an accumulation that adds up to 10 miles per day and more than 300 miles a month. His mother, on a busy shopping day, may walk 10 miles. A police officer, in common with all of his or her fellow officers, <u>walk</u> about 15
₁₆
miles on the beat.

16. F. NO CHANGE
    G. walked
    H. walks
    J. was walking

(2)

The foot is a complicated structure of twenty-six small bones linked by many joints, attached to each other and to the leg bone by numerous ligaments, moved by muscles and tendons, nourished by blood vessels, controlled by nerves, <u>and a covering of skin
₁₇
protects it</u>. In a newborn infant, some of the bones are
₁₇
merely bone-shaped pieces of cartilage, a gristle-like substance. As a child <u>grows, however, real</u> bone appears
₁₈
within, and gradually spreads throughout the cartilage

17. A. NO CHANGE
    B. and a covering of skin has protected it.
    C. and being covered by a covering of skin.
    D. and protected by a covering of skin.

18. F. NO CHANGE
    G. grows, however. Real
    H. grows, however real
    J. grows however, real

form. The heel, the largest bone, is not completed until the age of about 20 years. [19]

(3)

During all this walking, feet carry the weight of the body, and provide means to propel a person when he or
                            20
she walks, climbs, and jumps. As a person steps out, the body weight travels down through the heel, along the outside of the foot to the ball, across the heads of the long bones to the first metatarsal, and to the big toe. The big toe launches the walking motion. One after the
                                                          21
other, each foot in turn bears the total weight of the
  21
body. If your feet ache, try massaging them for 20
       22
minutes. You will be amazed at the results. [23]
  22

(4)

Because a 7-year-old boy weighs 55 pounds, he puts
  24
more than 800 tons of weight on his shoes every day (55 pounds times 30,000 steps), or about 24 tons a month. But a boy does more than walk. He jumps, kicks, and often has waded through puddles. His shoes
                    25
lead a rough life. Estimates of the active life of a pair of

19. Suppose that at this point in the passage the writer wanted to add more information about foot anatomy. Which of the following additions would be most relevant to the passage as a whole?
   A. A discussion of common foot ailments and their treatment.
   B. An account of foot operations on some well-known athletes.
   C. More specific details about the muscles that control the feet, the bone tissue, the nerves and tendons.
   D. A brief account of some famous myths involving the feet, such as the one about Achilles.

20. F. NO CHANGE
    G. body. And provide
    H. body and provide
    J. body, and, provide

21. A. NO CHANGE
    B. OMIT the underlined portion.
    C. One after the other—
    D. One after the other:

22. F. NO CHANGE
    G. If your feet ache, massage them!
    H. OMIT the underlined portion.
    J. If your feet ache, try massaging them, and you will be amazed at the results.

23. Is the description of the physical functioning of the foot appropriate in the passage?
    A. Yes, because the passage is actually about sports medicine.
    B. Yes, because the passage is about the stresses on the foot and footwear that are brought about by walking.
    C. No, there is no relevance to the rest of the passage.
    D. No, because it is already well understood that the foot exerts pressure.

24. F. NO CHANGE
    G. If
    H. Being that
    J. Since

25. A. NO CHANGE
    B. wades
    C. waded
    D. will have waded

shoes ranges from 20 days to 7 or 9 months; the average
        26
is about 10 weeks. In fact, no single component or

characteristic determine the life of a shoe. Fit is most
                  27
important, and usually only the wearer can tell whether

a shoe fits. Price alone certainly does not guarantee a

good fit! [29] [30]
     28

26. F. NO CHANGE
    G. would range
    H. range
    J. has ranged

27. A. NO CHANGE
    B. determines
    C. will determine
    D. is determining

28. F. NO CHANGE
    G. fit."
    H. fit?
    J. fit.

29. Are the statistics in the first sentence of the paragraph appropriate and meaningful?
    A. Yes, because the passage is about the stresses to the feet brought about by walking, jumping, and other physical activities.
    B. Yes, because the figures help us understand that everything has a physical consequence.
    C. No, because the passage is basically about the anatomy of feet.
    D. No, because the physical activity of a 7-year-old boy is irrelevant to the discussion.

30. Choose the sequence of paragraph numbers that makes the structure of the passage most logical.
    F. NO CHANGE
    G. 1, 2, 4, 3
    H. 1, 4, 2, 3
    J. 1, 3, 2, 4

Passage III

(1)

A park in the old part of Philadelphia not only is

preeminent among the sites associated with the signers

of the Declaration of Independence, but also notably

commemorates other major aspects of the nation's
    31
founding and initial growth and many momentous

national events. These include meetings of the First and

Second Continental Congresses, the Declaration was
                     32   33
adopted and signed, which marked the creation of the
        33

31. A. NO CHANGE
    B. commemorate
    C. will commemorate
    D. has commemorated

32. F. NO CHANGE
    G. Congresses—
    H. Congresses;
    J. Congresses

33. A. NO CHANGE
    B. The Declaration was adopted and signed.
    C. the Declaration, adopted and signed,
    D. the adoption and signing of the Declaration,

United States; and the labors of the Constitutional Convention of 1787, which perpetuated it. [34]

(2)

Independence Hall was originally the statehouse for the province of Pennsylvania. In 1729 the provincial assembly set aside funds for the building, designed by lawyer Andrew Hamilton. Three years later, construction began under the supervision and overview of master carpenter Edmund Wooley. In 1736 the assembly moved into the statehouse, which was not fully completed until 1756. Thomas Jefferson was a boy of thirteen at the time. As American opposition to British colonial policies mounted, Philadelphia became a center of organized protest. To decide on a unified course of action, in 1774 the First Continental Congress met in newly finished Carpenters' Hall, whose erection the Carpenters' Company of Philadelphia had begun four years earlier. In 1775 the Second Continental Congress, taking over the east room of the ground floor of the statehouse from the Pennsylvania assembly, moved from protest to resistance; Congress had created an army and appointed George Washington as commander

34. Is the reference to the park a meaningful way to begin this passage?
   F. No, because the passage is not about recreational sites, but about the significance of Independence Hall.
   G. No, because everything it signifies is covered elsewhere in the passage.
   H. Yes, because the general reference to scenery is a good way to begin any discussion.
   J. Yes, because the park is the site of fundamental historical events described in the passage.

35. Does the first sentence of the paragraph provide a general basis for the specific supporting details which follow?
   A. Yes, the sentence is a classic topic sentence followed by supporting details about the province of Pennsylvania.
   B. Yes, the sentence suggests a plan, and the rest of the paragraph spells out the plan.
   C. No, the sentence refers to a building that is mentioned again in the paragraph, but it does not adequately prepare the reader for the historical narrative that comprises the main part of the paragraph.
   D. No, the sentence does not relate to any supporting material.

36. F. NO CHANGE
   G. supervision
   H. supervision as well as overview
   J. supervision, and overview,

37. A. NO CHANGE
   B. Thomas Jefferson had been a boy of thirteen at the time.
   C. OMIT the underlined portion.
   D. Thomas Jefferson would be a boy of thirteen at the time.

38. F. NO CHANGE
   G. began
   H. had began
   J. has begun

39. A. NO CHANGE
   B. will have created
   C. has created
   D. created

in chief. Thus, the final break with the Crown had not
                40

come; not until a year later would independence have
                                                    41
been declared. [42]
    41

(3)

On July 2, 1776, Congress passed Richard Henry Lee's resolution of June 7 recommending independence. The delegates, then turning their attention to Thomas
                                                                                                                                                             43
Jefferson's draft of the Declaration, which had been
                                                 43
submitted on June 28. After modification, it was
       43
adopted on July 4. Four days later, in Independence Square, the document was first read publicly to the citizens of Philadelphia. In a formal ceremony on August 2, about fifty of the fifty-six signers affixed their signatures to the Declaration, the others apparently did
                                                 44
so later. [45]

40. F. NO CHANGE
    G. Finally,
    H. Nevertheless,
    J. In addition,

41. A. NO CHANGE
    B. be declared.
    C. declare itself.
    D. been declared.

42. This paragraph is organized according to which of the following schemes?
    F. A series of chronological references to Independence Hall, each at important historical junctures.
    G. A general statement about Independence Hall, followed by specific information about the structure.
    H. A series of statements comparing and contrasting Independence Hall with other structures.
    J. A series of arguments about the historical importance of Independence Hall, followed by answers.

43. A. NO CHANGE
    B. Then turning the delegates' attention to Thomas Jefferson's draft of the Declaration, which had been submitted on June 28.
    C. The delegates then turned their attention to Thomas Jefferson's draft of the Declaration. Which had been submitted on June 28.
    D. The delegates then turned their attention to Thomas Jefferson's draft of the Declaration, which had been submitted on June 28.

44. F. NO CHANGE
    G. Declaration the
    H. Declaration—the
    J. Declaration; the

45. Choose the sequence of paragraph numbers that makes the structure of the passage most logical.
    A. NO CHANGE
    B. 2, 1, 3
    C. 1, 3, 2
    D. 2, 3, 1

Passage IV

(1)

The greatest problem with the abortion issue is that it is far more complex than it first appears. It is a moral issue, because it involves what both sides admit is a decision to begin or terminate a life; it is a political issue, because many laws encourage or discourage the practice of <u>abortion; finally,</u> <u>social concerns are</u>₄₆ <u>addressed</u>, because all human beings are affected by the number of people born into the world.

46. F. NO CHANGE
G. abortion finally,
H. abortion: finally,
J. abortion, finally,

47. A. NO CHANGE
B. social concerns have been addressed,
C. it is of social concern,
D. it is a social issue,

(2)

One of the central issues of the modern era is abortion. On one side of the question <u>is</u> the pro-lifers, a minority who believe that abortion is the taking of a life and that the government must protect the rights of all its citizens, including the right of an unborn infant to live. On the other side are the pro-choice advocates, comprising a majority of <u>Americans who</u> believe that abortion should be legal under certain <u>circumstances, (particularly those involving the health of the mother).</u> Researchers and pollsters have been surprised at the strength of these convictions and at the extent to which most people have pondered their beliefs.

48. F. NO CHANGE
G. have been
H. will be
J. are

49. A. NO CHANGE
B. Americans (who
C. Americans, who
D. Americans. Who

50. F. NO CHANGE
G. circumstances, particularly those involving the health of the mother.
H. circumstances (particularly those, involving the health of the mother).
J. circumstances particularly those involving the health of the mother.

(3)

<u>However,</u> the majority group that <u>believes</u> in some form of abortion is also willing to describe the medical

51. A. NO CHANGE
B. Because
C. For example,
D. Although

52. F. NO CHANGE
G. believe
H. believed
J. is believing

process as when a life ends. A woman's decision to abort her pregnancy can be viewed, according to more than half of all the pro-choice people polled, as a choice between two evils and a conscious acceptance of guilt in the necessary termination of life. [54]

(4)

The pro-lifer or anti-abortionist tends to be on the right side of the political spectrum, sometimes believing that social programs are inherently no good and impeding human progress because they tend to discourage initiative. Using the rule of common good, pro-lifers ask what decision made by a woman contemplating abortion would bring about the greatest number of positive consequences that are beneficial for all concerned—one of those concerned, of course, being the unborn fetus. A baby's fine features, such as eyelashes and fingernails, are fully developed by the age of ten weeks. [59] [60]

53.
- A. NO CHANGE
- B. where a life ends.
- C. when you end a life.
- D. the end of a life.

54. Suppose that at this point in the passage the writer wanted to add more information about the abortion issue. Which of the following additions would be most relevant to the passage as a whole?
- F. A brief summary of views on the issue held by significant religious and political leaders.
- G. A list of hospitals that perform abortions.
- H. An expose of unlicensed or substandard abortion clinics.
- J. A case history of an abortion.

55.
- A. NO CHANGE
- B. ill advised
- C. bad news
- D. forbidden

56.
- F. NO CHANGE
- G. impeded
- H. impede
- J. impedes

57.
- A. NO CHANGE
- B. beneficial
- C. also beneficial
- D. OMIT the underlined portion.

58.
- F. NO CHANGE
- G. OMIT the underlined portion.
- H. A baby's fine features, for example, eyelashes and fingernails, are fully developed by the age of ten weeks.
- J. A baby's fine features, such as eyelashes and fingernails, being fully developed by the age of ten weeks.

59. For the most part, this passage is written according to which of the following strategies?
- A. Comparison/contrast
- B. Argument
- C. Description
- D. Narration

60. Choose the sequence of paragraph numbers that makes the structure of the passage most logical.
- F. NO CHANGE
- G. 1, 4, 3, 2
- H. 2, 3, 4, 1
- J. 2, 1, 3, 4

Passage V

(1)

The California Constitution requires that the governor submit a budget with an explanation to both houses of the legislature before January 11 of each year. The explanation must contain a complete spending plan, as well as an itemized statement of all expenditures provided by law or proposed by the governor, <u>and the proposed budget must be compared with last year's.</u>
₆₁
After the governor has submitted the budget, an appropriation bill, known as the Budget Bill, which reflects the proposed budget, is introduced into each house of the legislature and referred to the Assembly Ways and Means Committee and the Senate Finance Committee, respectively. The constitution requires that the legislature pass the Budget Bill by midnight, June 15. Until the Budget Bill <u>will have been enacted,</u> neither
₆₂
house can send to the governor any other appropriation bill, other than emergency measures. [63]

(2)

<u>Being</u> a budget approaching 20 billion dollars, the
₆₄
five months allowed by the constitution for all the item disagreements, resolutions, lobbying by special interest groups, and "dealing" by the legislatures on behalf of their constituents is hardly enough time. Yet, if the budget is not passed, the state of California literally ceases to function. All state employees are asked to stay

61. **A.** NO CHANGE
    B. and it must be compared with last year's budget.
    C. together with a comparison of the proposed budget with last year's.
    D. and it should contain a comparison of last year's and this year's budget.

62. **F.** NO CHANGE
    G. has been enacted,
    H. would have been enacted,
    J. was enacted,

63. Which of the following statements is best supported by the details supplied in this paragraph?
    A. The California Legislature and the governor are in contention.
    B. The California Constitution punishes lawmakers who violate its rules.
    C. The California Constitution places a high priority on timely passage of the state budget.
    D. The California budget process is hopelessly politicized.

64. **F.** NO CHANGE
    G. Due to its being
    H. Being as how it is
    J. For

home. Traffic on the freeways is measurably reduced.
                                                 65

All state government offices and agencies close and even
                                                 66
the legislature with its heavy responsibilities has to

operate with a minimal staff. When an absolute halt in
                                   67

services and business is so disruptive, and due to the
                                                 68
very fact that no other appropriation bill can be sent to
     68
the governor until the budget is passed, both the assembly

and the senate usually stay in session continuously until
                                        69
the impasse, whatever its genesis, is solved. It is not

surprising, under such conditions, that the legislature

and the governor seem to find solutions rather quickly

to disputes and stalemates that have been festering for
                                  70
months. [71]

(3)

The orderly operation of the government of California

depends on the state budget, a document controlling

expenditures that are larger than those of any American
                                              72
governmental jurisdiction with the exception of the U.S.
          72
government. Each year, the process of creating

the many parts of the budget begins in January with the
        73
governor's message to the legislature. [74] [75]

65. A. NO CHANGE
    B. Traffic, because it is on the freeway, is measurably reduced.
    C. OMIT the underlined portion.
    D. Traffic is reduced, especially on the freeways.

66. F. NO CHANGE
    G. close. And even
    H. close: Even
    J. close, and even

67. A. NO CHANGE
    B. If
    C. Because
    D. Until

68. F. NO CHANGE
    G. unless
    H. although
    J. because

69. A. NO CHANGE
    B. continually
    C. interminably
    D. repeatedly

70. F. NO CHANGE
    G. have been solved
    H. have been unresolved
    J. have been unknown

71. This passage was probably written for readers who:
    A. are tax accountants seeking to learn more about their vocation.
    B. are taxpayers and voters interested in how a state government works.
    C. enjoy scientific and quantitative facts.
    D. enjoy works of inspiration and solace.

72. F. NO CHANGE
    G. any other American governmental jurisdiction
    H. any, American governmental jurisdiction
    J. any American, governmental jurisdiction

73. A. NO CHANGE
    B. so many part of the budget
    C. a budget
    D. the workings of the budget

74. This paragraph emphasizes the importance of:
    F. the government of California.
    G. the size of the budget.
    H. the budget.
    J. the governor's message to the legislature.

75. Choose the sequence of paragraph numbers that makes the structure of the essay most logical.
    A. NO CHANGE
    B. 3, 2, 1
    C. 3, 1, 2
    D. 2, 3, 1

Answer Explanations TEST A

1. **D** The singular subject *one* requires a singular verb, so A and C are wrong. Choice B is incorrect because both the verb *totaled* in the same sentence and the verb in question refer to the year 1988, which is in the past.

2. **H** An objective-case pronoun is required after the preposition *of;* hence choices F and G are wrong. The comma in G and J is unnecessary.

3. **A** The dash is appropriately employed here to dramatize the pathos of *or can*.

4. **J** The first sentence of the paragraph mentions *images,* and therefore calls for description.

5. **C** To present an orderly and economical review of both nursing home extremes, with details characteristic of each type, the best choice of those given is the comparison/contrast strategy.

6. **J** The adverbial clause *than they once were* helps maintain the sequence of tenses in this paragraph.

7. **C** This passage is characterized by quick summaries and sparse detail. It would not be consistent with the rest of the passage to include detailed material.

8. **J** The clause *many of them have unclean and unhealthy conditions* is the best choice because the pronoun *them* refers to the existing *nursing homes;* the other choices introduce a new subject.

9. **D** Parallel adjectives occurring before a noun must be separated by commas.

10. **H** The paragraph is about conditions within nursing homes; the other options touch on related but basically irrelevant subject matter.

11. **B** If the noun *qualities* is used as the subject (A and C), the introductory phrase becomes a dangling participle. *Interested parties* is a better choice of subject than *the patient* (D) because, as the passage makes clear, choosing a home is usually a family undertaking.

12. **H** The phrase *behooves us* (F) is archaic; *best suits us* (G) and *is not a bad idea* (J) depart from the serious tone of the passage.

13. **C** This article is almost journalistic in style, given to quick summary and unembellished detail. Only a sparse summary paragraph would be appropriate in this context.

14. **F** The relative pronoun *which,* preceded by a comma, is needed to introduce a nonrestrictive clause.

15. **C** Paragraph 5 begins with the phrase *For these reasons*. With a quick scanning of the passage, it is clear that the reasons referred to are given at the end of paragraph 3, and that paragraph 5 should follow.

16. **G** The metaphor in this sentence is that of a loom; the verb *can be woven* maintains the metaphor.

17. **A** The dash correctly sets off examples.

18. **G** The term *cultural activities* is the focus of this passage, and yet it is not clearly defined.

19. **D** Only the phrase *rural people* clarifies which antecedent is correct (the same words in this case).

20. **H** Paragraphs 1 and 2 both deal with the concept *cultural activities* and belong together.

21. **B** The word *that* is needed before the last clause to make it a noun clause. The conjunction *when* (A), *because* (C), or *for* (D) cannot introduce a clause used as a predicate nominative.

22. **H** *Farther* is used to refer to a measurable distance or space. *Further* means "greater in measure, time, and degree."

23. **C** Use digits for dates; years are almost never spelled out.

24. **F** Hyphenate a compound adjective that precedes the noun it modifies.

25. **B** The first sentence suggests that a heritage festival may begin economic development, but the paragraph as it stands does not pick up that idea.

26. **J** The preceding sentence makes the point that farms in this area employ a third of the work force. Here the conjunction should be *thus* for that reason. The other options suggest contrast, which is meaningless at this point.

27. **B** The repetition of the preposition *in* and the noun *farming* or *production* results in parallelism.

28. **G** The three awkward options employ the phrase *spent its years of existence* in various versions, all of them unnatural sounding. The correct choice is a strong, clear statement.

29. **C** The pattern in this paragraph has been to give each accomplishment of the Council its own sentence. Also, choices A and B are run-on sentences.

30. **H** The paragraph does describe economic development, but does not explain how cultural activities "supplied the drive" for such development.

31. **D** All choices but "most distinguished" are either awkward or unnecessarily wordy.

32. **J** The most familiar idiom using these words is *method of playing*.

33. **D** Fine shades of meaning separate these words, but the only sound one to use here is *developed*.

34. **H** The participle *accomplished* modifies *musician* and is the most sensible choice. *More accomplished* compares *two* musicians.

Answer Explanations TEST A

35. A Classifying and dividing is the strategy that permits a writer full scope in exploring three or more subjects in one passage.

36. H The only meaningful choice is *quality*.

37. B Only the correct phrase conveys meaning that relates to the point being made in the paragraph—the difference in sound between the human and the mechanical piano player.

38. F The statements listing the three most distinguished musical instruments and comparing a player piano with a concert pianist are very opinionated; the passage would be more substantial if some hard data accompanied the opinions.

39. B The statement about the organ is in contrast to those made about other instruments, so a transitional word that indicates contrast is required.

40. H The other options are either redundant (F and G) or inferior (J).

41. A The word *whether* signals the need for the subjunctive mood at this point.

42. F Two characteristics are being considered in the sentence; *pressure* ("hard or soft") and *speed* ("slow or quick"), so each pair should remain intact, the pairs separated by a comma.

43. D *Most acutest* (A) is a double superlative, *more acute* (C) incorrectly suggests that there are only two listeners, and *acute* (B) lacks the force of the superlative and is therefore misleading.

44. H All the other options are awkward and wordy, and are not parallel to *the human organist*.

45. A The point of the passage is to persuade potential buyers to consider an organ.

46. F This phrase, not a common one in popular English, is appropriate to the deliberate, reflective tone of this passage.

47. B Quoted material, when available, is one of the most effective means of representing a person's thought and personality.

48. F The dash is appropriately used here to punctuate a parenthetical aside.

49. C This sentence consists of three clauses ending with predicate adjectives—*broad, accumulating,* and *intricate*. The only choice that maintains this parallel structure is C.

50. J The pronoun *that* does not have a clear antecedent here, so a noun should be supplied.

51. D This sentence is in contrast to the ideas expressed in the preceding paragraph.

52. H The past tense is appropriate here. The historical present is usually reserved for discussions of what a writer says or thinks in a particular work of literature.

53. B The pronoun *this* almost never is adequate by itself; a noun is required here for clarity.

54. J This sentence is incompatible in style and content with the rest of the passage.

55. C If no coordination is possible, that is, joining two independent clauses with a comma and a conjunction, then two complete sentences will work.

56. H Three parallel prepositional phrases modify the noun *problems* in this sentence: problems of *variability, (of) heredity,* and *(of) isolation*. The object of the preposition is always a noun.

57. D The pronoun *that* refers to the plural *problems,* and the verb must agree. The tense must be the present perfect (*have occupied*) since the reference is to the immediate past.

58. H The present tense is required because natural selection still stands as a general law today.

59. B The statement regarding Darwin's place in history *depends upon* how his theories are regarded in the future—thus the need for the *if* clause at the beginning of the sentence.

60. H If nothing else, this passage praises Darwin.

61. C The use of *throughout* is clear and direct; the other options are awkward or wordy.

62. J There is no need for any punctuation between the parallel adjectives *governmental* and *(many) private*.

63. B The verb *described* completes the parallel pair of passive verbs *are...marked* and *(are) described*.

64. H The word *unattended* in the preceding clause renders the word *unsupervised* redundant.

65. B An understanding of the word *antiquities* is essential to the understanding of the passage.

66. H Word combinations containing an *-ly* word should not be hyphenated. The adverb *carefully* modifies the adjective *carved*, and there should be no hyphen between them.

67. B Instead of a subordinating conjunction indicating *cause*, what is required here is a conjunction signaling *contrast* (*vertical* versus *horizontal*).

68. G This question involves a simple series of three items that must be separated by commas: *menhirs, lintels, and walls*.

69. A Spell out an occasional number that can be expressed in one or two words; with the exception of numbers from twenty-one through ninety-nine, which are always hyphenated, compound numbers are not hyphenated.

Answer Explanations TEST A

70. **J** *In which* is the only prepositional phrase that draws focus to the structure itself.

71. **D** The subject of this sentence is the singular *series*.

72. **G** This passage has all the characteristics of a scholarly paper, including assumption of some sophistication on the part of the reader, close attention to detail, and esoteric language.

73. **C** The paragraph begins with a bare statement about a significant prehistoric stone, one of the earliest erected. A younger reader would require more detail to understand the significance of such early monoliths.

74. **H** This paragraph seems to have two main ideas needing development: the stone first mentioned, and the development of Christianity in the region. With two main ideas, the structure is deeply flawed.

75. **B** The paragraph needs either to be restructured or to be introduced by a general statement that could accommodate both of the ideas present in the paragraph.

Answer Explanations TEST B

1. **D** All meanings carried by the underlined portion are implicit in the words preceding it. The entire portion is redundant.

2. **J** The quotation is pertinent, short, and authoritative. As such, it is a sound way to begin the passage.

3. **B** The antecedent of the pronoun in question is the singular *someone*.

4. **G** The phrase *lacking merit* at the end of the clause is adequate characterization of the type of case under discussion.

5. **D** As idealistic as the thought is, it is off the topic and has no place in this passage.

6. **H** The logic of this sentence requires that a transitional word indicating *cause* be employed in this spot.

7. **C** Three or more items in a series must be set off by commas.

8. **F** The phrase *changing attorneys* is a gerund phrase, that is, a *noun* phrase. Since it is an activity of the noun *client*, that noun requires the possessive apostrophe and final *s*.

9. **A** Dashes are appropriate marks to set off a parenthetical phrase, especially if one intends to emphasize the phrase.

10. **J** All other options are wordy or redundant.

11. **C** Colloquial and whimsical language is not in keeping with the matter-of-fact tone of the passage.

12. **G** Coordinate clauses must be separated by a comma.

13. **C** A new sentence begins at this point.

14. **J** At this spot a third noun—namely, *premium*—should parallel the objects *salary* and *rent*.

15. **D** Paragraph 3 begins with a clear signal that it should follow paragraph 4 rather than precede it, specifically the word *Finally*.

16. **G** The adverb *more* and the comparative adverb ending *-er* are equivalent, and cannot be used together. The result is a double comparison.

17. **B** The subject of this clause is the singular *person*.

18. **H** There is no suggestion or clue to suggest that the passage is intended for any one group.

19. **D** As it stands, the text contains a comma splice at this point; of the options, only the period break is correct.

20. **J** The present-tense, passive-voice verb is appropriate because the focus is on the toys, and the passage is written in the present tense. As it stands, this is a sentence fragment.

21. **C** The fact that the sentence later mentions that the rooms are "slightly askew" is reason enough to avoid the modifiers of the word *rooms*.

22. **J** The logic of this sentence requires that a conjunction indicating time be used at this transition; *when* is the only choice that makes sense.

23. **A** The verb agrees with the nearer subject (two) and is in the present tense.

24. **G** As interesting as the information may be, this sentence is wholly off the topic and must be removed.

25. **B** The notion of children marking their territory with smudges and smears is humorous and whimsical. The other options do not suggest humor.

26. **G** A compound adjective preceding the noun it modifies is hyphenated, but the two words before *homes* do not comprise a compound adjective; one, *finely*, is an adverb modifying the adjective *furnished*.

27. **C** The enormous difference in the size of these paragraphs, as well as the amount of data they contain, shows the writer's bias.

28. **G** The noun *difference* clearly indicates that two kinds of people are being compared; *distinguishing* is not needed.

Answer Explanations TEST B

29. **C** — Compound adjectives that *precede* the noun are hyphenated; ones that *follow* the noun usually are not.

30. **G** — The word *Conversely* is a clue that paragraph 2 must occur after paragraph 3; the words *another great difference* at the outset of paragraph 4 place it after paragraph 2.

31. **C** — The subject of the sentence is the singular noun *idea*. The prepositional phrase *of a community among nations* is a modifier of that noun. When the entire passage is read, it becomes apparent that the present tense is correct.

32. **J** — The only tense that conveys past action over a span of time to the present is the present perfect tense of the verb, that is, *have had*.

33. **B** — The parenthetical phrase *a free association based on shared principles and an increasingly shared way of life* has been set off by dashes rather than by brackets, an option generally chosen by writers to emphasize a phrase. There must be a dash at the end as well as the beginning of the phrase.

34. **F** — When a collective noun such as *people* clearly refers to individual members of a group, it takes a plural pronoun. Here the plural verbs *argue* and *choose* indicate reference to individuals.

35. **D** — The subject of the verb is the plural noun *ideals*. The prepositional phrase *of freedom* is a modifier of that noun.

36. **J** — The writer is attempting to establish a precedent for nations to join forces; reference to the cooperation of Greek city-states is logical and meaningful.

37. **B** — When a sentence has two or more subjects joined by *and*, the verb almost always is in the plural form. The present tense is correct.

38. **G** — Here the past participle of the verb *to shake* acts as an adjective modifying the noun *heritage*.

39. **B** — The subjects of this verb are the plural nouns *graves* and *camps*, not the noun *Reich*, which is part of a prepositional phrase modifying the noun *camps*.

40. **J** — An adverb is needed to modify the participle *standing*. Choice G is wordy; *mute* and *silent* (H) mean the same thing.

41. **B** — The antecedent of the pronoun is the singular noun *regime*, not the pronoun *they*.

42. **J** — The Berlin Wall is a very direct example of the evidence mentioned in the paragraph's first sentence, and the reference is therefore meaningful.

43. **B** — The statement is followed by a list that supports the assertion that the number of "like-minded nations" is increasing.

44. **H** — A colon is often used to introduce an appositive more dramatically or emphatically at the end of a sentence. A comma would be ineffective here.

45. **B** — The first paragraph introduces the notion of "a community among nations." Perusal of the passage quickly reveals that paragraph 4 begins with the words *This community* and belongs in position 2. Paragraphs 2 and 3 follow with appropriate clues at the beginning of each ("our community" and "other evidence") which point to the preceding paragraph.

46. **H** — This verb must be in the present tense to express what is still true.

47. **B** — The name *Antonia Shimerda* is in apposition with *protagonist* and is properly set off with two commas.

48. **J** — The adjective *actual* is the only choice that indicates what is intended, that the girl was a genuine Bohemian girl. The other choices are either redundant or misleading.

49. **C** — This "summary" is inconclusive; it should include more information about the story.

50. **H** — Commas and periods are *always* placed *inside* quotation marks, even when there are single and double quotation marks because the sentence contains a quote within a quote.

51. **A** — The word *albeit* means literally "although it be," a meaning that is required for the sense of the clause to remain intact, and which is not repeated in the other options.

52. **H** — The prefix *multi* is most often incorporated with another word as a unit.

53. **C** — Since the paragraph deals with Cather's preference in the novel to the country over the city, and since the entire passage is about the novel *My Ántonia*, the quotation is clearly meaningful.

54. **G** — This passage represents a relatively concentrated discussion of other critical works, and is likely to interest only readers who are knowledgeable about and interested in critical essays.

55. **C** — The passage is written in the present tense, and employs the historical present whenever necessary.

56. **F** — *Employed* in this sentence is a participle modifying the noun *symbols*.

57. **C** — To be parallel with the phrases naming the first two cycles, this one must begin with the noun *cycle*, rather than a clause describing it.

58. **G** — Only the comma, introducing a restrictive clause, is correct. Choice F results in a sentence fragment beginning with *In which*, and neither the semicolon (H) or the dash (J) is appropriate.

59. **D** — The body of the paragraph does a comprehensive job of developing the beginning generalization.

60. **G** — Paragraph 2 begins with broad, general statements about the novel, and spells out what the passage will be about. Accordingly, it is the introductory para-

Answer Explanations TEST B

graph, and is logically followed by paragraph 3, which develops the critical analysis begun at the end of paragraph 2. The summary paragraph logically follows.

61. C The word *concrete* is clear; added words with the same meaning are unproductive and uneconomical.

62. J The adjective *clear* is meant to modify the noun *notion* and so must be placed before it. When *clear* is placed in other positions, it modifies other nouns and creates confusion.

63. B The introductory paragraph of this passage might well have spelled out the meaning of *translating philosophy into concrete action,* rather than leaving the expression in its somewhat unclear form.

64. H In its original form, this sentence creates an error in *predication,* that is, an error in which the beginning of the sentence is not consistent with the end.

65. B The other choices are colloquial and inconsistent with the rather formal and businesslike tone of the passage.

66. J The pronoun *this* seldom is adequate, especially since the antecedent is *cronies. Their independence* provides the strongest logical transition.

67. C Any mark of punctuation weaker than a period or semicolon creates a run-on sentence. Two completely independent clauses are joined here.

68. G The logic of the sentence requires a conjunction signaling *condition,* such as *if,* in this spot. Conjunctions signaling other logical shifts, like *contrast* (F or H) or *restriction* (J) render the sentence meaningless.

69. C There is no point in repeating the meaning of a word redundantly. The word *nation* is clear; neither its meaning nor the meaning of the sentence is enriched or clarified by the additions of synonyms.

70. F The passage is clearly an attempt to demonstrate a peaceful foreign policy to the world.

71. B The attempt in this sentence and throughout the passage is to persuade more conservative Americans that we cannot be what we were after World War II.

72. F Coordinate clauses, that is, independent clauses joined together by a coordinating conjunction (*and, but, for, or, yet*) are separated by a comma.

73. C As truthful as the statement may be, and as related to world politics, it has nothing to do with the point of the passage and must be removed.

74. F The passage progresses from the statement that *We have now grown beyond the era* (of unchallenged power) to the recognition that *we must move toward appreciation* (of our role as conciliators).

75. D The clue at the beginning of paragraph 3, *At the outset*, indicates the placement of the paragraph just after the introduction. The beginning of paragraph 2 is meaningful only if one has read paragraph 3.

Answer Explanations TEST C

1. D Use a comma between the parts of a simple series.

2. H It is important to maintain the established subject—the forces that influence the way a child handles money; the other options are all off the topic.

3. D There is no need for *and* before the adjective clause *that children need to learn.* Choices B and C repeat the error. Choice C is wrong also because the pronoun *whom* is used to refer to a person, and the antecedent here is *principles.*

4. H There is a parallel series of sentences in this paragraph, all employing the infinitive. For this reason, the infinitive *to understand* is correct.

5. C The first sentence of the paragraph is a clear topic sentence that prepares the reader for the series of principles that forms the body of the paragraph.

6. J The antecedent of the pronoun is the plural noun *children* at the end of the preceding paragraph.

7. B The phrase *being as how* is substandard English; the other words create an illogical statement.

8. G The subject of the sentence is the singular noun *rise.*

9. D The pronoun *this* is almost never adequate by itself; the sentence requires a more complete statement. The point made in the preceding sentences is that money is more available.

10. H *Major* is more in keeping with the tone of the passage. The other words do not mean the same as *major* and are less preferable in this context.

11. C The underlined statement is off the topic and so must be eliminated.

12. H The subordinating conjunction *when* forms a logical link with the rest of the sentence; the other options do not.

13. A An introductory adverbial clause, except a very short one, is set off from the main clause by a comma. A stronger mark of punctuation in this place, such as choice D, would create a sentence fragment.

14. G The phrase *material possessions* makes a clear point; *worldly goods* is redundant.

15. C Paragraph 2 ends with a mention about *pressures*, a train of thought that leads directly to paragraph 5, which begins with the statement *These pressures are*

Answer Explanations TEST C

strong. In the same manner, the thought about managing money at the end of paragraph 5 is picked up in the first sentence in paragraph 3; the notion that children need experience in managing money is echoed in paragraph 4, and the emphasis on adults in paragraph 4 is continued in the first words of paragraph 6.

16. H A singular subject—in this case, *police officer*—followed by such a phrase as *in common with, accompanied by, in addition to*, or *together with*, takes a singular verb.

17. D To be parallel with the rest of the sentence, this part must begin with the participle *protected*, which modifies the noun *structure*.

18. F A parenthetical expression such as *however* is set off by commas.

19. C This choice is the only one that bears on anatomy.

20. H Compound verbs are not normally separated by a comma.

21. B The words *One after the other* are redundant; the phrase *in turn* means the same.

22. H This sentence has no bearing on the topic of the paragraph or passage and must be removed.

23. B Because the entire passage deals with the great stress placed on the foot, this description of the physical process of using the foot is meaningful.

24. G The word *if* is necessary at this point if the sentence is to be logical. Not all 7-year-old boys weigh 55 pounds.

25. B A present-tense verb is necessary to agree with the other verbs in the sentence.

26. H The subject of the verb is the plural noun *estimates*; the present tense is correct.

27. B When parts of a compound subject are joined by *or* or *nor*, the verb agrees with the nearer part—in this case, *characteristic*. The simple present tense is correct.

28. J The sentence is a simple declarative statement that requires a period.

29. A The figures provided are quite impressive and clearly dramatize the point of the passage.

30. J Paragraph 3 is a more general statement about the foot and should precede the very specific, detailed paragraphs 2 and 4. Note the clue in *During all this walking*.

31. A The subject of the verb *commemorates* is the singular noun *park*; the present tense is correct (note *is* in the same sentence).

32. H Items in a series are separated by semicolons if they contain commas within themselves. This sentence, when correctly constructed, includes a series of direct objects—*meetings, adoption,* and *labors*—the last two of which introduce clauses set off by commas.

33. D To be parallel with the direct objects *meetings* and *labors,* this item must begin with a noun.

34. J The park is the site of Independence Hall, around which most of the historical events described in the passage revolve.

35. C The topic sentence of this paragraph is flawed; the general point it makes is not broad enough to embrace the historical events described. A better topic sentence would be this: *Independence Hall, originally the statehouse for the province of Pennsylvania, was the site of an important event in early American history.*

36. G The word *supervision* is adequate; *overview* is repetitious.

37. C Although Thomas Jefferson figures importantly in the events later described in the passage, how old he was in 1756 has no bearing on this paragraph.

38. F The past perfect tense is required in this sentence because the action described took place *before* the past action that is the subject of the passage.

39. D All the actions in the sentence are in the simple past.

40. H The word *Nevertheless* provides the contrast that is needed in a sentence describing an unexpected consequence. The other connective words do not provide the contrast, and so make no sense in the context.

41. B In combination with the word *would, be declared* signals an event in the future; note "not until a year later."

42. F The paragraph, flawed because of a weak topic sentence, presents historical events that occurred in and near Independence Hall. Of the choices given, this is the only one that makes that point.

43. D This is the only correct, complete sentence. Choices A and B are sentence fragments. Choice C is a sentence plus a sentence fragment.

44. J A semicolon joins two main clauses; there is no conjunction. Anything weaker in this spot results in a run-on sentence.

45. A The paragraphs are correct as they stand. Since this passage is in chronological order, the sequence is self-explanatory.

46. F Items in a series are separated by semicolons if they contain commas.

47. D To be parallel with the other clauses in the sentence, this one must maintain the same pattern, *it is a . . . .*

48. J The subject of the verb is the plural noun *pro-lifers;* the present tense is needed.

Answer Explanations TEST C

49. C The comma is needed after *Americans* to set off the participial phrase *comprising a majority of Americans*. Otherwise, the sentence can be misread to mean that pro-choice advocates comprise a majority of all Americans who believe that abortion should be legal under certain circumstances, falsely implying that a minority of these Americans are not pro-choice.

50. G This phrase is not a digression but rather is information essential to the point being made, and so should not be enclosed in parentheses.

51. C This sentence needs to be introduced by a transition that signals the introduction of an example; the other transitions denote contrast *or cause,* and choices B and D result in sentence fragments.

52. F The subject of the sentence is the singular noun *group;* the present tense is correct.

53. D The word *process* is a noun; it must be described or restated as a noun, not as an adverbial clause.

54. F The views of leaders would be useful in this passage about opinions. The information in the other options would be off the topic.

55. B The adjective *ill advised* is clear and direct; the other options are colloquial or misleading.

56. H The subject of the sentence is the plural noun *programs*. The passage is written in the present tense.

57. D The clause *that are beneficial* merely repeats the meaning of the word *positive,* and so should be removed.

58. G This sentence has nothing to do with the point of the passage.

59. A For the most part, one view of the abortion issue is compared with the other in this passage.

60. H Paragraph 2 clearly introduces the topic and suggests the structure of the passage; paragraph 3 begins with an example of the quality of the thought mentioned at the end of paragraph 2; paragraph 4 presents the other view of the issue, and paragraph 1 sums up the complexity of the issue.

61. C The sentence in which this question appears ends with a series of noun objects, in which *comparison of the proposed budget* should be included. Note that the correct choice is the only one that is not a clause.

62. G The present perfect tense is required in this sentence because the action referred to extends, at least in its consequences, to the present.

63. C The entire passage emphasizes the point that no legislation is more important than the budget.

64. J Only the use of the preposition *For* creates a logical, correct sentence; the other choices are substandard English.

65. C The statement about traffic on the freeways has no bearing on the point of the passage.

66. J Use the comma before a coordinating conjunction linking main clauses.

67. C The logic that lies behind each of the options changes the meaning of the sentence dramatically. Only the use of *Because* results in a meaning consistent with the rest of the paragraph.

68. J The word *because* here creates an adverb clause that is parallel with the adverb clause that begins the sentence. Also, the other choices are either substandard English (F) or alter the meaning (G, H) of the sentence.

69. A *Continually* means "occurring in steady, rapid succession," while *continuously* means "occurring in uninterrupted duration," the latter meaning being preferable in this context.

70. H The idea of disputes and stalemates festering borders on a mixed metaphor. More sensible in this very businesslike passage is the use of the term *unresolved*. The other options make no sense in the sentence.

71. B The tone and message of the passage seem to be directed at constituents seeking to be informed.

72. G When the comparative (here, *larger*) is used for more than two, it is necessary to exclude from the group the object compared. In the original sentence the expenditures of the government of California would be included in the group *those of any American governmental jurisdiction . . . U.S. government*.

73. C The word *budget* is what is intended; additional words are distracting.

74. H The passage makes clear in several ways the importance of the state budget as an entity.

75. C Paragraph 3 is clearly the introductory paragraph for this passage. In addition, it refers to early January and the governor's message, two items mentioned also in the first sentence of paragraph 1. Paragraph 2 continues the chronological narrative, and even ends with a closing statement.

INDEX

Active voice verb form preferred, 49, 50
Adjectives, 175, 176
Analytic essays, 15–18, 60–63
Analyze, 4, 15
Anxiety, test, 1–3
Argue, 4, 18–21
Attitudes, 1
Audience, 30, 31, 40, 197–199

Before the exam, 2

Cause-effect essay, 192
Classification essay, 191
Closings to essays, 194
Clustering, 6
Coherence, 45
Comma splice, 171
Compare/contrast, 4
Comparison/contrast
    Essay, 12–15, 57–59, 191
    Topics, 68, 69
Comparisons, incomplete, 178
Conjunctions, subordinating, 50, 51, 172, 173
Conjunctions or connectives, 172, 173
Connectives or conjunctions, 172, 173
Contrast, 12–15
Coordination, 50, 172

Dangling constructions
    Gerunds, 178
    Infinitives, 178
    Participles, 177, 178
Dangling modifiers and verb forms, 177, 178
Deadlines, 2
Define, 5
Definition essay, 191
Describe, 5
Description, 190
Diction, 199
Discuss, 5
Drawing a blank, 43

English Review and Practice, 145–211
Error areas, 40–52
Errors
    Coordination, 50
    Parallelism, 51
    Predication, 46
    Subject-verb agreement, 47
    Subordination, 50
    Typical, 43–52
    Verb tense, 48
ESL concerns about English, 1, 78–112
ESL Practices, 2, 78
Essay question samples, 67–72
Essay samples, 53–67, 68–72
Essay types, 9–20
Essay writing procedure, 23–30, 39
Evaluate, 5
Exam requirements, 2
Exemplification, 7

Explain, 5
Explanatory essays, 15–18, 60–63

Figurative language, 203
Finding a topic, 43
Formality, 197
Fragments, 170
Freewriting, 6, 7
Fused sentences, 171
Future perfect, 49

Gerunds (noun type), 159, 167 (See, also, Verbs)

Holistic scorers, attitudes, 31, 40, 41
Holistic scoring
    Error values, 31, 32, 41, 42
    Procedures, 31, 32
    Rubric, 33
How to answer, 34–36
How to use this book, xi

Identify, 5
Infinitives, dangling, 178
Informality, 197
Introductory paragraphs, 10, 12, 36, 37

Key words in prompts, 4, 5

Language
    Appropriateness, 34
    Imagery, 203
    Sexist, 207
Legibility, 35
Listing, 5
Logic in comparisons, 178

Mapping, 7, 26, 29
Mechanics, 35
Mixed sentences (a type of error), 46
Modifiers
    Adverbs, 175
    Adjectives, 175, 176
    Dangling or misplaced, 47
    Misplaced, 47, 177
Multiple-Choice Test Samples, 113–144, 222–261

Narration, 190

Omissions
    Conjunctions, 206
    Prepositions, 206
    Transitions, 206
    Verbs, 206
Openings to essays, 194, 195
Organization, 34
Organizing, 193

Paragraph structure, 36–39
Paragraphing, 194, 195
Paragraphs, introductory, 10, 12, 36, 37
Paragraphs, supporting, 37, 38

Index

Parallel rule, 51
Parallelism, 185, 186
Participles, 159–161
Passive voice, overuse and thoughtless use, 49, 50
Past perfect, 48
Perfect tenses, 48, 106, 107
Personal experience, 9–11, 53–57, 67, 68
Persuasion essay, 18, 63–66, 192
Prewriting, 5, 36
Predication, 45, 46, 184, 185
Pregnant sentence or thesis, 24–28
Present perfect, 48, 49
Process essay, 190, 191
Prompt, addressing the, 21, 23
Prompts, 21, 22
Pronouns, 164
    Demonstrative, 166
    Interrogative, 166
    Nominative (See Subject case), 165
    Possessives, with pronouns and gerunds, 165–167
    Object case, 165
    Subject case, 165
Prove, 5
Punctuation, 145–155
Purpose, 44

Question types
    Structured, 3, 4
    Unstructured, 4

Readers, 31, 40, 197–199
Relate, 5
Rhetorical
    Skills, 190–199
    Strategies, 190ff.
Rubrics, 33, 34 (See Scoring guides)
Run-ons, 171

Sample essay questions, 67–72, 77
Sample essays, 53–66
Scoring guides, 33, 34
Semicolon, misuse or overuse, 47, 48
Sentence
    Compound, 172, 173
    Errors, 45
    Fragments, 170
    Fused, 171
    Run-on, 171
    Structure, 170
Sentences, 170, 171
Spelling, 42
    Generally, 200–202
    Common errors, 200, 201
    Incorrect and idiomatic, 200, 201
Starting or prewriting, 5–7, 23, 26–28
State of mind, 1, 2
Strategies, 190
Style, 197, 198
Subject-verb agreement, 47, 157–159
Subjunctive verb form, 182, 183
Subordination, 50, 79–82, 84, 85, 172, 173
Summarize, 5
Survey of Current CSU Requirements, x

Tactics, 3
Test anxiety, 1–3
Thesis, 10, 12, 19, 23–26, 36, 37, 39, 43, 44
Time budgeting, 35, 39
Time line for verb tense, 86, 87, 102–104, 106
Transitions, 187, 194
Transitions and coherence, 44, 45

Unity, 44

Verb tenses, 48
Verb tenses, time lines, 86, 87, 102–104, 106
Verbs
    Consistency, 181–183
    Gerunds, 163
    Infinitive, 162, 163, 182
    Subjunctive, 182, 183
    Subordinated, 181, 182
    Tense, 48, 49, 181
Verbs, verbals, 162–164

Word choice, 199–204
Word use, 199
Wordiness, 205, 206

NOTES

NOTES

NOTES

No One Can Build Your Writing Skills Better Than We Can...

Essentials of English, 5th Edition
$9.95, Can. $13.95 (0-7641-1367-4)
The comprehensive program for effective writing skills.

Essentials of Writing, 5th Edition
$10.95, Can. $15.50 (0-7641-1368-2)
A companion workbook for the material in *Essentials of English*.

10 Steps in Writing the Research Paper, 6th Edition
$10.95, Can. $15.50 (0-7641-1362-3)
The easy step-by-step guide for writing research papers. It includes a section on how to avoid plagiarism.

How to Write Themes and Term Papers, 3rd Edition
$11.95, Can. $16.95 (0-8120-4268-9)
The perfect, logical approach to handling theme projects.

The Art of Styling Sentences: 20 Patterns for Success, 4th Edition
$8.95, Can. $11.95 (0-7641-2181-2)
How to write with flair, imagination and clarity, by imitating 20 sentence patterns and variations.

Writing The Easy Way, 3rd Edition
$14.95, Can. $21.00 (0-7641-1206-6)
The quick and convenient way to enhance writing skills.

Basic Word List, 3rd Edition
$6.95, Can. $8.95 (0-8120-9649-5)
More than 2,000 words that are found on the most recent major standardized tests are thoroughly reviewed.

BARRON'S EDUCATIONAL SERIES, INC.
250 Wireless Boulevard • Hauppauge, New York 11788
In Canada: Georgetown Book Warehouse
34 Armstrong Avenue • Georgetown, Ontario L7G 4R9
Visit our web site at: www.barronseduc.com

Prices subject to change without notice. Books may be purchased at your bookstore, or by mail from Barron's. Enclose check or money order for total amount plus sales tax where applicable and 18% for postage and handling (minimum charge $5.95). All books are paperback editions. $ = U.S. Dollars. Can. $ = Canadian Dollars.

(#15) R 5/03

BARRON'S POCKET GUIDES—

The handy, quick-reference tools that you can count on—no matter where you are!

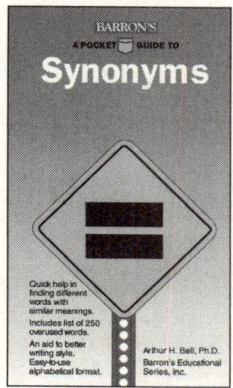

ISBN: 0-8120-4843-1
$7.95 Canada $11.50

ISBN: 0-8120-9816-1
$7.95 Canada $11.50

ISBN: 0-8120-9815-3
$7.95 Canada $11.50

ISBN: 0-8120-9814-5
$6.95 Canada $8.95

ISBN: 0-7641-1995-8
$7.95 Canada $10.50

ISBN: 0-8120-9813-7
$6.95 Canada $8.95

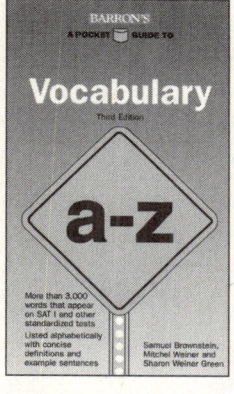

ISBN: 0-8120-9818-8
$8.95 Canada $12.50

ISBN: 0-8120-9812-9
$6.95 Canada $8.95

BARRON'S EDUCATIONAL SERIES, INC.
250 Wireless Boulevard, Hauppauge, New York 11788
In Canada: Georgetown Book Warehouse
34 Armstrong Avenue, Georgetown, Ontario L7G 4R9
Visit our website at: www.barronseduc.com

Prices subject to change without notice. Books may be purchased at your bookstore, or by mail from Barron's. Enclose check or money order for total amount plus 18% for postage and handling (minimum charge $5.95). New York State residents add sales tax. All books are paperback editions.

#18 R 5/03

ISBN: 0-7641-0672-4
$7.95 Canada $11.50

GRAMMAR GRAMMAR & MORE GRAMMAR

For ESL courses . . . for remedial English courses . . . for standard instruction in English grammar and usage on all levels from elementary through college . . . Barron's has what you're looking for!

501 English Verbs, *Thomas R. Beyer, Jr. Ph.D.* An analysis of English verb construction precedes 501 regular and irregular verbs presented alphabetically, one per page, each set up in table form showing indicative, imperative, and subjunctive moods in all tenses.
ISBN 0-7641-0304-0, paper, 552 pp., $14.95, Can$19.95

Grammar in Plain English, 3rd Ed., *H. Diamond and P. Dutwin* Basic rules grammar and examples clearly presented, with exercises that reflect GED test standards.
ISBN 0-8120-9648-7, paper, 304 pp., $13.95, Can$19.50

Painless Grammar, *Rebecca Elliott, Ph.D.* Focused mainly toward middle-school students, this book takes a light, often humorous approach to teaching grammar and usage.
ISBN 0-8120-9781-5, paper, 224 pp., $8.95, Can$11.95

1001 Pitfalls in English Grammar, 3rd Ed., *V.F. Hopper and R.P. Craig* Covers those trouble spots, including use of negative forms, noun and verb agreement, much more.
ISBN 0-8120-3719-7, paper, 352 pp., $11.95, Can$16.95

A Dictionary of American Idioms, 3rd Ed., *A. Makkai, M. Boatner, and J. Gates* More than 5,000 American idioms and slang expressions are defined and explained.
ISBN 0-8120-1248-8, paper, 480 pp., $13.95, Can$19.50

A Dictionary of Homophones, *Leslie Presson, M.A.* Presented are more than 600 sets of words that sound alike but are spelled differently, with different meanings.
ISBN 0-7641-0168-4, paper, 224 pp., $8.95, Can$12.50

Barron's Educational Series, Inc.
250 Wireless Blvd.
Hauppauge, NY 11788
Order toll-free: 1-800-645-3476
Order by fax: 1-631-434-3217

In Canada:
Georgetown Book Warehouse
4 Armstrong Ave., Georgetown, Ont. L7G4R9
Canadian orders: 1-800-247-7160
Fax in Canada: 1-800-887-1594

Visit us at www.barronseduc.com

BARRON'S

(#90) R 5/03